Second Language Needs Analysis

THE CAMBRIDGE APPLIED LINGUISTICS SERIES

Series editors: Michael H. Long and Jack C. Richards

This series presents the findings of work in applied linguistics that are of direct relevance to language taching and learning and of particular interest to applied linguists, researchers, language teachers, and teacher trainers.

Recent publications in this series:

Second Language Needs Analysis

Edited by

Michael H. Long

University of Maryland, College Park

CAMBRIDGE
UNIVERSITY PRESS

CAMBRIDGE UNIVERSITY PRESS
Cambridge, New York, Melbourne, Madrid, Cape Town, Singapore, São Paulo

Cambridge University Press
The Edinburgh Building, Cambridge CB2 2RU, UK

www.cambridge.org
Information on this title: www.cambridge.org/9780521618212

First published 2005

Printed in the United Kingdom at the University Press, Cambridge

A catalogue record for this publication is available from the British Library

Library of Congress Cataloguing in Publication data
Second language needs analysis / edited by Michael H. Long.
            p.   cm. – (The Cambridge applied linguistics series)
Includes bibliographical references and index.
ISBN-13 978-0-521-85312-5 hardback
ISBN-10 0-521-85312-5 hardback
ISBN-13 978-0-521-61821-2 paperback
ISBN-10 0-521-61821-5 paperback
1. Language and languages – Study and teaching.   2. Needs assessment.
I. Long, Michael H.   II. Title.   III. Series.
P53.55.S43   2005
418′.0071–dc22   2005020624   CIP

ISBN-13 978-0-521-85312-5 hardback
ISBN-10 0-521-85312-5 hardback

ISBN-13 978-0-521-61821-2 paperback
ISBN-10 0-521-61821-5 paperback

Contents

Contributors

Nicola J. Downey Bartlett, *Los Angeles, California*

Richard D. Brecht, *Center for the Advanced Study of Language, University of Maryland, College Park*

Craig Chaudron, *Department of Second Language Studies, University of Hawai'i*

Catherine J. Doughty, *National Foreign Language Center, and Center for the Advanced Study of Language, University of Maryland, College Park*

Roger Gilabert, *Blanquerna Communication Studies Department, Universitat Ramon Lull*

Janet Holmes, *Victoria University of Wellington*

Rebeca Jasso-Aguilar, *University of New Mexico*

Eric Kellerman, *Departments of English and Applied Linguistics, and Centre for Language Studies, University of Nijmegen*

Youngkyu Kim, *Department of Korean Studies, Ehwa Woman's University, Seoul*

Dong-kwan Kong, *Department of East Asian Languages and Literatures, University of Hawai'i*

Hella Koonen, *Department of English, University of Nijmegen*

Jinhwa Lee, *Department of Second Language Studies, University of Hawai'i*

Young-geun Lee, *University of Hawai'i Korean Flagship Overseas Program*

John A. Lett, *Research and Analysis Division, Defense Language Institute, Foreign Language Center, Monterey*

Michael H. Long, *School of Languages, Literatures, and Cultures, University of Maryland, College Park*

Rachel Rivers, *College of Education, University of Hawai'i*

William P. Rivers, *Center for the Advanced Study of Language, University of Maryland, College Park*

Ken Urano, *Faculty of Business Administration, Hokkai-gakuen University Sapporo, Japan*

Sonja Vandermeeren, *Germanistisches Seminar, Christian-Albrechts-Universitadt zu Kiel*

Monique van der Haagen, *Department of English, University of Nijmegen*

Michelle Winn, *University of California, Berkeley*

Acknowledgments

I would like to thank all the authors for allowing me to include their work; Jane Walsh and Geraldine Mark of Cambridge University Press for their patience and assistance in preparation of the manuscript; the anonymous reviewers for constructive comments on the first version of the text; and Cambridge Applied Linguistics Series co-editor, Jack Richards, for handling the review process itself.

Overview: A rationale for needs analysis and needs analysis research

Michael H. Long

In an era of shrinking resources, there are growing demands for accountability in public life, including education. In foreign and second language teaching, one of several consequences is the increasing importance attached to careful studies of learner needs as a prerequisite for effective course design.

Successful language learning is vital for refugees, immigrants, international students, those receiving education or vocational training through the medium of a second language in their own country, and individuals in occupations requiring advanced foreign language proficiency, among others. The combination of target language varieties, skills, lexicons, genres, registers, etc., that each of these and other groups needs varies greatly, however, meaning that language teaching using generic programs and materials, not designed with particular groups in mind, will be inefficient, at the very least, and in all probability, grossly inadequate. Just as no medical intervention would be prescribed before a thorough diagnosis of what ails the patient, so no language teaching program should be designed without a thorough needs analysis. Every language course should be considered a course for specific purposes, varying only (and considerably, to be sure) in the precision with which learner needs can be specified – from little or none in the case of programs for most young children to minute detail in the case of occupationally-, academically-, or vocationally-oriented programs for most adults.

A one-size-fits-all approach has long been discredited by research findings on the *specificity* of the tasks, genres and discourse practices that language learners encounter in the varied domains in which they must operate.[1] It is not simply that the *language* and *skills* required to function successfully, and the *texts* encountered, vary greatly for an overseas college student within discipline A, B or C, for a foreign tourist, for an immigrant construction worker, jeweler, hospital porter, union organizer, nurse, or emergency room physician, or for an illiterate newly-arrived refugee struggling with social survival

1

tasks (opening a bank account, renting an apartment, gaining permission for a child to start school, etc.) during the first months in an alien culture. The variation in language, skills and texts reflects underlying differences in the *roles* such individuals occupy, and in the *beliefs, practices, ways of speaking*, and *cultures* of the often overlapping *discourse communities* of which they seek to become members. As a recent discussion of discourse communities in academic disciplines concluded:

> Communities ... differ from one another along both social and cognitive dimensions, offering contrasts not just in their fields of knowledge, but also in their ways of talking, their argument structures, aims, social behaviors, power relations, and political interests.   (Hyland & Hamp-Lyons, 2002, p. 6)

Given such a broad range of phenomena, an ability to perform linguistic analyses of texts (telephone conversations, service encounters, academic lectures, scientific journal articles, office e-mail messages, purchase orders, driver's license application forms, etc.), even when an analysis is computer-assisted, will alone clearly be insufficient. Language teachers and applied linguists need to be familiar with the history of needs analysis (see, e.g., Swales, 1985, 2001; West, 1994) to avoid repeating mistakes of the past and reinventing the wheel. They also need familiarity with the wide array of sources and methods available to them today, and with appropriate combinations thereof, i.e., with source x method interactions.

Unfortunately, while books and journals are replete with reports of NAs (needs analyses) each year, with very few exceptions (see Van Els & Oud-de-Glas, 1983; Van Hest & Oud-de-Glas, 1990) relatively little attention is paid to needs analysis itself. In some respects, the NA literature is reminiscent of writing on language pedagogy 20 years ago, when authors wrote data-free books and journal articles recounting their alleged success at teaching this or that structure or skill, while offering no evidence that what they described had worked at all or worked better than alternative 'methods'. There is an urgent need for a serious research program (as distinct from one-off studies) focused on methodological options in NA itself. Hence, *methodological issues* in NA constitute a major focus of this volume, and contributors include explicit discussion of their very varied methodologies in their chapters.

The increasing importance attached to professionally-conducted NAs comes at a time when the theory and practice of NA itself, and of language teaching in general, are in flux, as educators respond to theory change and research findings in SLA and L2 syllabus design.

To illustrate, for some 30 years now, researchers have repeatedly shown that learners do not acquire a new language one structure at a time (nor could, since so many structures are inter-dependent). Nor do they acquire in the theoretically and empirically unmotivated structural or notional-functional sequences found in linguistically-based syllabuses and textbooks. This is true even when teachers and textbook writers attempt to teach them that way (see, e.g., Ellis, 1989; Hyltenstam, 1977; Lightbown, 1983; Pienemann, 1984). Learners are far more active and cognitively-independent participants in the acquisition process than is assumed by the erroneous belief that what you teach is what they learn, and when you teach it is when they learn it.

Nor do learners move from a state of zero knowledge of a structure to native-like mastery in one step, as is assumed possible by the many superficially different language teaching 'methods' – from ALM to Silent Way – that demand immediate forced production of the structure of the day to native-like accuracy levels, with 'error correction' prescribed when things go wrong. In reality, sudden categorical learning appears to be very rare, even in cases where theorists sometimes claim it does occur, e.g., (putative) parameter-resetting (see Hilles, 1986). Rather, language learning both inside and outside classrooms is a gradual, cumulative, often non-linear process. It involves zig-zag developmental paths, U-shaped behavior, passage through fixed developmental sequences in such areas as negation, interrogatives and relative clauses, plateaus, restructuring, lengthy periods when non-target forms and constructions are the norm, fluctuations in error rate, and only gradually improving accuracy (see, e.g., Huebner, 1983; Kellerman, 1985; Long, 1990, 2003; McLaughlin, 1990; Perkins, Brutten, & Gass, 1996; Pica, 1983; Pishwa, 1993; Sato, 1988, 1990; Shirai, 1990; Stauble, 1984; Zobl, 1982, 1984).

These and many other SLA research findings cast doubt on the validity of synthetic, especially grammatical, syllabuses, and have been partially responsible for the miscellany of syllabus types – lexical, structural, notional-functional, relational, topical, procedural, process, content, and task, plus hybrids – now on the table in applied linguistics (see, e.g., Long & Crookes, 1992; Robinson, 1995, 1998). The findings also delegitimize related synthetic 'focus on forms' language teaching methodology.[2] Equally, if structures or other linguistic elements (notions, functions, lexical items, etc.) are not to be the units of analysis in a syllabus, it throws into question the relevance of continuing to conduct needs analyses – the output of which will be the input to syllabus design – in terms of the structures or other linguistic forms most likely to be encountered in the domains of interest to a particular learner group. Structurally based NAs, even good ones (see, e.g., Cameron, 1998), tend to produce lists of forms similar to, but far less detailed than, the table of contents of most commercially-published pedagogic grammars, leading one to question their value. That sort of information may still be useful, but it will not be the most important information and, unattached to functional data (see, e.g., Cathcart, 1989) and/or cross-referenced to some other non-linguistic unit of analysis, it will often be meaningless.

Adding independent, converging motivation for a shift towards analytic, e.g., task-based, syllabuses of some kind, a variety of studies have suggested that it is often not lack of linguistic competence *per se* that renders learners unable to perform adequately at work or on an overseas university course. To cite just one of many such examples in the literature, an Australian duty-free store salesman studied by Marriot & Yamada (1991; see, also, Marriot, 1991) knew sufficient specialized Japanese lexical items relevant for selling opals to tourists, but missed sales opportunities for lack of awareness of cross-cultural pragmatic differences in making a sale. Rather, it is learners' inability to accomplish the *tasks* required of them, for which language use is often highly differentiated and both field- and context-specific, and for which much more than L2 linguistic knowledge is needed (see, e.g., Arden-Close, 1993; Bosher & Smalkoski, 2002; Jacobson, 1986; Jacoby, 1999; Jacoby & McNamara, 1999; Marriot, 1991; Medway & Andrews, 1992; Miller-Retwaiut, 1994; Mohan & Smith, 1992; Selinker, 1979). Hence, many modern NAs, including several reported in this volume, use *task* as the unit of analysis, with analysts (and sometimes the students themselves) out in the field collecting samples of the *discourse* typically involved in performance of target tasks relevant for the communicative needs of particular groups of learners.

There is more than one way to conduct a NA, however, just as there is more than one way to teach a language. Not all the studies reported in this volume share the same psycholinguistic underpinnings. By design, they illustrate a wide variety of task-based and non-task-based methodologies. It would be unnecessarily limiting, unreflective of the current state of the art, and a disservice to the reader to present multiple examples of just one approach, whatever the editor's personal preferences and beliefs. Readers sufficiently interested in the issues to work through a book like this will certainly be capable of forming their own judgments as to the relative merits of the different approaches.

Modern needs analysts owe a considerable debt to the pioneers in this important sub-field of applied linguistics, many of them still active: Jordan, Mackay, Mountford, Munby, Strevens, Swales, Trim, Van Eck, Van Els, Van Hest, Oud-de-Glas, Johns, Hutchison, Waters, Richterich, Chancerel, Jupp, Hodlin, Selinker, Candlin, Trimble, Brindley, Hyland, Flowerdew, and Dudley-Evans, among others, and to those associated with such early publications as *ESPMENA Bulletin, Lenguas Para Objectivos Específicos, English for Specific Purposes*, and the more recent *English for Academic Purposes*. They have laid the foundations in the form of conceptual ground-clearing, concrete examples of needs analyses, and insights into the complexities of domain-specific language use. What is needed now is a serious effort by applied linguists to identify generalizations that can be made about how best to conduct needs analyses for populations A or B, in sectors C or D, given constraints E or F. However detailed and insightful they may be, particular findings about the language, genres, tasks, etc., encountered in this or that domain are often only of use to others with the same or similar students. Of greater relevance to a far wider audience are the methodological lessons arising from such studies, and especially, research on the methodology of needs analysis itself. Yet such work is scarce. A principal aim of this volume is to indicate by example the potential scope of a needs analysis research program.

In the opening chapter, 'Methodological issues in learner needs analysis', I provide a summary and evaluation of various *sources* of information for a NA (published and unpublished literature, the learners, applied linguists, domain experts, triangulated sources); *methods* of obtaining that information (expert and non-expert intuitions, interviews, questionnaire surveys, language audits, participant and non-participant observation, ethnographic methods, journals and logs, language proficiency and competency measures); and *source x method combinations*. The three areas are considered with respect to the potential of different options for obtaining reliable, valid, and usable data about the *language* and *tasks* required for successful performance within a target academic, occupational, vocational, or other discourse domain. The review is based on a survey of literature in applied linguistics and social science research methods, supplemented by findings from a data-based study of methodological issues in a task-based NA of airline flight attendants. Several sources, methods, and source x method interactions, as well as the reliability of insiders and outsiders in NAs, were the primary foci of the flight attendant study. More case studies are needed to test the generalizability of the study's methodological findings to less neatly circumscribed, less public occupations than that of flight attendant, and to other sectors altogether.

Most contributors to this book, and most NAs, are concerned with needs specification at the level of individuals or, more often, learner types. In an era of globalization and shrinking resources, however, language audits and NAs for whole societies are likely to become increasingly important. Good (or bad) NAs at this level can greatly affect federal, state, or local government language policies, with far-reaching consequences for millions of people for years to come. The broad scope of such analyses presents peculiar methodological difficulties, with scientific sampling being especially important, and relatively large sample size making (telephone or written) questionnaire surveys and studies of government publications and other written documents likely to figure among the favored methods and sources. Furthermore, since primary audiences for findings from NAs in the public sector include politicians, economists, bureaucrats, and others seldom known for their understanding of the role of language in society, findings and rationales for recommendations need to be explicit, empirically-supported and expressed using concepts and terminology familiar to them.

Such was the case in two ground-breaking studies reported in the chapter by Richard Brecht and William Rivers. In what is a potentially precedent-setting innovation in foreign language needs analysis, Brecht and Rivers adopt an economic approach to analyzing the language 'market' in the USA, operationalizing 'supply' and 'demand' at the tactical level, and 'capacity' and 'needs' at the strategic level. This and an accompanying cost-benefit analysis allow them to distinguish 'private marginal value' – what an individual considers when deciding to learn or maintain skills in a language, and 'social marginal value' – the *societal need* for that language. They apply the model to two quite different cases: (i) language needs for US national security, and (ii) the accessibility of social services to speakers of languages other than English (LOTE) in the US state of Maryland. It is safe to predict that both studies will serve as models for work of this kind in many countries for years to come.

A second chapter dealing with NA in the public sector involves one of the largest foreign language teaching operations in the world, the Defense Language Institute (DLI) in Monterey, California. With some 800 faculty members providing instruction in 22 languages to 3,300 students for six hours each day – both staff and students funded by the US government, and ultimately by the American taxpayer, to the tune of tens of millions of dollars per year – it is vital to know that what is taught will satisfy the future communicative needs both of the students themselves and their sponsoring agencies. Not surprisingly, therefore, needs analysis at DLI is accorded considerable importance. The Director of its Research and Analysis Division, John Lett, reports three recent NAs conducted at DLI. Sources were domain experts familiar with students' future work, and experts in language proficiency assessment, using the ILR (Interagency Language Roundtable) scale; methods utilized included document analysis, retrospection, and unstructured interviews. After joint group discussions among the subject matter and testing experts, tasks were rated for frequency and criticality, and in some cases classified in various ways. They were then assigned a consensus language proficiency rating in each skill modality, taking into consideration the typical conditions under which those tasks are carried out and the standards of performance required. Subsequent reviews of the tasks and ratings often produce recommendations for policy makers as to the global language requirements for various military careers.

Having described the NAs themselves, Lett moves on to discuss several important reliability and validity issues that should be of concern to needs analysts everywhere, but which have very rarely been discussed in the NA literature. These include the use of convenience samples of subject matter experts, the lack of ready external criteria for assessing the validity of analyses, the lack of independence of proficiency level ratings obtained via the collaborative group process, possible response bias, and the halo effect. He identifies potential solutions to several of the problems, e.g., stratified random sampling, use of surrogate or partial test-retest and modified split-half procedures for improving reliability, and relating DLI graduates' language proficiency ratings to supervisors' field reports on their subsequent job performance in predictive validity studies. He points out, however, that the increased costs in time and personnel, among other problems, would often render them inadequate, or in some cases preclude their adoption altogether.

The next four contributions deal with NA in the occupational sector. In one of the few NAs to date to employ multiple sources and methods – and one of the very few to utilize participant observation, in the form of on-the-job training, to do the work being studied – Rebeca Jasso-Aguilar reports a study she conducted of the target tasks and language needs of maids ("housekeepers") in a large Waikiki hotel, part of a chain employing approximately 1000 maids. They are typically female, low income immigrants (or in some parts of the US, often illegal aliens). Participant observation (with tape-recording and note-taking), unstructured interviews and questionnaires were the methods Jasso-Aguilar used. Sources included three hotel maids, various supervisors, the executive housekeeper, a human resources staff member, daily shift briefings for the maids, and work-related documents, such as job descriptions. Methods and sources were triangulated to help guage reliability, and considerable disparities emerging between what supervisors confidently believed the maids' work to involve and what it actually involved. Jasso-Aguilar concludes with a critique of the unbalanced distribution of power in such settings, and a call for researchers to adopt a more critical perspective in NA – one which allows for the inclusion of a wider range of participants' voices and assessment of their needs beyond the workplace.

Working in a very different social and cultural setting, Sonja Vandermeeren begins with a brief introduction to problems in identifying objective, subjective, unconscious, subjective unmet, and objective unmet foreign language needs in the business world. Some useful sources are described, including business clients who are native speakers of the foreign language concerned (in this case, German), along with some methods for accessing their expertise. In one of the non-task-based NAs described in the book, Vandermeeren then reports results from two questionnaire surveys she conducted of the quantitative and qualitative language needs of 112 Finnish companies wishing to sell their products in German markets. Among other interesting findings was the existence of unmet needs for German of which many companies were unaware, but which Vandermeeren's methodology revealed. Also of note, and reminiscent of Marriot & Yamada's findings, was the relatively greater importance attributed by German clients to the Finns' knowledge of German business culture and practices than to their knowledge of the German (or English) language itself. Vandermeeren underscores the importance of NA not only for foreign language teachers, but for those who train them. She notes an innovative course in international business writing that has students conduct field research on foreign language needs as one of three tools used to develop the required cultural knowledge.

In another European study, this time of the English language needs of Catalan journalists operating in nine sub-domains of their profession, Roger Gilabert begins by drawing a useful, operationalizable distinction between target tasks and target sub-tasks. He then proceeds to demonstrate, first, that some sources and methods were more revealing than others in absolute terms. Second, he shows how triangulation by sources (scholars, company representatives, domain experts, and documents) and methods (unstructured and structured interviews, introspections, non-participant observation, and questionnaires) can improve the reliability and validity of NA findings in general. In the journalism study, the triangulation was supplemented by further non-participant observation of specific target tasks, which turned out to be especially useful, and by the collection of additional discourse samples. Gilabert also identifies some source x method interactions in his study, e.g., the greater productivity of insider introspections with domain experts than with company representatives. He offers useful suggestions concerning the relatively greater value of (i) responses to questionnaire items that probe judgments of frequency and perceived need, compared with harder-to-define 'difficulty,' and (ii) analysis of target discourse (in this case, e-mail messages) over self-report data by their sender.

In the fourth and final chapter on occupational needs, Eric Kellerman, Hella Koonen and Monique van der Haagen report an interesting study of a topic that has rarely, if ever, featured in applied linguistics, the language needs of professional footballers. With the internationalization of many professional sports, the communicative needs of professional athletes is a topic likely to grow in importance. In another non-task-based study, Kellerman et al employed multiple methods and sources: a telephone questionnaire (a form of interview schedule) with Dutch soccer club managements; a written questionnaire in both English and Dutch for foreign players; and unstructured interviews with two teachers of Dutch attached to top professional clubs in Holland, a club press officer, and two well-known coaches, including Arsene Wenger, the world-famous French manager of 2002 English Premiership champions, Arsenal. The sometimes strikingly different findings for English and Dutch as target languages, for players from different L1 and cultural backgrounds, and between language policies at Dutch and English clubs, underscore the importance of sampling in all NA studies. The study also illustrates how important personal insider contacts can be for what ethnographers (and perhaps security personnel at some clubs) refer to as 'gaining entry to the field.'

In a lengthy report on NA in an academic setting, focusing on foreign language learners, Craig Chaudron et al describe a NA conducted in the University of Hawai'i's Korean as a foreign language (KFL) program as part of the first stage of a federally funded three-year pilot study of Task-Based Language Teaching for Korean. The NA began with unstructured interviews of a stratified random sample of students enrolled in KFL classes, followed by a survey of the entire population using a questionnaire based upon the interview findings. The study shows how even students in what foreign language teachers often assume to be homogenous groups, and/or groups having no real need for a language beyond satisfying a college language requirement, in reality often do have definable, and varied, present or future communicative needs – needs that will often not be adequately met through use of a one-size-fits-all curriculum and set of teaching materials. Then, in a foretaste of work reported in the book's final section, the second half of the paper describes procedures employed by the University of Hawai'i team for collection and analysis of target discourse samples surrounding performance of two elementary-level 'social survival' target tasks for visitors to Korea. The final part of the paper describes how results of the analysis of target discourse were combined with SLA theory and research findings to motivate the design of two modules of prototype task-based teaching materials, each consisting of seven pedagogic tasks, the last also serving as an exit test, for classroom use in Korean courses.

The fifth and final section comprises three chapters, two from the USA and one from New Zealand, which focus on the collection and analysis of samples of language use in target discourse domains. After target tasks for a particular group of learners have been identified, the second stage of a thorough task-based NA involves collection and analysis of authentic samples of discourse surrounding accomplishment of those tasks. The first step, data-collection, is rarely without problems. For instance, quite apart from the usual technical difficulties surrounding audio or video recordings in the field, discourse samples may be lacking in the immediate environment of the language teaching institution, as is often the case when listening or speaking materials are required for foreign language learners headed for a second language environment. On other occasions, there may be difficulty in gaining access to sensitive service encounters, especially those involving confidentiality.

An example of the latter type, the US naturalization interview, was the focus of the study by Michelle Winn. Winn provides a detailed description of what was involved in her 'gaining entry to the field,' and identifies nine factors that facilitated the success of this and other aspects of her work. These included use of an inside connection, positioning herself as a learner rather than as an expert or evaluator, and use of immediate 'debriefing' interviews with INS (Immigration and Naturalization Service) interviewers. Winn finishes by showing how tasks and sub-tasks identified from the discourse analysis can be translated into task-based pedagogic materials and classroom activities.

Nicola Downey Bartlett reports a detailed study of what might at first seem an easy-enough task in a fairly straightforward service encounter: ordering coffee. The complexities she uncovers provide compelling evidence of the need for specificity in course design, even for seemingly mundane everyday tasks. Bartlett recorded 168 conversations at three sites where coffee was sold. She analyzed the resulting transcripts using a system partly inspired by pioneering work on service encounters by Ventola (1983), eventually producing a distillation of the findings in the form of an empirically based *prototypical dialog* of the kind that can provide a useful basis for the design of teaching materials. Finally, Bartlett compared her findings with dialogs in several current ESL textbooks, some claiming to model authentic native speaker use. As has been found in every previous study of this issue of which I am aware (see, also, Long, this volume), the discrepancies she identifies provide further evidence of the need to go beyond textbook writers' intuitions if a program (or publisher) is serious about meeting learner needs.

Bartlett's chapter offers a good example of how the second phase in task-based NAs, analysis of target discourse, can be conducted. A potentially complementary non-task-based approach is provided in the final chapter in this section. Over the five years of its existence, Victoria University of Wellington's government-funded Language in the Workplace (LWP) project has amassed a very large, very valuable corpus of audio- and video-recordings of talk in a variety of New Zealand workplaces. In her paper for this volume, the project's Director, Janet Holmes, focuses on a particularly important, yet often neglected, aspect of work-place communication: small talk.

As Holmes points out, small talk is the language that greases interactional wheels; failure in this area can sometimes be as important as an employee's substantive job performance (see, also, Bosher & Smalkoski, 2002; Svendsen & Krebs, 1984). The background knowledge, cultural knowledge, and sociolinguistic and pragmatic skills required are sometimes difficult even for native speakers to acquire, and harder still for the two populations targeted in her study: recent immigrants, and workers with an intellectual disability. Holmes provides an important discussion of the research methods utilized by the LWP project team, in particular, procedures that can be employed to enhance the validity of field recordings for that kind of work. This is followed by qualitative linguistic analysis of the target discourse samples. She reports the LWP team's findings concerning common topics for small talk, typical distributional patterns, and functions of small talk at work, before closing with some practical pedagogic suggestions for teachers involved in pre-experience and in-service training for students of these kinds.

The contributors to this volume do not toe a party line in the way they go about their work. Nor do they pretend to have answers to all the many complex methodological questions remaining in learner NA – questions concerning such matters as appropriate sampling procedures, the relative merits of various units of analysis, and optimal choices and triangulation among sources and methods, let alone what must eventually follow: predictive validity studies. As part of an embryonic collaborative research program, however, it is to be hoped that some of the studies reported here will inspire replications with different populations in different sectors, as well as new work designed to put NA on as sound a theoretical and empirical base as is expected in other areas of applied linguistics. Better-conducted needs analyses, after all, will enhance the quality of language teaching programs based upon them and, thereby, success rates for language learners.

Notes

1 By way of illustration, for examples of differences within and among academic disciplines, see Braine (1995); Dudley-Evans (1995); Dudley-Evans & St. John (1998); Flowerdew (2000); Horowitz (1986); Hyland (2000); Johns (1997); Prior (1998); and Swales (1981, 1990). For an excellent discussion of the need for specificity in course design, see Hyland (2002).
2 For empirical findings and arguments against synthetic syllabuses, 'focus on forms,' and also its opposite, a pure 'focus on meaning,' and in support of analytic, especially task-based, syllabuses and 'focus on form,' see, e.g., Doughty & Long (2002); Doughty & Williams (1998); Long (1985, 1991, 2000); Long & Crookes (1992); Long & Norris (2000); Long & Robinson (1998); Norris & Ortega (2000); Skehan (1998).

References

Arden-Close, C. (1993). Language problems in science lectures to non-native speakers. *English for Specific Purposes* 12, 3, 252–61.
Bosher, S., & Smalkoski, K. (2002). From needs analysis to curriculum development: Designing a course in health-care communication for immigrant students in the USA. *English for Specific Purposes* 21, 59–79.
Braine, G. (1995). Writing in the natural sciences and engineering. In D. Belcher & G. Braine (eds.), *Academic writing in a second language: Essays on research and pedagogy.* NJ: Ablex.
Cameron, R. (1988). A language-focused needs analysis for ESL-speaking nursing students in class and clinic. *Foreign Language Annals* 31, 2, 203–18.

Cathcart, R. L. (1989). Authentic English and the survival English curriculum. *TESOL Quarterly* 23, 1, 105–26.

Doughty, C. J., & Long, M. H. (2002). Optimal psycholinguistic environments for distance foreign language learning. Plenary address to the conference on 'Distance Learning of the Less Commonly Taught Languages.' February 1–3, 2002. Arlington, VA. *Second Language Studies* 20, 1, 2002, 1–42. Also in *Forum of International Development Studies* (Nagoya University) 23, 2003, 35–73. Also in *Language Learning and Technology* Volume 7, Number 3 (September) 2003, 50–80. (http://llt.msu.edu)

Doughty, C. J., & Williams, J. (1998). *Focus on form in classroom second language acquisition*. Cambridge: Cambridge University Press.

Dudley-Evans, T. (1995). Variations in the discourse patterns favoured by different disciplines and their pedagogic implications. In J. Flowerdew (ed.), *Academic listening* (pp. 146–58). Cambridge: Cambridge University Press.

Dudley-Evans, T., & St. John, M.-J. (1998). *Developments in English for specific purposes*. Cambridge: Cambridge University Press.

Ellis, R. (1989). Are classroom and naturalistic acquisition the same? A study of the classroom acquisition of German word order rules. *Studies in Second Language Acquisition* 11, 3, 305–28.

Flowerdew, J. (2000). Discourse community, legitimate peripheral participation, and the non-native English-speaking scholar. *TESOL Quarterly* 24, 1, 127–50.

Hilles, S. (1986). Interlanguage and the pro-drop parameter. *Second Language Research* 2, 1, 33–52.

Horowitz, D. (1986). What professors actually require: Academic tasks for the ESL classroom. *TESOL Quarterly* 20, 445–62.

Huebner, T. (1983). Linguistic systems and linguistic change in an interlanguage. *Studies in Second Language Acquisition* 6, 1, 33–53.

Hyland, K. (2000). *Disciplinary discourses: Social interactions in academic writing*. London: Longman.

Hyland, K. (2002). Specificity revisited: How far should we go now? *English for Specific Purposes* 21, 385–95.

Hyland, K., & Hamp-Lyons, E. (2002) EAP: issues and directions. *Journal of English for Academic Purposes* 1, 1–12.

Hyltenstam, K. (1977). Implicational patterns in interlanguage syntax variation. *Language Learning* 27, 383–411.

Jacobson, W. H. (1986). An assessment of the communication needs of non-native speakers of English in an undergraduate physics lab. *English for Specific Purposes* 5, 2, 189–95.

Jacoby, S. (1999). Rethinking EST: What can "indigenous assessment" tell us about the communication culture of science? Ms. Department of Communication, University of New Hampshire.

Jacoby, S., & McNamara, T. (1999). Locating competence. *English for Specific Purposes* 18, 3, 213–41.

14   *Michael H. Long*

Johns, A. (1997). *Text, role and context: Developing academic literacies.* Cambridge: Cambridge University Press.

Kellerman, E. (1985). If at first you do succeed ... In S. M. Gass & C. Madden (eds.), *Input and second language acquisition* (pp. 345–53). Rowley, MA: Newbury House.

Lightbown, P. M. (1983). Exploring relationships between developmental and instructional sequences in L2 acquisition. In H. W. Seliger & M. H. Long (eds.), *Classroom-oriented research in second language acquisition* (pp. 217–43). Rowley, MA: Newbury House.

Long, M. H. (1985). A role for instruction in second language acquisition: task-based language teaching. In K. Hyltenstam and M. Pienemann (eds.), *Modeling and assessing second language development* (pp. 77–99). Clevedon, Avon: Multilingual Matters.

Long, M. H. (1990). The least a second language acquisition theory needs to explain. *TESOL Quarterly* 24, 4, 649–66.

Long, M. H. (1991). Focus on form: A design feature in language teaching methodology. In K. de Bot, R. B. Ginsberg and C. Kramsch (eds.), *Foreign language research in cross-cultural perspective* (pp. 39–52). Amsterdam: John Benjamins.

Long, M. H. (2000). Focus on form in task-based language teaching. In R. L. Lambert & E. Shohamy (eds.), *Language policy and pedagogy* (pp. 179–92). Amsterdam and Philadelphia: John Benjamins.

Long, M. H. (2003). Stabilization and fossilization in interlanguage development. In C. J. Doughty & M. H. Long (eds.), *Handbook of second language acquisition* (pp. 487–535). Oxford: Blackwell.

Long, M. H., & Crookes, G. (1992). Three approaches to task-based language teaching. *TESOL Quarterly* 26, 1, 27–56.

Long, M. H., & Norris, J. M. (2000). Task-based teaching and assessment. In M. Byram (ed.), *Encyclopedia of language teaching* (pp. 597–603). London: Routledge.

Long, M. H., & Robinson, P. J. (1998). Focus on form: Theory, research and practice. In C. Doughty and J. Williams (eds.), *Focus on form in second language acquisition* (pp. 15–41). Cambridge: Cambridge University Press.

Marriot, H. (1991). Language planning and language management for tourism shopping situations. In A. J. Liddicoat (ed.), *Language planning and language politics in Australia. Australian Review of Applied Linguistics* (pp. 191–222). Series S, No. 8. Melbourne: ALAA.

Marriot, H., & Yamada, N. (1991). Japanese discourse in tourism shopping situations. In *Japan and the World Vol. 3.* Proceedings of the Biennial Conference of the Japanese Association of Australia. Canberra: Australia-Japan Research Centre.

McLaughlin, B. (1990). Restructuring. *Applied Linguistics* 11, 113–28.

Medway, P., & Andrews, R. (1992). Building with words: Discourse in an architect's office. *Carleton Papers in Applied Language Studies* 9, 1–32.

Miller-Retwaiut, H. L. (1994). Cross-cultural communication difficulties of some Micronesians in entry-level employment interviews in Hawai'i. M.A. in ESL thesis. Honolulu, Hawai'i: Department of Second Language Studies, University of Hawai'i at Manoa.

Mohan, B., & Smith, S. M. (1992). Context and cooperation in academic tasks. In D. Nunan (ed.), *Collaborative language learning and teaching* (pp. 81–99). Cambridge: Cambridge University Press.

Norris, J. M., & Ortega, L. (2000). Effectiveness of instruction: A research synthesis and quantitative meta-analysis. *Language Learning* 50, 3, 417–528.

Perkins, K., Brutten, S. R., & Gass, S. M. (1996). An investigation of patterns of discontinuous learning: Implications for ESL measurement. *Language Testing* 13, 1, 23–51.

Pica, T. (1983). Adult acquisition of English as a second language under different conditions of exposure. *Language Learning* 33, 4, 465–97.

Pienemann, M. (1984). Psychological constraints on the teachability of languages. *Studies in Second Language Acquisition* 6, 186–214.

Pishwa, H. (1993). Abrupt restructuring versus gradual acquisition. In C. A. Blackshire-Belay (ed.), *Current issues in second language acquisition and development* (pp. 143–66). Lanham, MD: University Press of America.

Prior, P. (1998). *Writing/disciplinarity: A sociohistoric account of literate activity in the academy.* Mahwah, NJ: Lawrence Erlbaum.

Robinson, P. J. (1995). Current approaches to syllabus design: A discussion with Ron White. *RELC Guidelines* 17, 1, 93–102.

Robinson, P. J. (1998). State of the art: SLA theory and second language syllabus design. *The Language Teacher* 22, 4, 7–13.

Sato, C. J. (1988). Origins of complex syntax in interlanguage development. *Studies in Second Language Acquisition* 10, 3, 371–95.

Sato, C. J. (1990). *The syntax of conversation in interlanguage development.* Tubingen: Gunter Narr.

Selinker, L. (1979). On the use of informants in discourse analysis and 'language for specialized purposes'. *International Review of Applied Linguistics* 17, 3, 189–215.

Shirai, Y. (1990). U-shaped behavior in L2 acquisition. In H. Burmeister & P. L. Rounds (eds.), *Variability in second language acquisition. Vol. 2* (pp. 685–700). Eugene, OR: Department of Linguistics.

Skehan, P. (1998). *A cognitive approach to language learning.* Oxford: Oxford University Press.

Stauble, A.-M. (1984). A comparison of the Spanish-English and Japanese-English interlanguage continuum. In R. W. Andersen (ed.), *Second language: A cross-linguistic perspective* (pp. 323–53). Rowley, MA: Newbury House.

Svendsen, C., & Krebs, K. (1984). Identifying English for the job: Examples from healthcare occupations. *The ESP Journal* 3, 153–64.

Swales, J. (1981). Definitions in science and law – Evidence for subject-specific course components? *Fachsprache* 3, 106–12.

Swales, J. (1985). *Episodes in ESP.* Hemel Hempstead, UK: Prentice-Hall.

Swales, J. (1990). *Genre analysis: English in academic and research settings.* Cambridge: Cambridge University Press.

Swales, J. (2001). EAP-related linguistic research: An intellectual history. In J. Flowerdew & M. Peacock (eds.), *Research perspectives on English for academic purposes* (pp. 42–54). Cambridge: Cambridge University Press.

Van Els, T., & Oud-de-Glas, M. (eds.) (1983). *Research into foreign language needs.* Augsberg: University of Augsberg.

Van Hest, E., & Oud-de-Glas, M. (1990). *A survey of techniques used in the diagnosis and analysis of foreign language needs in industry.* Brussels: Lingua.

Ventola, E. (1983). Contrasting schematic structures in service encounters. *Applied Linguistics* 4, 3, 242–58.

West, R. (1994). Needs analysis in language teaching. *Language Teaching* 27, 1–19.

Zobl, H. (1982). A direction for contrastive analysis: The comparative study of developmental sequences. *TESOL Quarterly* 16, 2, 169–83.

Zobl, H. (1984). The wave model of linguistic change and the naturalness of interlanguage. *Studies in Second Language Acquisition* 6, 2, 160–85.

PART I:
METHODOLOGICAL ISSUES

1 Methodological issues in learner needs analysis

Michael H. Long

Introduction

In an era of shrinking resources, there are growing demands for accountability in public life, with education a particularly urgent case and foreign language education a prime example within it. Many secondary school students and, especially, adults with serious academic, occupational, vocational, or 'survival' needs for functional L2 proficiency, as well as their sponsors, are increasingly dissatisfied with lessons, materials and methodology developed for someone else or for no-one in particular. There is an urgent need for courses of all kinds to be relevant – and to be seen to be relevant – to the needs of specific groups of learners and of society at large. This is especially, but not only, true of advanced courses, which by definition (should) involve specialized instruction for specific purposes. General (language for no purpose) courses at any proficiency level almost always teach too much, e.g., vocabulary, skills, registers or styles some learners do not need, and too little, e.g., omitting lexis and genres that they do. Instead of a one-size-fits-all approach, it is more defensible to view every course as involving specific purposes, the difference in each case being simply the precision with which it is possible to identify current or future uses of the L2. This varies from little or no precision in the case of most young children, to great precision in that of most adult learners.

One of the ways in which foreign and second language educators have responded to the changing situation is by basing more of their courses on the findings of surveys of learner needs. However, as in the teaching of English as a Second Language (ESL), too many of the needs analyses are carried out via semi-structured interviews or, more commonly, written questionnaires. Moreover, while exceptions exist and the situation is slowly improving, in the past the instruments have often been devised by teachers or applied linguists with limited expertise in research methods, little or no insider knowledge of the field concerned, and with the learners themselves as the primary, sometimes the only, respondents (see, e.g., Alalou, 2001; Lepetit &

Cichocki, 2002). The reliability and validity of the findings produced by such procedures are rarely discussed.

Regardless of the *methods* used to obtain it, the sufficiency of language students as *sources* of information about their present or future communicative needs is a complex and sensitive issue. To be sure, learners sometimes not only wish to be consulted, but also are well informed. In most cases, however, while they can identify their general reasons for language study (to visit country A, to study for a masters degree in subject B in country C, to work in occupation D, etc.), it will be the analyst's job to identify needs, administer tests, and generally complete the diagnosis. This is no different from what happens in any walk of life where specialized knowledge is involved. A physician, for example, typically begins with a general question asking a patient what brought him or her to the clinic today, but then assumes responsibility for the diagnosis itself, as well as for selecting an appropriate course of treatment.

While it would be comforting to assume otherwise, learner expertise is by no means guaranteed. Learners may be 'pre-experience', or 'pre-service', e.g., international students preparing for graduate studies in the USA, refugees in holding camps awaiting permission to emigrate to a country they have never seen, European or North-American students or management trainees headed for internships and business experience in Asia, or volunteers off to work in a refugee camp in another country. Alternatively, they may be 'in-service', e.g., teachers, scientists, businesswomen, diplomats, or military personnel about to move overseas. All these individuals can sometimes provide useful information on such matters as their learning styles and preferences, i.e., partial input for a *means analysis*. Understandably, however, they tend to make inadequate sources of information for a *needs analysis* (NA), since most in-service learners know about their work, but little about the language involved in functioning successfully in their target discourse domains, and most pre-experience or pre-service learners know little about either.

While a substantial number of NAs have been reported in the literature (and many more, conducted for private businesses or for very specialized groups of learners, remain unpublished), there has been surprisingly little research, despite its obvious and growing importance, on NA itself. Most of those writing on the topic either report the results of NAs, with little by way of generalizable findings or principles, or make unsupported assertions about appropriate or 'successful' NA methodology. With very few exceptions (see, e.g., Van Els & Oud-de-Glas, 1983; Van Hest & Oud-de-Glas, 1990), reviews of the L2 NA literature (e.g., Berwick, 1989; Brindley, 1984, 1989; West, 1994) make little or no reference to research in foreign language education or in ESL on the *methodology of NA* itself for the simple reason that hardly any such research has been conducted.

The limitations of current approaches are compounded by the continued tacit or explicit reliance by most needs analysts on the model provided by the project conducted for the Council of Europe in the early 1970s by Wilkins, Richterich and others (e.g., Richterich & Chancerel, 1977/1980; Wilkins, 1974), and related studies (e.g., Munby, 1978). As is well known, that work was designed to produce a unit credit system for describing language proficiency and use chiefly by individuals whose jobs led them to cross linguistic borders within the (then) European Economic Community. The desirability of some degree of standardization across countries and languages resulted in Wilkins et al opting for a putatively universal, i.e., non-language-specific, *semantically* based, 'notional-functional' system. NAs, together with the syllabuses and pedagogic materials based upon their findings, focused on the notions and functions supposedly required to satisfy various occupational language needs. While innovative and important in its time, and while undoubtedly an improvement on the dominant register analyses and structural sylla-buses of the day, such NAs and resulting curricula were typically based on *intuitions* about the notions and functions required, not empirical studies – and the intuitions of applied linguists, not domain experts, at that. Moreover, the courses, lessons, and materials that embodied the findings still assumed the validity of *synthetic* sylla-buses (Wilkins, 1976), i.e., those in which target language items are presented separately to learners, who are later required to synthesize them for communicative purposes. Like the NAs themselves, such syllabuses are built around *linguistic* (in that case, semantic) units of analysis. As with all synthetic approaches, the sequence of lexical, structural, notional and/or functional syllabus items is fixed *a priori*, thereby often conflicting with well-attested developmental sequences in both foreign and second language learning (for review, see, e.g., R. Ellis, 1994; Larsen-Freeman & Long, 1991; Towell & Hawkins, 1994), and disregarding cognitive processing constraints on learn-ability and teachability (Clahsen, 1987; Pienemann, 1984, 1998), about both of which, to be fair, little was known at the time of the Council of Europe work.

Twenty-five years and much data-based research on foreign and second language acquisition later, few serious scholars maintain that such approaches to language teaching are justified. Most argue instead either for what Wilkins (1976) called *analytic* syllabuses, i.e., those in which, using some *non-linguistic* unit of analysis, learners are presented with holistic samples of L2 use and helped to induce the rules of the grammar, as in, e.g., procedural (Prahbu, 1987), process (Breen, 1984) or task (Long, 1985) syllabuses, or else for some oil and water combination of analytic and synthetic syllabuses, e.g., task and structural (R. Ellis, 1993) or task and lexical (Willis & Willis, 1988). Whatever their respective merits and limitations, the new approaches to second and foreign language instruction require NAs to be conducted using units of analysis that are compatible with the ensuing syllabus specification, methodology, materials and assessment, and *all* approaches to NA, new or old, could benefit from some serious work on issues of reliability and validity.

Units of analysis in NA: The case for task

There are several independent motivations for *task* as the unit of analysis in NA. Most fundamentally, if the rationale offered for adoption of an analytic syllabus of some kind, and/or, in particular, for task-based language teaching is convincing (see Doughty & Long, 2002; Long, 1985, 1998, 2000, to appear; Long & Crookes, 1992, 1993; Long & Norris, 2000; Robinson, 1998, 2001; Skehan, 1998), then task-based NA will allow coherence in course design. It would be of little use to analyze learner needs in terms of linguistic units, such as words, structures, notions or functions, if syllabus content is not to be specified in such terms.

Beyond that basic motivation, however, task-based NAs offer a promising alternative (although not the only one, to be sure) for at least five additional reasons:.

(i) Most 'ready-made' job descriptions produced by domain experts in other sectors, including government, business, craft unions, education, psychology, and the military, are typically formulated in terms of background knowledge, performance standards, and tasks (for examples and discussion, see Long, to appear, chapter 4). So are occupational definitions in the US Department of Labor's *Dictionary of Occupational Titles* (*DOT*, a victim of federal budget cuts in the early 1990s). While an empirical question, it is reasonable to expect that expert insider analyses will more likely be valid than those produced by language teachers and applied linguists, who are outsiders – even the tiny minority of teachers and applied linguists with substantial time, money, and research methods expertise at their disposal.

(ii) However well carried out, linguistically based NAs (for a recent example, see Cameron, 1998) tend to result in lists of decontextualized structural items, not unlike the table of contents of any grammatical syllabus *not* based on a NA, and are of little use to a course designer or materials writer because they provide scant, if any, information on how, or to what ends, the structures are used in the target domain. Filling in the gaps with guesses about use can be highly misleading, as Cathcart (1989) documented in a study of doctor–patient communication. In the terms introduced by Widdowson (1972), real world "uses" of grammatical constructions often differ from the "usages" modeled in grammar-based language teaching materials.

(iii) Similar problems afflict linguistic analyses, and courses based on them, at the supra-sentential, i.e., text, level. Task-based analyses reveal more than text-based analyses about the dynamic qualities of target discourse. Traditional linguistic, or *text*-based, programs reflect a static, product orientation. Texts, after all, whether simplified or genuine, are the *result* of people's attempts to communicate with one another. In the broadest sense, they are the means by which actors no longer present once tried to accomplish communicative tasks. It was the tasks that motivated the texts, not the other way around (for examples and discussion, see Doughty & Long, 2002; Long, 1997, to appear).

(iv) Where ready-made analyses are lacking, new ones are required. Since there is some reason to believe that, with few exceptions, domain experts can provide valid information about the work they do in terms of tasks, but not in terms of language, about which they typically know very little, conceptualizing needs that way helps circumvent two notorious bottlenecks in program design (see Hutchinson & Waters, 1987; Selinker, 1979), the domain expert's usual lack of linguistic knowledge and the applied linguist's usual lack of content knowledge.

(v) The results of task-based needs analyses readily lend themselves as input for the design of a variety of analytic, task-based and/or (a small minority of) content-based second and foreign language courses, whose delivery can be harmonized with what language acquisition research has revealed about universal L2 developmental processes in and out of classrooms. Task-Based Language Teaching (TBLT), in particular (see Doughty & Long, 2002; Long, 1998, 2000, to appear; Long & Norris, 2000), is radically learner-centered not only in its reliance on NA findings to determine syllabus content, but also psycholinguistically, in the steps taken to cater to the learner's internal developmental syllabus, e.g., in its rejection (unlike almost all so-called 'task-based' commercially published materials) of externally imposed linguistic syllabuses of all kinds, overt or *covert*, in favor, among other things, of learner-driven 'focus on form' (Doughty & Williams, 1998; Long, 1991, 1998; Long & Robinson, 1998; Norris & Ortega, 2000).

The study

Given the paucity of information and of research on methodological issues and options in NA, the developments in SLA and L2 syllabus design noted above, and the potential advantages of task-based syllabuses in particular, a two-part study was undertaken to address the following general research question: What are the relative merits of various sources (especially, insiders and outsiders), methods (both qualitative and quantitative), and source x method combinations, in learner NA in general, and in identifying the language and tasks of airline flight attendants in particular. (Reasons for the choice of this specific target group are explained below.) The research consisted of (i) an extensive survey of the scholarly literature on NA and social science research methods; and (ii) collection and analysis of primary data on the language and tasks of flight attendants.

The literature survey

As was to be expected, the literature survey produced a wealth of information – far too lengthy to be presented here in its entirety. What follows is but the briefest summary, with selected references, where available, to useful original sources on possible NA procedures, and to sample studies (sometimes one or two out of a dozen or more reported) utilizing the procedures. For a more detailed account, see Long (to appear, chapters 4 and 5).

Sources for NAs

Five major options emerged from the survey with regard to sources for NAs (see Figure 1, opposite). The middle column in Figure 1 contains references to useful discussions and evaluations of the source concerned. The right-hand column lists references to sample NA studies utilizing that source (and sometimes other sources in the same study). Choice among sources is an important issue if, as Chambers (1980, p. 27) asserts, "whoever determines needs largely determines which needs are determined."

Source	Source/evaluation	Sample use
Published and unpublished literature	Crookes (1986) Long (to appear)	numerous LSP programs
Learners	Brindley (1984) Brindley & Hood (1990) Nunan (1988)	Beatty & Chan (1984) Ramani et al (1988) Savage & Storer (1992)
Teachers and applied linguists	Lamotte (1981) Selinker (1979) Zuck & Zuck (1984)	Numerous LSP programs
Domain experts	Huckin & Olsen (1984) Selinker (1979) Zuck & Zuck (1984)	Bosher & Smalkoski (2002) Coleman (1988) Ramani et al (1988) Tarone et al (1981)
Triangulated sources	Lincoln & Guba (1985) Long (this volume) Lynch (1995)	Cumaranatunge (1988) Gilabert (this volume) Jasso-Aguilar (1999) Long (this volume) Sullivan & Girginer (2002) Svendsen & Krebs (1984) Zughoul & Hussein (1988)

Figure 1   Sources of information for NA

Published and unpublished literature

If only to avoid reinventing the wheel, it behooves course designers to familiarize themselves with at least the scope of what has over the past 30 years become a vast store of published and unpublished NAs.[1] In addition to NAs themselves, numerous other written sources exist in both the public and private sectors. Most medium-sized and large corporations, for example, maintain detailed job descriptions for their employees. Where a unionized workforce is involved, union offices and/or contracts will usually contain similar information. The same is true of government departments, education departments and universities, militaries (see, e.g., the US Army's *Soldier's Manual of Common Tasks*), hospitals, and many other large institutions. Most are written as lists of *tasks* a job entails, sometimes taxonomized, and sometimes accompanied by minimum *performance standards*, usually expressed in terms of speed and accuracy. *Skill Level 1* of the *Soldier's Manual*, for example, deals (in 528 pages) with such matters as loading an M203 grenade launcher, identifying terrain features on a map, engaging targets with an M60 machine gun, reacting to a nuclear hazard, and giving first aid for frostbite. Each task lists conditions under which performance is to be assessed, the performance standards expected, training exercises, examples, any specific language to be used while doing the task, and an evaluation procedure and checklist. A useful general source, and one available in most reference libraries, is the US Department of Labor's *Dictionary of Occupational Titles*, which lists task descriptions for some 12,000 occupations based on tens of thousands of on-site job-analysis studies and other data (see the *DOT* entry for flight attendant, below). Such *occupation*-level descriptions, however, are almost always more general, and less detailed, than particular *job* or *position* descriptions.

Learners

It goes without saying that learners have special rights when it comes to deciding the content of courses they are to undergo, ideally assessed before classes begin, at their inception, and as they proceed. Discussions of perceived and/or actual needs among teachers and students can also raise the level of awareness of both parties as to why they are doing what they are doing, lead them to reflect usefully on means and ends (Nunan, 1988, p. 5), constitute one component in learner training (Ellis & Sinclair, 1989), and especially in courses implementing a process syllabus (Breen, 1984), serve as a vehicle for language learning itself. This does not mean, however, as some have suggested (see, e.g., Auerbach, 1995), that learners will necessarily constitute a reliable source, the best source, or the only legitimate source.

Some learners have been surveyed *in situ*, and found to be both articulate and familiar enough with a target discourse domain to provide usable, valid information (see, e.g., Ramani, Chacko, Singh, & Glendinning, 1988; Tarantino, 1988; Tarone, Dwyer, Gillette, & Icke, 1981), but others, e.g., immigrants and recent arrivals in Australia's Adult Migrant Education Program, have proved less able, and believed that teachers should decide what form a program should take (Brindley, 1984; Brindley & Hood, 1990). For obvious reasons, pre-experience learners will usually constitute unreliable sources, even when highly educated. Thus, PRC (People's Republic of China) graduate students provided very different information about their academic purpose English language needs when surveyed before leaving China, and then again after spending a year at US universities (Beatty & Chan, 1984). Moreover, while experienced 'in-service' informants often make excellent sources on the *content* of their job, training course, field of study, etc., they are more often (understandably) inadequate when it comes to intuitions about their *language needs*. It has, however, occasionally been found possible to improve educated in-service workers as sources on language through use of various elicitation methods, e.g., role-play and guided participant observation activities with a group of Thai aquaculturalists (Savage & Storer, 1992), or a series of carefully planned initial and follow-up questions about the meanings of a journal article in his field with an Israeli geneticist (Selinker, 1979). Finally, even when learners are indeed able to provide useful and valid insights about their present or future needs, better and more readily accessible sources may be available, including experienced language teachers and graduates of the program concerned, employers, subject-area specialists, and written sources of the kinds mentioned below.

Applied linguists

It is absurd to expect applied linguists to know much, if anything, about work in a specialized domain in which they have no training or experience. While few and far between, every comparison of the intuitions of applied linguists and domain experts in this regard that I am aware of has reported serious mismatches (see, e.g., Huckin & Olsen, 1984; Selinker, 1979; Zuck & Zuck, 1984). Such findings accentuate the risks involved in continuing to rely on applied linguists' intuitions in course design and materials writing.

Domain experts

After completing a study of the rhetorical structure of two astrophysics texts, Tarone et al (1981) were clear about the critical importance for NA of expert insider knowledge:

> We cannot stress enough the importance of [the specialist informant's] contribution to our analysis. His knowledge of the subject matter was absolutely essential to our analysis of the rhetorical structure of these papers.   (1981, p. 125, fn. 2)

When it comes to language, conversely, the picture is very different. Although exceptions have been reported (Ramani et al, 1988; Tarone et al, 1981), when asked about their language needs, most domain experts have proved unreliable, not just at the detailed linguistic level, but also where higher discourse events are concerned. For example, Marriot (Marriot, 1991; Marriot & Yamada, 1991) described how a monolingual English-speaking Australian shop assistant in a duty-free store failed to make sales of watches to Japanese tourists (who were in reality interested in buying) due to her lack of Japanese, compounded by her additional failure to recognize discourse cues when the tourists attempted to complete the transaction in English. Interviewed subsequently, the woman (who had worked in the store for four years) claimed she was able to 'get through' transactions with Japanese customers despite their poor English (*sic*), and that their politeness made them easy to serve. She was simply unaware of how her own language and cross-cultural awareness limitations were diminishing her effectiveness. Using task as the unit of analysis (as opposed, say, to asking them about structures, notions, and functions) enables domain experts to provide quality information of the kind they do possess, with linguistic information to be obtained via analyses of target discourse samples (see below). Combining domain experts and language proficiency experts in a team can produce successful task-based language NAs (Lett, this volume).

Triangulated sources

The value of triangulating perceived and/or objective needs among learners and other informants should be obvious, despite its rarity in the NA literature until recently, but the triangulation process itself can take different forms and deserves some elaboration (see Denzin, 1970; Lincoln & Guba, 1985; Lynch, 1995). *Triangulation* is a procedure long used by researchers, e.g., ethnographers, working within a qualitative, or naturalistic, tradition to help validate their data and thereby, eventually, to increase the credibility of their interpretations of those data. The process involves the researcher comparing different sets and sources of data with one another, e.g., by presenting workers', management's, and the observer's own perspectives on the causes of a labor dispute and on changes needed to the parties involved, and asking them to reflect on those interpretations (see Greenwood & Gonzalez Santos, 1992). Triangulation can involve comparisons among two or more different sources, methods, investigators or (according to some experts) theories, and sometimes combinations thereof (Lincoln & Guba, 1985, pp. 305–7).

A hypothetical illustration might help. A NA might sample the opinions of Chilean medical faculty members and students as to the nature and extent of the students' reading needs in English, and compare one with the other, and/or either or both with the reading requirements for a national medical examination. If faculty and student views were both assessed via a questionnaire, i.e., if method were held constant, that would be a case of triangulation by *sources*. If the faculty and/or student views (sources held constant) were studied via a questionnaire and interviews, that would constitute triangulation by *methods*, as would the comparison of faculty and student opinions as shown by the questionnaire and interview findings with the findings of a document analysis (study of the examination requirements). A comparison of results from faculty interviews, student questionnaires, and the document analysis would be triangulation by *sources and methods*. Not to be confused with any of the above, checking findings from two (or two hundred) more individuals of the same type using the same procedure, e.g., the findings from one faculty interview against those from another faculty interview, simply constitutes what Lincoln & Guba (p. 305) call 'multiple copies' of one type of source, not triangulation of different sources. Similarly, comparing findings from faculty interviews with reading requirements listed on course syllabuses written by the same faculty members would be a case of comparing different methods of accessing the same information from the same source, not triangulation of sources.

Triangulation of methods can involve use of different data-collection procedures, such as logs, non-participant observation, interviews, questionnaires, and testing, or, for those working within a quantitative paradigm, different research designs, e.g., a multiple case study of EAP students' progress through a medical course, and a quasi-experimental, criterion groups design comparing examination scores of students able and unable to read medical texts in English. Researchers in the qualitative, naturalistic mode, Lincoln & Guba (p. 306) point out, could not avail themselves of this option since the design in naturalistic inquiry is emergent, not pre-specified.

Triangulation by sources and/or by methods is an important procedure whose use, to the best of my knowledge, has with very few exceptions been ignored in the literature until recently (see Bosher & Smalkoski, 2002; Jasso-Aguilar, 1999/this volume; Svendsen & Krebs, 1984), although it has been employed in SLA and classroom research (see, e.g., Hawkins, 1985; Johnson Nystrom, 1983; Lynch, 1995). Many NA's for ESP programs involve data from different sources and/or data gathered via different methods. Such studies have found differences, often large differences, in the views of different classes of informants (see, e.g., Iwai, Kondo, Lim, Ray, Shimizu, & Brown, 1999; Markee, 1986; Ogata, 1992; Orikasa, 1989), but most have stopped there, content to report the differences and leave it at that. Jasso-Aguilar's (1999, this volume) study of the language and tasks performed by maids in a Waikiki hotel was an exception. Jasso-Aguilar utilized multiple sources (hotel maids, supervisors, the executive housekeeper, and a human resources staff member) and multiple methods (participant observation, unstructured interviews, and questionnaires), followed by triangulation of sources and methods to help determine the dependability of the findings obtained. She reports that triangulation enabled her not only to identify discrepancies, but to *explain* several of them. They were due to such factors as racial differences among sources; differences in typical guest requirements across shift times; difficulty with English, and with the written mode, in particular, making questionnaires and unstructured interviews differentially effective data-gathering procedures for informants of varying L2 proficiency; and differing interests and perspectives of employers and employees concerning such matters as the importance of the maids being able to 'chit-chat' with guests.

When different sources and/or methods produce conflicting findings, it is important to pursue the matter. Which sources are right, or more likely to be, and which to be followed when designing a program? Are none of them right? Or are all of them right (at least those involving different sources)? Assuming one rejects the postmodernist and epistemological relativist view that different views of reality, including tasks, simply reflect the fact (*sic*) that all of them are 'socially constructed' (in which case, there would be no such thing as 'facts', and one would not be bothered by conflicting findings, or indeed by 'findings' at all), this is exactly where triangulation, as opposed to informal cross-checking, can help the needs analyst. So, too, can one or more independent measures of the variable concerned, e.g., students' L2 proficiency or a flight attendant's knowledge and competence.

Methods of NA

In addition to substantive findings about the discourse of physics lectures, chemistry textbooks and the like, applied linguists have developed a considerable body of expertise in the various procedures available for NA, building on NA methodology in education (e.g., Stufflebeam, McCormick, Brinkerhoff & Nelson, 1985) and (insufficiently, in my view) on social science research methods in general (e.g., K. E. Bailey, 1982; Bernard, 1994; Lincoln & Guba, 1985; Reinharz, 1992; Strauss & Corbin, 1990). Several alternatives exist (see Figure 2 below), some requiring more expertise or time than others, and some being more appropriate than others for different situations or for use with different kinds of informants. They include both inductive and deductive procedures (Berwick, 1989). The former involve use of expert intuitions, participant and non-participant observation, and unstructured interviews, from which categories of needs are derived; the latter include use of devices and instruments, such as structured interviews, questionnaires, and criterion-referenced performance tests, with pre-set categories.

Procedure	Source/evaluation	Sample use
Non-expert intuitions	Auerbach & Burgess (1985)	Numerous (most?) LSP textbooks
Expert practitioner intuitions	Huckin & Olsen (1984) Lamotte (1981)	Lamotte (1981) Tarone et al (1981) Lett (this volume)
Unstructured interviews	Bailey, K. E. (1982) Spradley (1979) Hoadley-Maidment (1983)	Ramani et al (1988) Fixman (1990)
Structured interviews	Bailey, K. E. (1982) Bernard (1994)	Mackay (1978) Brindley (1984)
Interview schedules	Bernard (1994)	Mackay (1978) Tarantino (1988)
Surveys and questionnaires	Bailey (1982) Bernard (1994) Johnson (1992) Oppenheim (1966)	Horowitz (1986) Ferris & Tagg (1996) Iwai et al (1999) Mackay (1978)
Language audits	Coleman (1988) Watts (1994)	Mawer (1991) Watts (1994)
Ethnographic methods	Bernard (1994) Watson-Gegeo (1988)	Boswood & Marriot (1994) Mohan & Smith (1992) Roberts et al (1992)
Participant observation	Bailey, K. E. (1982) Bernard (1994) Lincoln & Guba (1994)	Hodlin (1970) Jasso-Aguilar (1999/this volume)
Non-participant observation	Bernard (1994) Lincoln & Guba (1985)	Bosher & Smalkoski (2002) Cumaranatunge (1988) Jacobson (1986) Jupp & Hodlin (1975) Svendsen & Krebs (1984)
Classroom observation	Chaudron (1988) Van Lier (1988)	Schmidt (1981) Allen et al (1984)

Diaries, journals, and logs	Bailey & Oschner (1983)	McDonough (1994) Reves (1994)
Role-plays, simulations	Berwick (1989)	Berwick (1989) Roberts (1982)
Content analysis	Braine (1988) Flowerdew (1994)	Benson (1991)
Discourse analysis	Sinclair & Coulthard (1975) Hatch (1992)	Crookes (1986) Ventola (1983)
Analysis of discourse	Jacoby (1999) Long (to appear)	Marriot & Yamada (1991) Medway & Andrews (1992) Sullivan & Girginer (2002)
Register/ rhetorical analysis	Biber (1988) Selinker (1988)	Conrad (1996) DeCarrico & Nattinger (1988) Trimble (1985)
Computer-aided corpus analysis	Flowerdew (1994) Sinclair (1991)	Kennedy (1990) Willis (1990)
Genre analysis	Swales (1990)	Swales (1986) Thompson (1994)
Task-based, criterion-referenced performance tests	Brown & Hudson (2002) Hudson & Lynch (1994) Norris et al (1998) Norris et al (2002)	Brown et al (2002) McNamara (1996) Norris et al (1998) Robinson & Ross (1996) Teasdale (1994)
Triangulated methods	Long (this volume)	Bosher & Smalkoski (2002) Gilabert (this volume) Jasso-Aguilar (1999/this volume) Long (this volume)

Figure 2   NA data-collection procedures

Use of multiple measures

It is difficult to overemphasize the likelihood that use of *multiple measures*, as well as multiple sources, will increase the quality of information gathered, whether or not the findings are used for triangulation by methods. Until recently, few studies had availed themselves of this option, Cumaranatunge's study of the needs of Sri

Lankan 'domestic aides' in Kuwait (Cumaranatunge, 1988) and Jasso-Aguilar's study of Waikiki hotel maids (Jasso-Aguilar, 1999, this volume), being notable examples. The practice has become far more common of late, however (see, e.g., Chaudron et al, this volume; Gilabert, this volume; Sullivan & Girginer, 2002), which is a very positive development. In particular, carefully *sequenced* use of two or more procedures can be expected to produce better quality information.

To illustrate, given adequate time and resources, a study of the language needs of tourist industry workers might usefully begin with a *literature survey* to preempt wheel-reinvention. If information of the type needed does not already exist, the next step might be to conduct in-depth *unstructured interviews* with members of different categories of stakeholders, such as one or more operators of different sized hotels, souvenir shops, restaurants, tour companies, rental car services, etc., as well as with tourists themselves. The purpose of this set of interviews would not be to produce a final inventory of target needs, but merely to obtain a better idea, based on insider knowledge, of the scope and dimensions of the sampling elements and sampling frame to be covered in a survey. Summarizing findings from Massey University's audit of language use in New Zealand's tourist industry, Watts (1994) noted that tourism involves many service categories, including formalities (consulates, customs, immigration), transport (airlines, railways, taxis), accommodation (hotels, condominiums), sightseeing (travel agencies, guided tours), entertainment (casinos, concerts, theaters), food and drink (kiosks, restaurants, bars), shopping (duty free stores, chemists, department stores), and other services (hospitals, banks, post offices, information centers). He pointed out that such sectors would change with increased choice of so-called eco-tourism and other more specialized types of foreign travel.

In light of the Massey audit, a *questionnaire* might then be designed for broad coverage of representative members and numbers of each category, i.e., a stratified random sample of the total population. The questionnaire would be mailed out or, if possible, used as the basis of face-to-face interviews, i.e., an interview schedule. This would be combined with in-depth *structured interviews*, following up on the results of the earlier open-ended round, with small representative sub-groups of the same stratified random sample. Since all the information gathered thus far would involve introspection and retrospection, interim conclusions would preferably be cross-checked against results of *participant observations* and/or *non-participant observations* of actual native and foreign language use, e.g., through daily *logs* kept by members of the target groups. *Proficiency measures*, ranging from language self-assessment procedures to task-based, criterion-referenced performance tests (see Brown & Hudson, 2002; Brown et al, 2002), as exemplified by the road test component of the standard driver's license examination, would help elucidate the gap between needs and present abilities. Finally, analyses of representative *target discourse samples*, e.g., audio-taped or video-taped recordings of service encounters between foreign tourists and travel industry personnel would be collected, as in Marriot's insightful studies of communication between Japanese tourists and Melbourne shop assistants. The analysis of target discourse would provide useful additional information for training some categories of staff, and help in the preparation of pedagogic materials.

Sampling

Many NAs are conducted using a *convenience sample*, i.e., informants available and willing to participate, who may or may not be representative of the target population. A *purposive sample*, i.e., a group selected by the analyst as supposedly typical, is only as good as the criteria for judging typicality, which is unknown. Circumstances sometimes make one or other the only options (for discussion, see Lett, this volume). Where time and access are adequate, however, improvements can be made using standard sampling procedures (see, e.g., K. E. Bailey, 1982, pp. 83–108; Bernard, 1994, pp. 71–101). A *random sample*, where each member of the population had an equal chance of being selected, is much preferable, but costly in time and money if the population is large. The task is simplified in such cases by use of a *systematic random sample*, involving selection of every *n*th person from the *sampling frame*, e.g., every *n*th name on an alphabetized list of all faculty members in the electrical engineering departments at six universities accepting a group of international students whose needs are being studied. Such a procedure might still be problematic, however, since the randomness of the selection could result in, say, equal numbers of faculty teaching undergraduate and graduate courses, the target reading tasks for which are often different (e.g., involving different proportions of textbooks and journal articles), when 90% of the international students concerned would be taking higher degrees. Such problems can be solved through use of a *stratified random sample*, i.e., a random, but proportionate, sample within each sub-group, or strata, of the population of interest (see Chaudron et al, this volume). Should identifying the sampling frame prove problematic, e.g., because faculty lists for two of the universities were unavailable, the analyst might opt for a *cluster sample*, i.e., a random sample drawn from the sub-groups (here, the remaining four universities) for which the sampling frame can be determined.

Expert and non-expert intuitions

Their own non-expert intuitions about language use remain the stock in trade for many commercial textbook writers, despite being notoriously unreliable. Every comparison of the language of target situations and the language modeled for them in language teaching materials that I am aware of has documented major discrepancies (see, e.g., Ventola, 1987; and Bartlett, this volume). This may not affect profits for textbook writers and publishers, but it can have serious consequences for learners. Thus, with considerable justification, Auerbach & Burgess (1985, pp. 478–90) strongly criticized authors of 'survival English' texts for producing materials which modeled oversimplified language, inauthentic communicative structure, and unrealistic situational content.

It is not clear whether domain experts can do any better. Research on the issue is sparse. Although studies by Selinker (1979) and Savage & Storer (1992) mentioned earlier, offer some hope in this regard, in general there is as little reason to expect solid meta-linguistic information from domain experts as there is to expect valid domain-specific knowledge from applied linguists. In one small-scale direct study of the issue, Lamotte (1981) compared her written intuitions about the language used between a physical therapist and her patient and transcripts of therapist–patient conversation which she subsequently audio-taped at a hospital. Lamotte found that her linguistic intuitions were quite unreliable, this despite being a year into a masters degree in applied linguistics at the time, and being herself a fully qualified physical therapist with five years' experience. (Conversely, her introspections about the *tasks* performed by a therapist proved fairly accurate.)

Interviews

One of the more direct ways of finding out what people think or do (in some cultures, at least) is to ask them, a function served by various kinds of interviews and questionnaires. The interview is a key data-gathering tool in many branches of the social sciences, most notably in anthropology and linguistics fieldwork. With suitable modification for informants from cultures in which formal structured interviews are not a recognized speech event (see Wolfson, 1976), it can serve the applied linguist well, too. Needless to say, allowances must be made for cross-cultural differences which may exist between interviewer and interviewee in value systems, in beliefs about such matters as teacher and student roles and relationships, in the appropriateness of discussing certain topics (e.g., age, religion, politics) at all, and of great importance for a NA, in notions of relevance, views about the significance of criticism, and truthfulness. Interviews are more open to bias and inconsistency of various sorts than questionnaires: among other ways, through interviewers communicating their attitudes about the matter at hand (e.g., the importance of the language they teach to the interviewee's work) to interviewees, thereby influencing their responses; interviewees telling interviewers what they think they want to hear; and by interviewers leading respondents, asking different questions or the same questions in different ways, and unintentionally distorting data by filtering the way they report or interpret responses through their own perceptions. Many of these potential problems can be avoided if the needs analyst is aware of them and, if need be and numbers warrant, by interviewer training. Having interviewers of the same race, ethnicity, sex, social class and cultural background as interviewees also increases the likelihood of obtaining good data, especially where attitudes and opinions on sensitive issues are involved. (For helpful reviews of research findings on these and related issues, see K. E. Bailey, 1982; Briggs, 1986.)

Although time-consuming, *unstructured*, or open-ended, interviews allow in-depth coverage of issues and have the advantage of not pre-empting unanticipated findings by use of pre-determined questions, categories and response options, a potential limitation of structured interviews and questionnaires. Unstructured interviews are exploratory, use no fixed format and allow the interviewee's notion of relevance to prevail, instead of being constrained by a set of pre-planned questions (see Chaudron et al, this volume; Kellerman et al, this volume). In Lincoln & Guba's words, unstructured interviews are appropriate when the interviewer "*does not know what he or she doesn't know* and must therefore rely on the respondent to tell him or her" (1985, p. 269, emphasis in the original). The quality of information produced can be greatly enhanced by awareness of basic interviewing micro-skills, such as initial use of a few general 'warm-up' or relaxation questions ("How do you like living/teaching here?" "How does working here compare with country/institution X?"), making sure the interviewee does the talking, and using follow-up probes when further detail or explanation is sought, including explicit requests for more information, 'pumps', like "uh huh" and other encouraging verbal and non-verbal back-channel signals, and silences which the interviewee fills. Many valuable insights on these and other matters are available to the serious needs analyst (see, e.g., K. E. Bailey, 1982, pp. 181–217; Bernard, 1994, pp. 208–55; Reinharz, 1994, pp. 18–45; Spradley, 1979).

Once unstructured interviews have been completed and the data from them analyzed, semi-structured or *structured* interviews may follow. As the names imply, these differ from unstructured interviews and from each other in the degree to which questions have been pre-formulated (and hence, the issues partly pre-determined) by the interviewer. In extreme cases, structured interviews are oral administrations of a questionnaire, then sometimes referred to as an *interview schedule*, as exemplified by some telephone interviews or by census takers who visit sample respondents' homes with a lengthy list of printed questions on a form which the interviewers fill out. Structured interviews and interview schedules have the advantage of being swifter to conduct, and of producing data that, because organized, will not require hours to categorize, and because standardized, will allow easy comparison across respondents.

Use of interviews is widely reported in NAs in ESP. Ramani, Chacko, Singh and Glendinning (1988) conducted unstructured interviews with Indian scientists. Fixman (1990) summarized findings of 32 semi-structured interviews, mostly with middle and senior managers, in nine companies of different types and sizes, designed to identify FL needs of US corporations. Brindley (1984) described the development, piloting and use of structured interviews in NA and objective setting for Australia's Adult Migrant Education Program (AMEP). Cumaranatunge (1988) employed structured and unstructured interviews, respectively, with, among others, Sri Lankan domestic 'aides' and various kinds of civil servants. Use of an interview schedule was reported by Tarantino (1988) with Italian physicists, chemists and computer scientists at the University of Bari. And in one of the earliest NAs in the professional literature, Mackay (1978) discussed use of an interview schedule with the Veterinary Medicine faculty at the National Autonomous University of Mexico (UNAM), noting three important advantages of structured interviews over questionnaires: they allow interviewers to make sure all questions are answered, to clarify any misunderstood or ambiguous items, and to follow up avenues of interest disclosed by answers that were unforeseen when the questionnaire was designed.

Questionnaire surveys

The advantages and disadvantages of questionnaire surveys are in large part the mirror image of those of unstructured interviews. Questionnaires, especially if mailed, group-administered or administered by third parties, can procure sizeable amounts of focused, standardized, organized data, potentially from a large sample of respondents, and do so relatively quickly and cheaply. They can accomplish all this, moreover, with the option of anonymity (should that be important to respondents) and with less chance of interviewer bias, since the questions asked, the order in which they are asked, and the precise way they are asked can all be carefully planned and fixed. On the other hand, response rates can be low, and the type of information and range of responses obtained are likely to be limited by the use of pre-determined questions and response options and formats. In a sense, that is, unstructured interviews serve to identify relevant questions, whereas questionnaires assume knowledge of the right questions and test hypotheses about answers.

Considerable expertise exists in questionnaire design and item-writing in the social sciences (see, e.g., Babbie, 1973; K. E. Bailey, 1982, pp. 109–80; Bernard, 1994, pp. 256–88; Oppenheim, 1966). Some pitfalls to avoid (most of which apply to interviews, as well) include double-barreled questions ("Do you read and write letters to customers in English?" "Are your students able to understand your lectures in English and ask clarification questions clearly when necessary?"), overly complex or technical wording ("Do you ever have difficulty with telephone pre-closings?"), leading questions ("Should sales staff be able to speak Spanish fluently?"), ambiguity ("Do you have difficulty understanding everyday French?"), abstractness ("Do you find reading English difficult?"), sensitive or threatening questions ("Do you skip reading assignments if they are in English?"), and especially, irrelevant questions. Items suffering from one or more of these flaws will usually surface quickly if writers try to answer them themselves or else when the instrument is pilot-tested.

Items may be open, with no pre-specified response categories or choices, or closed, where the respondent must choose from one or more specified options. As might be imagined, the strengths and weakness of each type roughly parallel those of unstructured interviews and questionnaires themselves. Open questions, for example, can elicit a wider range of information and more detail, and may be more suitable for complex issues, but they involve loss of standardization and are more difficult and time-consuming to code and interpret. Closed items provide standardized, easily coded and quantified data, but they may limit possible responses and may result in overly simple treatments of complex issues.

Administration of a questionnaire is among the most widely used procedures in NA (see, also, Brecht & Rivers, this volume; Chaudron et al, this volume; Gilabert, this volume; Kellerman et al, this volume; Kim et al, this volume; Vandermeeren, this volume). Mackay (1978) describes three uses of questionnaires (and provides the instruments themselves), one as the basis of the interview schedule for veterinary faculty at the National Autonomous University of Mexico (UNAM), a second with students from the same university department, and the third for a survey of ESP needs and program resources in SEAMEO (Southeast Asian Ministers of Education Organization) countries. Mackay makes the important point (*op. cit.* p. 23), potentially true of *all* NA methodologies, that, because of the way language teachers make their living, there is a danger they will exaggerate the importance of and need for their particular language for groups of learners, and he illustrates some steps that can be taken to help avoid the problem. A questionnaire on EAP reading needs, for example, should not 'lead' respondents by asking about how much reading they assign or do in English for their courses or research right away. Instead, they can be asked about the availability of relevant literature in the faculty members' or students' L1, and then about such matters as required course readings in 'other languages', before any mention is made of English. Mackay also noted how a faculty member having done graduate work overseas could easily influence his or her personal use of professional literature in a foreign language (FL) and choice of any L2 readings assigned to students – another example to support Coleman's claim (1988) about how one sector in a large institution, such as a university, can influence language use in another.

Several writers, notably Braine (1988, 2001) and Horowitz (1986), have pointed out that the rapid and extensive coverage achievable through questionnaires can lead analysts to overlook potentially serious issues of validity. In a study of academic writing tasks, for example, jumping straight to the design of a questionnaire for faculty in the disciplines of interest will likely simply reflect the applied linguist's preconceived notions about what goes on there. The needs analyst will do better to begin with interviews of faculty and students, or with study of syllabuses and actual writing tasks. This is a more valid starting-point, and one that can inform subsequent questionnaire construction. Horowitz began a study of tertiary academic writing needs by highlighting the variable nature of the lists of skills and tasks that had figured in previous questionnaire surveys of EAP writing, and recalling the concern expressed by Johns (1981) and Zemelman (1978, cited in Johns, 1981, p. 52), among others, as to whether the results of such studies reflect what the respondents do, think they do, think the researcher thinks they ought to do, or want the researcher to think they do. Horowitz also noted the danger that questionnaire items may reflect analysts' invalid, preconceived notions as to the relevant categories of tasks in an unfamiliar domain. A logically prior activity to asking respondents about *those* tasks, he suggested, should be to discover and classify (in that case, EAP writing) tasks from the perspective of those assigning and doing them. To that end, Horowitz collected and examined a corpus of actual writing assignments and essay examinations at a US university. Of approximately 750 faculty members contacted, 36 responded with usable data (a 4.8% return rate).[2] The data represented assignments from 29 courses (28 undergraduate and one graduate) in 17 departments. Aside from 'essay questions', seven major categories (target task types) emerged from the data: summary of / reaction to a reading; annotated bibliography; report on a specified participatory experience (e.g., a field observation); connection of theory and data; case study; synthesis of multiple sources; and research project. Many assignments specified expected content through sets of questions to be answered or detailed headings and sub-headings, and as such were very controlled. Recognition and reorganization of data were emphasized, rather than invention and personal discovery.[3] Replications of Horowitz's study are clearly needed with undergraduate and graduate courses from a systematically sampled range of disciplines and universities. (See Braine, 1995, for a modified replication with a study of the writing tasks of undergraduate students in engineering and natural science at the University of Texas, Austin.) Meanwhile, the differences between the task types Horowitz identified through surveying domain experts and those typical in lists presented to respondents based on the intuitions of applied linguists are a salutary reminder of the importance of working on quality before turning to quantity in a NA.

Language audits

A related use of questionnaires is to conduct a *language audit* (see, e.g., Coleman, 1988; Mawer, 1991; Sefton & O'Hara, 1992; Vandermeeren, this volume; Watts, 1994). Language audits are difficult to define because in practice they often include some activities and produce some of the same data typical of a NA. However, whereas a NA usually provides detailed information about the needs of individuals, and occasionally of much larger social groups (Brecht & Rivers, this volume), a language audit takes institutions or organizations as the unit of analysis and is usually conducted through a quantified general survey. Coleman (1988) effectively recommends that a language audit precede a NA in large institutions, partly in order to identify the individuals whose needs should be targeted for analysis. An audit produces (i) a target situation analysis (TSA) in the form of the language skills required by an organization, as determined, e.g. by job descriptions and records of current language *use*; (ii) a profile of existing language abilities, assessed by language test scores or proficiency self-ratings; and (iii) a recommendation concerning the amount and form of language training (or external provision of language assistance), if any, required to raise the profile to the standards identified by the TSA. In the business sector, Utley (1992, pp. 34–5) characterizes an audit as an exercise in defining any FL skills existing in a company, present and future needs for FL skills, the staff likely to require them, to what extent and for what purpose, and the options available to the company (e.g., instituting a FL training program, or buying outside translation and interpreting services) to deal with any gap identified between present abilities and current and future needs. An audit is useful for providing a quick overview of a situation and identifying mismatches between perceptions and reality, between what is going on and what should be.

By way of illustration, in the Massey study referred to earlier, Watts (1994) reported on a pilot language audit of the New Zealand tourist industry that employed a questionnaire to survey 96 major tourist organizations and companies, including airlines, information centers, duty free shops and hotels in five main tourist centers. The questionnaire was designed to assess the value respondents attached to FL proficiency, which languages were most important, the proficiency levels felt desirable and those actually held by industry staff, the kinds of FL materials produced for visitors, the arrangements made for business-related communication in FLs, and the degree to which staff recruitment and training policies recognized FL skills in applicants. 59 questionnaires were returned for a high 61% response rate. FLs were shown to be important for tourism (notably Japanese, German, French, Chinese, and Spanish, paralleling findings in Australia), especially for tour operators, airlines and hotels. The audit revealed discrepancies, between, first, the relatively high importance tourism organizations said they attached to FLs and the rather minor role FL ability actually played (relative to commercial experience and technical skills) in recruitment and training, and second, the FL proficiency levels perceived as desirable for staff and the abilities they actually possessed. Only certain specialist, 'front-line' staff positions, e.g., tour guides, front desk staff in hotels, and duty free shop assistants, were perceived as requiring higher proficiency, and few staff overall reported themselves as having such proficiency. Watts noted that such findings required detailed follow-up studies of language needs in the tourist industry, similar to those in Australia by Marriot (1991) and Marriot & Yamada (1991).

Participant and non-participant observation

Interviews and questionnaires involve informants (i) introspecting about tasks, and (ii) reporting on them, and researchers (iii) interpreting those data, three processes that can filter or distort even *perceived* reality. They tap respondents' perceptions, attitudes and opinions. Document study, as illustrated by Horowitz's (1986) examination of university writing assignments contained in syllabuses, course handouts, etc., can provide a more direct glimpse of what happens in a target domain (see, also, Benson, 1991; Flowerdew, 1994). Participant and non-participant observation have the advantage of allowing direct, in-depth, contextualized study of what participants actually do, of the activities of interest in their natural environment (natural, that is, except for the presence of the outside observer in the case of non-participant observation).

Non-participant observations as part of NAs have been reported for some time (e.g., Allwright & Allwright, 1977; Bosher & Smalkoski, 2002; Courtney, 1988; Cumaranatunge, 1988; Franco, 1986; Jacobson, 1986; Jupp & Hodlin, 1975; Mohan & Smith, 1992; Ramani et al, 1988; Savage & Storer, 1992; Svendsen & Krebs, 1984). Participant observation as part of a NA is much rarer. A study by Hodlin (1970, reported in Roberts et al, 1992, pp. 185–88) constitutes one of the earliest examples. Hodlin spent a week working in the packing department of a British factory which made cake mixes and breakfast cereals. She was presented to, and accepted by, the other workers as a temporary student employee, although her supervisor knew that she was really also conducting a field observation in preparation for an anti-racist training course to be run by the Pathway Industrial Unit. Hodlin employed a combination of participant observation, (presumably surreptitious) tape-recordings, and field notes to produce job descriptions, vignettes of some of her co-workers, and data on the kind of work-related and 'social' language required for the job, as well as the range of attitudes towards racial issues among line workers and supervisors, comparing the atmosphere in three sections where she worked. More recently, in addition to conducting interviews, attending personnel office meetings and the like, Jasso-Aguilar (1999, this volume) worked three day and two evening shifts as a trainee housekeeper, taking notes and making tape-recordings as she did so, as part of the multi-method, multi-source analysis she conducted of the needs of Waikiki hotel maids. She reported participant observation as having been by far the most valuable source of data, enabling her, among other things, to verify (as false) some outsider (human resources person) intuitions about language use, and to identify relevant sources, e.g., morning briefings, telephone calls to the housekeeping room, and paged messages, which she had not considered at the outset of the study.

Ethnographic methods

Ethnographic procedures, of which some kinds of participant and non-participant observation are two, are designed to lessen the cultural distance between *outsider* (observer) and *insider* (observed). They are used to seek out insider views of the culture. Crucially, this involves eschewal of pre-conceived, outsider, or etic, analytic categories of events, formulated before observation begins, in favor of emic categories, those considered relevant by insiders, which emerge from the data and the observer's developing interpretation of them – interpretations which are validated reflexively against insider views, e.g., through triangulation. Note that many forms of non-participant observation, such as the use of pre-determined categories in coding systems like the Communicative Orientation to Language Teaching (COLT), (Allen et al, 1984) to record, and simultaneously analyze, classroom talk, may be very valuable for some kinds of research or for teacher education, but have nothing to do with ethnography. There is a vast literature on both participant and non-participant observation, and the interested reader is again referred to texts on qualitative research methods in general (e.g., K. E. Bailey, 1982, pp. 247–82; Bernard, 1994, pp. 136–64; Kirk & Miller, 1986; Lincoln & Guba, 1985; Reinharz, 1992, 46–75; and Strauss & Corbin, 1990), as well as to work on ethnography and ethnographic methods in particular (e.g., Agar, 1986; Goetz & LeCompte, 1984; Hammersley & Atkinson, 1983; Hymes, 1962; Noblit & Hare, 1988; Shieffelin & Ochs, 1986; Spradley, 1980; Spradley & McCurdy, 1972; Watson-Gegeo, 1988, 1992, 1997).

To my knowledge, despite liberal use of the term in the NA literature (as in the applied linguistics literature, as a whole), there have been no NAs to date that meet the criteria for true *ethnographies*. For most writers on the subject (see, e.g., Hammersley & Atkinson, 1983; Watson-Gegeo, 1988), those criteria usually include micro-analysis of social patterns within a cultural group, and of the values and beliefs underlying them, in context. That typically requires lengthy immersion in the target setting, sometimes for periods of years; use of multiple data-collection procedures, especially, but not only, participant and non-participant observation, recordings and note-taking; entering the field 'unbiased', e.g., without fixed hypotheses to test, and instead allowing meaningful units of analysis, and often the research questions themselves, to emerge from the data; adoption of an insider's perspective on events, including use of emic categories in the description and analysis, i.e., units with meaning for the participants within their, not (necessarily) the analyst's, culture; validation of interim analyses by trialling them on participants, often through a process of triangulation; and in general focusing on the particular, not the universal, seeking *understandings* of events rather than generalizations valid beyond the original setting, and in some cases believing such generalizations to be impossible in principle where human behavior is concerned. As distinct from ethnography, *per se*, several researchers have advocated use of *ethnographic methods* as part of their approach to NA, on the other hand, including Boswood & Marriot (1994) in their important work on the socialization of business English teachers in Hong Kong.

Journals and logs

The use of different kinds of diaries, journals and logs for pedagogic purposes, in teacher education, and for research, has been reported and discussed in applied linguistics and language teaching since the early 1980s (see, e.g., K. M. Bailey, 1990; K. M. Bailey & Oschner, 1983; C. Brown, 1985; Parkinson & Howell-Richardson, 1990; Jarvis, 1992; McDonough, 1994). 'Dialog journals', in which students submit entries about their experiences inside and/or outside the classroom, and teachers write regular responses, usually to content rather than form, have been found to play a useful role in writing courses (Spack & Sadow, 1993), and more generally to serve as a valuable source of information for developing learner-centered curricula (Auerbach, 1992). The use of logs and journals described here, however, is narrower, in that the main purpose is to gather information for a NA. In most cases, learners are aware of that, and it influences the content of at least part of what they write (and sometimes are asked to write), as well as the focus of teachers' written responses. Dialog-journals sometimes contain logs, but logs can also be used separately in NAs. Logs are records, usually audio-taped or in the form of written notes, which learners make of their own language use, perhaps over a week at the office or university, perhaps longer. They are like language audits of individuals.

Successful use of diaries and logs in NAs and/or as sources of informal feedback for teachers and students about the degree to which needs are being met have been reported by Lundstrom (1994), McDonough (1994), Parkinson & Howell-Richardson (1990), Reves (1994), and Savage & Whisenand (1993), among others. As part of a five-day workshop in the EOP program for Thai aquaculturalists described earlier, for example, Savage & Whisenand had learners keep 'logbooks', student–teacher journals used to record language learning and teaching experiences. Student entries were reviewed daily by teachers in order impressionistically to assess (i) problems students felt they had with English, and (ii) the degree to which they saw that day's classroom activities as helping to resolve those problems. In other words, the logbooks served for work-related writing practice, as a partial basis for an informal analysis of perceived student needs, and as a continuing formative evaluation of attainment of program objectives as the five-day workshop pro-gressed.

These studies and others show diaries and logs to be potentially rich sources of insights into learner (and teacher) needs. They have the important advantage of preserving insider notions of what is relevant. They have the obvious disadvantage, on the other hand, of being time-consuming both to write and to analyze. What is recorded may be idiosyncratic and impressionistic and will need confirmation via other sources and methods.

Tests

Tests of various kinds constitute another valuable option for the needs analyst, but the kinds of tests available are as varied, and in some cases as problematic, as those employed for traditional assess-ment purposes. Few would deny that students in any kind of language teaching program should be tested using measures whose reliability and validity are established for the population concerned, (i) for diagnostic and placement purposes before a program begins, or, where that is impossible, soon after it starts, and (ii) again before exiting the program, for their readiness to perform adequately in the target domain(s). What is harder for some to accept is the proposition that, certainly for achievement testing, and arguably for diagnostic and placement purposes as well, measures of the ability to perform target tasks or task types identified as relevant by the NA should take precedence over general linguistic proficiency measures, and that if linguistic abilities are tested at all, it should be as integrated with task performance, and using real-world, not purely linguistic criteria. Such views are still controversial, yet the reality is that there is no such thing as abstract 'language proficiency', 'listening skill', 'reading ability', 'accuracy' or 'fluency'. Communicative ability is, by definition, 'task-related, context-related, specific, and local' (Jacoby & McNamara, 1999, p. 234; see also, e.g., Jacobson, 1986; Swales, 1985). The case for task-based testing in needs analysis, in other words, is the same as that for task-based language teaching and assessment in general (see Long & Norris, 2000; Brown et al, 2002).

In task-based NA, traditional language tests will ideally be superceded by task-based, criterion-referenced (direct or indirect) performance tests (see Brown & Hudson, 2002; Brown, Hudson, Norris, & Bonk, 2002; Norris, 2001; Norris et al, 1998). As part of a NA for a group of university EAP students, for example, the learners may be required to watch a graded series of (simulated or authentic) video-taped lecturettes and to answer a set of multiple-choice questions on the *information* contained in them, the key information-bits and test items having been identified by domain experts as those which NS students in the area of specialization would be expected to handle. In an elementary JSL (Japanese as a second language) course, a tourist-to-be might be required to role-play purchasing specified items from a Japanese shop-keeper, the shop-keeper's role being presented on audio- or video-tape, and the student's performance measured by his or her ability to identify from what the seller said such things as which items were and were not available, the cheapest product among a set of options for a needed item, and the total cost. (For another example, see Pedagogic Task (PT) 7 in the task-based module of Korean language teaching materials described in Chaudron et al, this volume.) In either case, such matters as the accuracy with which students supplied English articles, their ability to recognize grammatical and ungrammatical relative clauses, or their performance on a close test, would be irrelevant. Recognizing that native and non-native speakers alike have varying language abilities, and that individuals with lower linguistic abilities can often compensate for that with additional content knowledge, superior inferencing skills, etc., the focus would be on whether learners could handle the tasks, not the language in isolation, and hence, what additional instruction, if any, was required.

While the majority of language assessment specialists still maintain the field's traditional emphasis on developing *reliable* tests of linguistic proficiency, measured in the abstract (an orientation encouraged, of course, by equally traditional synthetic approaches to syllabus design and teaching methodology), a small but growing minority have undertaken the more challenging task of developing *valid* measures of task performance.[4] This is proving no easy matter. Thus, even in the context of an *integrated* performance test, the Occupational English Test (OET, an Australian measure of immigrant healthcare workers' language abilities), and even when domain experts (medical doctors) and applied linguists could be shown (see McNamara, 1996) to coincide in their judgments using the same general assessment of candidates' overall communicative effectiveness (which would certainly not always be the case), discrepancies were still reported between examinees' assessed performance and their subsequent perceived communicative abilities in the workplace. One explanation, Jacoby & McNamara (1999) suggest, is that the predictive validity of such performance measures may be reduced by use of simplified simulations (in that case, role-plays) of real world tasks, rather than the tasks themselves, and/or through the assessment criteria used to rate performance on those simulations differing from the criteria considered relevant by insiders in the target discourse community (see, also, Elder, 1993).

Support for the latter interpretation was provided by the findings of a pioneering study, utilizing a combination of ethnographic and discourse analytic procedures, of the 'indigenous' assessment criteria of a North American research team of solid state physicists preparing for upcoming conference presentations (Jacoby, 1999; Jacoby & McNamara, 1999). Whereas the OET concentrated on NNS (non-native speaker) deviations from native speaker linguistic norms, Jacoby found that non-/nativeness was all but irrelevant for the physicists (save for some feedback on minor linguistic errors on some overheads).[5] The physicists' assessment criteria were highly localized (making generalization by outsiders, applied linguists, difficult), were applied to native and non-native speakers alike, and were all inextricably related to content, argumentation structure, and multi-modality (in this case, speech accompanying technical graphics) embedded in the specific target task of presenting a mostly mono-logic, multi-media scientific report before a live conference audience. Unlike traditional linguistic proficiency tests, and even some supposed measures of communicative ability, there was no separation of communicative and professional performance. Jacoby & McNamara (1999, p. 236) suggest that efforts to do so, along with attempts to generalize away from task-specific assessment criteria, may prove counter-productive.

Findings such as these are important, and potentially ominous for task-based needs analysis and task-based assessment in general. Clearly, the single biggest question facing researchers in this area remains whether *construct-centered* assessment is feasible. Can common knowledge and abilities underlying several tasks be identified and measured, and the results used to predict learners' real-world performance on the tasks themselves? To what degree is it possible to use assessment data from student performance on one set of tasks to predict how those (or other) students will perform on 'similar' tasks possessing certain common characteristics, i.e., reflecting the same underlying 'construct'? (See Brown et al, 2002; Mislevy, Steinberg, & Almond, 2002; Norris et al, 2002; Norris, Brown, Hudson, & Yoshioka, 1998, for some pioneering work on this problem, and Bachman, 2002, for a critique of the program.) If no generalizability is possible, or only very weak generalizability, the needs analyst, like the assessment specialist in general, will be faced with *task-centered* assessment, i.e., with testing learner ability to perform a potentially daunting list of particular target tasks, which would clearly be uneconomical in terms both of students' time and test construction. Put another way, must needs analysts focus their assessments on learners' current abilities to perform *tasks* or *task-types*?

The flight attendant study

As with the literature review, the general research question motivating the second phase of the study, that concerning flight attendants, was: What are the relative merits of various sources (especially, insiders and outsiders), methods (both qualitative and quantitative), and source x method combinations, in learner NA in general, and in identifying the language and tasks of airline flight attendants in particular. Flight attendants (FAs) were selected as a test case for the second stage of the research for three basic reasons.

First, impressionistically, at least, their work is carried out in a relatively circumscribed discourse space, as compared, say, with that of arms dealers, missionaries, or politicians, thereby making the project more manageable.

Second, many outsiders, including language teachers and materials writers, would consider themselves relatively familiar with FAs' work and language use by virtue of having flown as passengers, often many times, with ample opportunity to observe FAs going about their duties. If teachers' or applied linguists' *intuitions* about language or tasks can provide a satisfactory basis for materials and course design at all, therefore, it should be in a case like this of a relatively familiar, 'public' occupation which they have experienced frequently as consumers. Conversely, if outsiders' intuitions fail them in such a simple case, the burden of proof shifts to those publishers and textbook writers who continue to produce language teaching materials ostensibly catering to far more specialized domains (business offices, computer science, medical practice, engineering lectures, etc.) by relying for the most part, and sometimes exclusively, on outsiders' intuitions about authentic language use in those areas.

Third, the writer's friendship with a key FA union leader would facilitate access to several important data sources. In what follows, it needs to be remembered that the focus of the research was *not* the needs of FAs *per se*, however (there was no interest in producing a language or task inventory for the occupation, for instance), but *methodological options* in identifying those needs.

Sources

Written sources

A number of written sources were consulted. These included the *Dictionary of Occupational Titles*, FA training manuals, a FA union contract, and several FA competency and re-certification tests. The *Dictionary of Occupational Titles (DOT)* provided a thumb-nail sketch of the occupation of FA, and did so in terms of *tasks* (see Figure 3). The vignette turned out to be accurate enough as far as it went, and potentially useful to help get a naive NA under way. However, it was limited to tasks performed in-flight, viewed from an outsider's perspective, without position-specific duties (e.g., reference to cabin class or exit door for which a FA is responsible), with no indication of relative frequency or importance, and with most of the 15 tasks listed involving FA–passenger interaction and services, all of which would subsequently be shown by triangulation with other methods and insider sources to be inadequate and unrealistic, although closer to reality than the breakdown of the work that would later be elicited from the applied linguists in this study.

Other written documents consulted (from a total of four airlines, including the two for which the four FA informants worked) were: a cabin crew organizational chart, a flight operations manual, standard forms and routine flight paperwork, pre-service FA training manuals, in-service re-certification manuals and tests, and a book-length union contract. In addition to diagrams and other visuals, these mostly

(1) 352.367-010 AIRPLANE-FLIGHT ATTENDANT (air trans.)
alternate titles: airplane-cabin attendant

Performs variety of personal services conducive to safety and comfort of airline passengers during flight: Greets passengers, verifies tickets, records destinations, and directs passengers to assigned seats. Assists passengers to store carry-on luggage in overhead, garment, or under-seat storage. Explains use of safety equipment, such as seat belts, oxygen masks and life jackets. Walks aisle of plane to verify that passengers have complied with federal regulations prior to take off. Serves previously prepared meals and beverages. Observes passengers to detect signs of discomfort, and issues palliatives to relieve passenger ailments, such as airsickness and insomnia. Administers first aid according to passenger distress when needed. Answers questions regarding performance of aircraft, stopovers and flight schedules. Performs other personal services, such as distributing reading material and pointing out places of interest. Prepares reports showing place of departure and destination, passenger ticket numbers, meal and beverage inventories, palliatives issued, and lost and found articles. May collect money for meals and beverages.   *DOT* (1991), p. 255

Figure 3   *DOT* entry for Airline Flight Attendant

took the form of statements about the *tasks* involved in, and *knowledge* required for, the job of FA. Their completeness made them much the richest sources of information for the tasks involved in a FA's work, for domain-specific technical/sub-technical language, and for explaining procedures, rules of conduct, and much of the background knowledge FAs access to do their job, e.g., information on computerized bidding, scheduling, pay calculation, service flow patterns for different types of aircraft, equipment location and checking, safety, in-flight emergencies, and basic medical procedures. The superiority of found written sources was to be expected due to their sheer length and because they represented insider-to-insider communication.

Informants: Insiders and outsiders

There were eight informants, all native speakers of English: four *insiders*, US FAs from two US airlines, ranging in age from the late 20s to late 40s, with from three to 25 years of experience; and four *outsiders*, US graduate students in applied linguistics, ranging in age from the mid-20s to mid-30s, all frequent domestic and inter-national air travelers. All data-collection sessions were conducted individually.

Each informant first provided *written introspections* in response to two prompts:

(i) Describe as many aspects of the job of a flight attendant as possible. Be concise. You don't need to write elaborately, but be specific. Notes will be sufficient.
(ii) Try to write down verbatim, or as accurately as possible, some of the language said, heard, read or written by flight attendants or encountered by flight attendants in any aspect of the job. Please be sure to label the speaker or hearer or type of material the language comes from.

The prompts, and subsequent interview questions, deliberately avoided use of 'task', in order to test an earlier claim that "tasks are the things people will tell you they do if you ask them and they are not applied linguists" (Long, 1985, p. 89). A few days later, each informant took part in an *unstructured interview* lasting about an hour, which was then transcribed. Written introspections and inter-view transcripts were analyzed in terms of tasks, lexis (technical/sub-technical, and other), and reported language use (range and type), as well as with respect to their various logistical qualities.

Insiders and outsiders were found to differ considerably (in both sets of data, written introspections and unstructured interviews, but especially the latter) in their conceptualization of a FA's job: its scope, the importance they attached to different components within it, their attitudes to it, etc. On *tasks*, they differed in the detail and com-plexity of their descriptions, the insiders providing much more, as shown, e.g., by the numbers of tasks, and numbers of different tasks, mentioned (see Tables 1 and 2).[6] The outsiders tended to describe only those tasks they could see as passengers (the same vantage point adopted by the *DOT*), mostly those that affected them personally, mostly those occurring in flight, and often idiosyncratically, some-

Table 1 Total tasks noted

	Written introspection	Interview	Total
FA ($n = 4$)	40	77	117
AL ($n = 4$)	60	48	108

Table 2   Total different tasks noted

	Written introspection	Interview	Total
FA ($n = 4$)	32	57	89
AL ($n = 4$)	30	33	63

times influenced by isolated (usually negative) episodes recalled from past flights (see Figure 4 opposite). Insiders, conversely, were able to produce generalizations and patterns: compare, e.g., (4a) and (4b). The narrow focus and perspective persisted even when outsiders were pushed by an interviewer to think of other aspects of a FA's job perhaps not directly visible to passengers (see, e.g., 4c).

Insiders surpassed outsiders in their knowledge of the *language* involved in a FA's work, too, as shown, e.g., by the numbers of technical and sub-technical terms, and numbers of different technical and sub-technical terms[7] utilized, both approximately five times as great (see Tables 3 and 4), the types of topics treated, and (see Figure 9, below) the relative importance attributed to FA–passenger and FA–co-worker communication.

Table 3   Total technical/sub-technical terms noted

	Written introspection	Interview	Total
FA ($n = 4$)	115	188	303
AL ($n = 4$)	35	26	61

Table 4   Total different technical/sub-technical terms noted

	Written introspection	Interview	Total
FA ($n = 4$)	89	134	195
AL ($n = 4$)	23	22	39

The *relative importance* attributed to different components of the FA's job also differed. *Safety* is the clear priority from the FAs' and airlines' point of view, as evidenced in all FA data, both written introspections and interviews, in training manuals, and on FA

(4a) AL1: maybe put big items in the closet for you, like my guitar, one time they took it, put it away for me ... once they put it behind seats [continues with long story about problems with retrieving his guitar at the end of the flight] ...

(4b) FA1: You check in with scheduling. Then the first flight attendant does a briefing of the flight – number of passengers, gate number, cockpit crew, review of the last in-flight bulletin and manual revision, service flow and procedure ... Then you go through security, enter your pin number and board the plane. Depending on the position that you fly, each flight attendant is assigned to check the emergency equipment (life vests, life rafts, flashlights, megaphones, oxygen, etc.) for that area. You also have to prepare the liquor carts (ice, beverages, etc.) for the in-flight service. Certain flight attendants are assigned boarding responsibilities (telling passengers the location of their seats) and others are assigned to the doors. After boarding, certain FAs do an infant count and verify special meals (vegetarian, child, low fat, etc.) with passengers, and others brief passengers near emergency doors on how to assist a flight attendant with emergency evacuation (check for fire and water level before opening the door, how to open the door and to take the flight attendant with them if she's incapacitated, and how to open her seatbelt to release her since it's different from the passengers' seatbelt) {snip: much more}

(4c) AL3: ... basically that type of stuff kind of like ... waitresses, or waiters ... in the air
Interviewer: Is there any other parts to the job that you might ... think of?
AL3: Anything else that they do? Gosh, I don't know anything else for them to do. Uh they seem to, uh ... the flights that I've been on, it seems that they basically give- give the food, make sure that you have plenty to drink ... basically they give things to you, and tell you what you need to do.
[later in the interview]
Interviewer: ... can you imagine any of the things that would happen outside of an airplane? ... like the role of the flight attendant ... or in the job?
AL3: Let's see ... I don't normally think about that because they're just kind of ... hands that come around and give you things. They don't have much of a personality ... they're just kind of roaming hands uh s- servodroids, kind of, but uh let's see. OK, sometimes I see them walking around with suitcases with the uh captain and uh co-pilot. And they look tired. Or they look glamorous and sexy. Because they're all very tall and ... uh ...

Figure 4   Insider and outsider perspectives

competency tests, with much of this part of a FA's work being done before and after flights, not just during them. Yet outsiders see a FA's job first and foremost in terms of provision of *services to passengers in the air*. See, e.g., AL3's comments above about 'waitress-in-the-sky' duties, and compare, for instance, the excerpts from written introspections by FA1 and AL1 in response to the first prompt in Figure (5a) and (5b). FA1 included information in terms of roles, positions and tasks, drew on considerable background knowledge, and did not mention in-flight service-related tasks until the unstructured interview; whereas AL1's entire response consisted of a list of 26 rather menial, in-flight, service-related tasks (more than most ALs), all visible to, and involving, passengers:

> (5a) FA1: A flight attendant's main role is to provide safety in case of an emergency. Flight attendants have been trained how to deal with specific situations on each of the aircraft – what to do in case of a ditching or bomb discovery or hijacking or fire on board. Flight attendants have been trained in CPR and in treating some medical problems . . .
>
> (5b) AL1: 1. greet passengers as they enter the plane
> 2. help passengers find seats
> 3. help put stuff in overhead compartments
> .
> .
> .
> 24. put movie screen 'down'
> 25. pass out customs forms
> 26. sell in-flight (no tax?) merchandise.

Figure 5   Insider and outsider priorities (written introspections)

The same pattern was observed in the unstructured interviews, as shown in Figure (6a) and (6b):

> (6a) FA2: Um well the way to think of my job is you know like I'm a flight attendant and I take care of people on the plane. But I don't-the safety part is there, but it's in the back of my mind, but actually it's the part that's really emphasized because like I said we go to re-con training every year. And then before we go on the plane we do briefings and stuff and during take-offs and landings we're supposed to be doing our twenty-second review during that time where we kind of picture where the equipment is located for emergency and how to operate it.

(6b) AL1: And they just kind of stand there and smile at you, unless you ask him, "Where is this?", which I always do … I have seen them help other people with big stuff. And they start looking for empty containers after a while, after the plane starts to go up …

Figure 6   Insider and outsider task priorities (unstructured interviews)

Even when explicitly prompted by the interviewer to think about other aspects of the job perhaps *not* heard or seen by the passengers, outsiders were usually at a loss, sometimes producing guesses that were highly inaccurate. See Figure (7a), (7b) and (7c):

(7a) AL1: I don't know what goes on when they go into the pilots' room [in fact, FAA regulations do not allow FAs to enter the cockpit], so there might be some pilot language they would have to know … and some baggage kind of language … just because there is that counter-check kind of deal, whatever it's called, gate-check that they sometimes have to do [work actually done by other ground staff and gate agents, not FAs] … know the immigration law at least on the surface

(7b) AL2: The five sections of the flight attendant's job would be one taking care of the emotional needs of the passengers [some correct items, like greeting them] physical needs of the customers [some correct items, like serving them food and drinks] taking care of the .. pilots [wrong], pre-boarding duties, preparing the cabin, doing like cleaning – I just suppose this, I have never seen it – and then probably after the flight, again cleaning the cabin and readying it for the next flight [mostly wrong items]… and possible emergency situations [vague] …

(7c) AL3: Anything else happens in their life? … You mean what do they do before they get on the plane and after they get off? … Ah, Ok, Ok, so maybe they walk ar- maybe they, I don't know, maybe they walk around and check the seats and see if there's anyone sleeping or uh someone forgot something, like a wallet or a bag or a baby or something, I don't know. Something like that. Uhm maybe they check for bombs or something, too, I don't know, maybe they look around and look for suspicious stuff or … uh probably I suppose they'd check- make sure that the doors are closed or or that there aren't any problems with the uh pressure … I really don't think about what they do.

Figure 7   Limitations of outsider perspective on tasks
            (unstructured interviews)

Somewhat unexpectedly, FAs were far more reliable and informative than applied linguists, not only about tasks and language, but also about *language use*. The outsiders' field of expertise in this case might have been expected to produce better judgments in this area, but it did not. The applied linguists turned out to know very little of the language involved in a FA's work, even when it came to standardized cabin announcements about fastening seat-belts, etc., and they knew it far less accurately. They also knew virtually nothing about language use (or tasks) between FAs and the cockpit, or among FAs themselves. Compare, for example, the comments, during unstructured interviews, in Figure (8a) and (8b).

(8a) AL1: I don't know what goes on when they go into the pilots' room, so there might be some pilot language they would have to know ... Superficial pilot language what they'd need to know to communicate with them ...

(8b) FA2: OK well between the cockpit and the flight attendant there's very little communication because all you do is say hello or whatever, and then if they call you and they want certain things to eat you just, you know, send up the stuff, 'cos actually we're not allowed in the cockpit, you know ... Yeah because of FAA regulations. And um so the only exchange you have is before and after flight between them. But on the flight there's a lot of communication between the flight attendants ...

Figure 8   Insider and outsider knowledge of language use
(unstructured interviews)

Moreover, as shown in Figure (9a), almost everything applied linguists reported about language use (e.g., 96% in the case of AL1, 100% for AL2) involved general in-flight announcements or FA communication with passengers, mostly high frequency, service-related formulae (and sometimes specific things that a FA had once said to them), and virtually no FA–FA talk. The FA responses, conversely (see 9b), suggested that all this was quite unrepresentative. FA1, for example, was very detailed and specific in her response to the introspection question about in-flight communication. 64 of 140 interlocutor labels she listed involved communication among FAs, including the lead FA; 38 of 140 involved FA talk with personnel other than FAs and passengers (manager, caterer, gate agent, scheduler, etc.). That is, only roughly 27% of the talk involved passengers; 73% did not. The FAs' judgments were supported by the evidence provided by the in-flight and other tape-recordings. The detail, too,

LFA: lead flight attendant
PA: passenger
FAA: Federal Aviation Authority

(9a) (LFA→FA) "Big handle, big trouble", (FA→FA) "I'm gonna close out my beverage cart", (FA→FA) "Are you gonna take lead?", (LFA→FA) "Our load is 18 and 154", (FA→GA) "We have a double-seating assignment", (LFA→FA) "Doors for departure, cross check", (FA→FA) "Have you checked in the PSK?", (PA→FA) "I'm going to miss my connection", and (FA→PA) "That bag needs to go under the seat", (FA→FA) "FAA is on board", (FA→FA) "She must be pretty senior to hold that schedule!", and (FA→MCC) "Do you want us to do the squeeze?"

(9b) [All FA→PA] "Would you like (e.g.) chicken or (e.g.) pasta?", "I'll be back with that shortly", "Do you need help finding your seat?", "This way, sir/madam", "Meat or chicken?", "The captain has turned off the seatbelt sign ...", "Would you like headphones?", and [PA→FA] "Can I keep the can?"

Figure 9 Insider and outsider perspectives on language use (unstructured interviews)

actual time, all call, AOA badge, back-to-backs, bids, bid sheet, block in, block out, block time, briefing, cockpit briefing sheets, codes, code 2, code 4, curbside check, deadhead, EDT, ETA, easy rights, flight groupings, ground-holding time, hold better schedule, illegal rest period, infant count, 1 left, 2 right, jump seats, layover, lead, leg-body-leg, load, main cabin coordinator, mixed crew, mutual trade, overduty, PBE, piggybacking, PSE, PSK, seniority number, short call, scheduled time, seniority number, service flow, service procedure, SPIL (Special Passenger Information List), time in route, TR 29, TSU, walk through, water walk, widebody ... and many more.

Figure 10 Some technical and sub-technical terms in insider recall of FA language use

was far greater in the insiders' accounts. For example, whereas FA1 prefaced some utterances with "Certain FAs say ...," none of what the applied linguists said was position-specific. FAs' descriptions were peppered with technical and sub-technical terms, some of which were so familiar to them that they appeared no longer to be aware that they *are* technical. Just a few of those employed by the FAs are shown in Figure 10. Outsiders used *none* of these terms.

Target discourse samples

In addition to gathering written documents of various kinds for the project, participating FAs made surreptitious tape-recordings of a pre-flight briefing, segments of in-flight FA–PA service, FA–FA talk during in-flight breaks, and FA–FA conversation aboard an airport shuttle.

While limited in certain respects, the in-flight tapes generally exhibited proportions of talk between FAs and passengers, and among FAs themselves, similar to those suggested by the FA (but not the AL) introspection and interview data. In addition, more than any other source in this study, the audio-tapes exhibited complex levels of *implicitness, open-endedness* and *inter-textuality.* To illustrate, inter-textuality in the pre-flight briefing involved references to, and reliance on, FAs' shared background knowledge of various systems and procedures, including an on-line computerized scheduling system, upcoming meetings and events, the FA manual, appropriate Japanese expressions for use with non-English-speaking passengers, door-opening procedures and service-flow patterns for different aircraft, hypothetical emergencies, and a crew shortage for an upcoming flight. High degrees of implicitness, open-endedness and inter-textuality are qualities found in other workplace talk, e.g., at a rural US railway station ticket window, while attempting sales to Japanese tourists in a Melbourne duty-free shop, briefing a partner in a British architects' office, and writing letters of apology in a Japanese travel agency in Waikiki (see Long, to appear), but qualities notoriously rare to non-existent in commercially published FL materials. The FA recordings also revealed large amounts of the not obviously work-related 'social talk' so critical for satisfactory job performance in other contexts (see, e.g., Bosher & Smalkoski, 2002; Svendsen & Krebs, 1984; Holmes, this volume).

Methods

Written introspections

Responses to written introspections exhibited considerably more variability than interviews at the individual level. If an informant misinterpreted a prompt, or the level of detail sought, for instance, there was no-one present to salvage the data-collection session. Written introspections also produced fewer data than interviews, although data that tended to be denser and more concise in informa-tional terms (terser, and with fewer anecdotes than the interviews, for instance). The introspections often contained *proportionately* more (useful) technical information and technical terms (except where those were specifically solicited during an interview), and information rendered in more readily usable form. Written introspections led respondents to structure their replies more clearly, perhaps because the intended audience was less certain and/or because, in the absence of the interlocutor feedback that an interview provides, the writer was attempting to preempt ambiguity. However, while sufficient to elicit most, and a higher proportion, of what outsiders knew, written introspections were far less adequate than interviews with insiders (see, again, Tables 1–4), the depth and breadth of whose knowledge only became apparent in response to follow-up questions from interviewers.

Unstructured interviews

While interview data were more time-consuming and labor-intensive to obtain, requiring one-on-one, face-to-face encounters, transcription, etc., interviews were more effective than written introspection overall in most respects. The researcher could trigger specific examples and illustrative anecdotes where needed in interviews, the audience was clear, and the comprehensibility of what they were saying was easy for informants to monitor. Informants took off on the two prompt questions for the introspections, but took off in all directions. They sometimes did so in the interviews, too, but the interviewer's presence meant that follow-up questions and comments could be used to re-establish the intended focus, as illustrated in Figure 11.

(11a)
Interviewer: . . . What does your job as a flight attendant consist of?
FA2: OK well um our job is mainly um safety related. And um the main purpose we're on the plane for is supposedly to evacuate the plane in case of an emergency so we're trained for doing that. And um the whole job centers around um the evacuation of the plane and how it would be handled your responsibilities in evacuation and all that kind of stuff. But then a lot of it is service-related taking care of passengers and um doing the the the uh beverages and meal service on the plane.
Interviewer.: . . . So what would you say the main sections of the work? There's the safety stuff is one   FA2: Yeah
Interviewer: And uh what else the food and beverage stuff is another
FA2: Yeah

Interviewer: Any other big- sort of big areas like that?
FA2: Um well another thing is public relations. We're supposed to be able to handle passengers and leave a good impression ya know with the passengers about ABC airlines. So so actually the focus of the job would be safety related and then service, and public relations … {more}

(11b)
Interviewer: So this [the briefing] is one thing that we never see. In a way it sounds like you folks organizing yourself to do the job in the air. But are there other aspects of the job that you actually do that the passengers don't see? Not just organizational, but actually part of the work that you do which is stuff we don't get to see?
FA2: Um no because actually the only thing we do beforehand would be the determination of the um the positions, and um other than that, once we're on the plane, it's everything that you see, how we do the service.
Interviewer: What about before we get on the plane? I mean you folks get on the plane for an hour before we even get there, right? What happens in there? I always wanted to know.
FA2: OK, yeah. So what we do is … {long description of other tasks – food checks, guidance for any novice staff, equipment checks (headsets), paper work, safety checks (life vests, oxygen, fire equipment, etc.), training selected passenger in emergency procedure (chute operation, etc.), checking galley is operational, matching passenger and meal lists, filling out forms of several kinds, etc.)

Figure 11   Reorienting questions during unstructured interviews

Unstructured interviews also allowed some informal *triangulation*, as in Figure 12:

Interviewer: From the passenger's point of view what we see is you folks once we get on the flight, and then we get off, you say goodbye, and you're still on the plane. Is that- is what we see a flight attendant's job or is there a lot more to it than what we see?

FA2: Yeah. Actually there's a lot more to it than what you see because like for instance um as I explained in the thing that we did- that I did for the . you know, what the job consists of [the written introspection]. Before you get on the plane you have to be familiar with everything and then you also … {several minutes of explanation of other responsibilities}

Figure 12   Informal triangulation during unstructured interviews

Surreptitious audio-recordings

Surreptitious recordings of target discourse samples were, with the exception of some in-flight segments, relatively painless to collect, and some produced excellent baseline data against which to check informants' intuitions about language and language use (and, to a far lesser extent, tasks), as well as providing target discourse samples potentially usable as models in materials design. They were not without problems, however. In-flight recordings tended to suffer from engine noise, often leaving FA speech audible, but passenger responses hard, and occasionally impossible, to decipher. Moreover, quite lengthy gaps sometimes occurred between snatches of talk as FAs went about certain of their duties alone. In-flight FA–FA communication, much of it taped at close quarters in the galley area, was generally audible.

Source x method interactions for language and tasks

A small number of source x method interactions emerged from the data-collection, some expected, some not. Found written materials were the best sources on tasks (many were written in what amounted to task format) and on language, as might be expected, due both to the written materials' length and status as samples of insider-to-insider communication. Insiders were far richer sources than outsiders on tasks (totals of 117 and 108, respectively), and also on technical/sub-technical language (totals of 303 and 61, respectively), the latter being the one area where the applied linguists might have been expected to have had an advantage. As shown in Tables 2 and 4, however, the insiders' superiority in both instances tended to be masked by the written introspections. Written introspections were relatively more efficient than unstructured interviews with outsiders, mostly because they were sufficient for the applied linguists to display their limited knowledge of both language and tasks, but much less effective with the FAs, who showed the far greater depth and breadth of their knowledge of each when given the opportunity to do so by the open-endedness and follow-up questioning made possible by the unstructured interview format. Thus, applied linguists mentioned a total of 63 different tasks, with roughly equal numbers (30 and 33, respectively) in the written introspections and the unstructured interviews. Flight attendants mentioned a total of 89 different tasks, nearly twice as many (57, compared with 32) during the interviews as in the written introspections. Where language was concerned, the same tendencies were clear. Applied linguists mentioned a total of only 39 different technical and sub-technical terms, 23 in the written introspections, and 22 during the unstructured interviews, i.e., virtually the same (small) number regardless of method. FAs, by contrast, mentioned a total of 195 different technical and sub-technical terms, 89 in the written intro-spections, and 134 during the interviews, i.e., with method making a difference.

Surreptitious recordings were a better source of baseline data for language use than for technical/sub-technical language itself or for task analysis, and, along with participant observation, probably the only mechanism for obtaining data on some important aspects of a FA's work, e.g., the (closed) pre-flight briefing, and social-bonding talk with other crew members, as well as for revealing some of its subtler inter-textual, open-ended, and implicit qualities. Inferring tasks from conversational transcripts involved an undesirably high degree of inference on the analyst's part, and was also inefficient, due to the relatively high ratio of (especially in-flight) language use to task accomplishment, most obviously routine service tasks repeated with many passengers. Written introspections, interview data, and written material were all better sources for this purpose.

Conclusions and implications

An adequate NA will usually be a time-consuming undertaking, and one requiring some expertise in applied linguistics, including research methods. Large-scale language teaching programs and commercial publishers alike often invest considerable sums of money in curri-culum development and materials writing, yet neglect NA as the appropriate starting-point for both. When NAs are conducted, their likely validity can be enhanced by careful attention to sources, methods, and source x method interactions.

Some reasonably firm conclusions can be drawn with regard to *sources* for a NA, some from the literature survey, some from the FA study.

First, a thorough NA (one conducted for the purpose of course design, not, as here, as a test of methodological procedures) should employ stratified random sampling, not a convenience sample, as was the case with the FAs and applied linguists.

Second, NAs should involve insiders / domain experts, not, or not just, learners, language teachers, or materials writers. Outsiders were oblivious to several major aspects of a FA's work. If this was true of such an apparently familiar and 'public' occupation, of which all had had indirect experience as travelers, and when the outsiders were relatively linguistically sophisticated, how much truer must it be in other cases involving NA and course design for less familiar, or wholly unfamiliar, academic, occupational, vocational, or 'street survival' domains?

Third, unless time or resources dictate otherwise, multiple sources should always be employed, both because they add breadth and depth to an analysis, and because triangulation of sources offers an important means of validating findings.

Valuable sources will often include found written materials. Although the DOT provided a limited, somewhat misleading vignette of a FA's work, it could still make a useful first port of call for a needs analyst completely unfamiliar with the target domain, followed by perusal of other written sources, which were highly instructive in this case, before wasting the time of domain experts. In many cases, multiple sources can also mean audio-recorded samples of target discourse. These can be relatively easy to obtain and are potentially of value to the course designer in at least three ways: as baseline data against which to validate intuitions about target discourse (even the intuitions of domain experts); as models of target language use (adapted or not) for incorporation into the design of instructional materials (see, e.g., Chaudron et al, this volume; Downey Bartlett, this volume; Sullivan & Girginer, 2002; Winn, this volume); and as a means of accessing insiders' real-world criteria for evaluating task performance. Unlike the disembodied texts that are the starting-point in traditional forms-focused language teaching, transcripts resulting from such in situ recordings are tied meaningfully to the target tasks which gave rise to them, and of which they are a record. FA discourse, like every other domain-specific language use studied by applied linguists to date, is far more complex than what tends to appear in traditional, (non-expert) intuitions-based language teaching materials. Modeling formulaic utterances such as "Would you like the chicken or the fish?" just won't do.

Some tentative conclusions also emerged where *methods* are concerned. As is widely claimed in the literature, unstructured interviews were successful in obtaining important ideas and information in this study that it would not have occurred to the researcher to target for not knowing what he did not know. While offering rapid coverage of more informants, and so superficially more efficient, a questionnaire would have required prior understanding of what the relevant issues were, and could only have served to check, i.e., confirm or disconfirm, that understanding, or to ascertain the degree of agreement or disagreement with it. Questionnaires are valuable for ascertaining the pervasiveness of existing views, in other words, but less so for creating new knowledge about an unfamiliar field, which may be preempted by too early a rush to quantification – and learning about a largely unfamiliar field is the typical situation confronting the needs analyst. As with sources, it is difficult to over-emphasize the likelihood that use of multiple methods of data-collection and analysis will increase the quality, not just the quantity, of information obtained, not least for the option this provides for triangulation by methods. Methods must also be carefully *sequenced*, however, e.g., (usually) more 'open' procedures, like unstructured interviews, before more 'closed' ones, like questionnaires. Despite the quick and easy coverage they offer, questionnaire surveys undoubtedly constitute the most over-used and over-rated approach to NA at present, especially when deployed in an unfamiliar domain or alone.

As for *source x method interactions*, qualitative methods produced rich data overall in this instance, but some were vulnerable to misinterpretation by informants. Procedures which are *too* open-ended or unstructured and/or during the use of which the researcher is not present to act as a guide (not a control), e.g., in this case, the written introspections, may sometimes be inadequate for obtaining a rich data set from domain experts. It is conceivable that this and the few other source x method interactions that emerged in the FA study were due to the particular nature of the domain under investigation, the particular way the investigation was conducted, individual variation among the (relatively few) informants, or some combination thereof. However, this is an aspect of NA methodology rarely, if ever, discussed, much less studied, so the patterns that emerged do at least suggest that selection among sources and methods needs to be supplemented by careful consideration of which of each may make productive pairings.

It is currently fashionable in some quarters of applied linguistics, albeit for different reasons or for no apparent reason, (i) to advocate learners as the principal or even the sole sources on learner needs, and/or teachers as the principal or even the sole assessors thereof, (ii) to argue for the classroom, once a course has begun and thereafter, as the principal or even the sole place and time for NA, or (iii) to disparage pre-course NA, or NA altogether. As should be obvious by now, however, given (a) the logistics involved in gaining access to relevant sources, (b) the familiarity with at least basic research methods required of those conducting a NA, (c) the frequent inadequacy of pre-service or pre-experience learners as sources, (d) the superiority of domain experts over outsiders as sources, and (e) the time needed both for a thorough NA, involving multiple sources and methods, carefully sequenced, and for materials development and course design based on its results, all three positions are untenable. The value of NA might become more apparent to skeptics, however, were they seen to be conducted more scientifically. Numerous NAs are reported in the L2 literature, and there is small, but growing, as yet mostly data-free literature on NA itself. What is sorely lacking is a substantial, coherent applied linguistics *research program* (not one-off studies) on NA itself.

Notes

1 A comprehensive annotated bibliography, broken down by sectors, is sorely needed. Meanwhile, useful, if somewhat dated, lists of references can be found in several places, including Jordan (1996), Robinson (1991, pp. 110–19), and West (1994). See, also, Long (to appear).

2 Such a low response rate threatens the validity of any survey and requires that the researcher provide information as to the degree to which the minority of returns are likely to have been representative of the initial sample (for a simple statistical procedure, see Bernard, 1994, pp. 276–7). More recently, a useful survey of spoken language needs of EAP students at US universities (Ferris & Tagg, 1996) was also based on a low rate (25.4%). Applied linguists are clearly going to need to utilize proven procedures described in the social science research methods literature for improving response rates (see, e.g., Bernard, 1994, pp. 275–81; Dillman, 1978, 1983).

3 Other findings useful to EAP writing teachers, including examples of the task types and information about which categories of assignments were typical of which departments, need not concern us here. Interested EAP writing teachers should consult Horowitz (1986).

4 See, e.g., Brindley & Slatyer, 2002; Brown et al, 2002; Norris et al, 2002; Norris et al, 1998; McNamara, 1996; Robinson & Ross, 1996; and van den Branden, Depauw, & Gysen, 2002. For treatments of many of the same issues in the general field of educational measurement, see Kane, 2001; Kane, Crooks, & Cohen, 1999; and Messick, 1994.

5 As an anonymous reviewer of this volume noted, this is also the generally accepted view in the field of rhetoric and professional communication, much of which might be thought of as LSP (languages for specific purposes) for native speakers.

6 In fact, the figures in Tables 1 and 2 tend to flatter the applied linguists, who were given credit for naming several micro-level passenger-service tasks (show passengers to their seats, hand out bags of goodies, etc.) that were subsumed under larger categories (e.g., conduct meal services) in the FA data. The FAs also covered a far wider range of tasks, including whole areas (conducting pre-flight briefings, checking emergency equipment, etc.) not mentioned by the applied linguists at all.

7 The distinction between technical and sub-technical lexical items was dropped from this analysis, and the categories collapsed, after attempts

by the author and a research assistant to achieve satisfactory inter-rater reliability (90% or better) proved unsuccessful. Two leading authorities on the L2 lexicon who were consulted at that point informed us that classification of terms into these two categories by vocabulary specialists (unlike ourselves), while widespread, seems always to have been impressionistic.

Acknowledgments

Generous support for this project was provided by the National Foreign Language Center, Washington, D.C., in the form of a Mellon Fellowship to the author, and by the National Foreign Language Resource Center at the University of Hawai'i, and is gratefully acknowledged, as is the valuable help with data collection and analysis provided by Paul Sevigny and Tony Donnes.

References

Agar, M. H. (1986). *Speaking of ethnography*. Beverly Hills: Sage.
Alalou, A. (2001). Reevaluating curricular objectives using students' perceived needs: The case of three language programs. *Foreign Language Annals* 34, 5, 453–69.
Allen, J. P. B., Frolich, M., & Spada, N. (1984). The communicative orientation of language teaching: an observation scheme. In J. Handscombe, R. A. Orem & B. Taylor (eds.), *On TESOL '83* (pp. 231–52). Washington, D.C.: TESOL.
Allwright, J., & Allwright, R. (1977). An approach to the teaching of medical English. In S. Holden (ed.), *English for specific purposes* (pp. 58–62). Oxford: Modern English Publications.
Auerbach, E. R. (1992). *Making meaning, making change*. Washington, D.C.: Center for Applied Linguistics.
Auerbach, E. R. (1995). The politics of the ESL classroom: Issues of power in pedagogical choices. In Tollefson, J. W. (ed.), *Power and inequality in language education* (pp. 9-33). Cambridge: Cambridge University Press).
Auerbach, E. R., & Burgess, D. (1985). The hidden curriculum of survival ESL. *TESOL Quarterly* 19, 3, 475–95.
Bachman, L. F. (2002). Some reflections on task-based language performance assessment. *Language Testing* 19, 4, 453–76.
Babbie, E. R. (1973). *Survey research methods*. Belmont, CA: Wadsworth.
Bailey, K. E. (1982). *Methods of social research*. New York: Free Press.
Bailey, K. M. (1990). The use of diary studies in teacher education programs. In J. C. Richards & D. Nunan (eds.), *Second language teacher education*. Cambridge: Cambridge University Press.

Bailey, K. M., & Oschner, R. (1983). A methodological review of the diary studies: windmill tilting or social science? In K. M. Bailey, M. H. Long & B. Peck (eds.), *Second language acquisition studies* (pp. 188–98). Rowley, MA: Newbury House.

Beatty, C. J., & Chan, M. J. (1984). Chinese scholars abroad: Changes in perceived academic needs. *English for Specific Purposes* 3, 53–9.

Benson, M. J. (1991). University ESL readings: A content analysis. *English for Specific Purposes* 10, 75–88.

Bernard, H. R. (1994). *Research methods in anthropology: Qualitative and quantitative approaches*. Second edition. Thousand Oaks: Sage.

Berwick, R. F. (1989). Needs assessment in language programming: from theory to practice. In R. K. Johnson (ed.), *The second language curriculum* (pp. 48–62). Cambridge: Cambridge University Press.

Biber, D. (1988). *Variation across speech and writing*. Cambridge: Cambridge University Press.

Bosher, S., & Smalkoski, K. (2002). From needs analysis to curriculum development: Designing a course in health-care communication for immigrant students in the USA. *English for Specific Purposes* 21, 59–79.

Boswood, T., & Marriot, A. (1994). Ethnography for specific purposes: Teaching and training in parallel. *English for Specific Purposes* 13, 1, 3–21.

Braine, G. (1988). Academic writing task surveys: The need for a fresh approach. *Texas Papers in Foreign Language Education* 1, 101–18.

Braine, G. (2001). When professors don't cooperate: a critical perspective on EAP research. *English for Specific Purposes* 20, 293-303.

Breen, M. (1984). Process syllabuses for the language classroom. In C. J. Brumfit (ed.), *General English syllabus design. ELT Documents* 118, 47–60.

Briggs, C. (1986). *Learning how to ask*. Cambridge: Cambridge University Press.

Brindley, G. (1984). *Needs analysis and objective setting in the Adult Migrant Education Service*. Sydney: Adult Migrant Education Service.

Brindley, G., & Hood, S. (1990). Curriculum innovation in adult ESL. In G. Brindley (ed.), *The second language curriculum in action* (pp. 232–48). Sydney: NCELTR, Macquarie University.

Brindley, G., & Slatyer, H. (2002). Exploring task difficulty in ESL listening assessment. *Language Testing* 19, 4, 369–94.

Brown, C. (1985). Two windows on the classroom world: Diary studies and participant observation. In P. Larsen, E. Judd & D. Messerschmitt (eds.), *On TESOL '84* (pp. 121–34). Washington, D.C.: TESOL.

Brown, J. D., & Hudson, T. (2002). *Criterion-referenced language testing*. Cambridge: Cambridge University Press.

Brown, J. D., Hudson, T., Norris, J., & Bonk, W. J. (2002). *An investigation of second language task-based performance assessments*. Honolulu, HI: Second Language Teaching and Curriculum Center.

Cameron, R. (1998). A language-focused needs analysis for ESL-speaking nursing students in class and clinic. *Foreign Language Annals* 31, 2, 203–18.

Cathcart, R. (1989). Authentic discourse and the survival English curriculum. *TESOL Quarterly* 23, 1, 105–26.

Chambers, F. (1980). A re-evaluation of needs analysis in ESP. *The ESP Journal* 1, 1, 25–33.

Chaudron, C. (1988). *Second language classrooms: Research on teaching and learning*. Cambridge: Cambridge University Press.

Clahsen, H. (1987). Connecting theories of language processing and (second) language acquisition. In C. W. Pfaff (ed.), *First and second language acquisition processes* (pp. 103–116). Cambridge, MA: Newbury House.

Coleman, H. (1988). Analyzing language needs in large organizations. *English for Specific Purposes* 7, 155–169.

Conrad, S. (1996). Investigating academic texts with corpus-based techniques: An example from biology. *Linguistics and Education* 8, 3, 299–314.

Courtney, M. (1988). Some initial considerations for course design. *English for Specific Purposes* 7, 195–203.

Crookes, G. (1986). *Task classification: A cross-disciplinary review*. Technical Report No. 4. Honolulu, HI: Center for Second Language Classroom Research, Social Science Research Institute, University of Hawai'i at Manoa.

Cumaranatunge, L. K. (1988). An EOP case study: Domestic aids in West Asia. In D. Chamberlain & R. J. Baumgardner (eds.), *ESP in the classroom: Practice and evaluation. ELT Document 128* (pp. 127–33). London: Modern English Publications / The British Council.

DeCarrico, J., & Nattinger, J. R. (1988). Lexical phrases for the comprehension of academic lectures. *English for Specific Purposes* 7, 91–102.

Denzin, N. K. (2001). Interpretative interactionism. *Applied Social Science Research Methods*, 16. Thiousand Oaks, CA: SAGE.

Dictionary of Occupational Titles. (1991). Fourth edition, revised. Washington, D.C.: US Employment Service, US Department of Labor.

Dillman, D. A. (1978). *Mail and telephone surveys: The total design method*. New York: Wiley.

Dillman, D. A. (1983). Mail and other self-administered questionnaires. In P. H. Rossi, J. D. Wright & A. B. Anderson (eds.), *Handbook of survey research* (pp. 359–378). New York: Academic Press.

Doughty, C. J., & Long, M. H. (2002). Optimal psycholinguistic environments for distance foreign language learning. Plenary address to the conference on Distance Learning of the Less Commonly Taught Languages. February 1–3, 2002. Arlington, VA. *Second Language Studies* 20, 1, 2002, 1–42. Also to appear in *Language Learning and Technology*, 7, 3 (September) 2003, 50–80 (http://llt.msu.edu).

Doughty, C., & Williams, J. (eds.) (1998). *Focus on form in classroom second language acquisition.* Cambridge: Cambridge University Press.

Elder, C. (1993). How do subject specialists construe classroom language proficiency? *Language Testing* 10, 3, 235–54.

Ellis, G., & Sinclair, B. (1989). *Learning how to learn.* Cambridge: Cambridge University Press.

Ellis, R. (1993). The structural syllabus and second language acquisition. *TESOL Quarterly* 27, 1, 91–113.

Ellis, R. (1994). *The study of second language acquisition.* Oxford: Oxford University Press.

Ferris, D., & Tagg, T. (1996). Academic oral communication needs of EAP learners: What subject-matter instructors really require. *TESOL Quarterly* 30, 1, 31–55.

Fixman, C. S. (1990). The foreign language needs of US-based corporations. In Lambert, R., & Moore, S. (eds.), *Foreign language in the workplace. Annals of the American Academy of Political and Social Science* 511, 25–46.

Flowerdew, J. (1994). Specific language for specific purposes: Concordancing for the ESP syllabus. In R. Khoo (ed.), *LSP: Problems and prospects* (pp. 97–113). Anthology Series 33. Singapore: SEAMEO Regional Language Centre.

Franco, A. L. (1986). Beyond the classroom: Monitoring at industry. *The ESP Journal* 4, 153–60.

Goetz, J. P., & Le Compte, M. D. (1984). *Ethnography and qualitative design in educational research.* NY: Academic Press.

Greenwood, D. J., & Gonzales Santos, J. L. (1992). *Industrial democracy as process: Participatory action research in the Fagor Cooperative Group of Mondragon.* Stockholm: Arbetslivscentrum.

Guba, G., & Lincoln, Y. S. (1994). Competing paradigms in qualitative research. In N. K. Denzin & Y. S. Lincoln (eds.) *Handbook of qualitative research* (pp. 105–17). Thousand Oaks, CA: SAGE.

Hammersley, M., & Atkinson, P. (1983). *Ethnography: Principles and practice.* London: Tavistok.

Hatch, E. (1992). *Discourse and language education.* Cambridge: Cambridge University Press.

Hawkins, B. (1985). Is an "appropriate response" always so appropriate? In S. M. Gass & C. G. Madden (eds.), *Input in second language acquisition* (pp. 162–78). Rowley, MA: Newbury House.

Hoadley-Maidment, E. (1977/1980). Methodology for the identification of language learning needs of immigrant learners of English through mother-tongue interviews. In R. Richterich & J.-L. Chancerel (eds.), *Identifying the needs of adults learning a foreign language* (pp. 39–51). Oxford: Pergamon.

Hodlin, S. (1970). Preliminary survey in a food factory: Introductory discussion, personnel records and participant observation. Southall, London: Pathway Industrial Unit.

70   *Michael H. Long*

Horowitz, D. M. (1986). What professors actually require: Academic tasks for the ESL classroom. *TESOL Quarterly* 20, 3, 445–62.

Huckin, T. N., & Olsen, L. A. (1984). On the use of informants in LSP discourse analysis. In Pugh, A. K., & Ulijn, J. M. (eds.), *Reading for professional purposes* (pp. 120–29). London: Heinemann.

Hudson, T., & Lynch, B. (1984). A criterion-referenced measurement approach to ESL achievement testing. *Language Testing* 1, 2, 171–201.

Hutchinson, T., & Waters, A. (1987). *English for specific purposes.* Cambridge: Cambridge University Press.

Hymes, D. (1962). The ethnography of speaking. In T. Gladwin & W. Sturtevant (eds.), *Anthropology and human behavior* (pp. 15–53). Washington, D.C.: Anthropological Society of Washington.

Iwai, T., Kondo, K., Lim, D. S. J., Ray, G. E., Shimizu, H., & Brown, J. D. (1999). *Japanese language needs analysis.* Ms. National Foreign Language Research Center, Honolulu, HI: University of Hawai'i at Manoa.

Jacobson, W. H. (1986). An assessment of the communicative needs of non-native speakers of English in an undergraduate physics lab. *English for Specific Purposes* 5, 2, 173–87.

Jacoby, S. (1999). Rethinking EST: What can "indigenous assessment" tell us about the communication culture of science? Ms. Department of Communication, University of New Hampshire.

Jacoby, S., & McNamara, T. (1999). Locating competence. *English for Specific Purposes* 18, 3, 213–41.

Jarvis, J. (1992). Using diaries for teaching reflection on in-service courses. *English Language Teaching Journal* 46, 2, 133–43.

Jasso-Aguilar, R. (1999/this volume). Sources, methods and triangulation in needs analysis: A critical perspective in a case study of Waikiki hotel maids. *English for Specific Purposes* 18, 1, 27–46.

Johns, A. (1981). Necessary English: A faculty survey. *TESOL Quarterly* 15, 1, 51–7.

Johnson, D. M. (1992). Survey research. In D. M. Johnson, *Approaches to second language learning* (pp. 104–29). White Plains, NY: Longman.

Johnson Nystrom, N. (1983). In H. W. Seliger & M. H. Long (eds.), *Classroom-oriented research in second language acquisition* (pp. 169–88). Rowley, MA: Newbury House.

Jordan, R. R. (1996). *English for academic purposes.* Cambridge: Cambridge University Press.

Jupp, T. C., & Hodlin, S. (1975). *Industrial English.* London: Heinemann.

Kane, M. T. (2001). Current concerns in validity theory. *Journal of Educational Measurement* 38, 319–42.

Kane, M. T., Crooks, T., & Cohen, A. (1999). Validating measures of performance. *Educational Measurement: Issues and Practice* 18, 5–17.

Kennedy, G. (1990). Collocations: Where grammar and vocabulary meet. In S. Anivan (ed.), *Language teaching methodology for the nineties* (pp. 215–29). Anthology Series 24. Singapore: SEAMEO Regional Language Centre.

Kirk, J., & Miller, M. L. (1986). *Reliability and validity in qualitative research*. Thousand Oaks, CA: SAGE.

Lamotte, J. (1981). Introspections and discourse in a physical therapy session. Unpublished term paper. Philadelphia: University of Pennsylvania, Graduate School of Education.

Larsen-Freeman, D., & Long, M. H. (1991). *An introduction to second language acquisition research*. London: Longman.

Lepetit, D., & Cichocki, W. (2002). Teaching languages to future health professionals: A needs assessment study. *Modern Language Journal* 86, 3, 384–96.

Lincoln, Y. S., & Guba, E. G. (eds.) (1985). *Naturalistic inquiry*. Newbury Park: Sage.

Long, M. H. (1985). A role for instruction in second language acquisition: Task-based language teaching. In K. Hyltenstam & M. P. Pienemann (eds.), *Modeling and assessing second language acquisition* (pp. 77–99). Clevedon: Multilingual Matters.

Long, M. H. (1991). Focus on form: a design feature in language teaching methodology. In K. de Bot, D. Coste, R. Ginsberg & C. Kramsch (eds.), *Foreign language research in cross-cultural perspective* (pp. 39–52). Amsterdam: John Benjamins.

Long, M. H. (1997). Authenticity and learning potential in L2 classroom discourse. In G. Jacobs (ed.), *Language classrooms of tomorrow: Issues and responses* (pp. 148–69). Singapore: SEAMEO Regional Language Centre.

Long, M. H. (1998). Focus on form in TBLT. *University of Hawai'i Working Papers in ESL* 16, 2, 35–49. Also in R. Lambert & E. Shohamy (eds.), *Language policy and pedagogy* (pp. 181–94). Amsterdam/Philadelphia: John Benjamins, 2000.

Long, M. H. (to appear). Chapter 4: Needs analysis, and Chapter 5: Analysis of target discourse. In Long, M. H., *Task-based language teaching*. Oxford: Blackwell.

Long, M. H., & Crookes, G. (1992). Three approaches to task-based language teaching. *TESOL Quarterly* 26, 1, 27–56.

Long, M. H., & Crookes, G. (1993). Units of analysis in syllabus design: the case for task. In G. Crookes & S. M. Gass (eds.), *Tasks in a pedagogical context. Integrating theory and practice* (pp. 9-54). Clevedon: Multilingual Matters, 1993.

Long, M. H., & Norris, J. (2000). Task-based language teaching and assessment. In M. Byram (ed.), *Encyclopedia of language teaching* (pp. 597–603). London: Routledge.

Long, M. H., & Robinson, P. (1998). Focus on form: Theory, research, and practice. In C. Doughty & J. Williams (eds.), *Focus on form in classroom second language acquisition* (pp. 15–41). Cambridge: Cambridge University Press.

Lundstrom, P. (1994). Task-based language teaching in a learner-centered setting: A case study. Term paper, ESL 750 (Task-based language learning). Honolulu, HI: ESL Department, University of Hawai'i at Manoa.

Lynch, B. K. (1995). Using triangulation in naturalistic research. Paper presented at the AAAL Conference, Long Beach, CA, March 27.

Mackay, R. (1978). Identifying the nature of the learner's needs. In R. Mackay & A. Mountford (eds.), *English for specific purposes* (pp. 21–42). London: Longman.

Markee, N. (1986). The relevance of sociopolitical factors to communicative course design. *English for Specific Purposes* 5, 1, 3–16.

Marriot, H. E. (1991). Language planning and language management for tourism shopping situations. In A. J. Liddicoat (ed.), *Language planning and language politics in Australia. Australian Review of Applied Linguistics.* Series S, No. 8. Melbourne: ALAA.

Marriot, H. E., & Yamada, N. (1991). Japanese discourse in tourism shopping situations. In *Japan and the World Vol. 3.* Proceedings of the Biennial Conference of the Japanese Association of Australia. Canberra: Australia-Japan Research Centre.

Mawer, G. (1991). *Language audits and industry restructuring.* Sydney: Macquarie University, NCELTR.

McDonough, J. (1994). A teacher looks at teachers' diaries. *English Language Teaching Journal* 48, 1, 57–65.

McNamara, T. (1996). *Measuring second language performance.* New York: Longman.

Medway, P., & Andrews, R. (1992). Building with words: Discourse in an architect's office. *Carleton Papers in Applied Language Studies* 9, 1–32.

Messick, S. J. (1994). The interplay of evidence and consequences in the validation of performance assessments. *Educational Researcher* 23, 13–23.

Mislevy, R. L., Steinberg, L. S., & Almond, R. G. (2002). Design and analysis in task-based language assessment. *Language Testing* 19, 4, 477–96.

Mohan, B., & Smith, S. M. (1992). Context and cooperation in academic tasks. In D. Nunan (ed.), *Collaborative language learning and teaching* (pp. 81–99). Cambridge: Cambridge University Press.

Munby, J. (1978). *Communicative syllabus design.* Cambridge: Cambridge University Press.

Noblit, G. W., & Hare, R. D. (1988). *Meta-ethnography: Synthesizing qualitative studies.* Beverly Hills: Sage.

Norris, J. M. (2001). Identifying rating criteria for task-based EAP assessment. In T. D. Hudson & J. D. Brown (eds.), *A focus on language test development: Expanding the language proficiency construct across a variety of tests* (pp. 163–204). Honolulu: University of Hawai'i Press.

Norris, J. M., Brown, J. D., Hudson, T. D., & Bonk, W. (2002). Examinee abilities and task difficulty in task-based second language performance assessment. *Language Testing* 19, 4, 395–418.

Norris, J., Brown, J. D., Hudson, T., & Yoshioka, J. (1998). *Designing second language performance assessments.* Technical Report No. 18. Honolulu, HI: University of Hawai'i, Second Language Teaching and Curriculum Center.

Norris, J. M., & Ortega, L. (2000). Effectiveness of L2 instruction: A research synthesis and quantitative meta-analysis. *Language Learning* 50, 3, 417–528.

Nunan, D. (1988). *The learner-centered curriculum.* Cambridge: Cambridge University Press.

Ogata, M. (1992). Language needs of EFL students in Japanese high schools. Scholarly Paper. Honolulu, HI: Department of Second Language Studies, University of Hawai'i at Manoa.

Oppenheim, A. N. (1966). *Questionnaire design and attitude measurement.* New York: Basic Books.

Orikasa, K. (1989). A needs analysis for an EFL program in Japan: A systematic approach to program development. *University of Hawai'i Working Papers in ESL* 8, 1, 1–47.

Parkinson, B., & Howell-Richardson, C. (1990). Learner diaries. In C. Brumfit & R. Mitchell (eds.), *Research in the language classroom ELT Documents 101.* Oxford: Pergamon.

Pienemann, M. (1984). Psychological constraints on the teachability and learnability of languages. *Studies in Second Language Acquisition* 6, 2, 186–214.

Pienemann, M. (1998). *Language processing and second language development. Processability theory.* Amsterdam/Philadelphia: John Benjamins.

Prahbu, N. S. (1987). *Second language pedagogy.* Oxford: Oxford University Press.

Ramani, E., Chacko, T., Singh, S. J., & Glendinning, E. H. (1988). An ethnographic approach to syllabus design: A case study of the Indian Institute of Science, Bangalore. *The ESP Journal* 7, 1, 81–90.

Reinharz, S. (1992). *Feminist methods in social research.* New York: Oxford University Press.

Reves, C. (1994). The use of journals in needs identification for academic reading. Term paper, ESL 750 (Task-based language learning). Honolulu, HI: Department of Second Language Studies, University of Hawai'i at Manoa.

Richterich, R., & Chancerel, J.-L. (1977/1980). *Identifying the needs of adults learning a foreign language.* Strasbourg: Council of Europe/ Oxford: Pergamon.

Roberts, C. (1982). Needs analysis for ESP programmes. *Language Learning and Communication* 1, 1, 105–20.

Roberts, C., Davis, E., & Jupp, T. (1992). *Language and discrimination: A study of communication in multi-ethnic workplaces.* London: Longman.

Robinson, Pauline. (1991). *ESP today.* Hemel Hempstead: Prentice Hall.

Robinson, P. (1998). SLA theory and second language syllabus design. *The Language Teacher* 22, 4, 1998, 7–14.

Robinson, P. (2001). Task complexity, cognitive resources and second language syllabus design. In P. Robinson (ed.), *Cognition and second language instruction*. Cambridge: Cambridge University Press.

Robinson, P., & Ross, S. (1996). The development of task-based assessment in English for academic purposes programs. *Applied Linguistics* 17, 4, 455–76.

Savage, W., & Storer, G. (1992). An emergent language program framework: Actively involving learners in needs analysis. *System* 20, 2, 187–98.

Savage, W., & Whisenand, R. (1993). Logbooks and language learning objectives in an intensive ESP workshop. *TESOL Quarterly* 27, 4, 741–6.

Schieffelin, B., & Ochs, E. (1986). Language socialization. *Annual Review of Anthropology* 15, 163–91.

Schmidt, M. (1981). Needs assessment in English for Specific Purposes: the case study. In L. Selinker, E. Tarone & V. Hanzelli (eds.), *English for academic and technical purposes. Studies in honor of Louis Trimble* (pp. 199–210). Rowley, MA: Newbury House.

Sefton, R., & O'Hara, L. (1992). Report of the work-place education project survey on behalf of the vehicle manufacturing industry. Melbourne: Victorian Automotive Industry Training Board.

Selinker, L. (1979). The use of specialist informants in discourse analysis. *International Review of Applied Linguistics* 17, 2, 189–215.

Selinker, L. (1988). Using research methods in LSP: Two approaches to applied discourse analysis. In M. L. Tickoo (ed.), *ESP: State of the art* (pp. 33–52). Anthology Series 21. Singapore: SEAMEO Regional Language Centre.

Sinclair, J. McH. (1991). *Corpus, concordance and collocation*. Oxford: Oxford University Press.

Sinclair, J. McH., & Coulthard, M. R. (1975). *Towards an analysis of discourse: The English used by teachers and pupils*. Oxford: Oxford University Press.

Skehan, P. (1998). *A cognitive approach to language learning*. Oxford: Oxford University Press.

Spack, R., & Sadow, C. (1993). Student–teacher working journals in ESL freshman composition. *TESOL Quarterly* 17, 4, 575–93.

Spradley, J. P. (1979). *The ethnographic interview*. New York: Holt, Rinehart and Winston.

Spradley, J. P. (1980). *Participant observation*. New York: Holt, Rinehart and Winston.

Spradley, J. P., & McCurdy, D. V. (1972). *The cultural experience: Ethnography in a complex society*. Chicago: Science Research Associates, Inc.

Strauss, A., & Corbin, J. (1990). *Basics of qualitative research: Grounded theory, procedures and techniques*. Beverly Hills: Sage.

Stufflebeam, D. L., McCormick, C. H., Brinkerhoff, R. O., & Nelson, C. O. (1985). *Conducting educational needs asessments*. Boston: Kluwer-Nijhoff.

Sullivan, P., & Girginer, H. (2002). The use of discourse analysis to enhance ESP teacher knowledge: an example using aviation English. *English for Specific Purposes* 21, 397–404.

Svendsen, C. & Krebs, K. (1984). Identifying English for the job: Examples from healthcare occupations. *The ESP Journal* 3, 153–64.

Swales, J. M. (1985). ESP: The heart of the matter or the end of the affair? In R. Quirk & H. G. Widdowson (eds.), *English in the world: Teaching and learning the language and literatures* (pp. 212–23). Cambridge: Cambridge University Press.

Swales, J. M. (1986). ESP in the big world of reprint requests. *English for Specific Purposes* 5, 1, 81–85.

Swales, J. M. (1990). *Genre analysis.* Cambridge: Cambridge University Press.

Tarantino, M. (1988). Italian in-field EST users self-assess their macro- and micro-level needs: A case study. *English for Specific Purposes* 7, 1, 33–52.

Tarone, E., Dwyer, S., Gillette, S., & Icke, V. (1981). On the use of the passive in two astrophysics journals. *The ESP Journal* 1, 2, 123–40.

Teasdale, A. (1994). Authenticity, validity and task design for tests of well defined LSP domains. In R. Khoo (ed.), *The practice of LSP: Perspectives, programmes and projects* (pp. 230–42). Anthology Series 34. Singapore: SEAMEO Regional Language Centre.

Thompson, S. (1994). Frameworks and contexts: A genre-based approach to analyzing lecture introductions. *English for Specific Purposes* 13, 2, 171–86.

Towell, R., & Hawkins, R. (1994). *Approaches to Second language acquisition.* Clevedon, Avon: Multilingual Matters.

Trimble, L. (1985). *English for science and technology: A discourse approach.* Cambridge: Cambridge University Press.

Utley, D. (1992). The language audit. In D. Embleton & S. Hagen (eds.), *Languages in international business: A practical guide* (pp. 33–46). London: Hodder and Stoughton.

Van den Branden, K., Depauw, V., & Gysen, S. (2002). A computerized task-based test of second language Dutch for vocational training purposes. *Language Testing* 19, 4, 438–52.

Van Els, T., & Oud-de-Glas, M. (eds.) (1983). *Research into foreign language needs.* Augsberg: University of Augsberg.

Van Hest, E., & Oud-de-Glas, M. (1990). *A survey of techniques used in the diagnosis and analysis of foreign language needs in industry.* Brussels: Lingua.

Van Lier, L. (1988). *The classroom and the language learner.* New York: Longman.

Ventola, E. (1983). Contrasting schematic structures in service encounters. *Applied Linguistics* 4, 3, 242–58.

Ventola, E. (1987). Textbook dialogues and discourse realities. In W. Lorscher & R. Schulze (eds.), *Perspectives on language in performance* (pp. 399–411). Tubingen: Gunter Narr.

Watson-Gegeo, K. A. (1988). Ethnography in ESL: Defining the essentials. *TESOL Quarterly* 22, 4, 575–92.

Watson-Gegeo, K. A. (1992). Thick explanation in the ethnographic study of child socialization: A longitudinal study of the problem of schooling for Kwara'ae (Solomons Islands) children. In W. A. Corsaro & P. J. Miller (eds.), *Interpretative approaches to children's socialization* (pp. 51–66). San Francisco: Jossey-Bass.

Watson-Gegeo, K. A. (1997). Classroom ethnography. In N. H. Hornberger & D. Corson (eds.), *Encyclopedia of language and education, Volume 8: Research methods in language and education* (pp. 135–44). Dordrecht: Kluwer.

Watts, N. (1994). The use of foreign languages in tourism: Research needs. *Australian Review of Applied Linguistics* 17, 1, 73–84.

West, R. (1994). Needs analysis in language teaching. *Language Teaching* 27, 1, 1–19.

Widdowson, H. G. (1972). The teaching of English as communication. *English Language Teaching* 27, 1, 15–19.

Wilkins, D. (1974). Notional syllabuses and the concept of a minimum adequate grammar. In S. P. Corder & E. Roulet (eds.), *Linguistic insights in applied linguistics*. AIMAV/Didier.

Wilkins, D. (1976). *Notional syllabuses*. Oxford: Oxford University Press.

Willis, D. (1990). *The lexical syllabus: A new approach to language teaching*. London: Collins.

Willis, D., & Willis, J. (1988). *Collins COBUILD English course*. London: Collins.

Wolfson, N. (1976). Speech acts and natural speech: Some implications for sociolinguistic methodology. *Language in Society* 5, 2, 189–209.

Zemelman, S. (1978). Writing in other disciplines: a questionnaire for teachers. Conference on Language Attitudes and Composition Newsletter (Portland State University) 5, 12–16.

Zuck, L. V., & Zuck, J. G. (1984). The main idea: specialist and non-specialist judgments. In A. K. Pugh & J. M. Ulijn (eds.), *Reading for professional purposes* (pp. 130–95). London: Heinemann.

Zughoul, M. R., & Hussein, R. F. (1985). English for higher education in the Arab world: A case study of needs analysis at Yarmouk University. *The ESP Journal* 4, 133–52.

PART II:
THE PUBLIC SECTOR

2 Language needs analysis at the societal level

Richard D. Brecht & William P. Rivers

Introduction

At the societal level, the need for language is generally defined within very general social goals, such as 'national security', 'social justice', or the like. The purpose of associating language with goals like these is to motivate policy and planning for language education at the national, state, or local level, or within the federal language education system. In an ideal world, every policy and intervention at the societal level would be discussed, based on an explicit cost-benefit analysis of the contribution of the intervention to the societal good. This would presume a clear specification of the contribution of the specific intervention domain (e.g., language) to the societal goal (e.g., national security), together with the qualifications of the responsible implementing agent (e.g., the Department of Defense and/or the higher education system). Such specification entails an economic approach, which involves specific description of the elements involved and the correlation of cost and benefit.

An economic approach to the language issue treats language as amenable to market analysis that describes its behavior and provides information to policy makers for their decisions on how to invest scarce public resources.[1] It starts from the perspective that there exists a market for language in a given country, one which can be more or less well described, and which can be influenced by policy interventions from a centralized government body.

In describing the behavior of language as a commodity in the United States, we operate within the familiar economic concepts of *supply* and *demand*, which "embody the very essence of economic reasoning and are the key ingredients of that quintessentially economic construct, the *market*" (Grin, 1999).[2] Breton (1998, p. 5) elaborates:

> When moving from a focus on "economic" phenomena to one on phenomena hitherto taken to be "non-economic" in nature, any aspect of the discipline of economics can be

brought to bear, but it is not possible to claim that an analysis of a political or of a social question is truly economic unless the basic methodology of the discipline is adhered to. One of the essential tenets of that methodology is that one should first analyze how individuals and organizations adjust to changes in the environment which is postulated to be theirs. In standard theory, this leads to the analysis of the demand for a good or a service by households and of the supply of the same good or service by firms.

Any policy application of economic analysis also entails a *cost-benefit analysis*, the common method for governments to allocate scarce public resources.[3] A cost-benefit analysis at the societal level involves the distinction between the "private marginal value" and the "social marginal value," introduced to the economic analysis of language policy by Jernudd & Jo (1985):

> ... the private marginal value and marginal costs (i.e., what the private individual takes into account in making a decision to learn or maintain skills in a language) will not be equal to the social marginal value and cost. Such a divergence between the private and social value and cost establishes a bona fide case for public (government) involvement ...
>
> (Jernudd & Jo, 1985, p.12; cited in Kaplan & Baldauf, 1997, pp.154–5)

We interpret social marginal value here as the more rigorous and positive statement of societal need for language, rather than the sum of private marginal value. Thus, as national security is often expressed as the need driving investment in language resources in the military and intelligence communities, we take it as a social marginal value, much like social justice or clean air.

Social marginal value in economics is a very knotty topic, often challenging the methodology to its full extent:

> Even if one could prove unequivocally – and one never can – that language treatment had a salutary effect it would be hard to calculate in any satisfactory sense the relative cost accrued for the benefits received.
>
> (Kaplan & Baldauf, 1997, p.163)

The difficulty referred to here is partially based on the fact that language concerns human capital development, as opposed to physical capital development.[4] In their study of the cost effectiveness of minority language revitalization policies in Western Europe, Grin &

Vaillancourt explicitly refuse to evaluate the social marginal value of language policies:

> The efficiency of a policy can only be judged in relation with society's objectives, and the formulation of these objectives is a political process ...   (Grin & Vaillancourt, 1999, p.3)

Grin & Vaillancourt demonstrate the feasibility of estimating, *post facto*, the unit cost of desired policy outcome, such as increased viewership of minority language television, or increased numbers of university graduates with certain proficiency levels in certain languages, but leave the specification of the *value* of those outcomes to policy makers and society at large.

In spite of this assertion with regard to society's objectives, the present paper is devoted to a methodology for laying out – to the extent possible – the social marginal value for language, as well as the market context in which it must be located. We shall exemplify this approach by addressing the social marginal value of a linguistically competent workforce responsible for national security and the social marginal value of multilingual access to state social services, attempting to move arguments for language to a level of specificity that can: (i) garner the support of policy makers because the actual demand for language is documented and the societal need or contribution of language is better understood; and (ii) target specific aspects of policy to specific intervention points because the supply is documented and existing strength and weakness of capacity is understood, thereby enhancing the effectiveness and cost-efficiency of the intervention.

Even when relatively weak, some understanding of the market and the need is a necessary basis for a cost-benefit analysis when allocating scarce resources.

The use of economic terms here, however, should not be taken to imply that we offer a rigorous economic analysis of the social marginal value of language in US society. Rather, our approach can be characterized as pre-theoretical, providing some basis for further exploration of the societal need for language in the US, as a social marginal value for this society. As noted above, in the discussion that follows we shall use two examples of social marginal value, or need, for language: a linguistically competent workforce responsible for national security and multilingual access to state social services guaranteeing social justice, the former at the national level, the latter at the state and specific agency level. We shall first present some rudimentary facts concerning the supply and demand for language within the national security domain, and then expand the concepts to include strategic considerations as the basis of a cost-benefit analysis. This will be followed by the social justice example, deriving from a recent project in the state of Maryland.

The market forces framework for language

In previous studies we have developed an overall economic framework for viewing the language 'market'.[5] These terms of reference we define as follows: *demand* refers to the specific tasks or interactions for which language competence is necessary or desirable;[6] *supply* refers to the available language competencies (human and technical), their sources, and modes of their storage. While supply and demand are immediate or tactical, the analysis of language and national security requires more strategic considerations. Accordingly, *need* represents the perceived or latent harmful conditions or beneficial social marginal value that can be mitigated or improved by language competence. *Capacity* is equally strategic, given the years it takes to acquire a language, and represents the ability of the nation (or other polity) to produce the supply of linguistic competence designed to meet demand.

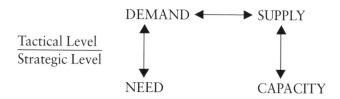

In terms of this framework, a functional or truly rational market would have *need* provoking real *demand*, for which an immediate *supply* is generated, which itself depends upon and defines an institutionalized *capacity* system. We have previously argued that the simple 'supply and demand' market model for language has serious flaws when it comes to strategic national needs, specifically that conditions in the US result in demand not adequately reflecting need, and capacity accordingly falling well short of producing the needed supply.[7]

As indicated above, in economic terms, national need can be seen as a positive specification – albeit approximate – of social marginal value, while the disjunction between demand and need is another way of stating that the sum of individual marginal values (for individuals or institutions) does not equal the social marginal value. Capacity, in turn, can be seen as the basis of the social marginal cost, since it represents the source of supply of language expertise available to the federal government, and, as such, constitutes a reasonable target of federal intervention and investment.

As noted above, justification for the cost investment in the form of federal intervention in the production of language expertise should proceed on the basis of an understanding of the language market and documentation of supply and demand. In addition, a cost-benefit analysis of the proposed intervention should follow, which presumes a reasonable assessment of current capacity, together with the cost of improvement, and some documentation of the need or social marginal value of language as the driving force for investment in language.

In Brecht & Rivers (2000), we proposed various forms of documentation against this framework. The following exemplify this kind of documentation; they are not, however, in any sense comprehensive or even adequately representative.

National Security Example

Demand

Currently, according to Crump (2001), some 80 federal agencies – from the State Department to the Patent and Trademark Office – depend in part on proficiency in more than 100 foreign languages. (Crump, 1985, reports only 19 agencies were identified as having such requirements.)

"More than 40,000 US troops are or have been stationed in more than 140 nations (excluding NATO countries and Japan) since 1991, including every nation in Latin America, all but two of the fifteen successor states to the USSR, some forty nations in Africa, and throughout South and Southeast Asia. More than 140 languages are spoken in these nations. The ability to communicate with military forces of other nations in a coalition, the ability to communicate with the people in a disaster stricken country, the ability to act as peacekeeper in situations such as Bosnia and Kosovo all of these demand higher skills in listening, understanding, and speaking." (Nordin, 1999)

Supply

The 'output' of the capacity system can be seen as the overall supply of linguistic expertise available for employment by federal agencies concerned with national security supplemented by the technical tools available, for example, machine translation and voice recognition software. (For illustrative purposes here, we will limit our notion of supply to human resources.) This supply of expertise, at the very least, must be specified according to the following parameters: the range of languages, the numbers of linguistically proficient professionals, and their levels of proficiency. Data that can be seen as indicating the level of existing supply of language expertise are the numbers and proficiency levels of graduates of the higher education system:

- Numbers: Enrollments in modern foreign languages in higher education declined from 16% of students in 1965 to 8% in 1994, and have remained at that level since then. Less Commonly Taught Languages (LCTL) (which include all of the languages critical to national security) account for less than 10% of these enrollments. *Fewer than 1%* of American college students are studying these critical languages. (Brod & Welles, 2000)
- Proficiency: Data from the American Council of Teachers of Russian and the National Security Education Program show that the median speaking proficiency of American college graduates after four years of language study, in five languages critical to national security (Chinese, Arabic, Russian, Korean, and Japanese) is 1 on a scale of 5, with 2 being the absolute minimum for functional proficiency, and 3 the minimum for professionals to practice in another language. (Brecht & Rivers, 2000, pp. 99–101) More specifically, after four years of university language study the percentage of learners reaching the minimal level proficiency (ILR 2) across three skills is the following:

  Reading: 35.4% at level 2 and above [$n=400$]
  Listening: 9% at level 2 and above [$n=378$]
  Oral: 12.5% at level 2 and above [$n=263$][8]

There is, in addition to the education system, another prime source of language supply in the US: the approximately fifty million speakers of languages other than English (LOTE) at home. According to a recent General Social Survey poll, approximately 25% of Americans claim to speak a foreign language, and approximately 11% of them say they speak it well. Of these who say they speak it well, the overwhelming majority declares that they learned it at home and, therefore, can be fairly viewed as heritage speakers. While there are no reliable data on the proficiency of these speakers, there is little doubt that they represent a major aspect of the language supply in the US.

While the numbers above give a fairly concrete, if only partial, picture of the supply and demand for language in the US, documentation in quantifiable terms of the strategic aspects of language in national security is much more difficult.

Capacity

Language capacity comprises five sectors: academic, federal, private, heritage, and overseas. The broadest of these, in the sense that it, in principle, touches all citizens of the US, is the academic sector, defined by the ability of the education system to graduate proficient bilinguals. These graduates may be Anglophones or may be speakers of LOTE from America's many heritage communities.[9] In either case, their bilingual ability is largely dependent upon instructional programs in our schools, colleges, and universities. We have shown in previous studies how these programs are supported by, and so largely dependent upon, the strength of the respective professional language 'fields' in the US, where strength is defined in terms of field 'architecture', consisting of base capacity, infrastructure, and flagship programs.[10] Very simply, effective instructional programs depend on expertise (researchers and teachers), professional organizations, materials development, teacher training, study abroad programming, testing and assessment systems, data collection and information-sharing networks, and nationally recognized flagship programs, among other elements.

The other capacity sectors are the heritage, federal, private, and overseas. The heritage capacity sector comprises the network of heritage language schools and school systems across the country in dozens of languages. The largest is that of the Chinese community, where at the last count approximately 100,000 students are enrolled in the Taiwan-related system and approximately 40,000 in the PRC-related system.[11] The government sector consists of the Defense Language Institute and the many language programs constituting the Command Language Programs in this country and around the world of the Department of Defense, the Foreign Service Institute School of Language Studies, near Washington, D.C., the language programs in the various intelligence agencies, as well as language programs in various government agencies, like the Department of Agriculture. The private sector is represented by language education companies, as well as by translation, interpretation, and localization firms. Finally, the overseas sector comprises study abroad and exchange programs around the world run by American, as well as foreign, management.

Need

If the precise specification of capacity is a challenge, it is easily outshone by the difficulty in determining need or social marginal value. In general, need can be broken down into political/military, social, and economic needs, as well as domestic and international needs. As noted above, the specification of need or social marginal value is extremely difficult. However difficult, social marginal value is the basis for government policy and intervention and so cannot be neglected, particularly given the fact that language is generally under-valued among policy makers in the US. Nevertheless, we propose to illustrate the documentation of linguistic need in the area of national security in four ways: shortfalls in supply; shortfalls in capacity; asserted need and demand; and declared national policy.

Shortfalls in supply

- The Foreign Service reports that only 60% of its billets requiring language are at present filled, with waivers applied to another 35% (Cohen & Kennedy, 1999).
- The Director of the Federal Bureau of Investigation made an unprecedented public plea for assistance in translation and interpretation, calling for volunteers fluent in Arabic, Farsi, and Pashtu, among other languages, in the wake of the events of September 11, 2001.[12]
- In recent testimony before the Subcommittee on International Security, Proliferation and Federal Services of the Senate Committee on Governmental Affairs, Ellen Laipson, Vice Chairman of the National Intelligence Council, noted shortfalls in the intelligence community in Central Eurasian, East Asian, and Middle Eastern languages, impacting collection, processing, exploitation, and analysis of data.[13]
- The testimony of a Drug Enforcement Administration (DEA) official in September, 1997, stated that the agency lacked sufficient Russian language expertise to combat organized crime groups from the former Soviet Union (Farah, 1997).
- The US Coast Guard recently completed an audit of its language requirements, finding that fewer than 50% were met; even in Spanish, the USCG met its language requirements only 75% of the time. Language requirements arose in all mission types – search and rescue, drug interdiction, ship inspection, and so forth.[14]
- The NTSB (National Transport Safety Board) found that the lack

of a common language contributed to the inability of the crew of the *USS Greenville* to mount rescue attempts after the *Ehime Maru* incident (Gordon, 2001).[15]

Shortfalls in capacity

- The Select Committee on US National Security and Military/ Economic Concerns with China (also known as the Cox Commission) cited the intelligence community's lack of capacity in language as a barrier to effective intelligence gathering and analysis of Chinese efforts in the proliferation of weapons of mass destruction. Representative Cox went so far as to state: "It is not unfair to say, if you are in the Ministry of State Security seeking to encrypt your conversation, speak Mandarin."[16]
- The National Foreign Language Center's 1998 national survey of Less Commonly Taught Language (LCTL) fields showed that for LCTLs with current enrollment levels of fewer than 10,000 (such as Arabic, Vietnamese, and Thai) inadequate resources existed for the development, publication, and distribution of teaching and learning materials.[17]

Asserted need and demand

- The recent Hart-Rudman report on National Security in the 21st Century states: "So, too, does government need high-quality people with expertise in the social sciences, foreign languages, and humanities. The decreased funding available for these programs from universities and foundations may threaten the ability of the government to produce future leaders with the requisite knowledge – in foreign languages, economics, and history, to take several examples – to meet 21st century security challenges."[18]
- An article by Luis Caldera (Caldera & Echevarria, 2001), recently retired Secretary of the Army, states "tomorrow's military force requires global capabilities, not only in terms of operational strength, but with regards to the quality of its people and their ability to adapt to different cultures and situations. In this dynamic and complex environment, regional expertise, language proficiency, and cross-cultural communications skills have become essential to our strategic success."
- The House Permanent Select Committee on Intelligence noted in its report on the 2002 Intelligence authorization that:
  > [t]here continues to be a great need throughout the Intelligence Community for increased expertise in a number of

intelligence-related disciplines and specialties. However, the Committee believes the most pressing such need is for greater numbers of foreign-language-capable intelligence personnel, with increased fluency in specific and multiple languages. The Committee has heard repeatedly from both military and civilian intelligence producers and consumers that this is the single greatest limitation in intelligence agency personnel expertise and that it is a deficiency throughout the Intelligence Community. The principle agencies dealing with foreign intelligence (CIA, NSA, FBI, DIA and the military services) have all admitted they do not have the language talents, in breadth or in depth, to fully and effectively accomplish their missions.[19]

Declared National Policy

The following policy statements all imply significant language requirements on the part of government agencies.

- The Clinton administration in 1998 announced a policy for enhancing economic ties with Africa (Hamilton & Duke, 1998).
- The White House's *National Security Strategy for a New Century*, mandated by the Goldwater-Nichols Department of Defense Reorganization Act of 1986, provides basic policy direction for strategic planning in national security.
- *United States Strategic Plan for International Affairs* is the Government Performance and Results Act-mandated strategic plan for international affairs.
- *DoD Quadrennial Review* constitutes a mandated review of Department of Defense capabilities.[20]

These policy statements essentially state that the security interests of the US involve virtually every area of the globe and, presumably, at least every principal language spoken in these areas.[21]

- In its report on the US Department of Education for the fiscal year 2002, the House Appropriations Committee issued a similar declaration, stating that the foreign language capacity of the United States was insufficient, and making it a policy to strengthen that capacity:

    The Committee is aware of the urgent need to strengthen instruction in foreign languages and related area studies that are less commonly taught. The Committee believes that foreign language skills and international expertise are essential factors in national security readiness. Ensuring US security, foreign policy leadership, economic competitiveness, an[d] our ability to solve global problems that affect the nation's well-being depend on Americans who have an understanding of and ability to function effectively in other cultural, business and value systems, as well as foreign language proficiency.[22]

The Congress thus identifies a shortfall in capacity and then addresses that shortfall with appropriations for Title VI programs, with instructions for the Department of Education to focus on specific languages and world areas:

> The Committee intends that the increase of $13,000,000 for the Title VI domestic programs be used first to strengthen foreign language training and related area studies in areas that are vital to our national security, including Central and South Asia, the Middle East, Russia, and the Independent States of the former Soviet Union.[23]

The Congress here reacts to the apparent need (documented above) for Arabic, Farsi, and other languages of Central and Southwest Asia by directing policy and investment at those areas.

The preceding analysis is directed at the need for a linguistically-capable federal workforce involved with national security. It depended upon existing data sources, which were considerable in view of the fact that the issue is national and most data available are oriented to that level. The problem is that the issue is very broad and the relevant data extremely general. In contrast to a cost-benefit analysis of supply and demand at the individual level dealing with private marginal value, this level of generality in detailing need or social marginal value leaves policy makers with little concrete information for directing policy and targeting interventions. The more information one has on need and on required capacity, the clearer policy and intervention can be.

In attacking a problem at a local level, the possibility of accurate targeting of interventions improves to the extent that data are collected on the specific social marginal value and the corresponding market (supply and demand, need and capacity). In the following example, the analysis is indeed targeted at the general goal of social justice and the particular social marginal value of multilingual access to social services in one state in the USA – Maryland.

Social justice example

The specification of domestic need can be illustrated in the social domain in the context of the dramatic rise in the number of speakers of a LOTE (Language Other Than English) that has taken place over the past three decades. The more than forty-five million residents in this country who speak a LOTE at home[24] affect almost every aspect of US society, impinging in particular on the medical, educational, judicial, and social service systems.[25] To the degree that these systems are subsidized by the Federal government, they are subject to Federal legislation embodying broad societal goals – for example, that society should be more just in its treatment of minorities.

As noted above, Grin & Vaillancourt (1999) assert that the specification of social marginal value is best left as official government policy, as long as the goal is generally understood and accepted by the citizenry. With respect to language and social justice, Presidential Executive Order 13166 of 20 August, 2000, requires all recipients of federal funding to comply with Title VI of the Civil Rights Act of 1964 with regard to LOTE speakers:

> The Federal Government provides and funds an array of services that can be made accessible to otherwise eligible persons who are not proficient in the English language. The Federal Government is committed to improving the accessibility of these services to eligible limited English proficient (LEP) persons, a goal that reinforces its equally important commitment to promoting programs and activities designed to help individuals learn English. To this end, each Federal agency shall examine the services it provides and develop and implement a system by which LEP persons can meaningfully access those services ... and thus [Federal agencies] do not discriminate on the basis of national origin in violation of Title VI of the Civil Rights Act of 1964. [26]

Simply put, the Executive Order reiterates earlier case law[27] to the effect that Title VI of the Civil Rights Act of 1964 prohibits discrimination based on a person's command (or lack thereof) of English.[28]

In the context of this social marginal value of a more just society, a broad policy is implemented that mandates that a just society does not discriminate against those who do not speak its language, or those who do not speak it well. Accordingly, the General Assembly of the State of Maryland passed a bill in its 2001 legislative session making explicit the state's policy with regard to the provision of services to LOTE speakers:

> The General Assembly finds that it is the policy of the State that departments, agencies, and programs are authorized to provide equal access to public services to persons with limited English proficiency.[29]

It further details an intervention:

> If, upon review, the Department of Human Resources determines that there is an increased need for interpretation and translation to assure equal access for limited English proficiency speakers, the Department of Human Resources shall make recommendations and prepare budgets for the implementation of comprehensive interpretation and translation services.[30]

Thus, the General Assembly of the State of Maryland (i) expressed the goal of inclusion of LOTE speakers in society, insofar as the State of Maryland and its agencies can effect that goal through the provision of services to Marylanders; (ii) recognized the desirability of a needs assessment at the state level in order (iii) to direct further policy development.

As a result of this federal directive and state legislation, the Department of Human Resources of the State of Maryland engaged the National Foreign Language Center (NFLC) to conduct a survey to determine the statewide demand, supply, capacity, and need for language in Maryland – in essence, a market analysis of language with respect to the operations of the government of the state of Maryland. One of the authors of this article (Rivers) served as the Principal Investigator for this project.

Data collection

The NFLC performed this project by collecting survey data in two phases: (i) a scientifically sampled statewide telephone survey administered to 200 front-line state employees; and (ii) a written general survey administered to all departments, agencies, and programs statewide. In phase I, the NFLC surveyed by telephone 200 randomly selected state employees in eight departments. The project team selected departments that had significant and frequent interactions with the general public. A total of 200 employees in 23 counties and Baltimore City were contacted; 173 employees agreed to complete the survey. In phase II, the NFLC sent a written, confidential survey to the secretary of all 18 cabinet departments, as well as the head of local and regional offices of those departments; department-wide units, state and gubernatorial boards; and independent agencies, commissions, and task forces. A total of 635 surveys were sent, of which 288 (45%) were returned.

Both surveys – the written survey of state offices and the telephone survey of state employees – asked for information on the demand for language, specifically for information on the languages encountered among the respondent's clientele and the frequency of LOTE-speaking clients. Equally important, the surveys targeted supply and capacity by eliciting information regarding the methods by which the responding employee or office removed any language barriers to the provision of services. These methods included using the services of bilingual caseworkers, police officers, clerks, cashiers, teachers, staff interpreters and translators, other bilingual staff in a volunteer capacity (that is, outside their normal duties), contractors, family members of the LOTE-speaking clients, community volunteers, or nothing at all. Finally, with regard to need, the surveys asked for the impact of language barriers on the provision of services, in terms of the delays the barriers created.

Findings

We present here exemplary data on language demand, supply, capacity, and need with respect to the operations of the government of the State of Maryland. A full presentation of the data appears in Rivers (2001).

Demand

Respondents to both surveys were asked whether they or their office had encountered LOTE-speaking clients during the past year, and if so, what language(s) the clients spoke. We take these data to represent current demand. In addition, we asked about the frequency with which speakers of a particular LOTE were encountered by Maryland state offices and employees. The overall findings on which languages are encountered might give a somewhat misleading picture of the demand for a particular language, overstating the demand in terms of the total number of client visits, whereas the data on frequency of contact give a preliminary indication of the magnitude of the impact upon the operations of the state government. Figure 1 shows the results for the frequency with which speakers of a particular language are encountered by state of Maryland offices. In Figure 1, 'sporadic' contact means less than one client interaction per month; 'infrequent' between one client interaction per month and one per week, and 'frequent' more than one client interaction per week.

Figure 1 demonstrates that Spanish is the language in most demand, with 60% of state offices reporting Spanish-speaking LOTE-speaking clients, with Asian languages (including Chinese, Vietnamese, and Korean) and Russian being the next most encountered, in approximately 20% of state offices. All other languages are seen by a handful of state offices. Figure 1 also indicates that all languages save Spanish appear in State of Maryland offices with similar frequency; that is, whether or not the language is encountered by a larger number of state offices (e.g., Vietnamese) or a smaller number (e.g., Tagalog), roughly a third of the offices encounter clients with a given language only infrequently, another third, sporadically, and the rest, frequently.

In addition, insofar as we collected data on respondents' job titles (from the survey of state employees) and as we can identify the responding department, office, or agency (from the survey of state offices), we can differentiate demand (and for that matter, supply, capacity, and need) among different types of employees, among agencies, and among geographic regions of the state. These analyses are reported in Rivers (2001).

Supply

The surveys elicited information on the methods used by employees and offices to facilitate interactions with LOTE-speaking clients. To the extent that these methods reflect the current language expertise available to the respondents' offices, we take these as indicating the supply of language expertise in the government of the State of Maryland.

Figure 2 presents results for the method most often used by state employees to meet LOTE-speaking clients' language needs. Figure 2 shows that bilingual staff are most often used, followed by client relatives or friends and community members. Employees report relatively low levels of utilization of contractors or staff interpreters.

Capacity

The survey requested information on the existence and knowledge of policies and procedures, and the training offered to employees in assisting LOTE-speaking clients. We take these as indications of the language capacity of the government of the State of Maryland, insofar as the state government and its employees are able to obtain a supply of language expertise or train employees in either the

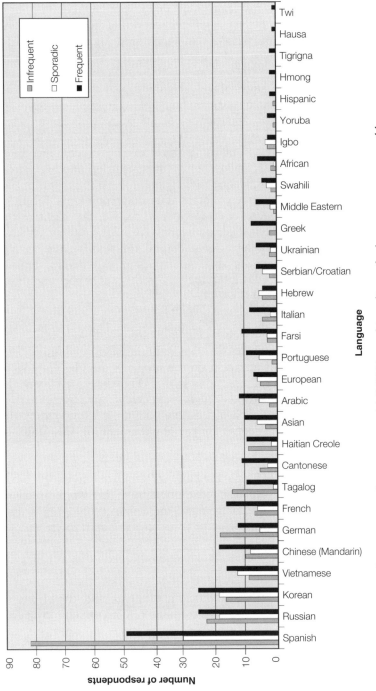

Figure 1 Demand: Frequency of encounters with LOTE-speaking clients, by language, as reported by State of Maryland offices

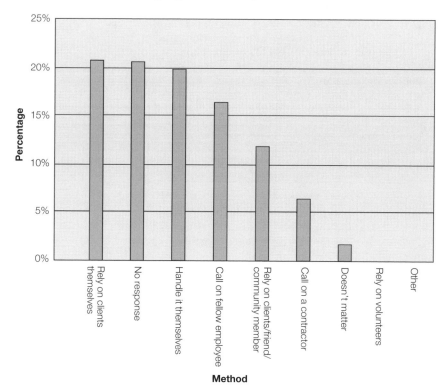

Figure 2 Supply: Most frequently used sources of interpreters and translators for interactions with LOTE-speaking clients, as reported by State of Maryland employees

languages required or the administrative procedures to secure language services.

State employees were asked if they knew of any policies or procedures for facilitating interactions with LOTE-speaking clients. Figure 3 presents the responses to this question. That fewer than half indicated any knowledge of policies or procedures is echoed in the data on the existence of training offered to State of Maryland employees. State of Maryland offices were asked whether they offer training to employees. Figure 4 shows the findings for that question.

Less that one-fourth of State of Maryland offices offer any training in language access for employees. Respondents indicated that this training consists exclusively of reimbursement for language courses, typically Spanish courses offered at local community colleges.

Additional data on capacity comes from free-response answers to questions on methods used to meet language needs and from the final

Figure 3   Capacity: State of Maryland employees' knowledge
of policies and procedures for ensuring access to
state services for LOTE-speaking clients

Policies or procedures?	n	%
Yes	83	48
No	54	31
Don't know	33	19
No response	3	2
Total	173	100

Figure 4   Capacity: State of Maryland offices that provide
training for employees in ensuring access to state
services for LOTE-speaking clients

Training available?	n	%
No	225	73
Yes	66	22
No response	16	5
Total	307	100

item on the survey, which solicited recommendations for statewide
policies. Among these responses is the promotion of the private
language services sector by senior management in state departments
as a resource for language supply. The state has awarded a statewide
blanket contract for telephone-based interpreting services to a
company located outside of Maryland; two departments, both
offering a broad range of social services, have contracted with
interpreting services located in the state; and some use is made of the
state's public universities and colleges as a capacity pool for interpreters and translators. For example, the University of Maryland
offers a technical translation course in Spanish each semester; the
faculty teaching that course has agreed to use materials from one
state department as part of the basic course materials, and to provide
the translations of the materials (in Spanish) to the department.

Finally, interviews with directors of local and regional offices in
areas with substantial LOTE-speaking populations indicate that
bilingual Spanish-speaking employees are recruited at the University
of Maryland, College Park. In follow-up interviews with a sample of
those bilingual employees, it became clear that all had taken courses
in the University's program for Spanish for Native Speakers. With

respect to the operations of the government of the State of Maryland, an active, if uncoordinated effort has been made to incorporate the resources of the University of Maryland into the supply and capacity of language for the state government. As we shall see below (Shortfalls in capacity), that effort, however fruitful, has been insufficient with regard to the capacity required to produce the supply of language needed by the state government.

Need

As noted above in the national security example, the specification of need comprises four categories of data: shortfalls in supply; shortfalls in capacity; asserted needs and demand; and declared policy statements. The data from the social services surveys provide some documentation in the categories of shortfalls in supply, and to a more limited extent, shortfalls in capacity. These can be supplemented by assertions of need and demand derived from informal interviews with departmental and local policy makers, as well as from some indirect data on the policy of the State of Maryland, as expressed in Senate Bill 543.

Shortfalls in supply

Both the written survey and the telephone survey asked those respondents with LOTE-speaking clients to provide quantitative information on the additional delay clients may experience in the provision of services due to language barriers. We take this as a prima facie indication that no language supply – no sufficiently qualified employee, or interpreter or translator from whatever source – was available at the time of the initial contact between a given LOTE-speaking client and the offices of the State of Maryland. The data indicate that fully one fourth of the offices and employees with LOTE-speaking clients cannot deliver services to those clients with the same efficiency with which services are delivered to non-LOTE-speaking clients.

Figure 5 reports the findings on delay of service by language as reported by State of Maryland offices. The data in Figure 5 indicate that delays are more likely to be encountered and are likely to be longer when the language of clients falls into the less-frequently encountered group – languages other than Spanish, Russian, Vietnamese, Chinese, and Korean – with delays from one day to one week occurring at least 50% of the time. It must also be noted that no language is free from some delay due to language barriers.

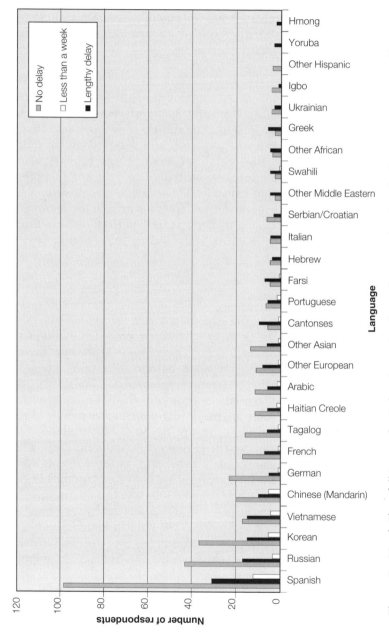

Figure 5   Need: Shortfall in supply: Delays in service due to language barriers, by language, as reported by State of Maryland offices

Shortfalls in capacity

Taken together, the data on delay by language indicate that certain languages pose significant problems for state offices in the provision of services. These languages tend to be those with smaller populations in the State of Maryland, or those whose populations are not concentrated in one geographic location. These languages (such as Twi, Hmong, Serbian) are also languages in which state offices are unlikely to have bilingual employees, and in which community resources are scarce. Finally, the interviews with directors of local and regional state offices also revealed that the directors felt that the pool of bilingual candidates with training in appropriate disciplines, whether from the University of Maryland or from the overall labor market, is limited, and that, due to its relatively low salaries, the state has difficulty attracting and retaining bilingual employees; several office directors indicated that they had unfilled bilingual positions.

Asserted needs and demands

To the extent that the surveys reveal assertions of needs and demand, they are found in the replies to the free-response item at the end of the survey, which asked for recommendations on improving access to services for LOTE-speaking clients, as well as any comments the respondent cared to make regarding the survey and language barriers in general. These have yet to be fully analyzed, but two trends have emerged: first, there are several offices which claim that there are no language needs or demands. These offices typically have no LOTE-speaking clients and are located in rural areas of the state with small immigrant populations. Second, a sizable number of responding offices asserted shortfalls in capacity – a lack of contract translation and interpreting resources, a lack of funds for desired training (typically in Spanish), and a lack of documents in other languages. These we take as assertions of need at the level of the director of the local or regional office.

Declared policy

During the course of the project, interviews with senior management in several state cabinet-level departments revealed that at least three departments (Health and Mental Hygiene, Human Resources, and Juvenile Justice) are in the process of developing policies to ensure access for LOTE-speaking clients. (The NFLC is assisting the Department of Juvenile Justice in their policy effort.) According to the interviewees, these policies are motivated in the greater part by a recognition that LOTE-speaking clients affect the operations of the department. Other motivations include pressure from community-based advocacy groups (such as the Baltimore Justice Policy Center and CASA of Maryland), as well as Executive Order 13166.

Conclusion

The current paper is an attempt to characterize language needs at the societal level in economic terms and to translate the argument for language policy in society into terms that policy makers would be more likely to accept as relevant and convincing. It makes clear that the first requirement for specifying needs, after adopting an economic model, is to gather data that an economic analysis requires. These data can be garnered from existing sources, as in the national security example above, or they can be obtained by dedicated research like that conducted for the social justice example. In settings where there is little understanding of the role of language in society and where there is, accordingly, little language capacity, the formulation of the argument for policy has to be as explicit as possible and supported by data. Finally, the driving force for any policy is need or social value, and the connection between basic societal values and language has to be made much more explicit before language will garner the support in the US it deserves.

Notes

1 There are, of course, other aspects of language that are of equal or higher value, for example, its cultural identity and aesthetic functions. They will not be discussed here. For examples from the successor states of the Soviet Union, see Davé (1997); Gorham (1995, 2000); Kopylenko (1997); Laitin (1998).

2 This general type of analysis – supply and demand – refers to *equilibrium* methods for describing and forecasting the behavior of some commodity or market. For its application to public economics, see Jha (1998).

3 See, for example, Folland et al (2001); Guitierrez (1995).

4 See, for example, Baldauf & Kaplan (1997, 150ff.) and Grin & Vaillancourt (1996).

5 Brecht et al (1995); Brecht & Rivers (2000); Brecht & Walton (1994).

6 Grin (1999) defines supply and demand either in terms of "... consumption of goods and services, non-material commodities, or production factors that embody some language-related characteristics ...," which he calls "language-specific commodities (LSCs)"; or as "... some *manifestation* of language, such as the continued existence of a

linguistic environment characterized by the presence of Welsh, Spanish or Inuktitut." We take the former as the operational concept for supply and demand, but narrow the "linguistic environment" to one in which specific tasks related to national security are performed.

7 Brecht et al (1995); Brecht & Rivers (2000).

8 Frank (2001).

9 We shall discuss the federal capacity sector in some detail below. We would only add here that the INS can be seen as part of the federal capacity picture, given the fact that they control the flow of H1B visas and other immigration to the US, some of whose holders can be hired by federal contractors.

10 Brecht & Walton (1994).

11 Carter (2001).

12 Colvin and Nelson, 2001.

13 Testimony of Ellen Laipson, Vice Chairman, National Intelligence Council, before the Subcommittee on International Security, Proliferation and Federal Services, Senate Committee on Governmental Affairs, September 14, 2000.

14 Crump (2001).

15 The *Ehime Maru*, a Japanese fishing vessel, was sunk off the Hawaiian islands with loss of life when struck by the *USS Greenville*, a submarine, surfacing rapidly without due caution.

16 http://cox.House.gov/press/coverage/2000/washposttranslators.htm

17 Cf. Brecht & Rivers (2000).

18 US Commission on National Security/21st Century. *Road Map for National Security: Imperative for Change.* p. 88.

19 House Permanent Select Committee on Intelligence (2001, p. 17).

20 National Defense Panel, 1997. *Transforming Defense: National Security in the 21st Century.* Washington, DC: Government Printing Office.

21 Fishman (2000) provides a taxonomy of global (at present, English), regional (lingua franca such as Hausa, Arabic, Russian, Spanish, Mandarin, Hindi, and so forth), and local languages. We take these declarations of US National Security interests in every world region to mean, de facto, that at least the regional lingua franca fall into the category of languages for which there is a declared national policy need.

22 House Appropriations Committee, 2001, p. 162.

23 House Appropriations Committee, 2001, p. 163.

24 Census 2000 Supplementary Survey, Table QT-02, Profile of Selected Social Characteristics 2000.
http://factfinder.census.gov/home/en/c2ss.html

25 A backlash against the growing presence of LOTE speakers in the US has occurred, spawning a political movement to establish English as the official language, as well as to mandate that all bilingual education programs adopt the subtractive mode by calling for quicker and more efficient transition to, rather than addition of, English. For concise presentations of these issues, see Crawford (2000); Tucker (1997).

26 *65 FR 50121* (August 16, 2000). The text of this Executive Order refers to LOTE speakers as "Limited English Proficient" (LEP) individuals. We use the term 'LOTE' throughout this article.
27 Lau *v.* Nichols, 414 US 563 (1974), Alexander *v.* Sandoval, 532 US 275 (1999).
28 Discrimination against the hearing-impaired is not included in this Executive Order, but rather in the Americans with Disabilities Act of 1990 (42 USC. 12181 et seq.).
29 Maryland Senate Bill 543, Section 1(a), Chapter 396 of the *State of Maryland Acts of 2001.*
30 Maryland Senate Bill 543, Section 1(d)(2).

References

Brecht, R. D., & Rivers, W. (2000). *Language and national security for the 21st century: The role of Title VI/Fulbright-Hays in supporting national language capacity* (pp. 85–88). Dubuque, IA: Kendall/Hunt.
Brecht, R. D., with J. Caemmerer & A. R. Walton. (1995). *Russian in the United States: A case study of America's language needs and capacities.* National Foreign Language Center Monograph Series. Washington, D.C.: National Foreign Language Center.
Brecht, R. D., & Walton, A. R. (1994). National strategic planning in the less commonly taught languages. *The Annals of the American Academy of Political and Social Science 532,* 190–212.
Breton, A. (1998). An economic analysis of language. In A. Breton (ed.), *Economic approaches to language and bilingualism.* Ottawa: Department of Public Works and Government Services Canada.
Brod, R., & Welles, E. (2000). Foreign language enrollments in United States institutions of higher education, Fall 1998. *ADFL Bulletin 31,* 2, 22–29.
Caldera, L., & Echevarria, A. J. (2001). The strategy-resource mismatch: The US Army is the nation's premier global engagement and operations-other-than-war force. *Armed Forces Journal International, March,* 32.
Carter, C. B. (2001). The US Coast Guard's foreign language needs assessment. Paper presented to the Federal Interagency Language Roundtable, National Foreign Affairs Training Center, September 21.
Cohen, B., & Kennedy, P. (1999). Comments before US Congress, House Appropriations Committee, Subcommittee on Commerce, Justice, State and the Judiciary, April 14, 1999. Reported by Federal News Service, Congressional Universe (online service). Bethesda, MD: Congressional Information Service.
Colvin, R., & Nelson, S. (2001). After the attack; Foreign Affairs; FBI issues call for translators to assist probe. *Los Angeles Times,* September 18, p. A1.
Crawford, J. (2000). *At war with diversity: US language policy in an age of anxiety.* Clevedon: Multilingual Matters.

Crump, T. (1985). *Translations in the Federal Government 1985.* Alexandria, VA: The American Translators Association.

Crump, T. (2001). *Translation and interpreting in the US Government 2001.* Alexandria, VA: The American Translators Association.

Davé, B. (1997). *The politics of language revival: National identity and state building in Kazakstan.* Unpublished Dissertation. Syracuse: Syracuse University.

Farah, D. (1997). Russian mob, drug cartel joining forces, *Washington Post,* September 29, A1.

Fishman, J. (2000). The new linguistic order. In P. O'Meara, H. Mehlinger, M. Krain & R. Newman, *Globalization and the challenges of a new century: A reader.* Bloomington: Indiana University Press.

Folland, S., Goodman, A., & Stano, M. (2001). *The economics of health and health care.* Upper Saddle River, NJ: Prentice Hall.

Frank, V. M. (2001). Language learning at advanced and above: Individual and programmatic characteristics. Presented at ACTFL 2001, November 16, Washington, D.C.

Gordon, M. (2001). Sub crew actively attempted to lend aid. *Honolulu Advertiser,* February 26.

Gorham, M. (1995). *Speaking in tongues: Language, culture, literature, and language of state in early Soviet Russia, 1921–1934.* Unpublished dissertation. Palo Alto: Stanford University.

Gorham, M. (2000). Mastering the perverse: State-building and language 'purification' in early Soviet Russia. *Slavic Review* 59, 1, 133–53.

Grin, F. (1999). The notions of supply and demand in the economic analysis of language. In A. Breton (ed.), *New Canadian perspectives: Exploring the economics of language* (pp. 31–61). Ottawa: Canadian Heritage.

Grin, F., & Vaillancourt, F. (1996). *Language revitalisation policy: An analytical survey. Framework, policy experiences, and application to Te Reo Maori.* New Zealand Department of the Treasury Working Paper 98/2. Wellington: New Zealand Department of the Treasury.

Grin, F., & Vaillancourt, F. (1999). *The cost-effectiveness evaluation of minority language policies: Case studies on Wales, Ireland and the Basque Country.* ECMI Monograph No. 2. Flensburg: European Centre for Minority Issues.

Guitierrez, B. S. (1995). Benefit-cost analysis with and without environmental preservation: A modified approach. *Revista Brasiliera de Economica* 49, 3, 483–98.

Hamilton, M. & Duke, L. (1998). Africa's potential as trade partner attracts corporate interest. *Washington Post,* March 23, A14.

House Appropriations Committee. (2001). *Report on Departments of Labor, Health and Human Services, and Education, and Related Agencies Appropriation Bill, 2002.* Washington, DC: Government Printing Office.

House Permanent Select Committee on Intelligence. (2001). *Report on the Intelligence Authorization Act for Fiscal Year 2002.* Washington, DC: Government Printing Office.

Jernudd, B., & Jo, S. (1985). Bilingualism as a resource in the United States. *Annual Review of Applied Linguistics* 6, 10–18.

Jha, R. (1998). *Modern public economics*. London, New York: Routledge.

Kaplan, R., & Baldauf, R. (1997). *Language planning from practice to theory*. Clevedon: Multilingual Matters.

Kopylenko, M. (1997). Gosudarstvennyj jazyk i oficial'nyj jazyk: razgraniče-nije pon'atija. [A differential definition of the terms 'state' and 'official language]: *Sajasat* [Journal of the Statistical Bureau of the Office of the President of Kazakstan], *May 1997*, 37–39.

Laitin, D. (1998). *Identity in formation: The Russian-speaking populations in the near abroad*. Ithaca: Cornell University Press.

Maryland Senate Bill 543, Chapter 396 of the *State of Maryland Acts of 2001*.

National security strategy for a new century. (1998). Washington, D.C.: The White House

Nordin, G. H. (1999). Language and the Department of Defense: Challenges for the 21st century. An interview with Glenn H. Nordin, Assistant Director of Intelligence Policy. (Language and Training) Office of the Assistant Secretary of Defense, C3I. *NFLC Policy Issues, Vol. 2 number 2*, December.

Rivers, W. (2001). *State Government survey of State departments, agencies, and programs – Persons with limited English proficiency. Preliminary Report to the General Assembly of Maryland*. ms. Washington: The National Foreign Language Center.

Tucker, G. R. (1997). Developing a language-competent American society: Implications of the English-only movement. In T. Bongaerts & K. De Bot (eds.), *Perspectives on foreign-language policy: Studies in honour of Theo van Els* (pp. 87–98). Amsterdam: John Benjamins.

United States Strategic Plan for International Affairs. 1999. Washington, D.C.: Office of Resources, Plans, and Policy, Department of State.

3 Foreign language needs assessment in the US military[1]

John A. Lett

Introduction

The process of language needs assessment (LNA) is of vital interest to the United States Government, which provides foreign language (FL) education and training to many thousands of individuals each year. A substantial portion of this education is provided by the Department of Defense (DoD) to members of the military services in order to ensure that language-related US security needs are met. The vast majority of military linguists[2] receive their initial language education at the Defense Language Institute Foreign Language Center (DLIFLC) in Monterey, California, where on any given day approximately 800 faculty members teach 22 languages to 3300 students, each of whom spends six hours daily in class for up to 63 weeks at a time. Clearly, the military services expend a great deal of money each year on language education, and they need to be sure that their funds are well spent, i.e., that students are being educated to appropriate FL skill levels. Also, systems are needed to manage large numbers of linguists, e.g., to specify how they will be deployed, what tasks they will perform and in which languages, and what proficiency level is needed to remain in good standing as a military linguist. Furthermore, and most importantly, the language proficiency requirements associated with a given military job must be known, because satisfactory job performance may well be a life or death matter. Thus, systematic procedures have been developed to assess the proficiency requirements of a given career field, or military occupational specialty (MOS)[3], and the resultant data have served to inform the development of regulatory policies regarding such matters as graduation standards at DLIFLC and retention and advancement of military linguists in various language-requiring career fields. In addition, these procedures have been adapted and applied to career fields in which FL proficiency is not officially required in order to hold the MOS, but is a definite enhancement to mission performance. In this chapter, the traditional DoD Language Needs Assessment (LNA) is described, along with a discussion of how LNA procedures are being adapted to respond to new and changing language-related requirements. As will soon become apparent, the LNA described here differs in some respects from the model that forms the framework for this book, beginning with the fundamental reason for which they are conducted. Their purpose is not to inform syllabus design or curriculum development, but to establish the language proficiency requirements of a given career field in terms of a known metric, one that is well known among foreign language professionals throughout the US Government.

Foreign language proficiency skill level descriptions

LNA procedures depend upon the use of a standard metric by means of which differing levels of language capabilities can be referenced and mutually understood. The metric of choice is that of the federal Interagency Language Roundtable (ILR) as set forth in the *Interagency Language Roundtable Language Skill Level Descriptions* (Interagency Language Roundtable, 1985).[4] As the label implies, these level descriptions are used widely throughout the US government. Originally developed by the Foreign Service Institute of the Department of State, they were gradually revised and expanded over more than two decades. The most recent version was endorsed by eighteen agencies in 1985. Separate descriptions are provided for each of the language skill modalities: speaking, listening, reading, and writing. In the late 1970s and early 1980s, the government descriptions were exported to and adapted by the academic community through a joint effort of the ILR, the American Council of Teachers of Foreign Languages (ACTFL), and the Education Testing Service (ETS). The resultant scale, originally known as the ACTFL/ ETS scale, is typically known today simply as the ACTFL proficiency scale (ACTFL, 1986, 1999, 2001). A similar scale was developed by the Bureau for International Language Coordination for NATO purposes.

The ILR scale is bracketed by level 0, meaning no proficiency at all beyond the occasional memorized word or phrase, and level 5, by which is meant an educated native speaker. Both threshold or base levels and intermediate levels ('plus' levels) are allowed, such that there are 11 possible scale values. In the ACTFL adaptation, ILR levels 3 through 5 were conflated into the superior level and the four ILR scale values of 0, 0+, 1, and 1+ were divided into two sets of low, mid, and high sub-levels. This was done to permit the more finely grained distinctions that were thought necessary to measure the progress that takes place during a typical academic language learning sequence. Originally, the ACTFL scale did not subdivide ILR level 2 because the focus was on accurate measurement at the lower levels. In succeeding years, however, as improved academic programs produced higher level learners and as both heritage learners and graduate students began to be tested in larger numbers, there was a felt need to more finely describe abilities at the advanced level. Thus, the 1999 and 2001 revised guidelines include advanced-low and advanced-mid sub-levels (Swender, 2002). The current ILR–ACTFL relationships are set forth in Table 1.

Table 1   Relationships among ILR and ACTFL scales

ILR	ACTFL
5	
4+	
4	
3+	
3	Superior
2+	Advanced High
2	Advanced Mid Advanced Low
1+	Intermediate High
1	Intermediate Mid Intermediate Low
0+	Novice High
0	Novice Mid Novice Low

Note. Table is configured per Swender, 2002.

A complete elaboration of what the various skill level descriptions mean is beyond the scope of this chapter; indeed, many chapters and complete books have been devoted solely to discussions of the level descriptions and of the proficiency construct in general.[5] However, the discussion of LNA procedures requires that author and reader share at least some heuristic notion of what is meant by a given level. One synthesis which has proved useful in introducing the proficiency construct to non-specialists is the 'functional quatrosection' of speaking proficiency which is presented in Table 2.[6]

Table 2　The functional quatrosection of speaking proficiency

	Function	Context/Content	Accuracy	Text produced
	Tasks accomplished, attitudes expressed, tone conveyed; what a person can do	Topics, subject areas, activities and jobs addressed; settings	Acceptability, quality and correctness of message conveyed	Length and organization of utterance; kinds of discourse
0	No functional ability	None	None	Individual words and phrases
1	Can create with the language, ask and answer questions, participate in short conversations, and resolve a basic situation	Everyday survival topics and courtesy requirements	Intelligible to a native speaker used to dealing with foreigners	Discrete sentences
2	Able to fully participate in casual conversations; can give instructions, describe, report facts, narrate in present, past and future, and resolve a basic situation with a complication	Concrete topics such as own background, family, interests, work, travel, and current events	Understandable to a native speaker not used to dealing with foreigners; sometimes miscommunicates	Full paragraphs, minimally cohesive

	Function	Context/Content	Accuracy	Text produced
3	Can converse in formal and informal situations, resolve problems in unfamiliar situations, deal with abstract topics, provide explanations, offer supported opinions, hypothesize	Practical, social, professional and abstract topics, particular interests, and special fields of competence	Errors virtually never interfere with understanding and rarely disturb the native speaker; only sporadic non-patterned errors in basic structures	Extended discourse
4	Able to tailor language to fit audience, counsel, persuade, negotiate, represent a point of view, and interpret informally for dignitaries	All topics normally pertinent to professional needs	Nearly equivalent to a well-educated native speakers; speech is extensive, precise, appropriate to every occasion with only occasional errors	Speeches, lectures, debates, conference discussions; well organized extensive discourse
5	Functions in a manner that is equivalent to that of a well-educated native speaker	All subjects	Performance equivalent to that of a well-educated native speaker	All text types controlled by a highly articulate, well-educated native speaker

Note: From the Defense Language Institute's *OPI 2000 Tester Certification Workshop Training Manual*, 1999, 42, as edited in 2002. Reprinted by permission

Introduction to LNA methodology

An LNA is performed by drawing together a group of individuals representing both the career field(s) in question and the language proficiency level guidelines. These individuals discuss the job tasks whose performance involves the use of the foreign language in any way. The outcome of the LNA is an array of job tasks, each one of which has been coded by the degree of language proficiency required in listening, reading, speaking, and writing, for the adequate performance of that task under stated conditions and to a stated standard. This information is then utilized by decision-makers to establish or revise official policies with regard to requirements for foreign language job performance and foreign language education for the career field(s) in question. In June 1985, DLIFLC and an agency of the Department of the Army hosted and conducted at DLIFLC an LNA in three major career fields. The procedures developed and applied in that LNA have served as the default point of departure for all subsequent LNA. They are summarized in the remaining paragraphs of this section.

Steps in conducting an LNA

Identify and obtain participants

A successful LNA requires the collaboration of two sets of individuals: a group of target career group subject matter experts (SMEs) who know the job(s) whose foreign language requirements are to be assessed, and a second group of SMEs with expertise in the assessment of language proficiency levels as described by the Federal Interagency Language Roundtable. Typically, the first set of SMEs is provided by the user agency and DLIFLC provides the second. At least two DLIFLC SMEs are required; three or more is optimal. The number of career group SMEs is a function of the number of career fields to be addressed in the LNA and the variety that exists within career fields, depending on such variables as theater of operations. For a single-career-field LNA, e.g., a traditional intelligence-related MOS, a group of six or eight SMEs may be adequate; for a multiple-career-field LNA (e.g., one addressing the needs of an Army Special Forces A-team), it may be necessary to convene a larger group, including at least two SMEs per specialty area. The typical LNA takes place over a week's time, not counting the pre-LNA preparations. Because each day's activities and deliberations build upon the shared context that has been created by the events of the preceding day(s), it is important that all participants be available for the entire LNA.

Identify relevant tasks

Career group representatives identify and array relevant doctrinal material with respect to the job tasks associated with the career field(s) whose language needs are to be identified. From this master list, the career group SMEs, assisted by DLIFLC SMEs if desired and convenient, select for analysis all and only those tasks whose performance requires some use of a foreign language. It is highly desirable that information about the career field and its job tasks be made available to the DLIFLC SMEs well in advance of the LNA, although this has not always been the case.

Apply non-language-related ratings

To facilitate interpretation and application of LNA findings, career group SMEs typically rate each task on such parameters as frequency of performance and criticality of successful performance. The inclusion of such a step is at the discretion of the career group representatives, and it may be performed during, prior to, or after the attachment of language proficiency requirements to the tasks.

Provide proficiency level training to career group SMEs

The career group SMEs must receive familiarization training in the use of the ILR Proficiency Level Descriptions adequate to prepare them for full participation in the LNA. In the first LNA, some SME groups received up to 40 hours of training (by comparison, to be provisionally certified as DLIFLC oral proficiency testers, candidates must successfully complete a 96-hour course). However, a two-day course now serves general LNA needs. This training may be provided at DLIFLC or at the career group site, typically by DLIFLC tester-trainers, who often serve as DLIFLC LNA SMEs themselves. The training may be provided either before or after the FL-requiring tasks have been identified.

Provide orientation to the career field for the proficiency SMEs

The proficiency SMEs must become familiar enough with the nature of the military duties involved to enable them to understand and interpret the statements of the military SMEs. In the original LNA, this process occurred simultaneously with the LNA itself. In subsequent LNAs, greater amounts of attention have been given to this requirement.

Provide for database support

As each task is discussed and its four FL requirements are identified, that information must be captured in a database so that tasks and requirements can be sorted and summarized in various ways at the conclusion of the LNA. To support this requirement, the career group supplies a computer, a database program, and a knowledgeable computer operator.[7] It is highly desirable that the operator meet with the SME groups throughout the LNA, inputting decisions as they are reached. A fall-back option is that data are entered in the evening after each day's work.

Conduct LNA itself

At the agreed upon time and place, the two groups of SMEs meet. The meeting may be chaired by a representative from either group. For each task, the career group SMEs consider aloud the task, condition, and standard, and discuss their experiences in the performance of this task. The DLIFLC SMEs participate by listening carefully and asking questions to elicit data that can be related to the ILR language proficiency descriptions. Ultimately, the group decides upon a rating ranging from 0 to 5, using plus-levels, for each task in each skill modality: listening, reading, speaking, and writing. Although it is highly desirable that the decisions be reached by consensus, and this is typically the case, the judgments of the DLIFLC SMEs are followed in the rare cases where consensus is not reached.

Determine language proficiency job performance requirements of the career field(s) in question

Career group SMEs, along with DLIFLC SMEs, study the results of the LNA judgments as sorted and printed out by the database operator. The combined group[8] analyzes the data from various perspectives, addressing questions such as:

- What proportion of all career field tasks require the use of a FL in their performance?
- Which skill modalities are most in demand?

- What is the most frequently observed proficiency requirement?
- What is the average (mean) proficiency requirement?
- How do mean and modal proficiency requirements vary across language skill modalities?
- What are the proficiency requirements of the most critical tasks?
- Are differing patterns of language skill requirements associated with different subgroups of career field tasks?

In light of these and other relevant considerations, the LNA report concludes with a recommendation to the career group policy makers regarding what the doctrinal language requirements of the career field(s) in question should be. At appropriate times and levels, language requirements policy is set by the career group.

Determine foreign language education requirements and policy

The establishment of foreign language education requirements and policy is separate from the determination of foreign language job performance requirements. For example, the June 1985 LNA concluded that in many areas, ILR level 3 was needed, but that it was not reasonable to require DLIFLC to graduate level 3 linguists from a basic language course.[9] Thus, job performance requirements were recognized as including level 3, but the educational policy established level 2 as the new DLIFLC graduation standard, placing responsibility on the services to raise personnel to the required higher levels in post-DLIFLC schools and through ongoing on-the-job training. DLIFLC personnel, whether LNA SMEs or others, may or may not be perceived as having a role to play in discussions of career group foreign language education policy. If desired, recommendations about language education policy can be made simultaneously with recommendations concerning foreign language job performance requirements.

Variability in the LNA process: three examples

The preceding section provided an overview of the ideal LNA process. In practice and over time, LNA procedures have had to be modified to fit differing circumstances. To illustrate some of these LNA variants, three LNAs are described below, beginning with the 1985 activity which established the ideal model.

The original 1985 LNA

This 'Cadillac' model involved a great deal of time, effort, and expense, and for good reason: its objective was to inform the establishment of education objectives and graduation standards for all basic program students at DLIFLC. US Army SMEs representing experience in numerous languages and assignments were brought to DLIFLC from a variety of locations for this activity. In all, 28 military SMEs and 11 DLIFLC proficiency SMEs participated, working simultaneously in four different working groups, each dedicated to a given career field or variant thereof. Each group analyzed each and every language-requiring job task as printed in the appropriate Soldier's Manual, beginning with the task, conditions, and standards as stated therein. Results were data-based, examined, discussed, and ultimately briefed to the highest appropriate policy-making level, then known as the General Officers Steering Committee (GOSC). The GOSC subsequently established new education standards for DLIFLC and directed DLIFLC to develop a plan to meet them. The implications have been dramatic and long lasting. For example, the DLIFLC graduation standard now provides the basis for the minimum language proficiencies which US Army linguists must demonstrate through annual testing in order to remain in good standing or to re-enlist in their career field. These same standards are used by commanders to report their degree of readiness, i.e., the proportion of their assigned linguists who meet or exceed (or fail to meet) the standard, and by personnel systems to award additional pay to qualifying linguists. No other LNA to date has had such far-reaching effects.

The 1999 riverine operations LNA

The US Marine Corps (USMC) is the executive agent for 'riverine operations', a term used to refer to military assistance provided by US forces to military and police forces in other countries in support of their counter-drug and counter-terrorist activities. The LNA which DLIFLC performed to assist the USMC in defining and meeting their language requirements for this mission differed in a number of ways from the default model described above. Three of them are described here: the source of raw material; the kinds of language proficiency recommendations made; and the larger context in which this LNA was conducted.

Normally, an LNA utilizes doctrinal material such as a Soldier's Manual as a point of departure, and participants discuss each of the stated tasks, conditions, and standards that are considered to require the use of a foreign language in their performance. In the present case, it was not possible to follow this procedure because such written doctrinal materials either did not exist or were not available. Therefore, the DLIFLC team had to develop its understanding of the kinds and variety of tasks that are involved in this career field via extensive interviews with the several experienced SMEs who were available at the USMC location where the LNA was performed. These individuals included some, but not all, of the kinds of personnel who are typically assigned to a particular mission. Fortunately, the personnel available included team leaders such as commissioned and non-commissioned officers (NCO) who had served in the capacities of Officer-in-Charge (OIC), Assistant OIC (AOIC), or Staff NCO in Charge (SNCOIC). They were able to compensate to a large extent for the unavailability of representatives of the remainder of a team's personnel, i.e., the NCO team members who teach their various specialties but do not serve in SNCOIC positions. These personal interviews constituted the primary source of information for the LNA.

In prior LNAs, a single set of recommendations emerged from the data, e.g., that holders of a given MOS must maintain at least a level 2 in listening and in reading. This kind of conclusion tended to be reached largely for practical reasons (systems were needed for managing substantial groups of individuals) and to be justified by pointing out that substantial numbers of tasks required similar language proficiency levels, despite the variability in the data set as a whole. In contrast, this LNA found that language requirements ranged dramatically, from straightforward 'show and tell' description to complex diplomatic and negotiation skills. The ultimate conclusion was that the OIC, AOIC, and SNCOIC required significantly greater amounts of language proficiency than the remainder of the team, and that all team members required extensive amounts of cross-cultural awareness and sensitivity.

The US Army Civil Affairs[10] LNA

This 2001 LNA, which addressed the language needs of a very complex career field, presented additional challenges to traditional LNA methodology but also led to certain improvements, particularly with respect to analysis and reporting of results. Of particular interest to this discussion is the way in which the task lists were developed and the way in which they were analyzed. Although there was a wealth of official documentation, it became clear as the LNA proceeded that the tasks that had been selected for examination were not so much individual soldier tasks as statements of what the team or unit as a whole needed to accomplish. Also, the essential question to be addressed for each task had to be rephrased to fit this particular career field, because FL proficiency is not a requirement for holding this MOS, despite the fact that many tasks can best be performed by language-capable personnel.[11] This means that the question addressed throughout these deliberations could not be the default, "What is the minimum FL proficiency required to do this task adequately?" but rather, "What is the minimum FL proficiency that this task needs *if it is to be done in a FL without the aid of an interpreter?*"

A complication which arose in the discussion of the tasks themselves led to a creative modification of the order in which tasks were discussed. Although personnel in this field are assigned to one or another teams, such as 'government', 'economics and commerce', or 'public facilities', many task statements were very similar across teams. Discovery of this fact provoked lively discussion and led ultimately to sorting the tasks, and sequencing them for discussion, by their sentential components rather than by their affiliation to a given team or category. For example, all the tasks beginning with "Advise and assist ..." were grouped together, and were further sorted by what came next ("in the technical administrative requirements" preceded "in locating, identifying, preserving, and protecting"), and again by the next element in the task statement, etc., so that both similarities and differences in the implications of the task statements could be seen at once while discussion was under way about how a given task had been performed by the SMEs who were gathered together.

This LNA also broke new ground in terms of the degree of analysis which was performed on the data. For each task, the data set included more than the traditional data elements, i.e., the proficiency levels required for listening, speaking, reading, and writing, plus an index of the frequency with which the task tends to be performed and the task's criticality to overall mission success. Each task was also coded for the 'team' to which it belonged and the major mission activity or activities it supported. Thus, it was possible to examine the data set from a greater variety of perspectives: the distribution of language requirements (by skill modality) for all tasks examined; the percent of tasks whose requirement would be met by a given proficiency level; the relationships among ratings of frequency and criticality; the distribution of language requirements for the subset of high frequency / high criticality tasks; and the distribution of tasks and their requirements across teams or supported mission activities.

The value of this approach is that the LNA report became a tool that can be used in a variety of ways. In addition to serving as a basis for establishing a foreign language education policy for the entire career field, the information as reported can, at least in theory, be used by commanders in forming teams and assigning personnel for specific missions.

Methodological issues and concerns

Classical approaches to establishing validity and reliability cannot readily be applied to LNAs as described herein. In these LNAs, validity, like beauty, is in the eye of the beholder. There is no conveniently-at-hand external criterion, and the determination of FL proficiency requirements for a given occupational community is determined by a sample of the members of that very community. If the final picture makes sense to them, and to their colleagues and their chain of command, then it is assumed that validity has been established, albeit in an admittedly tautological manner. Similarly, standard methods such as inter-rater reliability analysis do not obtain, because there is no pretense that judgments are rendered independently by the various members of the military and proficiency participants. To the contrary, the entire process is designed for and strives for consensus building, carrying with it the ever-present danger that a group will fall into a pattern, and everything will begin to look like a level this or a level that. These facts do not mean that validity and reliability are of no concern, of course, but quite the opposite. LNA managers alert each group of participants to the danger of the halo effect, and also attempt to include in each group of proficiency SMEs at least one strong personality who will not be at all hesitant to 'buck the crowd'. In addition, a prerequisite for selection as a proficiency SME is that the individual be an experienced and well-regarded oral proficiency tester.[12] Nevertheless, concerns remain with respect to both validity and reliability, each of which is further discussed below.

Reliability

Although traditional post-hoc inter-rater reliability analysis has been shown to be inappropriate for LNAs, it would be possible to conduct split-half or test-retest reliability studies of the LNA procedure. Unfortunately, the time and expense associated with bringing together the participants constitute a non-trivial impediment to such desires. The senior leadership of the career field being examined understandably authorizes the expense because he or she wants an answer on which to base policy decisions, not in order to support research studies requiring multiple iterations and twice the number of SMEs.

Of the two approaches, modified split-half procedures are more likely than test-retest studies to prove feasible operationally. For example, if an adequate sample of military SMEs could be obtained, two working groups could be formed. All participants would meet together, along with two teams of proficiency SMEs, to exchange initial orientation briefings and to reach agreement on the task lists to be examined, the nature of the question to be addressed, and any other procedures needing clarification. Then the group would split into two working groups, each of which would discuss the tasks and render independent judgments of the tasks' language requirements, coming together afterwards to compare and contrast and resolve differences. Although the ultimate product would be one of consensus, the original ratings of each working group would be preserved for further analysis. Examination of such data sets over time would provide ongoing insights into the reliability of each LNA's processes and of the procedure as a whole.

At even lower cost, surrogate or partial test-retest designs could be contemplated, such as video-taping the discussions and editing the tapes to delete overt statements by anyone regarding the proficiency levels being arrived at. The tapes could then be viewed by different groups of SMEs, whose proficiency judgments would be compared with those of the original LNA participants. Such a procedure would not be unproblematic, of course; for example, the proficiency SMEs in the post-hoc video-tape-mediated rating session would not have the benefit of the face-to-face orientation to the career field that was afforded the participants in the original LNA.

Meanwhile, on at least one occasion, the opportunity for a kind of test-retest reliability assessment presented itself automatically because the language needs of a given career field were reassessed. This was the case in the 2001 Civil Affairs LNA, because the field had been assessed also in 1988. At the conclusion of the 2001 LNA, the 1988 data and 2001 data were compared. The patterns of requirements were seen to be quite similar for two of the language skill modalities and to show substantial differences in the other two. The SMEs in the 2001 LNA expressed the opinion that the observed changes were consistent with changes in Civil Affairs doctrine due to world events and deployment experience during the intervening dozen years. Given that the 1988 LNA had been conducted with considerably less rigor than the 2001 one, and that there was no personnel overlap among the military participants and very little among the proficiency SMEs,[13] the comparability of patterns lent an aura of both reliability and face validity to the LNA process as a whole.

Validity

The derivation of task lists

A primary consideration regarding the validity of the LNA process concerns the nature and derivation of the task lists and the kinds of judgments to be made about each task. As discussed above, the methodological tension is between the use of a bottom-up strategy in which the tasks of the individual service member are examined versus a more global approach in which the task statements that are used as the point of departure for discussion have been taken from material written at the mission level. In both cases the military SMEs discuss their own experiences in the performance of the specific tasks at hand. However, the more human judgment that is required in extracting or synthesizing task statements from a larger corpus of written material (as opposed to simply examining every language-requiring task exactly as it is printed in a Soldier's Manual), the more danger there is that the tasks under examination will not adequately represent the universe of tasks associated with the career field under examination. This concern is exacerbated, of course, when no written materials are available for examination. Considerable care must be taken at the beginning of an LNA to ensure that the assembled military SMEs agree that the task list to be used adequately reflects their understanding of their professional area. Similarly, the essential question to be addressed for each task must be very clearly stated. This is especially important if the career field in question is one in which language proficiency is viewed only as an enhancement to mission performance, not as a requirement for holding the MOS.

The search for external criteria

It would seem logical to validate the findings of LNAs by relating the posited requirements of given tasks to supervisory perceptions of how well those tasks have been performed by personnel holding documented levels of language proficiency. If high-proficiency individuals receive higher marks for their performance of tasks requiring high levels of proficiency than those received by low-proficiency individuals who have performed the same tasks, this would tend to validate the proficiency level requirements that have been posited for those tasks. Both theoretical and practical constraints have impeded efforts to conduct these kinds of analysis.

At the theoretical level, it must be understood that language proficiency is but an enabling skill, to which technical job skills must be added.[14] Thus, a supervisory judgment that a task has been poorly performed may reflect inadequate capabilities in either language skills, job skills, or both. Separate measures of technical job skills are not readily available. Furthermore, many of the job tasks involved are classified, making it practically difficult to obtain reliable data at the task level. For example, in a large-sample longitudinal study of language proficiency change over time, linguists were sent an annual questionnaire on which they were asked how often they had performed specific job tasks during the preceding year. Their supervisors were asked to rate how well the linguists had performed those job tasks. These data were to be compared with the linguists' annual language proficiency scores. The research hypothesis was that there would be a higher correlation between language proficiency and supervisory ratings for those tasks whose performance required higher levels of proficiency. However, the task lists involved were classified as top secret, meaning that respondents had to take the questionnaires into a secure facility and cross-reference questionnaire items with classified reference material in order to know which tasks they were being asked about. Perhaps not surprisingly, too few questionnaires were returned to permit analysis, and the hypothesis remains untested.

Even at the macro level, such efforts are problematic. For example, one might posit that, all other things being equal, if a career field requires at least level 2s in listening and reading, the job performance of linguists with lower proficiency scores would be rated less positively than that of linguists with higher proficiency levels. However, the correlation of language proficiency scores with global ratings of supervisory satisfaction may be meaningless, because weaker linguists are often assigned to less demanding jobs, such that both the level 1+ linguist and the level 3 linguist may be perceived by their supervisors as doing an excellent job on their assigned duties.

Additional considerations

Several areas of concern address both validity and reliability. One such concern is the fact that the data being generated in an LNA are retrospective: the military SMEs are not directly observed in the performance of their duties, but rather recollect and describe what they have done. From a practical perspective, it is difficult to imagine any more direct way to obtain data; the job tasks are many, and as they are applied in different operations and under different circumstances, they become operationally defined in different ways. The only practical way to examine these disparate realities is to bring together an appropriate sample of individuals to pool their personal experiences. Nevertheless, it must be acknowledged that their recollections are post-hoc, and that the proficiency SMEs are limited to the data provided by these recollections.

It must also be acknowledged that the recollections and opinions of a different group of SMEs might lead to different conclusions because of the different experiences and recollections they would bring to the LNA. Normally, one would address such a concern by ensuring that the SMEs were a stratified random sample drawn to be representative of the population by controlling for such variables as language, theater of operations, rank, and gender. In practice, it has proved extremely difficult even to approximate such a sampling procedure because of practical impediments such as the lack of a convenient sampling frame and the unavailability of SMEs due to operational or personal considerations. Thus, in most cases, the SMEs must be considered convenience samples.

The degree to which the proficiency SMEs understand the military career field under examination is also emerging as more important than was originally thought to be the case. Such understanding becomes ever more critical as LNAs are applied to career fields in which language skills are viewed as an enhancement rather than a requirement. To respond to this growing need, procedures are being modified to place greater emphasis on the orientation of the proficiency SMEs to the career field well in advance of the LNA itself.

Finally, it should be acknowledged that the basic premises of LNAs are in a state of flux as a result of both experience in conducting them and changes in the kinds of language capabilities needed in the post-Cold War era. Traditionally, LNAs have been conducted solely to establish the officially required proficiency levels associated with a given career field or with a subgroup of practitioners thereof, not with the intent to influence language course curricula. As language needs become more diverse in the current environment, community concerns are beginning to shift toward an interest in greater specificity with regard to the kinds of language capabilities needed by a wider array of military personnel, not just those who are officially designated as linguists. It follows that LNAs can be expected to become more diverse in response, and that, in at least some cases, they will move toward the inclusion of a 'language for special purposes' orientation with overt curricular implications.

Summary and conclusions

Language needs assessments as described herein have provided an essential foundation for the development of language policy in various career fields of the US military. As they have been conducted with different groups of personnel over the past two decades, procedures have evolved and insights have grown into how best to conduct them. At the same time, and despite their demonstrated utility and perceived value to the community, evolving experience with LNAs has revealed several areas in which improvements are needed. Recommendations for additional improvements will be welcomed.

Notes

1 The views expressed in this chapter are those of the author and do not necessarily reflect the position of the Defense Language Institute Foreign Language Center, the Department of Defense, or the US Government.

2 In traditional US Government usage, this term denotes someone whose occupational specialty requires proficiency in a non-English language, not necessarily someone who possesses an advanced degree in linguistics.

3 Strictly speaking, the term *MOS* is appropriate to the US Army only, not to the other services. For convenience, however, it is used as a generic term throughout this paper.

4 The complete text of the *Descriptions* and a synopsis of their history are available at http://govtilr.org/

5 See, for example, Chapter 1 in Omaggio Hadley, 2001, for an excellent discussion and over six pages of references to works dealing with communicative competence, proficiency, and standards for foreign language learning.

6 This table, taken from the current DLIFLC tester certification training manual, is an adaptation of a similar table on page 31 of the 1999 ACTFL tester training manual, which in turn had adapted the table from Lowe's original *ILR handbook on oral interview testing*, first developed in the early 1980s. The original table did not have the fourth column and was known as the "Trisection of Oral Proficiency Levels" (Lowe, n.d., pp. 2–4).

7 In the early LNAs this was a non-trivial task; today it is a simple matter, easily accomplished with, e.g., a laptop with Excel™.

8 In more recent LNAs, questions such as these have been included in the data analysis and report produced by the DLIFLC LNA manager after

the LNA itself has been completed and SMEs have returned to their respective homes and duty stations.

9 At the time, the graduation standard was level 1.

10 Civil affairs units help military commanders by working with civil authorities and civilian populations to lessen the impact of military operations on them during peace, contingency operations and declared war ... [The 96% found in the Army Reserve] provide a prime source of nation-building skills. These reserve-component civil affairs units include soldiers with training and experience in public administration, public safety, public health, legal systems, labor management, public welfare, public finance, public education, civil defense, public works and utilities, public communications, public transportation, logistics, food and agricultural services, economics, property control, cultural affairs, civil information, and managing dislocated persons. http://www.soc.mil/usacapoc/capoc_default.htm

11 This apparent paradox is explained by fact that the missions can often be accomplished through the use of interpreters (despite the fact that military commanders may be skeptical of the reliability of local interpreters) or because enough relevant host nationals speak English to some extent.

12 As indicated above, these individuals have received special training in understanding and applying the ILR scale. As active testers, they apply this knowledge on a regular basis as they conduct high-stakes testing of DLIFLC students and other military personnel. Thus, they are presumed to be more qualified than others to serve as proficiency SMEs for an LNA.

13 Three proficiency SMEs were involved in the 1988 LNA. One of these three served as chair of the 2001 LNA and a second participated, primarily by providing proficiency orientation to the military participants. The majority of the proficiency judgments in the 2001 LNA were made by three additional proficiency experts who had had no role in the 1988 activity.

14 Most military linguists attend a separate school in which their MOS-specific job skills are taught. They are certified in their career field only upon successful completion of this additional course of study.

Acknowledgments

The author would like to thank colleagues and anonymous readers for their critical reviews and helpful comments. Any remaining errors or deficiencies are the fault of the author.

References

American Council on the Teaching of Foreign Languages. (1986). *ACTFL proficiency guidelines*. Hastings-on-Hudson, NY: Author.

124   *John A. Lett*

American Council on the Teaching of Foreign Languages. (1999). *ACTFL revised proficiency guidelines – speaking*. Yonkers, NY: Author.
American Council on the Teaching of Foreign Languages. (2001). *ACTFL revised proficiency guidelines – writing*. Yonkers, NY: Author.
Defense Language Institute Foreign Language Center. (1999). *OPI 2000 tester certification workshop training manual*. Monterey, CA: Author.
Interagency Language Roundtable. (1985). *Interagency Language Roundtable language skill level descriptions*. Washington, D.C.
Lowe, Jr., P. (n.d.). *ILR handbook on oral interview testing*. Washington, D.C.: CIA Language School.
Omaggio Hadley, A. (2001). *Language teaching in context* (3rd ed.). Boston, MA: Heinle & Heinle.
Swender, E. (ed.). (1999). *ACTFL oral proficiency interview tester training manual*. Yonkers, NY: ACTFL, Inc.
Swender, E. (2002). Personal communication, March 5.

PART III:
THE OCCUPATIONAL SECTOR

4 Sources, methods and triangulation in needs analysis: A critical perspective in a case study of Waikiki hotel maids[1]

Rebeca Jasso-Aguilar

Introduction

Several researchers have pointed to the inadequacy of outsiders' intuitions and the value of insiders' perspectives in needs analysis (NA), curriculum development and materials design for language teaching, as well as the importance of using multiple sources and methods (Long, this volume; Ramani et al, 1988; L. West, 1984; R. West, 1994). Few published studies on NA, however, have utilized multiple sources and methods, and of those that have (e.g., Cumaranatunge, 1988), fewer still have utilized triangulation. The purpose of this chapter is two-fold: (i) to compare several methods and sources available to needs analysts; and (ii) to report findings of a study of the needs of hotel maids which used multiple sources and methods, and triangulation.

NA and social engineering

Recently, a great deal of emphasis has been placed on NA for occupation-specific VESL (Vocational English as a Second Language) and other ESP (English for Specific Purposes) courses, often motivated by pressing time constraints, limited financial resources, and institutional and learner expectations (Chambers, 1980; Cumaranatunge, 1988; L. West, 1984). Institutional VESL and ESP curricula, however, face strong criticism from critical educators. Auerbach (1995) questions NA for the workplace as the basis for curriculum development for ESL students altogether, arguing that the process is often performed by outsiders whose information comes from institutions with clearly defined expectations of what they want the workers/students to do. Such information, she argues, can only be transformed into a curriculum whose goals are to serve the interests of institutions which have traditionally marginalized ESL speakers, socializing them into passive acceptance of subservient roles. Likewise, Tollefson (1989, 1991) denounces a covert policy in which language training for specific purposes channels immigrants into marginal occupations that offer no opportunity to gain additional language or job skills, ensuring that they will have enough English to perform adequately in minimum-wage jobs while avoiding any welfare dependency, yet not enough to move beyond those levels of employment. While these concerns regarding the occasional misuse of NA are valid, in this paper I explore a different methodology – different from traditional approaches to NA – and the possibility to use findings critically, so as to overcome the potential pitfalls.

The position taken in this paper follows Long (this volume, to appear), who acknowledges that institutional curricula could clearly lead to a potentially serious problem of "social engineering of the worst sort," but suggests that the possible exploitation of workers undertaking these courses:

> ... would be better seen as the result of Machiavellian government policy, pernicious business practices and gross dereliction of duty by educational administrators, not as the result of NA or specific purpose course design per se. It would involve an abuse of NA, but is neither its inevitable corollary nor reason to forego its positive effects.
>
> (Long, to appear, p. 10)

Although Auerbach opposes institutional NA and predetermined curricula, it is clear that the collaborative investigation of what is important to students, which she advocates, implies NA beyond the workplace (without excluding it), and that this NA is an ongoing process. Long advocates use of multiple sources and methods, insiders (with expertise) as better informants than outsiders, and triangulation of sources and methods. Triangulation, a commonly used procedure in anthropology, involves (with many variants) systematic comparison of interim findings from two or more sources, methods or combinations thereof, and an attempt to validate the researcher's (in this case the needs analyst's) interim findings by presenting them to the informants, and/or by seeking confirmation or disconfirmation of the current analysis. By using multiple sources and methods, and triangulation, Long believes that the main problem for which Auerbach opposes NA, that is, the learners' needs being identified only from the point of view of institutions and manipulated to their own advantages, can be overcome. Under the type of NA advocated by Long, Auerbach's approach falls short, since it considers the students and their lives and experiences the only source that should inform the curriculum. Long questions the reliability of many students as sources on their own needs, especially if they are new to the job or activity they are to perform, and Drobnic (1978, p. 320) reminds us that "linguistically naive students should not be expected to make sound language decisions concerning their training" (cited in Chambers, 1980, p. 26).

With these considerations in mind, this study set out to identify the tasks performed by the maids (or 'housekeepers') in a Waikiki hotel in order to complete their daily routine at the hotel, and the language involved in those tasks. One concern was to find out whether language was needed to perform the tasks, whether or not the maids perceived this need, and to what extent the lack of language abilities might have affected their performance. Another concern was to identify the needs and wants of both the maids and institutional representatives and to interpret any discrepancies.

Orientations in NA for the workplace: sources and methods

Some attempts have been made to identify efficient methods and sources of information for NA for the workplace. L. West (1984) suggests use of various sources, such as job description manuals, job site observations, tape-recording of conversations in the workplace, surveys, and specific questions that "can elicit key information about the language requirements of a job". For L. West, syllabus design derives from a logical analysis of the job. What that means, however, and who defines it, remain unclear.

Prince (1984) recommends *goal analysis*, which is what a company feels is the need for a course and its expected results, *job analysis*, which is the description of the job, and *language analysis*, which is the work-oriented language, which will include procedures, policies, etc., and which will emphasize the names of tools, supplies and other job terminology. In Prince's approach, workers are interviewed for information related to the job only, such as time spent on different tasks and to determine the degree of involvement. Prince also suggests that the analyst should consider the "company climate", tactfully asking workers questions about, for example, what they think the company values are. One presumes that these questions will be asked in the learners' native language, although this is not suggested and neither is any methodology for investigating "company climate".

R. West (1994) provides an overview of what has been done, said and written about NA. What is striking about his account, just like L. West's, is how little attention has been paid to learners as a source of information, especially compared to other sources. Little attention, either, has been paid to the sociopolitical environment of the workplace or to the sociopolitical environment of the workers outside the work-site. (Prince does seem to take the sociopolitical environment of the workplace into consideration, although it is not clear to what extent and how it is incorporated.) West enumerates ten different methods of data collection, suggesting that these methods ensure coverage of most of the (one presumes, crucial) areas. Of nine areas listed, only three (general personal background; language background; and attitudinal and motivational factors) seem to be related to issues outside the workplace. These areas, particularly attitudinal and motivational factors, suggest that a view of the workers' world outside the job is taken into account for NA purposes. R. West (*op. cit.*, p. 9) disagrees with adopting classification of language derived from social English, when the language used in real-world ESP situations differs from that predicted by some course designers, i.e., what Long refers to as using outsider intuitions to guess at the language used in specific work situations or for specific tasks.

R. West's state of the art NA in language teaching and Long's (to appear) chapters dedicated to NA have some points in common. They both agree on the advantage of utilizing multiple sources, and on the importance of selecting adequate information-gathering instruments. They regard the language intuitions of expert analysts and applied linguists as not necessarily reliable sources representative of language use in a field. They also agree that there is often a difference between learners' needs and learners' wants, although the degree to which they differ will vary among learners. Two crucial issues neglected by West (and indeed by the people he cites), but which Long treats in detail, are: (i) the need to establish a unit of analysis in terms of which needs will be identified, and (ii) the need for triangulation of sources.

Long (1985, and elsewhere) proposes *task* as the (non-linguistic) unit of analysis. For Long, task is a more viable unit of analysis than such options as situations or communicative events, among other reasons, because more relevant information for course designers is available in task-based occupational analyses by domain experts and other sources. Task-based occupational analyses reveal more about the dynamic qualities of target discourse than do text-based analyses; they also circumvent the domain expert's usual lack of linguistic knowledge and the applied linguist's usual lack of content knowledge. As such, they minimize the pervasive problem of finding informants who are competent in the academic, occupational or vocational area of interest and also knowledgeable about language use in that area. Once target tasks for a particular group of learners have been identified, domain experts (not necessarily the learners, unless they have expertise) can easily and reliably supply information which will later be analyzed by applied linguists, materials writers, teachers and learners. Another, and by no means less important, advantage of tasks is their role in preparing students as agents of social change:

> Steps are taken, both in pedagogic task design and in the area of methodology, to make learners aware of their potential as social actors, not merely passive observers, in determining task outcomes, and when necessary, in *redefining* tasks.
>
> (Long, to appear, p. 29)

Where sources are concerned, Long suggests appropriate combinations of language teachers with prior experience with learners in the program, people now undergoing or who have completed the education program, those already employed in the occupation for which the perspective learners are preparing, current or future subject area teachers or employers, documents, such as job descriptions and course reading lists, and published NA literature. Long emphasizes the need for triangulation, a process that involves the use of multiple-data-collection methods and may also involve the incorporation of multiple data sources, investigators, and theoretical perspectives. Triangulation contributes to the trustworthiness of the data and increases confidence in research findings (Glesne and Peshkin, 1992, p. 24). Prolonged engagement in the field, persistent observation and triangulation are procedures used by researchers working within the qualitative research or naturalistic research traditions to help them validate their data and to increase the credibility of their interpretations (Davis, 1992). 'Qualitative research' is an umbrella term for many kinds of research approaches and techniques, including 'ethnography', a term that has recently become fashionable in NA and ESL studies; 'naturalistic research' is a descriptive term that implies that the researcher conducts observations in the natural environment, that is, where people live and work (Watson-Gegeo, 1988).

Some case studies of NA for the workplace

Three case studies were selected, based on their methodology and the nature of the occupations investigated, to provide a framework for analysis and comparison in the present study.

Bell (1981) identified the tasks and sub-tasks demanded by the job specifications of a canteen assistant, as well as the knowledge and skills required to perform those tasks, choosing one task 'Dealing with complaints about cold food' to illustrate how to go about setting objectives, designing a syllabus, creating materials, etc. In a departure from a task-based approach, the *functions* involved in this task were identified: explanation, apology, offering, and reporting. For each of these, there were a number of speech acts and forms available which could lead to different interactions, depending on whether the client was satisfied or not, and at what point satisfaction had occurred. Materials were created by manipulating a conversation so as to create interactions which would necessarily contain speech acts qualitatively and quantitatively more complex. Bell predicted no less than six highly plausible interactions, and although he acknowledged that one could never be absolutely sure about a customer's reactions, he reported that conversations tended to keep fairly close to the predicted behavior. (It was not clear how these predictions were made.)

Svendsen & Krebs (1984) identified the language required for two health care occupations by using interviews with various people in the department where a job was performed, shadowing (following and observing) workers as they moved about the workplace at different times during the day, and tape-recording interactions among workers at the job site. They found that the language required for two occupations, central supply technician and hospital transporter, was quite different: while the technicians spent their day handling objects in a quiet and orderly fashion, the transporters interacted with others all day. There were frequent conversations amongst transporters and patients, nurses and co-workers; in addition, transporters were constantly checking on the phone for instructions. For job-related tasks in technicians' daily routines, which were also identified by Svendsen and Krebs, language was almost non-existent except when routines were interrupted (e.g., when they were out of some item, or when something was not working correctly). For the transporter, there were situations in which language needed to be used even though it did not interfere with the physical performance of the task. For example, a worker who was wheeling a patient to the x-ray room would want to tell the patient what was going to be done to her. Finally, Svendsen & Krebs also identified the need for social language, for small talk during break-time and also while work was being done (see, also, Holmes, this volume).

Cumaranatunge's (1988) goal of a learner-centered course catering to Sri Lankan women working as domestic aides in West Asia led her to conduct a NA using multiple sources (returning domestic aides, women currently working, agencies and employers, governmental officials, travel agents) and various methods (questionnaires, structured interviews, informal interviews, field study and participant observation), as well as various sites (e.g., the bank, the park, and the Sri Lankan embassy). The results not only provided information about the language used in their work, but also revealed problems and pressures faced by domestic aides while in employment, which in turn created additional situations in which English was needed. The use of multiple sources showed that the informants looked at problems and situations from their own perspective, and that these perspectives were rarely similar. This study was a good NA which fell one step short: there was no triangulation or evaluation of sources.

When the need arises for NA beyond the workplace

Goldstein (1992) provides an account of female factory workers learning English as a second language. Although hers is not a NA but a study of language choice, the use of ethnography allowed her to see the discrepancies between students situations for language use and the content of their ESL class: while lessons were composed of communicative tasks related to their work, such as polite ways to ask for tools, the particular socio-cultural environment of the workplace made it unnecessary for the women to be polite with one another, and it even made the use of English unnecessary. The majority of the women were Portuguese, their language choice was Portuguese, and they did not associate the use of English with getting ahead in the workplace. Their supervisor was a bilingual speaker of English and Portuguese, eliminating the need for English in supervisor–worker communication. On the assembly line, the use of Portuguese brought workers together, enabling them to meet efficiency and time standards, while the use of English generated conflicts, especially amongst the least proficient ones. Goldstein concluded that while English-language training is not always necessary for functioning well at work or for economic survival and/or mobility, there are still good reasons for women working and living in languages other than English to participate in ESL classes. She suggested looking at the larger picture of these (and other) women's lives and finding needs that can be addressed by providing language training to expand their options for functioning not just as a cheap labor force but as functional members of English-speaking societies. What she was arguing for, in fact, was NA beyond the workplace.

The study

The present study was mainly carried out at one of the many large hotels in Waikiki, one belonging to a well-known chain. In addition, two observations were performed at a smaller site belonging to the same company. The great majority of maids in these hotels are Filipino, Chinese, Korean, and Vietnamese women. As previously mentioned, the study set out to identify the tasks and language needed to perform a housekeeper's job. Two concerns guided the study: (i) to find out whether language was needed to perform the tasks, whether or not the maids perceived this need, and to what extent the lack of language abilities might have affected their performance; and, (ii) to identify the needs and wants of both the maids and the institutional representatives, and to interpret any discrepancies.

At the time I contacted the human resources person, Sandra, she was in the process of starting an English course for the hotel maids because, out of approximately one thousand housekeepers employed at the chain, "five hundred could benefit from learning English" (personal communication). She had begun to do her own NA of the language needs of the maids, and had already selected a consulting company to develop the curriculum. For this purpose, a task force had been assembled, composed of people with expertise in different areas who, in one way or another, had contact with the hotel maids: maintenance, security, housekeeping, front desk, and human resources. Sources for the study reported here included the human resources person, the executive housekeeper, various housekeepers and supervisors, task force meetings, morning/afternoon briefings, documents, such as job and routine descriptions, and the ESL curriculum designed by the task force. Sources will be discussed at more length in the following sections.

Methodology

Methods and sources used in this study were as follows.

Methods:
1 Participant observations (with tape-recording and note-taking)
2 Unstructured interviews
3 Written questionnaires (given to housekeepers and to co-workers)

Sources:
1 Three housekeepers (day and evening shifts)
2 Human resources person

3 Executive housekeeper: the person at the top of the housekeeping hierarchy
4 Various supervisors and housekeeper assistants: personnel between the executive housekeeper and the hotel maids in the housekeeping hierarchy
5 Task force weekly/biweekly meetings
6 Morning briefings
7 Housekeeping room
8 Documents (job descriptions, safety procedures, etc., all in English)

I conducted five participant observations, three observations corresponding to the day shift (8:00 am – 4:00 pm) and two to the evening shift (3:00 pm – 11:00 pm) between March and July, 1996. Unstructured interviews with the housekeepers were conducted as part of conversations during our work together; interviews with the human resources person and the executive housekeeper were more formal, in that time was set aside for the purpose, and some discussion of my ongoing research and findings took place during these sessions, as well. Written questionnaires for the housekeepers (Appendix A) consisted of 29 items aiming at identifying tasks and language use both at work and outside the job. Co-workers' questionnaires (Appendix B) contained 12 items aimed at identifying situations in which housekeepers needed English to interact with them, as well as the co-workers' perceptions of communication difficulties and language needs of the housekeepers. Both questionnaires were written in English.

The task force was composed of personnel with expertise in the areas of maintenance, security, housekeeping, front desk, and human resources. The NA process followed by the task force consisted of one-hour brainstorming sessions (most of which I attended), reflections and discussions of the previous session, more brainstorming, and so on, i.e., predominantly the use of intuitions. The results of these meetings were several lists of situations which, according to the task force, the maids were most likely to encounter on a regular basis, the tasks they were more likely to perform, the language they were more likely to hear, and language they should be able to speak, read or write in such situations. Aside from Chris, the housekeeper executive, most people participating in the task force could be considered outsiders to the housekeepers' group, in the sense that they were not housekeepers and had never worked as such. To one degree or another, all thought they knew the situations and the language that the housekeepers encountered on a daily basis. Participant observation would later disconfirm these intuitions.

Supervisors and housekeeper assistants, besides having experience and seniority as housekeepers, are fairly proficient English speakers. They may be responsible for answering the phone and performing duties in the housekeeping room, and may help in the training or supervision of new housekeepers. Supervisors also conduct the morning briefings at the smaller branches of the hotel chain, where there may not be an executive housekeeper. The morning briefings are conducted daily from 8:00–8:30 am. The executive housekeeper briefs the hotel maids on routine housekeeping issues, as well as special events in the hotel. The housekeeping room is the place where guests call with housekeeping requests; paged messages from and to the housekeepers are also received and sent here. Uniforms, pagers, keys and room assignments are kept and distributed here, which makes the place buzz with activity at the beginning and end of the work day.

Participant observation ranges along a continuum from observation to active participation (Glesne & Peshkin, 1992). I chose the latter because I was interested not only in identifying but in experiencing the tasks and situations that housekeepers face during a day's work, the language they hear, and the language they use. Because I also wanted to identify the language needed for training new personnel, I requested to be trained in the same fashion as a new housekeeper. This training essentially consists of pairing up the new housekeeper with an experienced one, after the apprentice has undergone a session on procedures and safety measures for the workplace with the executive housekeeper. If the apprentice's English proficiency is very low, this session will be conducted with the help of an interpreter, usually one of the housekeepers who speak the same language as the apprentice. The training occurs on the spot, the experienced housekeeper demonstrating how to do the job rather than explaining how to do it. Due to the context-embedded nature of the talk, names of objects are often substituted by "this" and "that", "go like this", "put like this". As found by Svendsen & Krebs (1984), nothing is expressed that cannot be seen. After the new housekeepers have mastered the routine tasks the job involves, descriptions and explanations are even less useful; housekeepers can go about their work with almost no need to speak, with the only item to read being their room-assignment sheet, and the only items to write being the times at which they start and finish a room, whether the safe box was opened, etc., on the same assignment sheet.

A day in the life of day-shift hotel maids at this hotel in Waikiki goes as follows: They arrive at the hotel, check their time cards at the clock located in the hall and change into their uniform in the locker room, where they place their belongings in a locker. They pick up their keys and room assignments (a sheet with the occupancy on their floor, names and number of guests, checkouts, etc.) at the house-keeping room, and join the rest of the maids in the dining-room, where they have some free coffee and chat until briefing time. Speakers of the same language tend to group together and converse in their native language. (This was a fact that seemed to bother some people, as indicated at a meeting by one member of the task force: "They don't want to learn English. If there's one who speaks a little English they'll rely on her for everything. They all hang out in their little groups. We're trying to break that up."). The executive house-keeper, Chris, comes into the dining room at 8:00 am and the morning briefing takes place. The briefing is in English, and Chris makes sure that there is at least one supervisor or assistant house-keeper (fairly proficient speakers of English) at each table, so they can translate and/or explain to the maids in case they find themselves unable to understand what Chris is saying.

After the briefing, the maids go to the housekeeping room to get their pagers (everybody carries one) and their keys and room assign-ments if they have not yet done so. Since they will have left every-thing ready for the next day (towels, sheets, supplies, etc.) at the end of their previous shift, they are ready to go straight to their floors. A particular floor is assigned to a housekeeper, and her daily workload is the cleaning of sixteen rooms on that floor. The amount of work required for each room is variable, depending on the type of room (single, double, extra beds added, children staying, etc.) and whether it is a checkout room or not. At one end of each floor there is a small room, a closet, where the housekeeper's cart is kept; there are also shelves of linens, towels, and other items, as well as cleaning supplies. Housekeepers are responsible for replenishing these items every day after they finish their rooms and before they go home, so as to avoid wasting time next day trying to collect all the needed supplies before work. The room-assignment sheet allows them to know the number and size of sheets, towels, and supplies (shampoo, hand lotion, shower caps, etc.) they will need to place on their carts.

Once they have packed their carts with everything they need, they go to the rooms, knock on the door and say "Housekeeping", wait a few seconds, and repeat the procedure before opening the door with their own key. They open the door slowly while saying "Hello", and, once they are convinced that the room is empty, they open the door wide, get the vacuum cleaner into the room, and station the cart in front of the door as if blocking it, a safety procedure specified in the housekeepers' manual. A complete, step-by-step set of the tasks involved in the process of cleaning rooms is included in this manual, which is given to the housekeepers during the initial session on procedures and safety measures. Cleaning routines as well as bed-making procedures are taught during the training period and their mastery encouraged, since they are designed to reduce time, effort and fatigue. Participant observation allowed me to witness that the housekeepers do in fact follow this routine in every room they clean.

At lunch time, which consists of 30 minutes between 11:00 am and 1:00 pm, the housekeepers usually sit together with speakers of the same language, share food and chat. After lunch they continue working until they finish cleaning their sixteen rooms, which usually occurs around 4:00 pm. Before heading down to the housekeeping room, they make sure that they leave everything ready for the next working day. They return their keys, pagers and assignment sheets to the supervisors at the housekeeping room, check their time cards, and head back home. These last activities are not performed silently, as the housekeepers turn the end of a day's work into an opportunity to socialize in their own languages.

Participant observation showed that the job of day-shift house-keepers occurs in solitude, with very few situations in which the need for English language arises. By the time they go up to clean their rooms, most of the guests have left, and even encounters with the few guests still around do not require more language than short greetings ("Hi", "Hello", "Good morning/afternoon").

While doing the participant observation, my informants (the hotel maids I had been paired up with) and I engaged in conversation. They were usually interested in my personal life, and willing to talk about their own. This is an important aspect pointed out by Gold-stein (1992), related to how newcomers are incorporated in the workplace network, and how friendships are formed and become the basis for support in the workplace. (See, also, Holmes, this volume.) Unstructured interviews were conducted between conversations about families and lives outside the workplace, including questions about the need for English in their work and the problems related to their lack of English proficiency, as well as what they thought it would be useful to learn in an English class. Conversations between my informants and myself, interactions that the housekeepers go through, and paged messages they receive in a day's work, were all tape-recorded. Morning briefings were tape-recorded, as well, and the desk clerk answering the phone in the housekeeping room was recorded during a one-hour session, too. These phone calls were mostly from guests who had some requests for the housekeeping department, or from housekeepers who were requesting something or reporting room discrepancies.

Triangulation and comparisons of sources and methods

Participant observation proved to be the most useful method, allowing me to experience first-hand the tasks involved in being a hotel maid, as well as the language and situations involved. Because it gave me access to various sources in similar situations, participant observation allowed me to triangulate sources and interpret discrepancies amongst sources' different perceptions of the same situation or issue. It also made it possible to confirm or disconfirm outsiders' predictions, as well as to explain some of those predictions. Sandra, for example, who had once dressed and worked as a housekeeper for a day to learn about their situations and language needs, had stated she was "amazed at how much interaction goes on with the guests" (personal communication). I, conversely, was amazed at how little interaction was going on between my informants and the guests, and between myself and the guests (see Appendix C).

In qualitative field work one must look for recurring patterns not only of what happens during observations but also of what does not happen, and try to understand why people do what they do (Wolcott, 1995). This led me to notice that the interactions between the guests and myself usually occurred after I made eye contact with them and smiled while keeping eye contact, a deliberate effort on my part to encourage interaction. Even this effort, however, did not result in anything more than a simple greeting, thus casting doubt on Sandra's generalization. An interpretation of this difference is that quite possibly Sandra was the one initiating the interactions, not to mention the fact that her physical appearance must have been an unusual sight in this environment. Sandra is an obviously Caucasian woman while the great majority of the housekeepers, as mentioned before, are Filipino, Chinese, Korean, and Vietnamese. I am not suggesting racist attitudes here, but rather an assumption on the part of guests that the housekeepers cannot speak English, and that, therefore, they choose not to interact unless they have a need. Because it must have seemed so obvious that Sandra could speak English, they probably felt more inclined to interact with her. (At this point, it should be mentioned that I am not, and do not look, Caucasian, a fact that could have led guests to believe that I was in fact a housekeeper, unable to speak much English). Neither am I implying that the housekeepers are unfriendly, or that they do not smile at the guests. My informants in fact smiled a lot, but one could hardly expect them to go out of their way to create opportunities for conversation, when they had sixteen rooms waiting to be cleaned.

Several task force predictions were cast in doubt by the results of participant observation. One situation, the one correct prediction, occurred twice: guests with no key asking to be let into their rooms. The prediction for the language most likely to be used by the guest (and heard by the housekeeper) was "But this is my room", spoken by an adult in an argumentative tone, to which the appropriate responses could be "Can you please run your key through the door?", "I need to see / check / be sure / verify that this is your room.", "I'm sorry, it's for your safety." and a suggestion that, if the guest continued arguing, the housekeeper should leave and call security. In the two cases in which this situation arose the guests were actually children who behaved more politely than the task force had predicted. The first situation arose during the day shift, when an approximately ten-year-old girl came back to her room and found nobody in. Josy (the day-shift housekeeper I was shadowing) and I were in the room across the hall, and the girl asked Josy, "Could you please open the door? (pointing to her door). My grandfather is not here." Josy, a fairly proficient speaker of English, just looked at her assignment sheet, verified that the guests in the particular room included a child, and opened the door for her. Notice that the prediction made by the task force was incorrect not only in the type of interlocutor and the tone of the request, but also in that they did not even consider that the guest might give an explanation for making such a request – in this case the girl explaining why she was asking to be let into the room.

The second instance occurred during the evening shift. A group of soccer players (three 13- and 14-year-old boys) came back to their rooms before the person in charge (and holding the key) did. The following is an excerpt from a rather lengthy conversation:

Boy 1:   Can you guys open it? (talking to Kris, the evening-shift house-keeper, and me, pointing at his door).
Kris: No. Sorry.
Boy 1:   But it's our room.
Kris: Can you call front desk? . . . They open it for you.
Boy 2:   What?
Kris: There's a phone over there (pointing at the phone at the end of the hall).
Boy 3:   What do we say, can you show us how to do it?
Kris: Just . . .

Boy 1:   How long will it take?

Kris: ... the room number (she tries to tell them what to say when calling the front desk, as they fight over who should make the phone call; they go to the phone and return to the cart).

Boy 1:   Today somebody just opened it for me.

Boy 3:   Can we show you like ... our names are there ... or ... look, I got something here (he shows Kris some kind of ID).

Boy 2:   Oh yeah! Oh let me tell you what's inside

Boy 3:   Look ... look ... right here ...I'm in the room (showing an ID with his name)... I don't know if you have like ... a list with names of people staying in the room.

The conversation continues for a while. The point is that, although the one prediction for this situation made by the task force was correct, it fell very short of providing an account of the type and amount of interaction and negotiation that occurred.

These two examples may lead us to reconsider Bell's prediction of the six highly plausible interactions, and his statement about customers' reactions tending to keep fairly close to the predicted behavior. As a source, the task force relied heavily on intuitions about hypothetical situations related to the task force members' own domains, and theorized about the language used in such situations. Their predictions concerning situations for small talk/greetings and closing a conversation with guests did not materialize during my participant observations. In cases of emergencies, however, people in specific departments do expect housekeepers who report them to use some formulaic language, especially in the area of safety. Whether this formulaic language is used or not remains unknown; these are situations which almost never arise.

Participant observation also led to the identification of sources which had not been considered initially, like the morning briefings and the housekeeping room. It was while working with my informants that the usefulness of the paged messages as a source of language needs became obvious, and I realized that while working with one informant would provide access to the messages she received, tape-recording the messages in the housekeeping room would provide access to the messages sent to all housekeepers in the hotel. This confirms the emergent nature of qualitative research, where the "selection strategy evolves as the researcher collects data" (Glesne and Peshkin, 1992, p. 25). In naturalistic inquiry, rarely does the researcher have a prespecified study design or a set of prespecified questions; responses to initial questions lead to new questions, and, coupled with observations, they allow discovery of alternative and complementary sources and methods which initially would have not been considered or even thought of (Glesne & Peshkin, 1992; Wolcott, 1995).

The following are examples of language used in paid messages to maids (1) and the language used to deal with guests' phone requests (2, 3) in the housekeeping room (for more examples see Appendix D). (XXX indicates unclear speech or difficult-to-transcribe words; the speaker is an evening supervisor, Celina):

(1) (Name), 719 would like service now. Room 719 service now. Thank you. Room XXX needs clean sheets.
(2) Good evening, housekeeping, Celina. Yes yes yes ... they want roll-away bed? OK, bye bye (she hangs up and pages the runner). The bedroom 602 need roll-away bed, 602 roll-away bed. Thank you.
(3) Good evening, housekeeping, Celina ... mhm ... two coffee mugs, OK ... Pardon? ... No it's not free, we just let you borrow ... OK thanks (hangs up and pages the runner). XXX also bring two coffee mugs in room 2706 ... two coffee mugs in room 2706. Thank you.

Although these requests usually go to the runner[2] first, what makes them very important as a source is that they are the type of request with which the guests approach the maids if they see them, before calling housekeeping.

Morning briefings were undoubtedly the most important source of English for the housekeepers. The issues dealt with at these meetings ranged from those strictly related to their daily work (like supplies and guests) to institutional information (such as surveys and new policies) and institutional 'bonding' (like reciting the company's values and practicing Christmas carols). Problems related to personal feelings and touchy situations on the job also have an important place in these meetings, making them potentially very rich situations for language learning and language socialization (see the excerpt from Sakamaki's briefing below). The following are excerpts of some of the briefings, conducted at the main branch by the executive housekeeper (Chris) and an assistant housekeeper (Maria), and by supervisors (Janet and Sakamaki) at a smaller branch of the hotel chain.

Chris:
OK I talk to XXX manager. Remember you folks brought up yesterday about the XXX combination, yeah? ... We have been ordering extra linen because is almost like four people per room, yeah? Four- four teenagers per room, OK? ... And it's a lot ... just ... take the stuff off the beds and put them back... as far as vacuuming ... if you cannot you cannot ... OK? ... because ... we cannot expect you to pick up and move their XXX bags and move all their shoes because that's four people yeah? ... If only one or two guests, no problem, but four, yeah?

Maria:
OK ... you can call in sick, yeah? ... Please try to call one day before in order that we ... will call for replacement, yeah? Right away ... cause it's very hard if you call us and let us know "I will call it back later" ... then try to re-do the schedule, yeah? Especially late at night when nobody, Chris, Lina or XXX are no here, yeah?

Janet:
Very good. OK let's make the briefing short. We got a couple of things more for you. Regarding supplies ... please, when you service your room, double check: toilet paper, kleenex, soap, shampoo. We're still getting calls from the guests early in the morning no more ... OK? ... always should have ... back up ... tissue paper, toilet paper, yeah? So please, take good care of your guests, OK?

Sakamaki:
... If you really need XXX or comments, please comment ... please comment with a supervisor, no ... no talking to other people ... OK? ... If you think is not right, is not fair, so ... XXX schedule and you now you talking to everybody ... please comment ... for example, Marasita, for example, "Ah is not fair how come I get too much check out and she only gets two." I talk to Marasita and Marasita not gonna help ... right? ... So you gotta go see who can help you out the problem ... OK? ... Understand, yeah?

Unstructured interviews provided more and better quality information than questionnaires. As mentioned before, questions to the housekeepers were asked informally, more as part of casual conversations during our work together, thus allowing me to begin the process of building rapport with my informants and developing trust, both crucial aspects of qualitative research (Glesne & Peshkin, 1992). The following responses provide some insight into various sources' perceptions of the need for English at work.

Josy (day-shift housekeeper):
Researcher: Do you think that to do your work, you need to speak English very well?
Josy: No (without hesitation). You mean the housekeepers?
Researcher: Yes, for example, for your job. How much do you use English?
Josy: Ah ... (she keeps working while she seems to be thinking).
Researcher: That you have to use English.
Josy: You have to (repeating my words) ... Ah! (seems to suddenly remember) because talk the guest, yeah? But they don't understand too English, yeah? They say, "Yes, yes, yes." You know, the Chinese, like that.
Researcher: And does that sometimes create problems?
Josy: Yeah problem, because they don't understand the ...

Lao (evening housekeeper in charge of the public area):
Because some guests, yeah, they asking me, you know uh uh plenty questions but I cannot answer. Some guests, they listen, yeah? They say, "Oh, you no talk nice." But I tell, you know, if you go English class, yeah, you can talk nice and you ... and when they listen, they feel comfortable. If no, you English class, yeah? You English no good, yeah? Some thinking like that, you know. I like help people, you know, but sometimes you don't understand. It's hard.

Celina (an evening supervisor):
... usually we just show it (the job) to them and they just follow, how to clean ... not too much problem ... they (the maids) get evaluated ... cleaning, bodysavers (procedures to increase safety, efficiency, and to reduce fatigue). Good in cleaning is what is important.

Sandra (the human resources person):
The reason we have an English program starting is the hotel's focusing on more guests services and trying to be friendly and be a host to everybody, to have each employee be a host to each guest rather than "Oh it's the front desk job to greet people and if I'm a housekeeper, I can just say hello and that's it." The way the company puts it, "to show our *aloha*[3]." Sometimes we get, ah, negative comments cards (regarding the housekeepers) They say things like "I asked for this and I didn't get it." But mostly is like "And can't you even get staff that speak English?" More like whiny, irritated.

Chris (the executive housekeeper):
To be able to explain to the guest that either because of their English or their understanding they're not able to help them, but maybe they can refer them or put them on the phone with the managers, you know, at least tell them that. If they can just put the guests at ease and let them know that although I cannot help you, I can have someone help. Yeah, that would be it. I'm sure the guests wouldn't be upset about that. As for emergencies, they know what to do. They know what to say. I think the more we practice with them, the more they will feel comfortable. Like towards the afternoon, when the guests will be coming back, even. You know. If you tell them just "Hi," they'll say something else, you know. "Hi, how are you today? I'm fine." And it goes on. You know (laughs) They [the housekeepers] might shy away from that. I don't want them to be worried about what the guests might say.

Josy's, Lao's, Celina's, Sandra's and Chris' responses are a clear example of the differences in perceptions that different sources can have of the same phenomenon (Cumaranatunge, 1988), and of how those perceptions can vary according to whether they are insiders or outsiders. It is clear that Josy, a fairly proficient English speaker, does not perceive English as necessary for the housekeeping job, nor regards chit-chatting with guests as part of her work. Celina seems to agree with Josy when she asserts that "Good in cleaning is what is important." Josy also hints that this pressure to talk to guests can generate problems since there are some guests who are not English speakers and engage in conversation when they in fact do not understand what the maid is asking or saying. Lao's perceptions of interactions with the guests as necessary for her job make sense for two reasons: the evening shift operates a schedule when the majority of the guests come back from the beach and get ready for dinner, and the public area includes places where there is constant traffic of guests, like the lobby, the front desk, the conference rooms, the halls, and the bathrooms. This causes Lao to have substantially more contact with guests than any of the day-shift housekeepers. Sandra, an outsider representing institutional interests who has no experience working as a housekeeper, seemed to regard the need for the maids to chit-chat as the most relevant need, while Chris, also an institutional representative, offered a different, more on-target perspective of the maids' English needs in their work. This should not be a surprise, however, for Chris is hardly an outsider. The executive housekeeper is at the top of the housekeeping hierarchy, with housekeeper assistants and supervisors between her position and the hotel maids. Her work involves a great deal of knowledge and performance of those occupations, besides interviewing and hiring new personnel and acting as a liaison between housekeeping and the rest of the departments. In part because of the nature of the job, and perhaps also because of Chris' personality (very involved with, and supportive of, the housekeepers), she is well aware of what goes on in a housekeeper's job on a daily basis, which makes her able to understand and share the insiders' perceptions. Also, it is not unusual for housekeepers to come to her with language questions related to dealing with doctors and other situations outside the workplace (personal communication). In addition, she is the person in charge of dealing with guests' complaints, which gives her an insight into their needs in terms of services provided by the housekeepers. It is this combination of knowledge that makes her responses more elaborated and focused on concrete facts, as compared to the responses from some other sources. Chris fits several criteria for Selinker's good informant: "... a NS, well trained and competent in the field of interest, used to dealing with NNSs attempting to function in that domain, caring about their success in doing so, able to explain what experts in the domain do, and willing to revise initial answers after follow-up questions if wrong the first time ... should have a feel for the technical language in the domain, an openness to language teaching and LSP" (Selinker, 1979). Chris was aware of how little interaction goes on between guests and maids, and also of the background knowledge and pragmatics involved in chit-chatting, which makes casual conversation more complex than it seems – a fact that can discourage the housekeepers in their language efforts. For both reasons, she did not regard it as a major need the way Sandra did. During the interviews, she often expressed a desire to help the housekeepers succeed at the job, although this desire was expressed rather in institutional than personal terms: "We want them to succeed."

The following responses address the question of what it was thought would be useful to learn in an English class. This question was oriented towards investigating the various sources' perceptions of the housekeepers' language needs.

Chris:
Work terminology, only because XXX they have a lot of communication with the clerk, and most of the XXX, the guest requests or discrepancies uh one example would be the parts of the XXX, the knob, the light bulb, the switch, whatever, outlet. We use the terminology that the guest would most likely use from the mainland. For example, we call uh the lanai (a Hawaiian word) 'lanai', whereas the guests call it 'balcony', so they (the housekeepers) should know both. I'm not saying that they should use the other term, but they should know both.

Kris (the evening-shift housekeeper in charge of rooms and non-public areas such as offices):
... to learn about the hotel, name of things. Some people don't know how to say it, like toilet paper. To practice the things in the hotel.

Lao:
Simple English like "go see doctor", yeah? Then uh, "Meet a friend". You know. I just want learn the simple English. You know. When we go travel, we need English. Oh, you know, where I stay now, you know, I need to go somewhere, you know, "Can you tell me, you know, this hotel?" You know.

Lao also mentioned the questions that guests usually ask her: "Where's the market?", "Where's ABC store?" (a popular souvenir store chain), "How can I get to Ala Moana?" (a very large shopping center), "What bus I take?", "Where can I eat the Chinese food ... the good ... the good one?", questions about safety of Honolulu, oh "Here at night 11 o'clock, can you go outside? Is dangerous?" You know, like that.

Again, discrepancies between Lao's and Chris' perceptions can be explained by the nature of their jobs. Chris' job takes place mainly in empty rooms and offices, which makes knowing names of items more necessary than knowing how to answer guests' questions. In addition, Lao's English proficiency is higher than Chris', a fact that could make her ready, and willing, to learn language beyond what is needed for the job. Chris agrees with Chris and once again offers a more on-target perspective when she suggests the need for housekeepers to learn the names of things and the terminology used by the guests. Appendix D shows that many of the interactions in the housekeeping room involve requests of specific items.

Questionnaires provided little information related to either language or tasks, confirming Long's assertion that domain experts (in this case, the housekeepers) who have reliable introspections about language are exceptions, not the rule (although, admittedly, these domain experts were ESL speakers, and the questionnaires were in English). The questionnaires were administered during three morning briefings, with Chris going over each question and having a supervisor or assistant housekeeper help at each table. Not surprisingly, there were several questionnaires which had similar answers, probably what the housekeepers had had explained or suggested to them by the supervisor at their table.

Responses to the questionnaires followed certain patterns according to nationality. All the Filipino housekeepers, for example, answered "yes" to question 4 (Did you study English in your home country?) and questions 8 and 9 (Do you speak English now? Do you speak English at work?), and reported not having any problems communicating with co-workers or guests (questions 11a, b, c). Most of the non-Filipino housekeepers, on the contrary, answered "no" to question 4 and left question 8 unanswered, or answered "a little", yet more than two thirds did not report having difficulties communicating (in English) with co-workers or guests (questions 9 and 11a, b, c). The English proficiency of the Filipino housekeepers varied, but it was higher than that of the rest of the housekeepers. Thus a similar answer among speakers of markedly different language proficiency is a discrepancy to be accounted for. A plausible explanation would depend on the language they use; if they communicate with co-workers using either a shared native language or Hawaii Creole English (HCE or 'Pidgin'), which most of the housekeepers (including the Filipinas) seem to speak better than so-called 'standard' English, then there seems to be no reason for having communication problems. Where communication with guests is concerned, if most of their communication is reduced to simple greetings, then it is understandable that they do not perceive any difficulty. This suggests more evidence of the unreliability of (many) learners' perceptions regarding their language needs.

Most housekeepers indicated their daily room assignment sheets and the surveys that the hotel conducts among workers as both reading and writing needs for the job (questions 12–15). Some indicated Saturday briefings and newspapers as reading needs as well. A variety of items were specifically indicated in answers to question 18 (What would you like to learn in an English class?): "writing," "spelling," "vocabulary," "correct grammar," "improve speaking," "learn everything at work." How many of these are objective needs and how many subjective needs or 'wants' (Long, this volume; R. West, 1994) cannot be determined, since it is difficult to know exactly what is meant by such responses as "improve speaking" and "correct grammar." They could refer to 'standard' English, which Lao hints at in a statement of hers about the need to learn to "talk nice," and which Chris clearly refers to in some of her comments on what the maids should learn.

Most of the housekeepers' co-workers' answers to their question-naires did not report any difficulty in communicating with the house-keepers (questions 6 and 8). However, all of them expressed a need for the maids to take English classes (question 12) "so they can understand", "so we can communicate", "improve English lan-guage", etc. These answers show a discrepancy which can only be partially accounted for with the same explanation given above for the housekeepers' answers (the use of HCE or 'Pidgin' facilitates communication between co-workers and housekeepers). It is possible that when co-workers answered "yes" to question 6 (Do you ever speak English to the housekeepers?), and "no" to question 8 (Is it difficult communicating with them in English?), they may have meant HCE (which is, after all, a variety of English) and 'standard' English when they answered question 12. This may explain why co-workers implied difficulty in understanding and communicating with the housekeepers (question 12) after denying such difficulty in questions 8 and 9, and it may imply a perception on their part of the housekeepers' need to learn 'standard' English. This explanation would agree with Lao's and Chris' perceptions mentioned above. These interpretations, however, remain speculative.

One particular questionnaire was quite informative in regards to the view of an outsider (the assistant general manager) as to the maids' language needs. This individual perceived the maids as able to 'get by' with their English skills, a fact that probably reflects the general feeling, and explains why most co-workers and maids did not perceive communication difficulties. This person also took into account the need for a "better command of the language" not only in the workplace but outside, as well, and seemed quite aware of the frustration that Lao expressed when she reported being unable to understand what guests wanted or liked.

A point of concern regarding the questionnaires was the number of questions that were not answered. Most housekeepers left questions 19–29, which refer to language use and needs outside the workplace, unanswered. A plausible explanation may be language difficulty, which highlights the importance of using the native language for written introspections. Lack of time may have played a role as well: the questionnaires were answered during morning briefings, which usually had a packed agenda. The lack of response to so many questions also highlights the importance of piloting questionnaires.

Conclusion

This study has shown the value of using multiple sources and methods for identifying learners' needs, the general reliability of insiders, and the frequent unreliability of outsiders. Participant observation proved to be crucial not only for familiarizing the researcher with the tasks and language involved in the maids' work, but also for identifying more sources, and triangulation allowed identification of the most reliable ones. This is bad news for applied linguists who make a living out of materials design and curriculum development based on their and other outsiders' intuitions: they are likely not providing their students with a realistic picture of the types of tasks, interlocutors, interaction patterns, and background knowledge involved.

The use of multiple sources also showed that different actors in a social setting have different perceptions of similar tasks and situations, which leads them to different objective and felt needs. Conflicts are bound to arise because their views often differ, and because the actors involved do not hold the same power in social settings. In this study, for example, it was found that the language necessary for the tasks that the hotel maids have to perform in their job is very limited, and a lack of English language skills does not affect their performance. Conversely, institutional representatives perceive a need for the housekeepers to develop better language skills that will allow them to engage in 'chit-chatting' with guests to show the company's 'aloha', a strategy geared towards increasing business. This should lead us as researchers and curriculum designers to reflect on "the very obvious question of whose needs are we concerned with and how they are determined" (Chambers, 1980, p. 26).

That an institutional need – clearly not perceived as such by the housekeepers – can be the motivation behind establishing a task force, a curriculum, and a language course, is a clear example of how power can be exercised in decision-making. Needs analyses are usually the result of institutional mandates, and are usually paid for with institutional money, but there is also the issue of who pays for language training. In this study, the company believed that the cost should be shared by itself and the housekeepers, on the basis that it would provide benefits to both (human resources person, personal communication). However, language training that does not meet the needs of students is a recipe for failure from the standpoint of motivational factors, and plain unfair when one considers that the housekeepers would be paying with both money and time.

There is no implication here that English language training is unnecessary or undesirable, and I would like to remind the reader of Goldstein's (1992) suggestion of looking at the larger picture to find needs that must be addressed in order to expand students' options in English-speaking societies. In conducting a NA, it is necessary to examine the social context in which actors live their lives critically, as well as the power differentials involved. As researchers and curriculum designers, we must strive for a critical perspective based on dialogue with, rather than observation and manipulation of, people (Comstock, 1982).

The use of qualitative research methods, and, more specifically, of ethnography, can help achieve this goal, by taking into account the social context of people's lives, and by allowing them to express their own voice and needs, as opposed to the researcher's, or the institution's. Although the study reported here was not an ethnography, the use of several qualitative research methods, multiple sources, and triangulation allowed for inclusion of learners' voices. These voices clearly disagreed with institutional needs and interpretations, and expressed their own. Further ethnographic research is suggested in order to identify language and literacy needs the housekeepers have outside the workplace, to create a curriculum that will truly engage them in language learning, so as to allow them to become active and functional members of an English-speaking society (Goldstein, 1992), not merely cheap labor capable of reporting cleaning discrepancies in their rooms and greeting guests in 'standard' English.

Acknowledgment

The author wishes to thank the University of Hawai'i's Department of Second Language Studies for its support. Special thanks to Professor Mike Long for his encouragement and advice.

Notes

1 This is a revised and expanded version of the paper with the same title that first appeared in *English for Specific Purposes* 18, 1, 1999, 27–46.
2 The runner is an employee who is dispatched to the rooms to deliver items requested by the guests.
3 *Aloha* is a Hawaiian word with several meanings. In this context, it would indicate the company's friendliness and desire/effort to make the guests feel at home and have a pleasant stay.

References

Auerbach, E. R. (1995). The politics of the ESL classroom: Issues of power in pedagogical choices. In R. Tollefson (ed.), *Power and inequality in language education*. Cambridge: Cambridge University Press.

Bell, R. T. (1981). *An Introduction to Applied Linguistics: Approaches and Methods in Language Teaching* (Appendix A). London: Batsford.

Chambers, F. (1980). A re-evaluation of needs analysis in ESP. *The ESP Journal* 1, 1, 25–33.

Comstock, D. E. (1982). A method for critical research. In E. Breedo & W. Seinberg (eds.), *Knowledge and Values in Social and Educational Research*. Philadelphia: Temple University Press.

Cumaranatunge, L. (1988). An EOP case study: Domestic aids in West Asia. In Chamberlain & Baumgardner (eds.), *ESP in the Classroom: Practice and Evaluation*, (pp. 127–33). ELT Document 128. London and Oxford: The British Council in Association with Modern English Publications (Macmillan).

Davis, K. A. (1992). Validity and reliability in qualitative studies. Another researcher comments. Research Issues. *TESOL Quarterly* 26, 3, 605–8.

Drobnic, K., Trimble, L. & Trimble, M. T. (eds.) (1978). Mistakes and modifications in course design: An EST case history, in *English for specific purposes: Science and technology*, 313–321. English Language Insitute, Oregon State University, Corvallis: Ore.

Glesne, C. & Peshkin, A. (1992). *Becoming qualitative researchers: An introduction*. White Plains, NY: Longman.

Goldstein, T. (1992). Language choice and women learners of English as a second language. In K. Hall, M. Bucholtz & B. Moonwoman (eds.), *Locating Power: Proceedings of the Second Berkeley Women and Language Conference*, Berkeley, CA: Berkeley Women and Language Group.

Long, M. H. (1985). A role for instruction in second language acquisition: Task-based language teaching. In K. Hyltenstam & M. Pienemann (eds.), *Modeling and assessing second language development*. (pp. 77–99). Clevedon, Avon: Multilingual Matters.

Long, M. H. (to appear). *Task-based language teaching*. Oxford: Blackwell.

Prince, D. (1984). Workplace English: Approach and analysis. *The ESP Journal* 3, 2, 109–15.

Ramani, E., Chacko, T., Singh, S. J., & Glendinning, E. H. (1988). An ethnographic approach to syllabus design: A case study of the Indian Institute of Science, Bangalore. *The ESP Journal* 7, 81–90.

Selinker, L. (1979). The use of specialist informants in discourse analysis. *International Review of Applied Linguistics* 17, 2, 189–215.

Svendsen, C., & Krebs, K. (1984). Identifying English for the job: Examples from the health care occupations. *The ESP Journal* 3, 153–64.

Tollefson, J. W. (1989). *Alien winds: The reeducation of America's Indochinese refugees.* New York: Praeger.

Tollefson, J. W. (1991). *Planning language, planning inequality.* New York: Longman.

Watson-Gegeo, K. (1988). Ethnography in ESL: Defining the essentials. *TESOL Quarterly* 22, 4, 575–92.

West, L. (1984). Needs assessment in occupation-specific VESL or how to decide how to teach. *The ESP Journal* 3, 143–52.

West, R. (1994). Needs analysis in language teaching. *Language Teaching* 27, 1, 1–19.

Wolcott, H. (1995). *The art of fieldwork.* Newbury Park, MA: Sage.

Appendix A: Housekeepers' questionnaire

Name_____

  1. Where are you from?
  2. What language do you speak?
  3. How many years did you go to school in your home country?
  4. Did you study English in you home country?   Yes_____ No_____
  5. How long have you been in the United States?
  6. How long have you been working as a housekeeper?
  7. What things do you do every day at work?
  8. Do you speak English now?
  9. Do you speak English at work?   Yes_____ No_____
 10. If you answered No, why not?
 11. If you answered Yes,
       a) Who do you speak English with?
       b) When do you speak English with them?
       c) Is it difficult communicating with them?
 12. Do you sometimes need to read English at work?   Yes_____ No_____
 13. If you answered Yes, what do you need to read?
 14. Do you sometimes need to write in English at work? Yes_____ No_____
 15. If you answered Yes, what do you need to write?
 16. Have you ever studied English in the United States? Yes_____ No_____
 17. Would you like to study English?   Yes_____ No_____
 18. If you answered Yes, what things would you like to learn in your
       English class?
 19. Do you speak English outside the job?   Yes_____ No_____
 20. If you answered Yes, when do you speak English?
 21. Does somebody help you with English when you go
       shopping, or when you go to the doctor, etc.?   Yes_____ No_____
 22. If you answered Yes, who helps you?
 23. What language do you speak at home with your family and friends?
 24. Do you have children?   Yes_____ No_____
       How many?
       What languages do they speak?
 25. Are your children in school?   Yes_____ No_____
 26. Do you sometimes go to meetings at your children's school?
 27. Can you understand what teachers and parents
       say at those meetings?   Yes_____ No_____
 28. Does somebody help you with English at those
       meetings?   Yes_____ No_____
 29. Did somebody help you answer this questionnaire? Who?

Appendix B: Co-workers' questionnaire

Occupation_____

1. Do you speak English?
2. What things do you do every day at work?
3. For reasons of work, do you need to speak with
   the housekeepers?   Yes_____ No_____
4. If you answered Yes, please describe the work situations in which you need to speak to them.
5. In what language do you speak to them? Please write as many languages as you use.
6. Do you ever speak English to the housekeepers?   Yes_____ No_____
7. If you answered Yes, in what situations?
8. Is it difficult communicating with them in English? Yes_____ No_____
9. If you answered Yes, can you explain the difficulties?
10. Do the housekeepers sometimes need to read messages
    from you, or write messages to you in English?   Yes_____ No_____
11. If you answered Yes, can you explain in what situations?
12. Based on you experience working at the hotel and with the house-keepers, what do you think it would be good for them to learn in an English class? What do you think are the languages that they need to learn most? Please give as many examples as you can think of. Thank you.

Appendix C: Examples of interactions with guests

Examples of interactions with guests that occurred during the five sessions of participant observation (interactions already included in the paper, such as those with guests asking to be let into their rooms, are not repeated here).

Interactions with guests during day-shifts. None of these interactions occurred because the guests stopped to chat; they interacted while passing by. FG = female guest; MG = male guest.

(1) MG: Hello.
    Researcher: Hello, how are you.
    FG: Hello, good morning.

(2) MG & FG: Good morning.
    Researcher: Good morning, how are you today.
    MG: Fine, yourself?
    Researcher: Fine thank you. Have a good day.

(3) MG: Finished for the day? (making a gesture)
    Researcher: I wish.
    MG: You wish! (laughs)

Interaction that took place when a guest wanted the maid (Shu) to wait a few more minutes before servicing the room:

(4) Shu: (Knocks on the door). Housekeeping.
    FG (Japanese): (Opens the door) Yes?
    Shu: Housekeeping.
    FG: How about 15 minutes ... we'll go out?
    Shu: OK.

Shu moves to another room, and a few minutes later the guest calls back:

    FG: OK lady.
    Shu: OK. Thank you.

Interaction that took place when two guests (Korean females) returned and their room was still being serviced.

(5) FG: For you (pointing at two dollar bills on the night table).
    Researcher: Oh, thank you.

Interaction that occurred during the evening shift. There was usually a housekeeper and a supervisor working together in the rooms during the evening shift. Chris is the housekeeper, Celina is the supervisor.

(6) Child: Excuse me, do you have a swimming pool?
    Chris: Yes, ten(th) floor.

Interactions that occurred between the housekeeper in charge of the public area (Lao), during the evening shift. There was only one maid working in the public area, and she would be 'pulled out' from her duties there during busy times when extra help was needed in the rooms.

While emptying ashtrays in the lobby:

(7) FG: Hello, how are you.
    Lao: Hi.

In the hall outside the meeting room, with guests coming out of a meeting:

(8) FG: Good evening.
    Lao: Hi, good evening.
    MG: Hello ... you got to clean up (smiling).
    Lao: Yes (she smiles and nods)
    Guest: I know what it is like. I have to do it sometimes.

Interactions while cleaning the women's bathroom in the basement, where there was a new Chinese–Japanese restaurant.

(9) FG 1:   Hello.
    Lao: Hi.
    FG 2:   Hi ... (she hesitates to come in since we are cleaning the floor) am I interrupting something?
    Lao: Hi.
    Researcher: No, just go ahead.

Interaction with the front desk clerk (FDC) when cleaning the front desk area:

(10) FDC: Hi Lao, how are you
    Lao: Hi XXX.
    FDC: How's your son?
    Lao: Very big! ... XXX pounds.
    FDC: Wow! He's soon going to outweight you.
    Lao: Yes! (laughing).
    FDC: (To me) Are you shadowing tonight?
    Researcher: Yeah.

Appendix D: Examples of phone calls and paged messages

Examples of phone calls and paged messages received and sent in the housekeeping room during an evening shift observation.

Examples of paged messages:

(1) (Name), 719 would like services now. Room 719 service now. Thank you.

(2) Room_____ needs clean sheets.

(3) Room_____ needs service. Room_____. Thank you.

(4) Call housekeeping, housekeeping, call housekeeping. Thank you.

Examples of the evening supervisor (Celina) attending phone requests from guests in the housekeeping room. Messages would then be paged to the runner or to the housekeepers:

(5) Good evening, housekeeping, Celina. Yes, yes, yes ... they want roll-away bed? OK, bye bye. (She then hangs up and pages the runner):

(6) The bedroom 602 need roll-away bed, 602 roll-away bed. Thank you.

(7) Good evening, housekeeping, Celina. Pardon me? What ... ah ... what do you want to ... oh we have only toothbrush, toothpaste ... that's all we have complimentary ... no we have only XXX mhm OK ... that's all we have I think. And besides that we have the lobby, we have the store in the lobby where you can buy those things ... we have toothpaste ... and we have toothbrush ... how about toothpaste ... OK ... bye bye.

She hangs up and turns to me "He's asking for deodorant", she says. She pages the runner:

(8) Call housekeeping please call housekeeping. Thank you.

The phone rings, it is the runner who had just been paged:

(9) Good evening, housekeeping, Celina ... XXX OK room 2706 ... ah they like toothbrush and toothpaste and comb.

(10) Good evening, housekeeping, Celina mhm two coffee mugs, OK ... pardon? No it's not free, we just let you borrow ... OK thanks.

Celina pages the runner:

(11) XXX also bring two coffee mugs in room 2706 ... two coffee mugs in room 2706. Thank you.

(12) Good evening, housekeeping, Celina mhm oh OK yeah we have do ...
we have vacuum too OK ... you need the ... to vacuum the carpet?
OK we have some ah some things to XXX up. OK. I'll page my runner
and sen(d) to XXX room XXX right? So you need a vacuum only ...
OK Thanks. (Celina pages the runner)

(13) XXX please bring one vacuum in room 2215, the guest would like to
borrow it. Room 2215 like to borrow vacuum.

(14) Good evening, housekeeping, Celina. Yes Kris ... OK is it occupied
room? OK thanks, bye.

This was a call from Kris, the evening maid, reporting a problem she
had encountered in one room. Celina pages maintenance:

(15) Room 2914 the bathtub stopper is not working ... Room 2914 the
bathtub stopper is not working. Thank you.

Example of Celina calling housekeeping to report discrepancies in a
room while working with Kris:

(16) Celina: 805 you said maid service, yeah? ... it's ah vacant room ... is it
XXX? Double check. (She hangs up and a few minutes later her pager
beeps with the following message):

(17) 805 continental room need to be cleaned before 9 o'clock. 805
continental room need to be cleaned before 9 o'clock.

After hearing the message she turns to Kris:

(18) So they want the room clean, Kris.

Example of Celina responding to the paged message "Call housekeeping, please call housekeeping."

(19) Renato, you paged me. Yeah ... 29? Right now? OK. OK. Goodbye. (A
TV repairer is going up to fix the TV in room 29 and Celina must let
him in and stay with him until he finishes his job.)

Example of Kris paging housekeeping to make a request:

(20) I need one shower curtain, 805.

5 Foreign language need of business firms

Sonja Vandermeeren

Introduction

This paper is organized into four sections. The first section provides a definition of foreign language need in the business context, catalogues types of this need and discusses its indicators. In the second section, some methods that can be employed in need analysis studies are presented. Section three provides illustrative material from two surveys that were carried out in Finland and Germany, respectively. The educational implications of the findings of studies into the foreign language need of companies are then dealt with in the fourth section.

When dealing with language need, terminological and conceptual difficulties arise. Firstly, the terms 'need' and 'needs' are only partially synonymous. The term 'language needs' can refer to language users' and learners' reported need, to what they think they need in relation to language use and training (e.g., better skills in a certain language, less teaching of grammar, etc.). The term 'need', which I use, is primarily used when need is seen as something objective, as something one objectively ought to have. Secondly, the concept of language need cannot be entirely 'objectivized'. It is never totally devoid of subjectivity. In my terminology 'objective need' is based on an objective criterion, not on somebody's opinion (see below). The choice of this criterion is, of course, subjective again. It is a vicious circle.

The concept of foreign language need

Many business activities require the use of foreign languages. Often, foreign language need is determined by commercial factors (for instance, when products need to be sold to potential customers from abroad). The decision not to use the company's local language can also be made for internal communication purposes (for instance, when subsidiaries are to report to their foreign Head Office). One of the reasons for writing manuals and contracts in their receivers' mother tongues is because this prevents those receivers from seeking redress in a court of law for any given ill consequences of their misunderstanding the specialized vocabulary (see Jörissen, 1991, for further discussion on product liability; see also Koch, 1991, p. 148). To compensate for insufficient foreign language proficiency, companies may make use of external resources for translating or interpreting. As a matter of fact, companies may conduct cost/benefit analyses regarding their language use with a certain market. For example, if the market in question is small and the use of its language is not widespread, the benefit from learning its language, or paying for translations, would not exceed the costs involved. On the other hand, when a company believes that using the language of a certain market will decisively optimize their profits, they may decide to do so.

The concept of business firms' foreign language need has many facets, all of which are to be mirrored by its definition. I propose defining it in the following way: The need of business firms for employees whose knowledge of foreign languages and of the cultures that these languages are embedded in suffices for establishing and maintaining business contacts with speakers of these languages (Vandermeeren, 1998, p. 60). The command company representatives have of a foreign language is not only the ability to find the appropriate (technical) word, pronounce/spell it correctly, connect it with other words in a sentence in order to say or write what they mean, but also awareness of the socio-cultural context of that language. Unfortunately, there is often a basic lack of knowledge of the socio-cultural norms native speakers follow and, hence, a misunderstanding of these speakers.

Language need has two dimensions. The quantitative dimension is revealed by asking questions of the following kind: "How often is language X needed?", the qualitative one by posing questions like "Which kind of competence in language X is needed?". Answers to these questions can be obtained from various informants, for instance, from sales/export managers, sales/export employees, or secretaries. Informants' statements are subjective and therefore disagreement-prone. A respondent's claim that his/her company has foreign language need originates in his/her attitudes towards the use, acquisition and perfection of foreign languages (Vandermeeren, in press). A concrete example: In the past British managers did not consider it necessary for their employees to learn foreign languages, due to the status of their mother tongue as an international business language (Reeves, 1985, 1990). In recent years they have come to realize that English alone does not suffice to initiate and consolidate contacts with overseas business firms (Metcalf, 1991).

It must be borne in mind that researchers, too, have attitudes concerning language need, which inevitably influence their choice of research objectives and their interpretation of the findings. Among most language need researchers there is a consensus about the positive effect of the use of foreign languages in corporate settings. As a matter of fact, foreign language skills are regarded as a prerequisite for economic success. Those who believe that a company's linguistic adaptation to its clients will decisively optimize that company's profits put forward the need for a wide range of foreign languages to be known by the company's employees. Others merely require language skills in English of company representatives, and some advocate relying entirely on receptive skills in foreign languages. The former stress the need for English as an extensively and exclusively used lingua franca. The latter see an advantage in shaping international business interactions in the following way. Acting as the originator of a communication, a company representative uses his/her own mother tongue and in the receiver role he/she is able to understand the mother tongue of the originator.

Language need researchers have to make sure that the indicators they want to investigate capture the true complexity of the concept and provide them with a detailed and comprehensive picture of the language need under investigation.

Vandermeeren (1998) describes a large research project, 'Foreign language use in European business' (financed by the German Research Council) established to measure, amongst other things, foreign language use and need in selected companies located in Germany, France, the Netherlands, Portugal and Hungary. The concept of foreign language need was operationalized using four questionnaire variables: the frequency of the companies' contact with foreign business environments, and their perceptions of their foreign language need and unmet foreign language need, as well as the frequency of their foreign language use. These variables drew on the following questions (matrices):

1 How often does your company have business relations with companies in the following countries (0 = never, 1 = occasionally, 2 = regularly)?
2 How often does your company need skills in each of the following languages in order to perform the following communication tasks (0 = never, 1 = occasionally, 2 = regularly)?
3 Does the foreign language proficiency available in your company suffice to perform these communication tasks (0 = no proficiency, 1 = too little, 2 = sufficient)?

4   How often does your company use the following languages in doing business with companies in the following countries (0 = never, 1 = occasionally, 2 = regularly, 3 = (almost) always)?

When used in a one-dimensional manner, the answers to the above questions indicate two types of need. First, the answer relating to the frequency of contact with a certain country indicates *objective need* (frequency of contact is an objective indicator; turnover in a certain national market is also a good objective indicator of language need). Second, informants' perceptions of foreign language need indicates *subjective need* (informants' perceptions are a subjective indicator). By using question 1 and 2 as filters, three more types of need are obtained:

Unconscious need: Companies who are in regular business contact with a certain country and claim that it is not/only occasionally necessary for them to use that country's language have an unconscious language need (= b as a percentage of the sum of b and d as shown in the cross-tabulation).

		objective need (business contact)	
		never/occasionally	regularly
subjective need	never/occasionally	a	b
	regularly	c	d

Objective unmet need: Companies who are in regular business contact with a certain country and do not / only occasionally use that country's language have an objective unmet need.

		objective need (business contact)	
		never/occasionally	regularly
language use	never/occasionally	a	b
	regularly/(almost) always	c	d

Subjective unmet need: Companies who state that it is necessary to use a certain language and that their employees lack (sufficient) skills in that language have a subjective unmet need.

		subjective need	
		never/occasionally	regularly
available language skills	none / too few	a	b
	sufficient	c	d

Empirical data on various indicators of these five distinct kinds of need, taken together, enable us to look at foreign language need of business firms in great detail. To exemplify some indicators more concretely:

- top managers' ideal of how competent their staff should be in a certain foreign language (= subjective need)
- sales managers' claims that their department does not need employees competent in a certain foreign language even though it is in regular business contact with speakers of that language (= unconscious need)
- secretaries' reports of the difficulties they encounter when using a certain foreign language orally or in writing (= subjective unmet need)
- export managers' statements that their department does not use a certain foreign language even though it has regular business contacts with speakers of that language (= objective unmet need)

As noted earlier, the need of companies for foreign languages has many aspects: phonological/orthographical, lexical, grammatical, pragmatic and cultural ones. The above-mentioned types of indicators can be related to all of these aspects, for instance, the subjective unmet need to the cultural aspect (e.g., middle management's statements that cultural barriers prevent joint ventures with companies in foreign countries becoming successful).

The maxim behind the differentiation between these five types of needs, whose indicators should be collectively investigated, is that 'linguistic adaptation is the best strategy to help in closing (good) deals with foreign trading partners; the use of English as a lingua franca is only second best'. There is a general consensus among linguists and non-linguists (e.g., Emmans et al, 1974; King, 1984; Hagen, 1988; Holden, 1989; Pearce, 1991) on the positive effect of linguistic adaptation, especially on export performance ('adaptation' is a term used in international marketing and refers to a company strategy of responding in an adaptive manner to national markets (different products, brands, prices, qualities, advertising campaigns, etc., for different markets)). This is supported by the survey 'Foreign language use in European business' (Vandermeeren, 1998). Alarmingly, French companies who relatively often use English when corresponding with German companies export lower percentages of their goods to Germany than companies who relatively often use German. The correlation is clear; the direction of the causality is not. Does adaptation lead to better export of performance, or do high export percentages lead to more adaptation? The two variables probably interact.

The use of English as a lingua franca, the use of the first language of the business partner, and the use of one's own first language compete with each other. These strategies are not 'all or nothing' phenomena. Most companies mix their strategies of language choice. Hagen (1993, p.10) states that "at the micro-level of companies, transactions are frequently carried out in a mixture of several languages". In addition, at the macro-level of international business communication, certain languages are more commonly used than others, a phenomenon that seems determined by factors such as the number of people who speak them, their potential as a lingua franca, or the purchasing power of their native speakers. For instance, linguistic adaptation is more often pursued with countries which have high involvement in international business activities as producers and purchasers of finished goods and/or providers of services (Holden, 1989). Vandermeeren's (1998) figures show that for both Dutch and German companies the percentage of those using German greatly exceeds the percentage of companies using Dutch. The explanation for this is that most Dutch companies are competent in German and that the use of German as a business language clearly dominates that of Dutch, a fact which is also accepted by the Dutch-speaking companies. In contrast, German is not that often used in German–French business dealings, because the French in general are not as fluent in German as the Dutch are, and because German is no more dominant than French in its use as a business language. In other words, German and French tend to have equal status in international business, whereas Dutch does not. Consequently, in German–French interaction, both sides either use English as a neutral lingua franca, or they use the language of their business counterpart, in a process of 'reciprocal linguistic adaptation'. Moreover, language use has to do with national identity. Not using the language of your business counterpart is, in a way, saying that his or her language, his or her national identity, is less important than yours. Using English as a lingua franca is a solution, but then the answer to the question

"Which socio-cultural norms are to be followed?" is even more complicated than in the case of adaptation: American or British norms? French or German norms?

Lingua franca use in business interaction is often affected by limited sociolinguistic and pragmatic knowledge. Non-native speakers tend to interact in accordance with the socio-cultural norms governing use of their own first language. In order to make sure that their communicative intentions are not misunderstood, business interactants must negotiate with their interlocutors as to which rules govern the conversation between them. In this way, a convergence of norms is achieved (Beneke, 1991, p. 60ff.). Business representatives belonging to a particular network (e.g., car components manufacturers and car manufacturers) who regularly meet and use a lingua franca on these occasions are perfectly able to negotiate a conversational style acceptable to all members. Over the course of regular (written and oral) communications within a network, a style becomes established which transcends cultural and linguistic boundaries (see, also, Firth, 1991, 1995; Pogner, 1999 for further discussion.

> Let there be no mistake: the use of an international language such as English is indispensable for the efficient handling of international affairs, broadly defined. However, it seems to me that the infallibility of English as a universal panacea to problems of cross-cultural communication has been greatly exaggerated. [...] As long as the lingua franca is used in a mechanical (and culturally impoverished) way, with a limited vocabulary, narrowly defined according to clearly understood conventions, then international business – commercial, scientific, technical – can be efficiently conducted. [...] For rich and intimate communication on complex, important issues something more is needed. [...] The solution to it [...] is the acquisition of several foreign languages, indeed the celebration of multilingualism.   (Cohen, 2001, pp. 89–91)

Methods in language need research

The research techniques that can be used in investigations of language needs are many: observation, interview, questionnaire, language test, etc. (see Long, this volume). In this section, I will describe some of the most important ones.

Participant observation

One of the indicators of language need, namely language usage, is directly observable. To prevent the target persons from manipulating their communicative practices for the researcher (Labov, 1978, p. 209), the latter collects data incognito in a natural situation or gathers 'naturalistic' data experimentally. Van Hest & Oud (1990) mention that the Scottish Association for Language Teaching instigated a participant observation of those working in the Scottish tourism sector. Germans, French and Spanish participants, etc., living in the United Kingdom pretended to be tourists in face-to-face interaction with this target group to be able to assess their foreign language skills. While the most naturalistic data may be collected that way, participant observation is an extremely time-consuming method, especially when the goal is statistical representativeness. Moreover, it must be remembered that we are dealing with researchers' perceptions (of, for instance, language competence on the basis of language usage), which do not necessarily reflect objective reality.

Interviews and questionnaires

Interviews and (postal) questionnaires serve to give the researcher a chance to confront informants with open or closed questions about their (or others') language need. Closed questions are easier to analyze and to score than open questions. In structured interviews researchers go through a questionnaire with the informants, who are able to explain and differentiate their answers. A rapid way of investigating language need is provided by scaling techniques, which can easily discriminate among respondents with different opinions. Subjects are asked to agree or disagree with negative and positive items (e.g., agree strongly, agree, undecided, disagree, and disagree strongly). A large portion of (social) psychological literature is devoted to this type of questionnaire and the danger of response bias. There is considerable discussion of the possibility that respondents are generally more inclined to acquiesce to a statement than to disagree with it (Schuman & Presser, 1981, p. 203ff.). Questionnaire-based surveys (Dannerer, 1992; Grinsted, 1993; Hagen, 1988; Vandermeeren, 1998; Verdoodt & Delbeke, 1983) only gain access to informants' real perceptions of language need when they are carried out with extreme methodological care. If questionnaires are sent to companies, a lot of persuasive work has to be done, as well. The informants have to be convinced to complete the questionnaire, in order to raise otherwise low response rates.

Job advertisements

To shed additional light on the foreign language need of companies, their newspaper job advertisements – which mention the foreign language skills required at recruitment – can be analyzed (Claessens, 1988; Drochner & Kirchberg, 1987; Glück, 1992). These analyses are not 100 per cent in accordance with the true situation, as there are a number of positions where foreign languages are tacitly required, and the position to be filled sometimes does not really demand the foreign language skills mentioned, but mentioning them is good for public relations (De Jager & Reunis, 1971).

Language tests

Language tests are educational tools, which are used in the second stage of corporate language audits. The four stages of an audit are as follows:

- identification of foreign language skills required of employees to complete their communication tasks
- determination of the foreign language proficiency of the employees
- comparison of the existing level of command with the required level
- proposal of the educational language policies to be adopted by the company to improve the foreign language proficiency of their employees

Language tests yield qualitative information on language skills. Fishman & Cooper (1978) recommend communicative tests which expose subjects to contextualized linguistic input, drawing on real-life situations. Three questions arise: "Which job situations are to be drawn on?", "How are they to be built into the tests?" and "Can the output be assessed in an objective way?" (van Els et al., 1984, pp. 312–32).

Anonymous questionnaires

The Delphi method gathers information from specialist informants, who are asked to fill out a questionnaire anonymously. They are given access to the answers of their fellow respondents and asked to fill out the questionnaire again in order to allow them to adjust their answers to those of the other respondents. The goal is to reach a general consensus (Atteslander, 1993, p. 172). Martin & Chaney (1992) relied on this method to develop an optimum curriculum for students of Intercultural Business Communication. They used the following respondents: business persons who were faced with cross-cultural communication as part of their jobs, lecturers in intercultural communication, and members of the Academy of International Business (AIB).

Language need analyses

The concept 'foreign language need' provides the theoretical starting point for the two language needs investigations that are presented in this section; (first a quantitative analysis then a qualitative analysis). They are operationalized in the form of a questionnaire that elicits in formation on the above-mentioned different types of language need.

Quantitative German language needs

First, the case of Finland is taken to illustrate the quantitative dimension of language need (Vandermeeren, 2002). A one-page questionnaire, which was written in Finnish and consisted of closed questions, was sent to a random sample of 300 Finnish companies, of which 112 completed it after one mail-shot. The original survey's figures for English and French are not dealt with here; only the numerical findings relative to the following German language needs are provided:

Objective German language need ($n = 112$)

Question: Please indicate how often your company has business relations (export, import, joint ventures, etc.) with companies in Germany: 0 = never, 1 = occasionally or 2 = regularly.

73% of the surveyed companies had regular business relations with Germany, whereas 21% only had occasional dealings. A further 6% of the responding companies were not in contact with German business firms at all.

Subjective German language need ($n = 112$)

Question: How often does your company need German language skills in order to perform the following communication tasks? (0 = never, 1 = occasionally or 2 = regularly)
How often did the responding business firms report the need for German language facilities (to be able to complete the tasks 'correspondence', 'telephone calls' and 'negotiations')?

According to informants' responses, approximately 5.5% of the surveyed companies did not need German language proficiency at all. About 30% claimed to need German occasionally, and some 64.5% regularly (see Table 1 for exact figures for correspondence, telephone calls, and negotiations, respectively).

Table 1 Subjective German language need of Finnish companies (*n* = 112)

Communication task / Need (frequency)	Correspondence	Telephone calls	Negotiations
never	5.6	4.6	6.6
occasionally	31.5	31.2	27.4
regularly	63.0	64.2	66.0

In light of the fact that it is dangerous to make inferences about companies' actual language need from their expressed need, evidence was sought of companies who were not aware of their German language need. As mentioned earlier, the subjective maxim 'Linguistic adaptation is the best strategy in international business' influences the interpretation of the data under investigation. The maxim 'English should be used as a lingua franca' would be equally subjective. Language need can be quantified, but not 'objectivized'. Indicators of need can be objective, but seeing a need is always subjective.

Unconscious German language need

(*n* = 82 companies who maintain regular business contacts with Germany)

Cross-tabulation of objective and subjective German language need indicated that, of the companies who were in regular business contact with Germany, 21.5% claimed only occasionally or never to need German language skills.

Let us now explore the issue of unmet needs.

Subjective unmet need for German language competence

(*n* = 72 companies who see a need for German language facilities)

Of the companies claiming that they regularly needed German language proficiency, approximately 49% stated that they had insufficient or no German language skills.

Some 6% reported a complete lack of skills, whereas close to 43% thought that there were insufficient German skills in the company (see Table 2).

Table 2   Subjective unmet need for German language skills in Finnish companies (*n* = 112)

Communication task / German language skills	Correspondence	Telephone calls	Negotiations
none	4.4	6.3	7.4
insufficient	42.6	41.3	45.6

Objective unmet need for German language competence

(*n* = 82 companies who maintain regular business contacts with Germany)

How many of those companies in regular business contact with Germany claimed that they only occasionally or never used German with German communication partners? Cross-tabulation indicated that this was the case for 24%. It was found that only 4% of the surveyed companies in regular business contact with Germany never used German. 20% merely used it occasionally.

The results of the survey which related to German language need can be summarized as follows. Two thirds of the responding Finnish companies (64.5%) claimed that a need for German language competence arose regularly. Half of those companies (49%) felt that they lacked (adequate) German abilities, which is too high a percentage in light of the maxim that adaptation is the best strategy. The situation was worse than that, however, since the percentage of those needing German language skills exceeded the percentage of those claiming to need them. One fifth of the companies who maintain regular business contact with Germany (21.5%) were unaware of their need for German. In addition, a quarter of the companies in regular business contact with Germany (24%) reported frequencies of German language use that were too low when compared to the frequencies of their business dealings with Germany.

Qualitative German language needs

The second research project presented in this section continues where the first one ended, not only in that it reveals information on qualitative German language need of companies who communicate with German firms, but also because the respondents themselves are German companies. As van Els et al (1984, p. 107) rightly observe: "Never has it been attempted to question the other side, their (future) communicative partners." According to Beamer (1992), intercultural communicative competence should be commented on from the receiver angle, since the communication is exposed to the receiver's socio-cultural norms. I shall look at primarily qualitative language need 'from the other side' by attempting to answer the following questions:

1 Which German language skills (in relation to text types) do they consider to be necessary?
2 Which level of German language command do they consider a prerequisite for successful communication?
3 Do they stress the need for their communication partners to follow German socio-cultural norms?

A two-page questionnaire containing only closed questions was formulated (see Appendix A). It elicited information on the attitudes of German firms towards linguistic and cultural adaptation on the part of their foreign business partners, i.e., subjective German language need, as seen from the German side, and was sent to 50 exporting companies in Schleswig-Holstein (Northern Germany). After one mail-shot, nine had replied. I telephoned the others asking them to complete the questionnaire if possible. A total of 34 did so.

First, let us explore the issue of linguistic adaptation. How did the responding companies evaluate the use of German instead of English by their foreign business partners? The answer was to be given on a six-point scale (1 = very positively to 6 = very negatively). An average rating of 2.5 was obtained. The standard deviation of only 0.9 indicated general agreement on the issue (see Table 3).

How did the respondents rate the use of German instead of English in terms of usefulness (1 = very purposeful to 6 = totally unnecessary)? An average rating was derived for each of the following communication tasks separately:

- inquiry (mean = 3.2)
- offer (3.3)
- order (3.2)
- acknowledgment of order (3.3)

- invoice (3.4)
- complaint concerning delay (3.1)
- explanation of delay (3.1)
- self-introduction (education/position with the company) (2.9)
- company depiction (3.0)
- product depiction (2.8)
- small talk (3.1)
- price/conditions negotiation (2.9)

These results suggested that Schleswig-Holstein companies rated the use of German less favorably on the usefulness dimension than in terms of general evaluation. They had a barely favorable attitude to the usefulness of German, regardless of the communication task or

Table 3   Breakdown of respondents by attitude to German language use
($n = 34$)

1 (very positive attitude)	6 respondents	
2	8 respondents	
3	17 respondents	Mean = 2.5
4	3 respondents	Standard deviation = 0.9
5	0 respondents	
6 (very negative attitude)	0 respondents	

the communicator. They even seemed to think that it did not make more sense for their suppliers to use German (when writing pre-sale documents, like offers) than for their customers (when writing documents, like orders). It is often claimed that adaptation is more typical of seller firms, because it is a prerequisite for successful selling. Interestingly, Vandermeeren (1999, p. 289) found that adaptation is more frequently pursued when writing before-sale documents, such as advertising brochures and catalogues, than when writing after-sale documents, such as confirmations of orders and invoices.

The third question measured respondents' attitudes to dealing with individuals with a limited command of German. The companies who responded to the questionnaire evaluated incorrect (but still intelligible) German language usage in business letters as not really annoying (1 = very annoying to 6 = not annoying at all). Ungrammatical word forms (e.g., wrong declension) (4.7) and incorrect spelling (4.7) scored slightly higher than inexact wording (wrong word (4.3), sentence construction (4.5)) and unsuitable style (e.g., too formal / not formal enough) (4.4).

One can deduce from the answers to the next question that German companies regard knowledge of German (corporate) culture as more useful than German language knowledge (a difference of up to 1 point):

- knowledge of German politics (2.9)
- economic geography of Germany (locations and imported/exported articles) (2.5)
- organizational structure of German companies (departments/company hierarchy) (2.4)
- German corporate culture (negotiating/managerial culture, etc.) (1.8)
- German cultural norms and customs (2.4)

As evident from the above, knowledge of German corporate culture is viewed as most useful.

Respondents also indicated their level of agreement with the following statements concerning linguistic and cultural adaptation (see question 5), via a scale from 1 (strongly agree) to 6 (strongly disagree):

- Knowledge of English suffices for initiating and securing business contacts with German companies (2.4)
- Command of German is a prerequisite for initiating and securing business contacts with German companies (4.3)
- Foreign firms should follow their own cultural norms as closely as possible in communication with German firms (3.5)
- Foreign firms should follow German cultural norms as closely as possible in communication with German firms (3.2)
- Foreign firms should follow German cultural norms and simultaneously show their own cultural identity in communication with German companies (2.2)

Schleswig-Holstein firms see only a little advantage in their business partners using German. More emphasis was placed on cultural adaptation. However, they endorse cultural adaptation unequivocally only when it is not too strong, i.e., when communication partners also show their own cultural identity. Among American business people, Francis (1991, p. 409) found a similar preference for moderate cultural adaptation on the part of their Japanese business partners.

When asked to evaluate traits and behavior of foreign business partners, respondents reported that they regarded hospitality (1.7), tolerance (1.9), professional experience (2.0) and flexibility (2.1) as most positive, followed by spontaneity (2.5) and straightforwardness (2.6). Formal politeness (3.1) and emotionality (3.5) were rated less favorably. The responding firms had negative perceptions of lacking self-confidence (4.6), lacking authority (4.6), unpreciseness (4.9), superficiality (5.0), aimlessness (5.1), lack of discipline (5.2) and unpunctuality (5.3). (1 = most positive, 6 = most negative)

The results of the second survey (the qualitative German language needs survey) show that the responding companies have a moderately positive attitude to the use of German by their foreign business partners. Apparently, English language use is very well received in the Schleswig-Holstein business community. They also provide us with information as to what is regarded as most useful: German language knowledge on the part of their foreign business partners or knowledge of German culture. Clearly, the respondents prefer the latter. In addition, they do not make strong qualitative linguistic demands, apart from intelligibility, on their foreign business partners who choose German in communication with them.

Educational implications of the findings of needs analysis studies

Many corporate activities require the use of foreign languages. The need for business-oriented foreign language skills has two major sources: corporate tactics of communicating successfully and strategies relative to market psychology. Firstly, foreign language use is a way of preventing miscommunication. Companies know that solid command of the mother tongue of their foreign business partners is especially valuable for writing text types with legal consequences, i.e., an offer, order, or sales contract. Secondly, foreign language use is a vehicle for commerce. For that reason, pre-sale text types, like offers, are more frequently written in the customer's mother tongue than post-sale documents, like order confirmations and invoices (Vandermeeren, 1999, p. 281). Linguistic adaptation is a way to communicate in a receiver-friendly style and to improve the atmosphere; it may help in closing a deal.

This section explores the relevance of needs analysis studies exemplified by the two surveys described in the previous section for the field of education. The study of the German language need of Finnish companies showed that half the responding firms who claimed that they needed German language competence reported that they were not able to correspond, telephone, or negotiate adequately about business-related subjects in German. Is this to be attributed to the fact that the Finnish education system does not produce a sufficient number of competent German speakers? In 1995, Finns who took German in secondary schools numbered 56,795 (1.1% of the population). Compared to the Netherlands with 540,000 pupils

(3.4%) in the same year, this is a relatively low number (Goethe-Institut, 2000). In addition, the vocational language policies adopted by the Finns probably do not fill the need for business-related German skills. The following question also arises: Do these language policies meet the qualitative need, i.e., do vocational institutions with business German courses in their curricular offerings emphasize communicative functioning in business situations enough?

Foreign language users in business settings face many problems entailed by a lack of (intercultural) communicative competence. Lacking knowledge of intercultural differences, for instance, different communication styles, also leads to miscommunication. Business German teachers should keep such problems realistically before them as they teach and should build remedies into the curriculum. Central to the demanding task for these teachers is the anticipation and ranking of learners' needs in their (later) careers. Because of the close relationship between language and culture, (future) users of Business German need to develop intercultural sensitivity and competency. They should be aware of the socio-cultural context of language and acquire acting abilities in intercultural professional situations.

How to equip Finnish learners of Business German? According to the reports from Schleswig-Holstein companies, foreign companies with business connections to Germany need knowledge of the economic geography of Germany, of the organizational structure of German companies, of German business culture and conduct, and of the German mentality (for discussion on cultural differences between Germany and Finland, see Reuter et al., 1991). It is of particular interest that, in the opinion of the respondents, cultural proficiency is even more important than language proficiency. So, Finnish students who take Business German need educational programs that help them to achieve intercultural communicative competence as applied to German–Finnish business contacts.

Foreign language pedagogues have proposed few models and educational tools which interweave language competence with cultural knowledge (Beamer, 1992; Bowe, 1994; Byram, 1989, 136ff.; Moureau-Martini, 1994; Murray et al, 1989; Verckens et al, 1998). The course in international business writing designed by Verckens et al works with three educational tools, in order to familiarize students in Belgium, Finland, and the United States of America with the cultural context of language: textbooks on the subject of cross-cultural communication, field-research (foreign language need analyses) and simulation games. As participants in the business games, the students have to produce written documents in English that are actually sent to each other and reacted to. The problem of cultural adaptation to the receiver is raised during an open discussion in class. Letters are evaluated with a view to establishing business contacts outside a student's own culture. What is extremely interesting is that need analysis is used as an educational tool by Verckens et al (p. 248):

> The field-research component makes students look *beyond the wall of the educational institution* to find out what goes on in the real world of business with regard to cross-cultural communication. The students, using a questionnaire, are asked to interview a manager who has to communicate internationally in order to perform his/her tasks. The results are used to critically reflect on the general theories, methods, and statements and particular anecdotes that our source books present.

Conclusion

Before learners of a foreign language for business purposes can be provided access to a foreign language and culture by their teachers, the teachers must know which business-related skills and knowledge their learners need. Instructional goals and subjects should be geared to learner needs. The findings of needs analysis studies such as the two described in this paper are very valuable for foreign language teachers who want to develop a curriculum that best suits student needs. Moreover, needs analysis can be used as an educational tool both in language instruction, as Verckens et al do, and in language teacher training.

The second study described above provided a preliminary investigation of qualitative need. Its purpose was to shed light on one of the factors which shape foreign language need, namely native speakers' attitudes towards linguistic and cultural adaptation on the part of their non-native communication partners. For foreign language educators, who train (future) foreign language teachers, knowledge of those attitudes is of great importance. Trainees must obtain that specific knowledge from them if they are to use it in instructional practice themselves.

References

Atteslander, P. (1993). *Methoden der empirischen Sozialforschung* Berlin: de Gruyter.
Beamer, L. (1992). Learning intercultural communication competence. *Journal of Business Communication, 29,* 285–303.

Beneke, J. (1991). *Englisch als lingua franca oder als Medium interkulturel-ler Kommunikation*. In R. Grebing (ed.) *Grenzenloses Sprachenlernen* (pp. 54–66). Oxford: Cornelsen & Oxford University Press.

Bowe, H. (1994). University courses – linguistics for business. In T. Bungarten (ed.) *Kommunikationstraining und -trainingsprogramme im wirtschaftlichen Umfeld* (pp. 41–55). Tostedt: Attikon

Byram, M. (1989). *Cultural studies in foreign language education*. Clevedon: Multilingual Matters.

Claessens Raadgevend Bureau (1988) *Onderzoek naar functie-eisen in personeelsadvertenties*. Amsterdam.

Cohen, R. (2001). Language and negotiation: a Middle East lexicon. In J. Kurbalija & H. Slavik (eds.) *Language and diplomacy* (pp. 67–92). Malta: Diplo Projects.

Dannerer, M. (1992). Wirtschaftsdeutsch in Ungarn. Eine empirische Studie über Bedarf und Probleme. *Informationen Deutsch als Fremdsprache* 19, 3, 335–349.

De Jager, E. & Reunis, A. (1971). Onderzoek naar de 'marktwaarde' betreffende de kennis der vreemde talen van HTS'ers en ingenieurs. Dordrecht.

Drochner, K.-H. & Kirchberg, E. (1987). Zum Bedarf an Fremdsprachen-kenntnissen. Statistische Untersuchung anhand von Stellenanzeigen in italienischen Tageszeitungen. *Scuola e lingue moderne* 3, 46–58.

van Els, T. et al. (1984a) *Applied linguistics and the learning and teaching of foreign languages*. London: Edward Arnold.

van Els, T. et al. (1984b) Research into foreign language needs. *Die Neueren Sprachen* 83, 1, 104–108.

Emmans, K. et al. (1974) *The use of foreign languages in the private sector of industry and commerce*. York: Language Teaching Centre, University of York.

Firth, A. (1991). 'Lingua franca' negotiations: towards an interactional approach. *World Englishes* 9, 3, 269–280.

Firth, A. (ed.) (1995). *The discourse of negotiation: Studies of language in the workplace*. Oxford: Pergamon Press.

Fishman, J. A., & Cooper, R. L. (1978). The sociolinguistic foundations of language testing. In B. Spolsky (ed.) *Approaches to language testing. Advances in language testing Series* 2, 31–38. Arlington: Center for Applied Linguistics.

Francis, J. N. P. (1991). When in Rome? The effect of cultural adaptation on intercultural business negotiations. *Journal of International Business Studies* 22, 403–428.

Glück, H. (1992). Die internationale Stellung des Deutschen auf dem europäischen Arbeitsmarkt. In W. Kramer & R. Weiß (eds.) *Fremd-sprachen in der Wirtschaft. Ein Beitrag zu interkultureller Kompetenz* (pp. 47–75). Köln: Dt. Inst.-Verl.

Goethe-Institut (2000). *Deutsch als Fremdsprache: Zahlen im Überblick*. Goethe-Institut: München.

Hagen, S. (1988). *Languages in British business: an analysis of current needs*. Newcastle: Newcastle upon Tyne Polytechnic Products Ltd.

Hagen, S. (ed.) (1993). *Languages in European business. A regional survey of small & medium-sized companies*. Dartford: CILT.

Holden, N.J. (1989). Toward a functional typology of languages of international business. *Language Problems and Language Planning* 13, 1, 1–8.

Grinsted, A. (1993). Southern Denmark. In S. Hagen (ed.) *Languages in European business. A regional survey of small & medium-sized companies* (pp. 48–58). Dartford: CILT.

Jörissen, H. (1991). Das Produkthaftpflicht-Risiko aus fehlerhaften Gebrauchsanweisungen, Instruktionen und Warnhinweisen. In E. Feldbusch et al. (eds.) Neue Fragen der Linguistik: Akten des 25. Linguistischen Kolloquiums Paderborn 1990 (pp. 385–391) Tübingen: Niemeyer.

King, T. (1984). The role of foreign languages in the Jaguar success story *The Incorporated Linguist* 24, 3–4, 154–159.

Koch, H. (1991). Legal aspects of a language policy for the European Communities: language risks, equal opportunities, and legislating a language. In W. Knapp et al. (eds.) Analyzing intercultural communication (pp. 147–161). Berlin/New York: de Gruyter.

Labov, W. (1978). *Sociolinguistic patterns*. Philadelphia: University of Pennsylvania Press.

Metcalf, H. (1991). Foreign language needs of business. *IMS Report 215*. University of Sussex, Falmer, Brighton.

Martin, J. S. & Chaney, L. H. (1992). Determination of content for a collegiate course in intercultural business communication by three Delphi panels. *Journal of Business Communication* 29, 267–284.

Moureau-Martini, U. (1994). Interkulturelles Training mit Video. Deutsch für Nachwuchskräfte französischer Exportfirmen. In T. Bungarten (ed.) *Kommunikationstraining und -trainingsprogramme im wirtschaftlichen Umfeld* (pp. 201–208). Tostedt: Attikon.

Murray, J. H. et al. (1989). The Athena Language Learning Project: design issues for the next generation of computer-based language learning. In W. F. Smith (ed.) *Modern technology in foreign language education: application and projects* (pp. 97–118). Lincolnwood/IL.: National Textbook Co.

Pearce, G. (1991). *Languages and the British manager*. Corby, Northants: British Institute of Management.

Pogner, K.-H. (1999). Discourse community, culture and interaction: on writing by consulting engineers. In F. Bargiela-Chiappini & C. Nickerson (eds.) *Writing business: genres, media, and discourse*. (pp. 101–127) Harlow: Longman.

Reeves, N. (1985). Education for exporting capability – languages and market penetration. *The Incorporated Linguist* 23, 3–4, 147–153.

Reeves, N. (1990). The foreign language needs of UK-based corporations. *ANNALS, AAPSS* 511, 60–73.

Reuter, E. et al. (1991) Zur Erforschung von Kulturunterschieden in der internationalen Wirtschaftskommunikation. In B.-D Müller (ed.) *Interkulturelle Wirtschaftskommunikation* (pp. 93–121). München: Iudicium.

Schuman, H. & Presser, S. (1981). *Questions and answers in attitude surveys. Experiments on question form, wording and context.* New York: Academic Press.

Vandermeeren, S. (1998) *Fremdsprachen in europäischen Unternehmen. Untersuchungen zu Bestand und Bedarf im Geschäftsalltag mit Empfehlungen für Sprachenpolitik und Sprachunterricht.* Waldsteinberg: Popp.

Vandermeeren, S. (1999) English as a lingua franca in written corporate communication: findings from a European survey. In F. Bargiela-Chiappini & C. Nickerson (eds.) Writing Business: Genres, Media and Discourses (pp. 273–291). Harlow: Longman.

Vandermeeren, S. (2002). Fremdsprachenbedarf in finnischen Unternehmen. In A. Nuopponen, et al. (eds.) Interkulturelle Wirtschaftskommunikation: Forschungsobjekte und methoden (pp. 207–223). Vaasa: University of Vasaa.

Vandermeeren, S. (in press). Research on language attitudes. In U. Ammon et al. (eds.) *Sociolinguistics.* Berlin/New York: de Gruyter.

van Hest, E. & Oud, M. (1990). Eine Untersuchung der bei der Diagnose und Analyse von Fremdsprachenbedarf in Handel und Industrie verwendeten Techniken. Luxemburg: Kommission der Europäischen Gemeinschaften.

Verckens, J. P. et al. (1998) The experience of sameness in differences: A course in international business writing. In S. Niemeier et al. (eds.) The *Cultural Context in Business Communication* (pp. 247–261). Amsterdam/Philadelphia: Benjamins.

Verdoodt, A. & Delbeke, L (1983). *Belangstelling voor en werkelijke behoeften aan moderne vreemde talen in België. Verslag 2. Een onderzoek naar de algemene behoeften aan talen in bedrijven en overheidsdiensten.* Leuven: Centrum voor Mathematische Psychologie en Psychologische Methodologie.

Appendix A: Survey questionnaire

This is the questionnaire, in translation, developed for the survey:

1. How do you evaluate the use of German instead of English by foreign company representatives for each of the following communication tasks? (+ 3 = very purposeful; –3 = totally unnecessary)

	+3	+2	+1	–1	–2	–3
writing inquiries	[ ]	[ ]	[ ]	[ ]	[ ]	[ ]
writing offers	[ ]	[ ]	[ ]	[ ]	[ ]	[ ]
writing orders	[ ]	[ ]	[ ]	[ ]	[ ]	[ ]
writing confirmations of orders	[ ]	[ ]	[ ]	[ ]	[ ]	[ ]
writing invoices	[ ]	[ ]	[ ]	[ ]	[ ]	[ ]
complaints concerning delays	[ ]	[ ]	[ ]	[ ]	[ ]	[ ]
explanation of delay	[ ]	[ ]	[ ]	[ ]	[ ]	[ ]
self-introduction (education / position with the firm)	[ ]	[ ]	[ ]	[ ]	[ ]	[ ]
company depiction	[ ]	[ ]	[ ]	[ ]	[ ]	[ ]
product depiction	[ ]	[ ]	[ ]	[ ]	[ ]	[ ]
small talk	[ ]	[ ]	[ ]	[ ]	[ ]	[ ]
price/conditions negotiation	[ ]	[ ]	[ ]	[ ]	[ ]	[ ]

2. How do you evaluate it when representatives of foreign companies in regular business contact with Germany have the following knowledge of Germany? (+3 = very purposeful; –3 = totally unnecessary)

	+3	+2	+1	–1	–2	–3
German politics	[ ]	[ ]	[ ]	[ ]	[ ]	[ ]
economic geography of Germany	[ ]	[ ]	[ ]	[ ]	[ ]	[ ]
organizational structure of German companies	[ ]	[ ]	[ ]	[ ]	[ ]	[ ]
German corporate culture	[ ]	[ ]	[ ]	[ ]	[ ]	[ ]
German cultural norms and customs	[ ]	[ ]	[ ]	[ ]	[ ]	[ ]

3. How do you evaluate the following mistakes in the language usage of foreign company representatives writing German in a poor but still intelligible manner to German company representatives? (+3 = very annoying; –3 = not annoying at all)

	+3	+2	+1	–1	–2	–3
inexact sentence construction	[ ]	[ ]	[ ]	[ ]	[ ]	[ ]
wrong word (the German word for '. . .' is not . . . , but . . .)	[ ]	[ ]	[ ]	[ ]	[ ]	[ ]
ungrammatical word forms (e.g. wrong declension)	[ ]	[ ]	[ ]	[ ]	[ ]	[ ]
unsuitable style (e.g. too formal / not formal enough)	[ ]	[ ]	[ ]	[ ]	[ ]	[ ]
incorrect spelling	[ ]	[ ]	[ ]	[ ]	[ ]	[ ]

4. How do you evaluate the following traits and behavior of foreign business partners? (+3 = very positive; −3 = very negative)

	+3	+2	+1	−1	−2	−3
lacking self-confidence	[ ]	[ ]	[ ]	[ ]	[ ]	[ ]
lack of punctuality	[ ]	[ ]	[ ]	[ ]	[ ]	[ ]
formal politeness	[ ]	[ ]	[ ]	[ ]	[ ]	[ ]
lack of discipline	[ ]	[ ]	[ ]	[ ]	[ ]	[ ]
straightforwardness	[ ]	[ ]	[ ]	[ ]	[ ]	[ ]
spontaneity	[ ]	[ ]	[ ]	[ ]	[ ]	[ ]
aimlessness	[ ]	[ ]	[ ]	[ ]	[ ]	[ ]
emotionality	[ ]	[ ]	[ ]	[ ]	[ ]	[ ]
lacking authority	[ ]	[ ]	[ ]	[ ]	[ ]	[ ]
hospitality	[ ]	[ ]	[ ]	[ ]	[ ]	[ ]
tolerance	[ ]	[ ]	[ ]	[ ]	[ ]	[ ]
unpreciseness	[ ]	[ ]	[ ]	[ ]	[ ]	[ ]
flexibility	[ ]	[ ]	[ ]	[ ]	[ ]	[ ]
superficiality	[ ]	[ ]	[ ]	[ ]	[ ]	[ ]
professional experience	[ ]	[ ]	[ ]	[ ]	[ ]	[ ]
the use of German instead of English	[ ]	[ ]	[ ]	[ ]	[ ]	[ ]

5. What is your opinion of the following statements (+3 = strongly agree; −3 = strongly disagree)

	+3	+2	+1	−1	−2	−3
Knowledge of English suffices for initiating and securing business contacts with German companies	[ ]	[ ]	[ ]	[ ]	[ ]	[ ]
Command of German is a prerequisite for initiating and securing business contacts with German companies	[ ]	[ ]	[ ]	[ ]	[ ]	[ ]
Foreign firms should follow their own cultural norms as closely as possible in communication with German firms	[ ]	[ ]	[ ]	[ ]	[ ]	[ ]
Foreign firms should follow German cultural norms as closely as possible in communication with German firms	[ ]	[ ]	[ ]	[ ]	[ ]	[ ]
Foreign firms should follow German cultural norms and simultaneously show their own cultural identity in communication with German companies	[ ]	[ ]	[ ]	[ ]	[ ]	[ ]

6 Evaluating the use of multiple sources and methods in needs analysis: a case study of journalists in the Autonomous Community of Catalonia (Spain)

Roger Gilabert

Introduction

The purpose of this paper is two-fold: (i) to describe a research project on the analysis of the English-language needs of journalists in the Autonomous Community of Catalonia, Spain; (ii) to evaluate the use of multiple sources and methods in needs analysis (NA).

The NA framework for this study was that provided by Long (this volume). Long suggests that previous NA models, such as that of Wilkins (1976) or Munby (1978) in the 1970s, although useful at the time, were in fact based on the intuitions of applied linguists about the notions and functions required by learners, and not on empirical studies. Since then, work on such models has generated pedagogical materials that have "focused on the notions and functions supposedly required to satisfy various occupational language needs." (Long, this volume, p. 21). Still today, the majority of NAs that can be found in the literature rely on outsiders' views (basically learners and applied linguists) rather than on insiders' views (domain experts). In addition, most NAs limit themselves to reporting findings and few ever discuss the reliability or validity of their methodology.

Long advocates use of multiple sources and methods, as well as triangulation by sources and/or by methods, in order to improve the reliability and validity of findings. In Long's model, linguistic units (such as words, structures, notions or functions) are replaced by 'task' as the unit of analysis. A few studies have started reporting the efficacy of multiple sources and methods (Svendsen & Krebs, 1984; Jasso-Aguilar, 1999, this volume). Jasso-Aguilar's study, for example, provides evidence of how triangulation by sources (domain experts, supervisors, human resources people, task force meetings, morning briefings, and documents) and by methods (participant observations, unstructured interviews, and questionnaires) can produce accurate and reliable information about language needs.

Long (this volume, p. 23) also suggests that task-based NAs

> readily lend themselves as input for the design of a variety of analytic, task-based and/or (a small minority of) content-based, second language and foreign language courses, whose delivery can be harmonized with what language acquisition research has revealed about universal L2 developmental processes in and out of classrooms.

The information obtained in this project has since been used to revise an existing English-language program for students of Communication Studies, and to inform an English-language course for professional journalists, each of which has been designed from a task-based perspective, both in terms of syllabus design and methodology.

Project description

The research project had two primary objectives. The primary aim was to obtain accurate information about the tasks that journalists carry out in English in journalism companies in Catalonia, Spain, and to obtain information about the language involved in those tasks. The second was the collection of task-related discourse samples – written texts, such as articles and e-mail messages, and samples of oral interactions, such as telephone conversations and interviews – for subsequent linguistic analysis. Related objectives included obtaining information from different domain actors about the importance of English within journalism companies, the role of English within the domain, the areas, sections or departments where English is used and needed most, the language requirements of such companies when hiring new employees, and information about their foreign language training policies. Finally, the intention was to conduct research on methodological issues in NA itself, and, thereby, test Long's model.

Preparation for field research

The research began with a survey of NA literature. Especially useful were the above-mentioned study by Jasso-Aguilar (1999, this volume), Long's analysis of the needs of flight attendants (Long, this volume), and Martin & Brodt's study (Martin & Brodt, 1973) for a task-based curriculum for hospital corpsmen. After considering the definitions of task provided by Crookes (1986), Swales (1990), and Long (to appear), two provisional units of analysis were established. These were *target tasks* and *target sub-tasks*. *Target task* was defined as a differentiated process domain experts have to carry out in English, which is divided into steps, each of which must have an outcome, and not be dependent on or part of other tasks. *Target sub-task* was defined as a differentiated process which, while having a number of steps and an outcome, is dependent on or part of another major target task.

Figure 1 shows the different steps involved in the *target task* of 'interviewing a source'.

Figure 1   Target task: 'Interviewing a source'
            (Spa = Spanish, Cat = Catalan)[1]

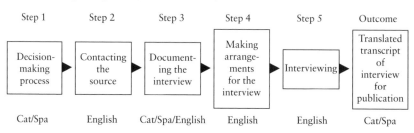

At this point, it is important to emphasize the fact, that in an EFL context like the one in which this study took place, the outcome of tasks is rarely in the target language. Catalonia is a bilingual community, the two languages being Spanish and Catalan, where only exceptionally some journalists in information portals need to write articles in English. As the research later revealed, the outcome of most *target tasks* in Catalonia is either in Spanish or Catalan. However, the likelihood of the outcome of a *target sub-task* being in English is considerably higher. This is the case, for example, with the *target sub-tasks* of 'Documenting the interview' or 'Making arrangements for the interview', as shown in Figures 2 and 3.

Before the actual field research started, a tailor-made database program was created for the collection and processing of data. Given the nature of the research objectives, the principles of naturalistic

Figure 2   Target sub-task: 'Documenting the interview'

Figure 3   Target sub-task: 'Making arrangements for the interview'[2]

Calling or e-mailing the source to request interview	→	Calling or e-mailing the source to arrange time, place, topics of the interview	→	Sending an e-mail or fax message to source to confirm arrangements
English		English		English

research, especially the concept of 'emergence' advanced by Lincoln (1985), also informed the project.

Prior to starting fieldwork it was important to describe the target discourse domain, or *discourse community* (Swales, 1990), of journalism. However, since journalism is a very broad domain, it had to be described by consulting several sources. The two most useful were the Internship Coordination Office and the Student Employment Office, two services that the Blanquerna School of Communication Studies offers to students enrolled in the program, and which act as links between our educational institution and the labor market. Both provided information about the different types of companies within the domain of journalism where students often work as interns or where they find jobs and which require interns or new employees to know English. Most importantly, they supplied company listings, as well as the names and phone numbers of contact people in those companies. Their information greatly facilitated access to companies and thus made the research easier. In contrast, whenever companies were contacted directly, without any referral, the process was a lot slower, and in some cases unsuccessful.

Nine sub-domains were identified within the domain of journalism: conventional newspapers; on-line newspapers; radio stations; TV networks; information web sites (portals); conventional magazines; on-line magazines; press offices; and production companies.

Conventional and on-line newspapers, information portals, radio stations, and television networks share several characteristics. They are divided into the same or similar sections (e.g. international, society, or sports, among others), have to update and provide information on a day-to-day basis, and employ journalists who work as researchers, interviewers, and writers (a minority work as announcers or anchors in radio and television).

With few exceptions, conventional and on-line magazines are not divided into information sections, but rather specialize in different sectors (e.g. medical, pharmaceutical, or fashion, among others). Journalists also research information, interview sources and write articles, but, unlike their colleagues in the other media, their work consists of slightly longer projects (ranging from week-long to month-long projects), and they tend to specialize in a single subject connected to the sector with which the magazine deals.

Finally, journalists in production companies and press offices, although still dealing with information, play a role closer to public relations. In these kinds of companies, most journalists provide the other media with information about the corporation they represent.

In spite of the similarities among some sub-domains as to their internal organization and the role of journalists within them, it was believed important to maintain the division into nine sub-domains provided by our specialist sources in order not to miss any information that might be specific to a particular sub-domain.

Sources and methodology

Once the nine sub-domains had been identified, a company from each domain was selected. The selection criteria were the largest readership (for both conventional and on-line newspapers, conventional and on-line magazines, and information web sites), the largest audience (for TV networks and radio stations), the largest number of employees and prestige within the field for press offices and production companies. Availability and access to companies, of course, also had to be considered.

After contact names and numbers were obtained from the above-mentioned student services, unstructured interviews started. First, three scholars (initially, a specialist in media distribution, the head of the Internship Coordination Office and, later in the research, an expert in new technologies) were interviewed. Interviews were usually first set up with company representatives and, through them, with domain experts. As shown in Table 1, a total of 19 unstructured interviews were carried out with company representatives and with one or two domain experts from each company. Specifically, eight company representatives and 11 domain experts were interviewed. These interviews were later transcribed for further analysis. In these first interviews, informants were asked a series of open-ended questions (e.g., Do you need to use English in order to do your job? How important is it to know English in your profession? What kind of things do you do in English?) and permission was asked for the interviews to be taped. Information was obtained about the views of the different actors on the importance and role of English within their company and position, the areas where English is needed and used the most were identified, information about

Table 1   Sources and interviews

Method	Unstructured interviews				Structured interviews	
Source	Co. Rep.	Role	Domain experts	Role	Domain experts	Role
Conventional newspaper	1	Sub-editor	2	Writer	1	Writer
On-line newspapers	1	Editor in chief	1	Writer	1	Writer
Radio stations	1	Head of International Section	1	Writer/announcer	–	–
TV networks	1	Head of International Section	1	Writer/anchor	–	–
Info portals	1	Sub-editor	1	Writer	1	Writer
Conventional magazines	1	Editor in chief	1	Writer	–	–
On-line magazines	1	Editor in chief	1	Writer	–	–
Press offices	1	Head of Press Office	2	Press Officer/Writer	2	Press Officer/Writer
Production companies	–	–	1	Press Officer/Writer	–	–
TOTAL	8		11		5	

company requirements regarding English and training policies was retrieved, and target tasks were identified. In some cases, second interviews with domain experts were carried out. The second time these interviews with domain experts took place literally at the desk of the domain expert. More specific questions were asked (e.g., How does an interview actually work? Do you contact the source yourself? Do you contact your sources via e-mail, telephone? How do you prepare for the interview?), so that domain experts would describe the tasks in detail. They indicated the purpose for which each task is carried out, the kind of interlocutor/s in the performance of the task (when appropriate), the context in which the task takes place, the language requirements of the tasks (such as the skills required to complete the task, the kind of language problems they encounter, and their evaluation of the linguistic difficulty of the task), as well as information about the frequency of performance of the task.

A number of structured interviews were also carried out to pre-test the questionnaires. They consisted of reading all the task statements drawn from unstructured interviews to informants for them to assess how frequently a task was carried out, how difficult it was to carry it out in English, and how necessary it was for them to be trained in English to carry out the task. They helped to make sure task statements were understandable, and also helped to eliminate or group some tasks statements, in order to make questionnaires more manageable. Out of the 43 task statements which were originally drawn from qualitative interviews, eight were eliminated, so the final version of the questionnaire contained 35 task statements.

Questionnaires to be sent via e-mail were created after analyzing the information obtained through unstructured interviews and domain experts' introspections about tasks. Information about e-mail addresses of companies was obtained by means of the trade directory published by the Professional Association of Journalists in Catalonia. The head of the Student Employment office selected 513 companies out of the 710 journalism companies registered in the Professional Association of Journalists of Catalonia, where students in the program may potentially find jobs. Sub-domains that neither the Student Employment office nor the Internship Coordination Service had ever supplied students with because they needed other kinds of student profiles (e.g., lawyers, statisticians, and business students) were omitted. Those 513 constituted the total population of journalism companies to be surveyed.

Following a suggestion by Martin & Brodt (1973), questionnaires were designed to obtain information about whether or not the tasks or sub-tasks identified during the qualitative part of the research were carried out in those companies, the frequency with which they are performed, the perceived difficulty for each task, and whether domain experts judge that training is required for each specific task. Statements were organized into six different blocks: e-mail communication, news writing, telephone communication, face-to-face communication (excluding interviews), interviewing, written documentation, and audio-visual documentation. For each of the 35 task statements in the questionnaire, participants were asked to indicate the degree of frequency, difficulty, and need for language training on a five-point scale (0 = never / very easy / not necessary, 4 = very frequently / very difficult / very necessary). Informants were asked to eliminate invalid answers. The following is an example of a task statement (translated from Catalan) that domains experts were asked to assess for frequency, difficulty, and need for training:

0000 Interview sources face-to-face (without an interpreter)
5151 Frequency: 0 1 2 3 4
5152 Level of difficulty: 0 1 2 3 4
5153 Need for training in English: 0 1 2 3 4

As shown in Table 2, 59 companies out of 513 companies com-

Table 2 Questionnaires

Sub-domains	Sent to companies	Failed or returned unanswered	Returned answered
Conventional newspapers	93	18	6
On-line newspapers	5	1	1
Radio stations	55	10	9
TV networks	19	4	4
Info portals	4	0	1
Conventional magazines	106	20	9
On-line magazines	10	1	3
Press offices	170	33	20
Production companies	16	3	2
TOTAL	513	90	59

pleted and sent back the questionnaires, which constituted a response of 11.5%.

Limited non-participant observation was also used in this research. Permission was granted by company representatives to send two researchers to observe the everyday work of a domain expert (either in newsrooms or offices) in each sub-domain except for one (a production company). The newsrooms of a major radio station and an on-line magazine were visited by two researchers who spent a whole morning observing the work of domain experts. Since the tasks that were observed took place predominantly in Catalan or Spanish, plans had to be adjusted. Domain experts were questioned about the tasks in which English played a major role, and identified interviews, press conferences, and event organizations. Permission was obtained from company representatives and domain experts to observe specific communication events which normally took place outside the newsroom or office. These were three face-to-face interviews, five press conferences, one event organization, and two campaign presentations by press officers. Permission was not granted by press offices to attend product launch meeting or company business meals.

Finally, textual samples were collected mainly during second interviews with domain experts. All of them were asked to provide examples of the written sources, links, written and recorded interviews, video footage, and e-mail messages connected with each task-type they described. The following samples were collected: 159 e-mail messages were collected from four different sub-domains (two press offices, an on-line magazine, a radio station, and a TV network); a large number of subject-specific articles were given to researchers by an on-line magazine and two press offices (a museum and a computer company); several product catalogues and press packs were provided by two press offices; all sub-domains supplied us with links to on-line sources they use on a regular basis; three recorded interviews (two face-to-face interviews and a telephone one) and their transcripts were lent to researchers by an on-line and a conventional newspaper, and an on-line magazine; a few hours of video footage (as sent by news agencies) and the scripts corresponding to each piece of news were obtained from the TV network; and a large number of news wires were provided by a radio station, a TV network, a conventional newspaper, and an on-line newspaper.

Evaluation of the use of multiple sources and methods

Multiple sources

The information obtained through this research confirmed Long's contention that interviewing several different social actors provides reliable and accurate results. Scholars, who have the responsibility of training future journalists, delivered useful insights about the domain. They outlined the organization of the domain, the synergies within the industry and the effects of those synergies on the role of journalists. For example, the fact that media companies tend to merge affects the role of journalists within the domain, multi-tasking being one of the consequences. They also pointed out the areas which are growing most rapidly (on-line journalism and press offices). Their information needs to be considered when making decisions about syllabus design. However, although they showed general agreement on the importance of English, the information about tasks that they supplied was too general and, as expected, their information about language needs was minimal.

Company representatives, who are either involved in the hiring process or at least had a say in it, provided useful information about the importance of English, their expectations and needs regarding interns and new employees, and some general information about the tasks performed by domain experts. Again, their task description was incomplete or imprecise and included very little information about language needs.

Finally, domain experts, who are the people who actually perform the job, proved to be the most useful sources. They shared their views about the importance of English within their sub-domain, they completed the information advanced by company representatives by describing the specific tasks they carry out in English, they provided their introspections about language use in those tasks and, in most cases, supplied materials, such as recorded interviews, e-mails, documents, links to web sites, among others. Transcript 1 shows how a domain expert (a correspondent for a radio station) confirms that 'skimming' is essential when documenting a piece of news:

> ... one must be able to identify from the context which the most important sentence would be ... for a correspondent that's essential ... because you must think that you must read 10 newspapers ... you don't read everything ... you just 'zap' through them ...
>
> Transcript 1. Source: domain expert. Sub-domain: radio station. Translated from Catalan.

By triangulating sources, accessing different views about how each task is carried out was made possible. In other words, the view of how English is used in the performance of tasks would have been partial if different sources had not been used.

In this particular research, information was cross-checked by interviewing two kinds of sources with very different, asymmetrical positions within each company on the same topics. This happened in all sub-domains but one, and, as seen in the transcripts below, it triggered considerably different views about how things are done or are supposed to be done. Also, whenever it was possible, a different researcher interviewed domain experts during second unstructured interviews. This allowed double-checking of some of the statements made by domain experts during the first unstructured interview. No major differences were found by using two different researchers to interview the same domain expert. Transcripts 2 and 3 below are an example of how two different sources, a company representative and a domain expert, provided two different versions of how pieces of news are produced. In Transcript 2, a company representative from a conventional newspaper talks about the different sources used when writing an article:

> (*about wires from news agencies*) ... this is like ... say ... our raw material for all the sections but mainly for the international section ...
>
> ... then we have the different TV networks ... our main source of information being CNN ... well ... in English ... because we have the other channels from here ... which are services that are used to learn about what we don't know or to have ... we could say ... to make a little evaluative comparison between pieces of news ... that's right ... the Herald Tribune which is the North American newspaper which is published in Europe and the press ... the British press ... The Guardian ... The Independent ... etc.
>
> Transcript 2. Source: company representative. Sub-domain: conventional newspaper. Translated from Catalan.

From the company representative's words, one might have gotten the impression that what a journalist does in an international section is to check different sources which are equal in importance when writing an article. However, this information seemed to be contradictory with what a domain expert working for the same newspaper reported:

> ... you must think that in a newspaper ... normally ... when

you're writing a piece of news, you don't compare anything ... I mean ... the news in the international section is not made by comparing wires from news agencies against newspaper articles ... in the international section it's done by taking the wire and translating it ... if it's not been sent to you by the correspondent ... it's a real shame but points of views about the news are being limited ... Anglo-Saxons have the monopoly and the news that comes up ...

Interviewer: ... maybe ... I've found that there are places like web-based magazines or on-line newspapers ... because maybe they have the limitation of time ... because it may be that they have to write an article from one day to the next, and there's no limitation of space ... they can sometimes use more sources ...
... or maybe they're not so burnt out by routines ... like this daily press we're doing ... there are some writing routines and nobody can change that ... on-line magazines have started from scratch ... with a different spirit ... so it's reasonable that they should try to do it in a different way ...

Transcript 3. Source: Domain expert. Sub-domain: conventional newspaper. Translated from Catalan.

The two descriptions provided by the two sources have different implications for task design. The process of writing an article described by the company representative may have led the researcher to think that the strategies involved in documenting an article are 'skimming' and 'scanning' different texts in order to select information for an article. However, the domain expert in the conventional newspaper reported that the 'routine' procedure is to 'translate' from a single text type, news wires in this case, rather than skim or scan different written texts or audio-visual sources. The domain expert certainly revealed what journalists actually 'do' in newsrooms. The ethical issue remains, however, of whether what one wants to teach students in the language class is the 'routine' practice in newsrooms or what scholars say they 'should' be doing. That debate, though, goes beyond the purpose of this paper.

Multiple methods

The use of different methods has also proven effective. Chronologically, this research started with unstructured interviews. Informants were asked to provide introspections about tasks and the language involved in them. In some cases, the interviews were accompanied by non-participant observation and the collection of target discourse samples. Structured interviews were conducted before questionnaires. Questionnaires were pre-tested in each sub-domain before being sent to the whole population. Once returned, further non-participant observation for specific target tasks was carried out, together with collection of additional discourse samples.

Unstructured interviews were useful for building rapport with informants, obtaining the necessary authorization to collect materials, forming a general idea about the role of English in each sub-domain, and, most importantly, for identifying additional informants. However, the information about tasks and language had to be completed by means of domain experts' introspections. It was by means of the second interviews with domain experts that each sub-task or task was given a context, the purpose of each task was defined, and the language problems with them identified. As mentioned before, domain experts are the people who actually carry out a job, and they know exactly what is done and needed. With respect to triangulation by source and method, the information retrieved by means of insider introspections certainly proved to be more reliable and to work better with domain experts than with company representatives. In this study, although most heads of department had been domain experts' at some point, they were in charge of coordinating and supervising the domain experts' job rather than involved in carrying out journalism tasks. Also, as seen in the previous section above, their role and position may have prevented them from revealing what actually takes place in newsrooms.

As expected, structured interviews did not provide any major changes in the content of the information already collected, but they were helpful for the design of quantitative questionnaires. The 35 task statements which made up the questionnaires were organized according to frequency. Thus, questions relating to documentation (14 out of 35) were placed at the beginning of the questionnaire since documentation is one of the most frequent tasks journalists carry out in most sub-domains. However, when pre-testing them in press offices, it was noticed that a significant proportion of the documentation tasks included in the task statements were not carried out in press offices. That meant that a journalist in a press office had to assess 14 task statements relating to tasks that he or she does not carry out in English. That, it was thought, could be discouraging, and may have triggered a lower response. Hence, the task statements relating to tasks which are carried out in all sub-domains, such as the ones relating to e-mail communication, were placed at the beginning.

When considering questionnaire findings, it is important to point out that, of the three variables informants were asked to assess with regard to each task statement, difficulty was the one that elicited least reliable information if we consider the feedback provided by informants. Despite testing it during structured interviews, in the 'open comments' section at the end of the questionnaire some informants reported that it was not quite clear what exactly was meant by 'difficulty', and whether they had to assess the difficulty of performing a task against their level of English. The contrast of frequency and need for specific training, however, proved to be particularly useful. Questionnaire results showed that the tasks rated as most frequent did not necessarily correspond to the ones they reported they needed training for. For example, it was found that of the ten most frequent tasks, six involved reading (web sites, magazines, official organization web sites, press releases, reports, etc.), whereas of the list of tasks for which training was most needed, a majority involved writing and speaking (interviewing sources face-to-face, requesting information from a source or institution via e-mail, entertaining visitors, interviewing sources over the phone, etc.). With regard to the low response obtained, it must be pointed out that unfortunately it is not uncommon either in needs analysis or in journalism. Questionnaires provided useful information about the frequency and need for specific language training in journalism companies in general, but it was not enough to make assessments about each particular sub-domain. Certainly, rather than surveying the whole population, a stratified random sample (in which each company in a population had an equal chance of being selected, in a proportionate way, in each sub-domain) would have been more reliable.

The example that follows shows how non-participant observation can elicit information which may be difficult to obtain through other methods. Two researchers observed the work of journalists in the international news section of the largest radio station in Catalonia. During the observation, the majority of tasks carried out by those journalists were performed in Catalan, and the texts involved were in French or Portuguese. English was only used to document a piece of news with information retrieved from news agencies. However, by means of non-participant observation, it was possible to define in more detail a sub-task that had previously been identified by means of an unstructured interview. The documentation of a piece of news from international TV channels had been roughly described as comparing information in order to support the information received from news agencies. However, a journalist who was working on a piece of news stopped to watch the event that was being broadcast live on TV. He then taped some of the declarations of the sources in order to include them in a radio broadcast. When asked to describe such a sub-task further, he confirmed that it is basically live declarations that are of interest, since they cannot be obtained from news agencies. Apart from this finding, which should be considered when designing pedagogic tasks, most sub-tasks that were carried out and which are performed on a regular basis are mainly passive. After a few hours, it was concluded that there was not much more for researchers to observe. Therefore, continued presence at company sites was not justified. Although prolonged non-participant observation in companies may not be particularly suitable for an EFL context, limited non-participant observation was useful with some specific tasks, such as interviews, press conferences, and presentations.

Finally, reference should be made to the collection of target discourse samples. As mentioned in the section above which describes the sources and methodology employed in this research, discourse samples (e-mails, reports, press releases, recorded face-to-face interviews, recorded telephone interviews, etc.) were collected during visits to journalism companies and were organized around the information obtained on each task. The linguistic (genre, textual and discourse) analysis, which started after the data collection concluded, has begun to reveal interesting information about the language involved in tasks. This is the case with e-mail messages collected from the press office of a well-known museum in Barcelona that regularly organizes exhibits of worldwide scope. The e-mails belonged to a sub-task labeled as 'Provide information about own institution via e-mail', which was a part of a major target task labeled 'Organizing an event'. During the unstructured interviews, the domain expert was asked to describe the above-mentioned sub-task. She said that when people request information, she sends it, and that she also often sends information about exhibits to regular and new contacts without them asking. She added that they sometimes ask for additional images or information, but that it is a quite standardized procedure. When asked to be more specific about the language involved in that kind of e-mail correspondence, she said that people asked for information and she replied with sentences such as "I attach the information you asked for." From the information in the interview, one may have deduced that basically people used the functions of 'requesting' and 'thanking', whereas she used the function of 'informing'. However, further linguistic analysis revealed that, although people mostly 'requested' information, they also used a wide variety of functions such as 'requesting to be updated', 'requesting permission', 'requesting clarification', 'thanking', 'urging', 'acknowledging', and 'apologizing', among others. The press officer, apart from 'informing', also used a rich variety of functions (even if she always used the same expression for each function) such as 'offering further information', 'apologizing', 're-directing', and 'granting permission', among others. The linguistic analysis of texts that the collection of samples permitted, together with the contextualization of texts within task processes, are there-fore essential for the creation of pedagogic tasks. The transformation of real *target task* into pedagogic tasks should be, however, the subject of a different paper.

Conclusions

In this paper a description of a task-based needs analysis of journal-ists in Catalonia has been presented and evidence provided of how the use of multiple sources and methods helped to obtain more reliable and validated findings.

As far as the use of multiple sources is concerned, it has been shown how, although all the social actors of a domain can provide useful information about the kind of tasks that are carried out within the domain, as well as about the language needs they have, it was domain experts who provided the most accurate and reliable infor-mation. This supports Long's claim that, if only one source is to be used in a NA, domain experts should be that source (Long, this volume), rather than students, scholars, company representatives, or applied linguists. It has also been shown how, in this study, tri-angulation by sources also produced more reliable findings, since company representatives, who are the usual sources in most NAs, may act as 'gatekeepers'.

With respect to methods, unstructured interviews allowed re-searchers to build rapport with informants, helped roughly to identify the tasks and sub-tasks carried out by domain experts, and were used to collect texts to which Catalan journalists are exposed. However, it was domain experts' introspections that helped the researcher to describe the tasks in detail, identify the different steps, identify the texts involved in them, define the outcome, ascertain the perceived difficulty of each task, and establish what are considered to be acceptable performance standards. This has important consequences for task design, and for the grading and sequencing of tasks as well as for assessment. Pedagogic task design is closely connected to the issue of complexity, a key concept in Robinson's framework for syllabus design (Robinson, 2001). If tasks are to be sequenced in a task-based syllabus according to increasing complexity, obtaining information about the number of elements involved in each task, the here-and-now, and the reasoning demands of each task, is particularly relevant. Using task as the unit of analysis has made it possible to collect information that can be used to define the complexity of each task and, therefore, to make decisions about grading and sequencing. The transformation of target tasks into pedagogic tasks and their grading and sequencing in a syllabus would be, however, the subject of a different paper. With respect to the consequences for assessment, if performance-referenced assessment is going to be applied in a task-based program, as opposed to system-referenced assessment, the information retrieved from domain experts about what are considered to be acceptable standards in the performance of a task can be especially useful.

Other methods, such as unstructured interviews, contributed to improving questionnaires used to obtain information about the frequency and need for specific training for each task. If a variety of methods had not been used, questionnaires alone would clearly have proven capable of obtaining only very limited information. Non-participant observation contributed to obtaining and completing information about specific tasks, which in this case were interviews, press conferences, and presentations.

Finally, the task-based needs analysis reported in this paper has revealed interesting information about the dynamic qualities of target discourse. These qualities were not obtained using previous text-based needs analyses employed in the creation of the English-language program described at the beginning of this paper. After all, it is tasks that drive texts, and not vice versa.

Notes

1 The different steps involved in the performance of the *target task*, 'Interviewing a source', do not necessarily follow the specific sequence shown in Figure 1. However, they are all steps in the process of accomplishing the target task.

2 Our research later showed that in small journalism companies, the journalist is in charge of the whole process of interviewing a source. However, in larger companies, journalists may count on their production teams to take care of some steps in the process, such as 'Making arrangements'.

References

Crookes, G. (1986). Task classification: A cross-disciplinary review. University of Hawaii at Manoa: Center for Second Language Classroom Research, Social Science Research Institute. Technical Report No. 4. Honolulu.

Jasso-Aguilar, R. (1999, this volume). Sources, methods and triangulation in needs analysis: A critical perspective in a case study of Waikiki hotel maids. *English for Specific Purposes* 18, 1, 27–46.

Lincoln, Y. S. (1985). *Naturalistic research*. London: SAGE.

Long, M. H. (this volume). Methodological issues in learner needs analysis.

Martin, M. C., & Brodt, D. E. (1973). Task analysis for training and curriculum design. *Improving Human Performance* 2, 113–20.

Munby, J. (1978). *Communicative syllabus design*. Cambridge: Cambridge University Press.

Robinson, P. (2001). Task complexity, cognitive resources, and syllabus design: A triadic framework for examining task influences on SLA. In P. Robinson (ed.), *Cognition and second language instruction* (pp. 287–318). Cambridge: Cambridge University Press.

Svendsen, C., & K. Krebs (1984). Identifying English for the job: Examples from healthcare occupations. *The ESP Journal* 3, 153–64.

Swales, J. (1990). *Genre Analysis*. Cambridge: Cambridge University Press.

Wilkins, D. (1976). *Notional syllabuses*. Oxford: Oxford University Press.

7 "Feet speak louder than the tongue": A preliminary analysis of language provisions for foreign professional footballers in the Netherlands

Eric Kellerman, Hella Koonen,
Monique van der Haagen

Introduction

Anyone interested both in second language acquisition *and* sport will surely have been impressed by the quality of the English spoken by international tennis stars like Kim Clijsters or Martina Navratilova. Or perhaps the excellent Japanese spoken by top *sumo* wrestlers Akebono (real name Chad Rowan) and Musashimaru (formerly Fiamalu Penitani), both born and raised in Hawai'i. Equally impressive are those professional footballers[1] and managers who become fluent idiomatic speakers of the languages of their host countries. One thinks of the fluent English of French forward Thierry Henry (Arsenal), and his compatriots Gérard Houllier and Arsène Wenger, managers of England's Liverpool and Arsenal football clubs respectively. How do they do it, we wonder, these conspicuous cases of highly successful foreign language learning? Are they naturally gifted, or are there special factors in their sporting worlds which promote proficiency? Is the fact that we tend to see interviews with foreign sporting stars who are usually also *linguistic* stars actually an indicator that the great mass of international sporting figures are no better at learning languages than the rest of us? In this chapter we consider the importance of the host language in the lives of foreign professional footballers, with particular emphasis on the situation in the Netherlands.

Language and professional football

There seems to be very little pertinent academic literature on the topic of language learning in international sports settings, with the partial exception of Miyazaki (2001), a book about non-Japanese

200

sumo wrestlers written for a mass audience by an academic. Most of what there is seems more sociologically oriented (e.g., Koutstaal, 1998, and various papers by Maguire and Stead: Maguire & Stead, 1996, 1998; Stead & Maguire, 1998, 2000a, 2000b). There is of course a great deal of important work on language acquisition by economic migrants ('guest workers') or political refugees such as those studied in the ESF (European Science Foundation) project (e.g., Perdue, 1993, and references to other projects therein). While it might be argued that professional sportsmen and women who move from country to country are also economic migrants (and like many ESF informants, professional footballers may not always have enjoyed high levels of education), they are of course considerably more mobile, sometimes awaking the impression that home is where the chequebook flaps loudest. Nicolas Anelka, for instance, still in his 20s, has now travelled from France to England to Spain and back again to France and England for transfer fees amounting to some $100 million. For this reason, 'itinerant' or 'peripatetic worker' might be a more apt term. On the other hand, there are players with less mercenary ambitions who are keen to leave their home countries to develop their skills by playing abroad. Such is particularly true of many of the Scandinavian players in England interviewed by Stead & Maguire (1998).

The European transfer market has become big business. The media and public alike relish news and rumour of impending moves involving major stars, especially when 'magnet countries' like Spain and Italy, and to a lesser extent England, Scotland, France and Germany, are involved. Clubs demand success, and the richest are willing to cast their net wide to achieve it.[2] In 2000, for example, Barcelona paid Arsenal about $33 million for Dutch winger Marc Overmars, making him at a stroke of a pen the most expensive Dutch player of all time. Unfortunately (from a Dutch perspective, that is), *most* of the best Dutch footballers end up in countries like Spain, Italy and Britain, where top players can earn well over $100,000 a month. What we have here, then, is not so much the 'brain drain' as the 'boot chute'.

As a consequence of this movement of resources, Dutch clubs (like clubs in other 'feeder countries') are themselves forced to look for their talent abroad. Some clubs, like Ajax, sponsor nursery clubs abroad (Ajax Cape Town, for example). Others make use of an ample stream of 'talent' from eastern Europe and Africa. According to the managing director of one leading Dutch club, to fill the gap caused by the dearth of local talent, mature foreign players will have to be paid at least $255,000 a year to come to the Netherlands. The downside of all this wealth, as the language teacher at another Dutch club maintained, is that some players cannot handle this rags-to-riches transformation and spend so freely on clothes, cars and friends they never knew they had, that at the end of the month they do not have enough left to pay their bills. Fortunately for them, Dutch clubs frequently take care of their players' banking, immigration, and housing problems.

Travelling footballers are nothing new. Since the second world war, players have regularly been lured abroad to earn their livings in Europe and beyond (notably those English footballers who fatefully went to Columbia in 1950 to escape an £8 a week maximum wage at home). But it was probably the Bosman ruling of 1995 that was responsible for the current heavy traffic in footballers within the European Union. The Bosman ruling states that players who are members of the European Union are free to leave an EU club at the end of their contracts and may freely negotiate new contracts elsewhere.[3] As an example of the current state of football in England, one of the top clubs, Chelsea, has regularly fielded a team with only one British player in it, while Arsenal may field as few as three British players (and as many as five Frenchmen).

This growing internationalisation presents us with a wonderful opportunity for studying second language acquisition and small-scale language planning in the workplace. While the standard of European club football may have benefited from the movement of so many foreign footballers, their presence nevertheless creates a special set of difficulties for player and employer alike. For instance, the press officer at Dutch club Ajax told us that in the days when foreign footballers were a rarity, they would learn the language of the club very quickly because it was the only way to survive. Now, the much larger groups of foreigners tend to stick together and the clubs have a linguistic problem on their hands.

But do the clubs recognise their foreign players' language needs, and if they do, what provisions do they make for them? To approach this question, we recently carried out a survey of Dutch clubs, players, coaches and teachers. Initially, for the sake of comparison, we wanted to tackle the English situation as well. However, after the consultation by telephone of a number of clubs in the second and third divisions of the Nationwide Football League,[4] we soon learned that most of these clubs did not have any provisions for the few foreign players they employed. What is more, the clubs in our target divisions (FA Barclaycard Premiership and Nationwide Football League Division One) have proved to be unco-operative (with the exception of Arsenal, to be discussed below). For the purposes of this paper, therefore, we will focus principally on the survey of Dutch clubs.

The study

In world terms, Dutch is a minority language with about 22 million speakers, 16 million of whom are squeezed into the Netherlands.[5] This probably makes the Dutch more aware than the English of the linguistic problems foreigners may encounter, because they, the Dutch, speak foreign languages (especially English) as a matter of course. The accommodating nature of the Dutch in this respect has led some of the English-speaking players in our survey to comment that they did not really see the need to learn Dutch at all. These comments are in line with one of the most frequently heard complaints about the Dutch (in actual fact a backhanded compliment to their linguistic abilities), their eagerness to switch to another language the moment they detect a foreign accent issuing from the person they are talking to.

As of September 1999, there were roughly 200 foreign footballers playing for 36 different clubs in the Netherlands. These clubs are equally distributed between the top division (*KPN-Telecompetitie*) and the second division (*Toto-divisie*). We constructed a telephone questionnaire for the club managements designed to provide us with information regarding the languages the clubs used, the importance they attached to Dutch being spoken by their foreign players, the facilities they had for the players to learn a language, and the way in which these facilities were organised for them. 28 of the 36 clubs (a remarkably high 78%) answered the questionnaires, and 21 (c. 58%) further promised to see to it that written questionnaires in both English and Dutch would be filled out by the foreign players (see Appendices for the English versions of these questionnaires). Eventually, we sent out 117 questionnaires to players, and 48 (41%) were returned; again a remarkably high yield. However, 10 questionnaires had to be discarded because they were either filled out by Dutch-speaking Belgians, or by someone acting on the players' behalf, a fact which may be construed as potential evidence of a problem of which we were aware, namely that some of the foreign players in the Netherlands may be pretty well illiterate. Thus we were left with 38 usable questionnaires (c. 34%). We also interviewed two coaches, two teachers of Dutch, and one press officer in order to obtain more background information on the language situation at the clubs.

Findings

The clubs

What follows are accounts of the most striking responses to these questionnaires. We will start off with the clubs. To the question "Does the club think it important for players to have a thorough command of Dutch?", the answer was almost uniformly affirmative. Only one club said "No", but added that players should "mingle and make themselves understood". All clubs reported that they used Dutch, even though some in the *KPN-Telecompetitie* said that they occasionally used other languages, such as English, as well. In response to the question as to why players needed to be taught Dutch, most of the clubs considered "communication in the workplace" to be the principal reason, with a smaller number also mentioning "integration into Dutch life". The clubs who referred to the workplace explained that foreign players are employees and are therefore expected to speak Dutch just like Dutch employees. Some of the remarks made were: "Players have to understand Dutch in order to follow instructions and conversations," and "It takes up too much time if players do not have a thorough command of Dutch." Although some clubs recognise that English could function as a lingua franca as well, Robby McDonald, former manager of *KPN-Telecompetitie* club De Graafschap and himself bilingual, said that since contracts usually last as long as four years, it is important for players to learn Dutch as soon as possible. Sef Vergoossen, former manager of *KPN-Telecompetitie* team Roda JC, and now working in Belgium, told his Dutch players to speak Dutch to the foreign players: "I tell them to speak slowly and to use gestures. Explain the message in English only if it is not understood."

Now, if clubs think it is important for foreign players to speak Dutch, what kind of facilities do they have for them to learn the language? 68% of the clubs we contacted provide their foreign staff with some sort of language instruction, but there are those who surprisingly lack these facilities. Some explain this away by claiming that all their players already speak Dutch, while others suggest that communication is simply not a problem at their club. Although clubs in the *KPN-Telecompetitie* are more likely to serve their foreign staff in a language they understand than *Toto-divisie* clubs, most of them provide their foreign players with language training, while fewer than half of the *Toto-divisie* clubs do so. Money, or the lack of it, is probably the most important reason for this difference between the divisions, and in any case there are fewer foreign players in the *Toto-divisie* than in the *KPN-Telecompetitie*.

It is also interesting to see what forms of language instruction clubs provide their players with. Some clubs hire their own teachers, while others work with schools in the area or with specialised language learning institutions. Lessons are planned around training and game schedules, but most clubs try to provide their foreigners with at least two lessons a week. Eight *KPN-Telecompetitie* clubs also offer players' partners the opportunity to follow courses. Clubs also realise that, for most players, following language courses is low on their list of priorities. Three clubs in the *KPN-Telecompetitie* stated that taking language lessons was a contractual obligation, while twelve said that lessons were 'compulsory'. However, while we were visiting Ajax, we came across one of the club's language teachers waiting to give a lesson to a star player who has been notoriously slow to learn Dutch. After half an hour, the teacher got fed up and decided to go home, leaving the team manager still out looking for the miscreant. Acts of truancy like this are fairly common, and the fines imposed by the clubs for failing to attend lessons are financially no more than fleabites. Els Herberichs, the Dutch teacher at *KPN-Telecompetitie* club Roda JC, notes a great difference in motivation between the footballers and other foreigners she teaches: "Footballers are in the spotlight and they know it. In the beginning it is very difficult to make contact with them. Therefore it is important to create an atmosphere in which these players feel comfortable. That is why I do not allow journalists or photographers in my classes." Leon Smeets (formerly a language teacher at PSV Eindhoven and Willem II, now at Ajax) agrees: "... players know they are good at football but hesitant when it comes to learning new languages, and they want journalists to write about what they are good at."

Clubs use a variety of materials for teaching language. Some use commercially available courses, while others design their own materials, for instance to teach players football terms. A few clubs use a combination of both. However, Herberichs believes that foreign footballers should do more than merely learn the language – they should also attempt to *integrate* into Dutch society, which is why in her classes she exploits differences between Dutch and other cultures. "I am a woman," she says, "and in some cultures, women do not have the same position as in the Netherlands. Talking about differences such as these is ten times more important than teaching them Dutch football terms." David Endt (Ajax) notes a further problem of integration: "There are players who come from a country where tribal hierarchies are very important. If there are two players from different tribes, one player may not take orders from the other, and this can be a problem on or off the field, something that we have no notion of." For Endt, being able to unpack the cultural baggage foreign players bring with them is essential; he for one would like to see suitably trained counsellors appointed by the clubs to help players. "Cultural and linguistic differences are equally important," he adds,

> ... but we should not forget that language is the bearer of the culture and culture is more complex than language alone. You have to learn more about different cultures to be able to guide these players. The football scene makes this rather difficult, because it is based on results at an extreme level. It is exceptionally demanding. If a player performs badly, he will be ignored. This is the law of football. There have to be people in such an organisation as Ajax to prevent this fall-out. I must not be swayed by the issue of the day. I have to look ahead and try to understand why someone is not performing very well. The club has to create conditions in such a way that a player starts to feel good. We have to see the player as a human being and not only as a footballer.

The players

Now let us turn to the players' responses. They were each presented with questionnaires dealing with their backgrounds, their knowledge of languages, the language instruction they may or may not be receiving, and their attitudes towards learning and speaking Dutch. The responses to the questionnaires showed that the 38 players in our final sample spoke 21 different native languages between them, ranging from Danish to Twi and from English to Bobo.[6] The players were, on average, between 20 and 24 years of age. *KPN-Tele-competitie* players tended to have been in the Netherlands longer (almost 4 years on average) than *Toto-divisie* players (about 2.5 years).

34% of the players said that they spoke Dutch 'well' or 'very well', as against the 36% who assessed their English at this level. Only four (10.5%) said they did not understand Dutch well. During training sessions, about half the players said they spoke Dutch only, with about 60% speaking only Dutch during team talks. During interviews, on the other hand, just under one-third (31.5%) used Dutch only. Only 26% reported using Dutch with other foreign players that do not have the same native language as the respondents, and only one player reported exclusively using Dutch with family, friends or partners. Most players reported using Dutch for shopping (79%), banking (65%), and immigration matters (63%).

In response to the question whether it was important to speak Dutch well, 37 out of the 38 agreed that it was. 20 (c. 53%) stressed the importance of Dutch at work, four pointed to the usefulness of Dutch while shopping, and "Dutch-speaking partners" and "the need to consult with teachers at their children's schools" were each mentioned by two players. 12 players gave less focussed responses, (e.g., "It is important to communicate better with other people"; "It is important to understand what is being said"), and only one specifically mentioned integration: "... so you can integrate more easily into society. It is also important for my own development." One player took an anthropologist's stance: "It is important to be able to observe and understand people interacting in their natural linguistic state." Two players seem to consider the Netherlands as no more than a port of call on the way to somewhere more prominent: "It is not important to speak Dutch when you are determined to leave the country again." "It is not important if you are only here for a few years." This attitude is probably more widespread than is evident from our survey, and the Dutch teacher at Ajax sees it as one of the main reasons why some players resist learning Dutch. Two players mention English as a preferable alternative: "Everybody speaks English." "It is important to speak Dutch in the Netherlands, but it is not important because everyone speaks good English." In the end, club management, coaches and players alike all considered good communication to be an essential component of good football.

We have already seen that most clubs provide their foreign players with some sort of language instruction. Nearly all the players indicated that they are receiving or have received language instruction in the Netherlands. There is, however, considerable variation in the frequency of these lessons. While players in the *KPN-Tele-competitie* are taught on average for two hours per week, players in the *Toto-divisie* reported an average of almost six hours per week. Some of these latter players might possibly have had intensive language training outside the club, because their clubs did not report as many hours.

Players were also asked if they were satisfied with the language instruction they received. Like students everywhere, two wanted "more listening and speaking", two wanted "more hours", and one player wanted a different tutor. Most players were, however, happy with their form of instruction (c. 86%).

The last question in the questionnaire dealt with more general issues about learning Dutch. The players were asked to indicate how important such factors as 'language training', 'having a partner who speaks Dutch', 'contact with team-mates', 'contact with friends', and the 'availability of Dutch-language media'. Unsurprisingly, most players (c. 87%) indicated that language training was 'important' or 'very important' in learning Dutch. And while most players did not report having Dutch partners (c. 68%), when they did, they were rated as 'important' or 'very important'. Dutch team-mates were uniformly considered (very) important, as were Dutch friends.

It is more difficult to establish how important the media are for learning Dutch. More than a quarter of the players indicated that neither Dutch radio, nor newspapers, books or magazines were important for learning Dutch. Unsurprisingly, Dutch television *was*, with one exception only, considered 'important' or 'very important' for acquiring the language. In a recent magazine interview, PSV's former Finnish winger Joonas Kolkka (now in Germany) described TV as a central component of acclimatisation: "There is hardly anything better for learning the language than television. And the language is very important for feeling good in your new culture." (Schouten, 1999, translation ours). Cultural and linguistic differences makes integration into a new society, even a small one like a professional football club, a very complex issue. Ajax' David Endt put it to us this way:

> New players find themselves in a different environment, a different culture and a different atmosphere. They also have to absorb a lot of information from the club and from the coach, who tells them what to do technically and tactically. And then there is the language. New players cannot achieve equilibrium with the environment in which they have to function because of the enormous amount of input they receive. This is reflected in their performance on the field. Concentrating on the trainer's explanations eats up the energy that the players consequently lack on the field.

The situation in England

Our survey suggests that the majority of Dutch clubs are well aware of the potential language and cultural problems facing their foreign imports and make provisions for their needs. We had originally intended to conduct a similar survey among English clubs, but, as we have indicated above, Premiership clubs were generally unco-operative. What information we do have on the English situation is sketchy but telling. One English club from the lower divisions of the Nationwide league justified its lack of foreign language facilities when a spokesperson claimed (thus inadvertently providing us with the title of this chapter) that "feet speak louder than the tongue", a proposition no Dutch club in our survey would subscribe to. Dutchman Willem Korsten (formerly of Leeds and Tottenham Hotspur) suggests that the English clubs leave language learning very much to chance. Korsten notes that, when he was playing for Dutch club Vitesse, *English* lessons were provided for players as training sessions were conducted in that language (the coach at the time was a German). Vitesse also provided Spanish and Japanese lessons 'just for fun', but perhaps with their players' further careers in mind. At Leeds, Korsten notes, language learning was left to its own devices. One foreign player had to learn English from fellow-players, as no English teacher was available at the club. As a Dutchman, Korsten notes that he and the Scandinavian players had far fewer language problems than players from southern Europe (cf. Stead & Maguire, 1998), though the various regional accents of British players constituted a substantial hurdle. Our Dutch respondents also note how relatively easy it is for Scandinavian players to adapt, and Co Adriaanse, former manager of Ajax, was quoted on Ajax' American website as saying, "It's hard to teach a player Dutch in such short time (*sic*). We did it with (the Danes) Laudrup and Grønkjær. But (Georgian) Shota Arveladze, for example, still calls an 'één-tweetje' a 'one-two' after four years" (www.ajax-usa.com/ajax/news.html).

However, it is *not* self-evident that mastery of the host language is essential, especially for a manager of a top club. This point is quickly forgotten in the public discussion of Chelsea's Claudio Ranieri, an Italian appointed in 2000 as manager of the London club with absolutely no knowledge of English. In the early days of his tenure, the press conducted a non-stop campaign of complaint and mockery, even to the extent of ridiculing the translations of Ranieri's reluctant 'interpreter', an English steward at the club with an Italian mother, who was rapidly pressed into service. Once Ranieri realised that journalists were judging him by the quality of the 'interpreting', the steward went back to stewarding (Glanville, 2000). The rectitude of press prejudices were amply confirmed by the club's less than stellar performances at the time. What is quickly overlooked is that many top European clubs like Chelsea are essentially foreign clubs in a local competition, with the players largely closeted away from the directors and administrative staff at their own self-sufficient training centres. As one English club official told us zeugmatically, "We only see the players on match days and television". In Chelsea's case, both coaching staff and a good number of the players are Italian or have played in Italy, a fact which prompted two of the regular English players to announce publicly that they were considering taking Italian lessons out of politeness to their manager. And, as Brian Glanville, one of the more experienced English football commentators, points out (Glanville, 2000), there have been conspicuous cases where football prowess has apparently not been undermined by deficient language skills, notably Jesse Carver[7] and George Raynor, two Englishmen who both successfully managed top Italian teams in the 1950s. In this century, the Turk, Fatih Terim successfully managed Fiorentina for a brief period while barely speaking Italian. Perhaps, then, Ranieri was being hounded by an insular press, anxious to see him fail and happy when he did. His English is certainly more than adequate now (2003). Similarly, the Englishman Bobby Robson, and his successor, the Dutchman Louis van Gaal, were both derided over their linguistic skills while at Barcelona, once the results stopped coming in. In the Netherlands, the initial failings of one expensive Greek import have also popularly been attributed to a lack of eagerness to acquire functional Dutch skills.

There is of course a whiff of hypocrisy in all this. Journalists and chatlist contributors blame foreign personnel who do not learn the host language fast enough, while they themselves are quite likely to be monolingual. In this respect, the following story about Dutch soccer star Dennis Bergkamp is quite instructive. Speaking in competent English, the Dutchman was just coming to the end of a first press conference in London shortly after his multimillion-dollar transfer from Inter Milan to Arsenal in 1995, when a journalist asked Bergkamp if he spoke any foreign languages. Bergkamp paused for a second or two as if to savour the profundity of the question before responding calmly, "Yes, I speak yours."[8]

One club at least in the English Premiership does take the language needs of its players seriously. This is Arsenal, which has a French manager, Arsène Wenger. Wenger was born in Strasbourg, and until he began schooling at six, spoke Alsatian at home. Later in life he learned German and English (a language he realised was essential if he was to get on), and in the mid-nineties went to Japan to manage the J-League side, Grampus 8. There he was provided with an English-speaking interpreter, which, he notes, meant that his English improved at the expense of his Japanese.[9] Yet his period in Japan, like Carver's and Raynor's, was marked by success. He returned to France to manage Monaco, before Arsenal signed him in 1996. His own English is fluent and idiomatic.

Arsenal, like many top European clubs, has amassed a considerable non-British playing presence at the club. At the time of writing, there are players on the books from Brazil, Cameroon (though, through early emigration this player, speaks Spanish), France, Germany, the Ivory Coast, Latvia, Lithuania, The Netherlands, Nigeria, Spain, Sweden, Switzerland and more. As at many Dutch clubs, it is stipulated in foreign players' contracts that they must learn English, and a teacher is regularly available. Players may take extra lessons if they wish. There is a strict English-only policy at the club, except when Wenger is engaged in one-on-one conversations with another Frenchman.[10] The multinational character of the club naturally raises certain problems of integration, with young players in particular having problems in adjusting to life abroad. Wenger believes that it takes at least six months for a player to begin to feel comfortable in his new environment, and a full two years to feel 'at home'. In such circumstances, Wenger stresses the need to develop what he calls a 'club culture', with its own norms and values operating independently of the dominant culture outside the gates of Arsenal's training centre. At the same time, he also realises that there are limits to what can be done to force players to integrate – at mealtimes for instance, players naturally tend to sit in national groups, or, in the case of the players from former Soviet republics, historico-political ones.[11]

Wenger does not see a need for a football-oriented English teaching syllabus, for although it is essential that players learn crucial technical expressions quickly (such as 'push up', 'drop back', 'lay the ball off'), they will do so in the best Total Physical Response manner – on the job (swearing in English, Wenger wryly notes, is mostly limited to variants on the F-word). Noting the variable progress made by his non-British players, he points to extroversion as a positive factor in language success, illustrating this by reference to the personalities of two of his players from the same country, the one outgoing and learning by leaps and bounds, the other, more retiring, making slow progress. He firmly believes that successful language learning is a prerequisite for acclimatisation – and an acclimatised player will give of his best. On Ranieri, he stated that, while the Italian might get by without too much English initially, in the long term it would prove detrimental to his position as manager of Chelsea if he did not improve (which he has).

Final thoughts

We have seen in our survey that clubs in the Netherlands consider host language provisions essential to foreign players' successful functioning, as does Arsenal's Arsène Wenger. Players too see the value of learning the host language, if only for instrumental reasons. Yet there is some very limited evidence, if only at managerial level, that footballing success and linguistic prowess do not need to go hand in hand, at least in the short term. But then managers and coaches are leaders who give directions, if necessary through interpreters, while players are the foot soldiers who carry the directions out on the field without the luxury of interpreter services at their elbows.

In a world of ever-increasing internationalism, we predict that the language needs of professional footballers, managers and coaches will become increasingly prominent in the formulation of club policy, especially as it is quite clear that Dutch clubs at least see Dutch language competence as a prerequisite for footballing success. Given the complexity of the issues involved – language and culture, the need for tangible achievement, integration in the workplace, relations with the world outside the confines of the club, and so on – there is clearly good reason for detailed investigation of language within professional football clubs. How this second language is acquired, in what is essentially a micro-multicultural environment, is a matter of considerable interest, and deserves to be taken beyond the anecdotal stage. Future research could perhaps also be undertaken in a more ethnographic framework to study the club and its members as a social group. But our experience is that gaining access to clubs is no easy matter for outsiders.[12] Perhaps European universities should copy certain of their American counterparts and nurture their own top sportsmen before selling them for vast sums to the Real Madrids, Manchester Uniteds and Barcelonas of this world on the strict understanding that they be permitted to conduct ethnographic research in exchange for scoring goals or saving penalties.

Notes

1 In this chapter, 'football' and 'footballer' are used in their British senses. Readers more familiar with American English should bear in mind that the equivalents are 'soccer' and 'soccer player'.
2 Only holders of passports of member states of the European Union may move freely to seek work within the EU. There is a quota on players from outside the EU and this has led to a spate of cases where players from outside the EU have claimed citizenship on the basis of spurious documentation.
3 After this paper was first drafted (September, 2000), radical new legislation affecting contracts was proposed within the EU which would considerably reduce the size of transfer fees.

4 In England, the professional scene is divided up into the FA Premier League and the three divisions of the Nationwide Football League. The Premiership and the Nationwide Football League are separate organisations, though promotion and relegation between them takes place every season.

5 Apart from the Netherlands, Dutch is also spoken in Flanders (Belgium), Surinam, and the Netherlands Antilles.

6 There were 6 speakers of English, 5 of Russian, 4 of Danish, 3 each of French and Romanian, 2 of Portuguese, and one each of Arabic, Bobo (Burkina-Faso), Bulgarian, Czech, Finnish, German, Ghanaian, Lithuanian, Manding Ko (Gambia), Polish, Slovenian, Spanish, Twi (Ghana), Ukrainian and Yugoslavian.

7 Glanville, a fluent speaker of Italian, cites Carver's favourite 'Italian' phrase, *Lui parlare me lo stesso*, presumably 'He always says the same to me'.

8 Personal communication, Ken Friar, Managing Director, Arsenal Football Club.

9 Japan, with its deeply-ingrained tradition of hospitality towards high-status outsiders, is an interesting case in this respect. The feat of a *gaijin* mastering Japanese essentially undermines one of the cornerstones of Japaneseness, as do Akebono's and Musashimura's achievements in reaching the highest sumo ranking of *yokozuna* (Surin, no date). Non-Japanese Asians can have a hard time of it in Japan, and even second- or third-generation Chinese and Koreans may hide their true identities in order to avoid discrimination. Frequently, the way to overcome these racial handicaps in Japanese society is to seek one's fortune in sport and entertainment. Once established, these stars can safely 'out' themselves, as was the case with the Korean-origin baseball pitcher Harimoto and the actress Keiko Matsuzaka (Keiko Yoshioka, personal communication).

10 If this seems axiomatic, it should be pointed out that a note on Fulham's club website once stated that Jean Tigana, the former French manager of the club, insisted on English being spoken, even between himself and his French coaching staff ('No tongue twisters for Fulham', www.fulhamfc.co.uk/news/02122000.asp).

11 A number of Dutch respondents specifically pointed to this phenomenon at their own clubs, and considered it a problem. At one club, it was forbidden for two foreign players to sit next to each other at lunch; others insist that players order their food in Dutch.

12 The principal data gatherer in this study is Hella Koonen. The decision to have a woman breach the male bastion of professional football was deliberately taken, and has paid off handsomely, we think, in terms of the access we have been granted to Dutch clubs. However, for obvious reasons, detailed ethnographic research would best be conducted by a male insider – as Hella herself put it in a spoken presentation of the results reported here, "I can hardly get in the showers with the players, now, can I!"

Acknowledgments

We would particularly like to thank David Endt (Ajax), Els Herberichs (teacher at Roda JC), Willem Korsten, Rob McDonald (former Manager, De Graafschap, now with Ajax Capetown), Leon Smeets (formerly language teacher at PSV Eindhoven and Willem II, now at Ajax), Sef Vergoossen (former Manager, Roda JC), and Arsène Wenger (Manager, Arsenal Football Club) for giving up some of their precious time to talk to us. Our thanks are also due to Ken Friar (Managing Director, Arsenal) for his assistance in facilitating the first author's visit to the Arsenal Training Centre, and to all those Dutch clubs and foreign players who answered our questionnaires. We are also grateful to Carel Jansen and Robin Leavis (University of Nijmegen), and David Stead (Loughborough University) for wise counsel.

References

Glanville, B. (2000). Ranieri and the Italian connection. *The SportsStar.* http://www.thesportsstar.com/tss2352/23520860.htm,   27 December 2000.

Koutstaal, I. (1998). Teambuilding in een cultureel divers samengestelde betaald voetbal organisatie ('Team building in a culturally diverse professional football organisation'). Undergraduate thesis, Free University of Amsterdam.

Maguire, J A. and & Stead, D. E. (1996). Far pavilions? Cricket migrants, foreign sojourns and contested identities. *International Review for the Sociology of Sport* 31, 1–24.

Maguire, J. A. and & Stead, D. E. (1998). Border crossings: Soccer labour migration and the European Union. *International Review for the Sociology of Sport* 32, 59–73.

Miyazaki, S. (2001). *Gaikokujin rikishi wa naze nihongo ga umai no ka* ('Why are foreign sumo wrestlers so good at Japanese?'). Tokyo: Nihongogaku Kenkyuujo.

Perdue, C. (ed.) (1993). *Adult language acquisition: Cross-linguistic perspectives.* Cambridge: Cambridge University Press.

Schouten, W. (1999). Door vreemde ogen ('Through foreign eyes'). *TV Studio* 31/07/99 – 06/08/99, 8–9.

Stead, D. E. and Maguire, J. A. (1998). View from the north: The experiences of Nordic/Scandinavian players in English soccer. In P. Murphy (ed.), *Review 1997–98 Association Football Season,* 34–36. London: Singer and Friedlander.

Stead, D. E. and & Maguire, J. A. (2000). No boundaries to ambition: Soccer labour migration and the case of Nordic/Scandinavian players in England. In *Soccer and Science in an Interdisciplinary Perspective,* J. Bangsbø, (ed.), Copenhagen: University of Copenhagen.

Stead, D. E. and & Maguire, J. A. (2000). Rite de Passage or Passage to Riches? *Journal of Sport and Social Issues*, 24(1), 36–60.

Surin, K. (no date). Afterthoughts on 'Diaspora'. www.duke.edu/literature/DIASPORA.htm

Appendix A

Telephone questionnaire for clubs (translated into English)

Good morning/afternoon. This is Hella Koonen from the University of Nijmegen. Could I speak to ... in the Press Office?

For my final thesis at the University of Nijmegen, I'm investigating the language needs of foreign players in the Netherlands and England and the language teaching provisions at various clubs. An increasing number of foreign footballers work in these two countries, but little is known about how they manage when it comes to language. That's why I'm interested in the ways in which clubs meet the language needs of their players.

May I ask you a number of questions?

1) *How many foreign players are there at your club?*
   a) If there are no foreign players, ask why.   END

2) *Which language is/was used the most?*
   a) On the pitch during training
   b) On the pitch during matches
   c) During team talks
   d) At press conferences
      i) By whom?
   e) During interviews
      i) By whom?

3) *Does/did the club offer language training?*
   a) If No, why not?
      i) Does the club think it important for foreign players to have a good command of Dutch? Why?
      ii) Ask whether we can submit a questionnaire to the players, then   END
   b) If Yes, what languages?

4) *What are the language classes like?*
   a) Type
      i) Teacher
      ii) 'Teach yourself'
      iii) Other?
   b) Frequency
   c) Location
   d) Method

5) *Who are the classes? for (Just the players?)*

6) *Are classes compulsory for players?*

7) *Does the club think it important for players to have a thorough command of Dutch? Why?*

I would also like to ask your foreign players a number of questions to find out what they consider to be their language needs.

May I send you a number of questionnaires to be filled in by the foreign players?

Thanks very much for your help.

Appendix B

The players' questionnaire

1 How old are you?

....

2 In which country were you born?

....

3 Which language is your mother tongue?

....

4 When did you move to the Netherlands?

.... / ....

    month   / year

5 Have you lived with a Dutch family?

- Yes, I have lived with a Dutch family since ....
- Yes, I lived with a Dutch family from ....
  until................................... .
- No

6 Do you (or did you) have a partner who speaks Dutch very well?

- Yes
- No (continue with question no. 8)

7 How long have you known (or did you know) this partner?

.... years

.... months

8 How well do you **understand** the following languages?
   (Example: Dutch: not very well – fair – well – very well)

   Dutch: not very well – fair – well – very well

   English: not very well – fair – well – very well

9 How well do you **speak** the following languages?
   (Example: Dutch: not very well – fair – well – very well)

   Dutch: not very well – fair – well – very well

   English: not very well – fair – well – very well

10 Which languages **other than Dutch and English** do you speak and how
   well do you speak them?

   (Example: ...*French*.................... : fair –(well)– very well)

   1) .... : fair – well – very well

   2) .... : fair – well – very well

   3) .... : fair – well – very well

---

11 For which of the above languages did you have classes **before you came
   to the Netherlands** and how long?

   1) Dutch   : .... years

   2) English   : .... years

   3) ....   : .... years

   4) ....   : .... years

   5) ....   : .... years

---

12 Which language is used most: Which language do **you** use most:

   During training: During training:
   • Dutch   • Dutch
   • English   • English
   • Other: ....   • Other: ....

   During matches: During matches:
   • Dutch   • Dutch
   • English   • English
   • Other: ....   • Other: ....

   During meetings: During meetings:
   • Dutch   • Dutch
   • English   • English
   • Other: ....   • Other: ....

   During press conferences /   During press conferences /
   interviews: interviews:
   • Dutch   • Dutch
   • English   • English
   • Other: ....   • Other: ....

                                          With Dutch players:
                                          • Dutch
                                          • English
                                          • Other: ....

With foreign players whose language
you don't speak:
- Dutch
- English
- Other: ....

With family, friends and/or partner:
- Dutch
- English
- Other: ....

13 Indicate which of the following activities you take part in and which
language you then use.

- Shopping:
  - Dutch
  - English
  - Other: ....

- Banking:
  - Dutch
  - English
  - Other: ....

- 'Vreemdelingendienst'
  (Immigration):
  - Dutch
  - English
  - Other: ....

- Housing:
  - Dutch
  - English
  - Other: ....

14 Do you find it important to speak Dutch well?

- Yes
- No (continue with question no. 16)

15 Why is it important for you to speak Dutch well?
(then continue with question no. 17)

....

....

....

16 Why is it **not** important for you to speak Dutch well?

....

....

....

17 Have you had any language classes in the Netherlands?

- Yes, I still do
- Yes, but not any more
- No (continue with question no. 22)

18 Indicate for which language(s) you have/had classes and how often.

- Dutch: .... hours per week

- English: .... hours per week

- Other language: .... : .... hours per week

19 How much attention in class is/was given to:
(Example: Reading: (much) – little)

Listening: much – little
Reading: much – little
Speaking: much – little
Writing: much – little

20 Are you in general satisfied with the classes you have?

- Yes (continue with question no. 26)
- No

21 How would you like to change these classes?
(then continue with question no. 26)

- more often, namely .... hours per week

- less often, namely .... hours per week

- classes for a different language, namely ....

- more listening and speaking

- less listening and speaking

- other: ....
  ....

22 Would you like to have language classes? If yes, for which language(s)?

- Yes: • Dutch
         • English
         • Other: ....
- No (continue with question no. 25)

23 How would these classes be organised?
(More than one answer can be possible.)

- Offered by the club
- Coaching by friends or relatives
- With teacher
- Without teacher
- Other; namely ....

24 How often would you like to have these classes?

.... hours per week (continue with question no. 26)

25 Why do you **not** want to have language classes?

....
....
....
....
....
....

26 Some people learn to understand Dutch by watching television.
Indicate how important the following are for you to learn Dutch.
(Example:
Radio: not applicable – not important – important – very important)

1) Language lessons:
not applicable – not important – (important) – very important
2) Dutch partner:
not applicable – not important – important – very important
3) Contact with team-mates:
not applicable – not important – important – very important
4) Contact with friends:
not applicable – not important – important – very important
5) Radio:
not applicable – not important – important – very important
6) Television:
not applicable – not important – important – very important
7) Newspapers:
not applicable – not important – important – very important
8) Books and magazines:
not applicable – not important – important – very important

This is the end of the questionnaire.
Thank you very much for your co-operation!

PART IV:
THE ACADEMIC SECTOR

8   A task-based needs analysis of a tertiary Korean as a foreign language program

Craig Chaudron, Catherine J. Doughty,
Youngkyu Kim, Dong-kwan Kong, Jinhwa Lee,
Young-geun Lee, Michael H. Long, Rachel Rivers,
and Ken Urano

Introduction

In 2002, a research team at the University of Hawai'i's National Foreign Language Resource Center (UH NFLRC) completed a three-year, federally funded[1] pilot project on a task-based approach to the teaching of Korean as a foreign language (KFL). The project covered all six components in the design, implementation, and evaluation of a Task-Based Language Teaching (TBLT) program (Doughty & Long, 2002; Long, 2000; Long & Norris, 2000): needs analysis; syllabus design; materials development; methodology and pedagogy; testing; and evaluation. Deliverables from the project included instruments and procedures for each component in both Korean and English, the latter intended as models for potential use in the teaching of other commonly and less commonly taught languages. This paper describes Stage 1 of the project, completed in the academic year 1999–2000: a task-based analysis of learners' target language needs, along with an illustration of the use of target discourse samples, collected as part of the needs analysis, in a module of task-based teaching materials. While some data are presented from the Korean study, the emphasis throughout is a practical demonstration of one process by which a task-based needs analysis (NA) can be carried out for any tertiary foreign language program. Since it was not the intention of the project at this time to develop an entire curriculum, only a selection of identified target needs was focused on to develop prototype task-based instruction.

The research team recognized that a complete NA for such learners should involve gathering information via various *methods* and from various *sources* (Long, this volume), e.g., through interviews with their teachers or future employers (domain experts), analyses of potential uses of Korean in target situations sampled

225

using participant and non-participant observation, as well as by soliciting the opinions of the students themselves through structured or unstructured interviews and survey questionnaires. While learners are not always very sophisticated judges of their own needs, it was deemed important to identify their perceived future needs:

> [T]he sufficiency of language students as *sources* of information about their present or future communicative needs is a complex and sensitive issue. To be sure, learners sometimes not only wish to be consulted, but also are well-informed ... [E]xpertise is by no means guaranteed. Learners may be 'pre-experience', or 'pre-service', ... Alternatively, they may be 'in-service', [and] ... can sometimes provide useful information on such matters as their learning styles and preferences, i.e., partial input for a *means analysis*. Understandably, however, they tend to make inadequate sources of information for a *needs analysis* (NA), since most in-service learners know about their work, but little about the language involved in functioning successfully in their target discourse domains, and most pre-experience or pre-service learners know little about either. (Long, this volume, p. 20)

The study

In the Fall semester, 1999, and Spring of 2000, a task-based NA was conducted for all students (*n* = 84) enrolled in 100-level through 400-level Korean classes at the University of Hawai'i (UH). The steps involved in this process are summarized here, and then described in detail in the following sections. First, unstructured interviews were conducted with instructional staff (not reported here), and with a stratified random sample of 25% of students enrolled in Fall of 1999. Next, the entire student population was surveyed using a written questionnaire based, in part, on findings from the interviews. Goals reported included visiting friends and relatives, tourism, academic research of various kinds, career enhancement, church-related activities, and military service requirements. Following an analysis of these goals and the interview tapes, in the interest of producing materials of relevance to the largest proportion of students, two target 'social survival' tasks were identified as relevant for over 90% of respondents, who reported having already visited Korea and/or planning to do so (again): 'Following street directions' and 'Shopping for clothing'. After English baseline data for those two target tasks had been gathered and analyzed, authentic Korean discourse samples surrounding their accomplishment were collected by native speakers of Korean in Honolulu and Seoul. Finally, steps in performing the two tasks were identified and the findings incorporated in two prototype modules of task-based materials, one designed for near beginners, and the other for second-year students of Korean.

Participants

The students involved in this research included all those in first- and second-semester classes in the first and second years of study of KFL (101, 102, 201, and 202), and in second-semester classes in the third and fourth years (302 and 402). A total of 84 students were enrolled in those classes in Fall, 1999, distributed by class level and academic status as shown in Tables 1a and 1b (one subject did not eventually participate, so that all tallies are based on a total *n* of 83).

Table 1a Students by course

Course (and section)	Number of students
101	9
102	12
201	16
202–1	12
202–2	13
302	8
402	13
Total	83

Table 1b Students by academic status

Academic status	Number of students
Freshman	13
Sophomore	19
Junior	18
Senior	16
Graduate	17
Total	83

Of those students, 51 were females and 32 males. With respect to their language backgrounds, 55 (66%) listed only English as their L1, and 15 (18%) both English and Korean as L1s, indicating an expected sub-population of heritage language students. Later analysis of the questionnaire and interview results suggested that, as over half of the sample had Korean-speaking parents or grandparents with whom they spoke on occasion or more frequently, then even among those who identified themselves as L1 English speakers, over half did speak Korean in the home or family. Among the ten students (12%) who did *not* list English as a native language, seven were native speakers of Japanese, one listed only L1 Korean, and one each listed only Russian or Tagalog as their L1. The remaining three students (4%) listed English and one of Chinese, French and Thai as their L1s.

Unstructured interview procedures and results

Interview sample

A stratified random sample ($n = 21$) of 25% was selected from the entire population of students in these courses for in-depth unstructured interviews. The procedure was as follows:

(i)   All students in each class level and section (there were two sections of Korean 202, so that seven class groups were involved) were listed and blocked both by class group and in terms of their status as either graduate or undergraduate, on the assumption that this known classification distinction would be influential in their uses of and needs for Korean, as has been shown to be the case for university students of English in the USA (Ferris & Tagg, 1996).
(ii) Alternating between males and females, each student within a block was assigned a number in sequence.
(iii) A table of random numbers was used to sample 25% of the students from each block, resulting, for example, in two out of eight undergraduates being sampled from Korean 101, six out of 23 from Korean 202, and one out of three graduate students from Korean 302.
(iv) In the event that any student might fail to appear for an interview, three additional students were randomly sampled from the entire pool as alternates.

The resulting sample consisted of 9 males and 12 females, out of the total of 32 and 51, respectively, of whom 13 were undergraduates and 8 graduate students.

Procedures

Two research assistants (a native speaker of English, and a Japanese–English bilingual) contacted students from the sample individually and arranged for approximately half-hour audio-taped interviews with each one. For the most part, interviews were carried out in the L1 of participants, i.e., English for the majority, plus Japanese for a small group. Participants were asked a sequence of questions concerning demographic characteristics (ethnicity, native or family language, and background in language studies), reasons they had been to Korea or were planning to go, reasons for studying Korean, current or future professional uses anticipated for Korean, specifics of language skills they expected to need, and task-related language abilities they could identify as necessary when in Korea or in future employment. The interviews were summarized and screened for specific information that would be relevant to describing students' perceived wants and needs in taking their Korean courses, and in order to develop a questionnaire for distribution to the entire student population in those courses.

Results

Demographic patterns and visits to Korea

Half the interviewees had some Korean heritage, and a quarter (5) were full Korean. Almost all had studied Japanese previously or spoke it well, and several were quite proficient (one of the interviewers was a native speaker of Japanese, and thus able to verify this fact). Reasons subjects cited for visiting Korea included that they had been born there, to visit relatives, to accompany a church group, for tourism, or to study. Reasons cited by those who had plans to go (or go again) included the above, as well as plans to move to Korea or to escort friends and/or family there.

Reasons for studying Korean

Reasons students mentioned for studying Korean included that they wished to communicate better with relatives, to understand their heritage, to use the language for research, and to speak with friends, and that they had a general interest in Korean culture and awareness of the usefulness of the language when seeking employment. Anticipating their potential career choices, they were able to suggest a number of future needs and uses: teaching English or Japanese in Korea; teaching Korean language and literature; jobs in the military, foreign affairs or diplomatic relations; research (with Korea or Korean as either a primary or secondary focus); and various other kinds of employment, such as backstage dancer on MTV, translator, tour guide, nurse, (Korean) restaurant employee, and hotel, bank, and office worker. Most of these suggestions appeared to be recognition of possibilities, rather than concrete plans under way. As one interviewer commented, "It seems to me that much of the population is looking for uses of Korean because they are interested in it, already know a little, or like it thus far, rather than having a use in mind and then pursuing [their studies]."

Language skills and tasks identified

Students were able to name a number of specific skills and applications for which they would be able to use Korean, including: reading in the field of Korean religion and history, and reading menus, notes and signs; writing e-mails and faxes, and notes or letters to family and friends; listening to song lyrics and radio or TV broadcasts; and linguistically focused uses, such as comparing Japanese and Korean structure and recognizing differences between speech patterns of men and women. Most of these interviewees had difficulty identifying any concrete *tasks* they might have to perform. However, in anticipation of visits to Korea, they did identify the following: using transportation (bus, taxi, and subway); getting around – asking for and understanding directions; ordering food in a restaurant; and buying things (asking for prices and bargaining). But with respect to employment-specific tasks, they were not very precise. One military respondent was perhaps the most articulate: "The most I'd be expected to do is to look at a document and figure it out." He later explained that as there would be other Koreans around, he might not have to do even that, but instead would talk with Korean generals about weapons, training, policy, and strategy.

The interviews identified several points that the researchers had not anticipated, in particular the following: (i) that, owing to the high percentage of heritage students, many had opportunities to speak with different relatives in their families; (ii) that the church was a frequent setting for contact with Korean; (iii) that students had multiple reasons for being interested in Korean; and (iv) that a number of respondents used Korean to engage in recreational activities. On the basis of these interviews, a questionnaire was designed and administered to the entire student population in the classes described above, for broader coverage and in order to obtain more detailed information on the settings and uses identified through the interviews. The observations from the interviews also allowed the researchers to use closed-response items for many of the questions.

Questionnaire procedures and results

Procedures

A questionnaire was provided to all students ($n = 84$) in the above-mentioned Fall, 1999, classes, either to be completed in class or taken home and returned to the researchers. (See Appendix A.) All but one student complied.

Results

The primary finding of the questionnaire survey was that responses matched those in the interviews quite closely, thereby triangulating and confirming the fruitfulness of the interview. (See Appendix B for summary tallies of responses to items concerning social uses and needs.)

Use of Korean with relatives

In keeping with the heritage-language background of many of the students, although 66% had identified English as their L1, a majority indicated that they spoke Korean at least sometimes with their mothers ($n = 52$, or 63%), while large numbers spoke at least sometimes with other relatives ($n = 38$, or 46%), with grandmothers ($n = 36$, or 43%), and with fathers ($n = 29$, or 35%). Correlated with these general family-oriented uses, similar percentages of respondents indicated that they wanted to learn Korean in order to use it (or use it more) with their relatives.

Travel to Korea

The results of the questionnaire indicated that the majority of students ($n = 62$, or 75%) had visited Korea at least once before, and 76 (92%) intended to visit Korea (for the first time or again). Reasons for visiting or intending to visit were ranked as shown in Table 2.

Table 2 Ranking of reasons for travel to Korea

Reason	n (% of 83)
Visit friends or relatives	55 (66%)
Tourism/vacation	42 (51%)
Born there	19 (23%)
To study there	19 (23%)
Military service	9 (11%)
Business/work	7 (8%)
Church group	4 (5%)
Others (academic research, sports, as an escort, attend a conference)	3, 2, or 1 each

Additional reasons for studying Korean

While use of Korean with relatives was cited as a reason for further study of the language, respondents indicated several additional reasons as having at least some importance for them. These are shown in Table 3 (the first percentage is for those indicated as being of at least some importance, the second percentage for those indicated as being of more than average importance).

Table 3 Ranking of other reasons for study of Korean

Reason	% at least some importance/ % more than average
Cultural interest	99% / 76%
Tourism/vacation	92% / 69%
Communicate better	90% / 81%
Business/employment	85% / 54%
Academic	84% / 59%
Language requirement	79% / 58%
Understand ethnic heritage	77% / 62%
Professional/vocational	71% / 43%
Religious	34% / 10%
Other	– / 9%

Identifying target tasks for materials development

Given that a large number of students had visited and/or were going to visit Korea (again), and that the most prominent reasons for learning Korean were better communication with family members, general cultural interest, and tourism/vacation, several 'social survival' target tasks for the development of beginning and intermediate materials were identified. As the research project was limited in available time and access to language classes for pilot work, these were gradually narrowed to two distinct tasks, each designed for two levels of learner. Initially, 'Making automobile rental reservations' was considered, along with 'Following street directions', as they could impressionistically be expected to be of greater and lesser complexity, respectively, and so allow more options in materials design than two tasks of comparable complexity. Twenty English language conversations involving these two tasks were surreptitiously[2] recorded in impromptu encounters in Waikiki by a NS (native speaker) and a NNS (non-native speaker) of English. These were used as the basis for prototypical discourse construction of the task materials. But after inquiries in Seoul revealed that automobile reservations there could often be conducted in English, and were, in any case, rare for visitors to Korea, the final target tasks decided on were two relatively simple ones, 'Following street directions' and 'Shopping for clothing' (henceforth *Directions* and *Shopping* tasks, respectively).

Collecting target discourse samples and identifying prototypical discourse structures

A framework for analyzing prototypical discourse structures was developed and first applied to the *Directions* data collected in English in order to provide a model for the process ultimately usable with any target language. The framework was then applied to the *Directions* data collected in Korean (Lee, 2002). Because understanding the nature of the target discourse is key to the development of sequenced pedagogic tasks, this analysis is described in some detail.

From transcriptions of audio recordings elicited respectively by a NS and a NNS of English who asked passers-by (always NSs) for directions to various locations in Waikiki, three typical direction-asking patterns were identified. Two situations were identified leading to three distinct types of interaction when both direction asker and direction giver were native speakers: (i) *nearby* destinations, and, therefore, easy-to-deliver directions, led to all-at-once or detailed, segmented patterns; and (ii) *distant* destinations, and, therefore, hard-to-deliver directions, led to simple, segmented patterns. In interactions with the non-native direction asker, direction-giving patterns were often different from those with the native speaker, and, notably, were relatively similar within the NS-to-NNS set, whether or not the destination was near or far. These three patterns will be discussed in more detail after some other less frequent, but still regular, patterns are noted.

If the person asked did not know the way, either the interaction ended with an apology, the person took the direction seeker to someone who did know, or else to a map, whereupon a quite different type of (visually supported) direction-giving ensued. If two people were asked, the interaction was different yet again, and seemingly more complex. In the case of distant destination, regardless of whether the directions-seeker was a NS or NNS, sometimes the person asked gave overly general directions that would never work, e.g., "You just head down that way and keep going for quite a ways," or first commented about how far and how difficult it will be to reach the place in question, and then tried to give very specific directions. Although these discourse structures each occurred more than once (and thus would merit further study), the three patterns described earlier were more prevalent, and only these were analyzed further for the development of prototype materials.

Close and easy directions

When the destination was close and easy, directions were delivered by NS–NS either all-at-once or in detailed segments, while NS–NNS directions were always delivered in simple segments (whether the destination was near or distant). The following schematic patterns describe the two NS–NS patterns (with inherent variations) in the close-and-easy situation:

English pattern (1): NS–NS All at once (simple)

Key: NS = NS direction-asker; NNS = NNS direction-asker;
      P = NS pedestrian respondent; (...) optional element;
      [...] variation point

NS: Asks for directions
P: Directions given in their entirety, but not particularly detailed.
     a. way to start off
     b. where to turn towards destination
     c. what to do or how far to go until standing right in front of it
NS: Rephrases to gain confirmation
     [Depending on whether NS is correct or incorrect in her understanding of the directions, either:]
P: Confirmation or
     Another go, with corrections at the point of error in the directions
NS: OK. Thanks.
P: Gives another direction detail, previously not included, unsolicited
NS: OK. Thanks. [or goes through a round of confirmation]

English pattern (2): NS to NSs Bit by bit (detailed)

NS: Asks for directions
P: Very detailed and specific directions, part 1
NS: Back-channels (uh huh) to show understanding
P: Very detailed and specific directions, part 2
NS: Back-channels (uh huh) to show understanding
P: Very detailed and specific directions, part *n*
NS: OK. Thanks.

When giving close-and-easy direction to NNSs, NSs either automatically broke up the directions into more easily digestible segments, or the NNS back-channeled, such that the directions were likewise broken up. This was akin to the second kind of NS–NS interaction just described above, in the sense that the directions were provided segment by segment. However an important difference was that compartmentalized, easy-and-close directions given to NNSs were very always very simple, in contrast to the very detailed segments provided by NSs to NSs. Also, in the sample set of recordings, the NS used only one back-channel (uh huh), and then only occasionally, whereas the NNS used several (uh huh, OK, oh oh, oh, I see), and used them a great deal, reflecting his L1 norm.

Far and hard directions

The far and hard situation seems to over-ride the interlocutor factor in that, regardless of native or non-native interlocutor status, directions are delivered in simple segments, as shown here (using the NNS direction-asker case as the example):

English pattern (3): Bit by bit (simple)

NNS: Asks for directions
   (When the place is far and hard: Comment about this)
P: Directions, part 1
NNS: Back-channels (uh huh, OK, oh oh, oh, I see) to show understanding
P: Directions, part 2
NNS: Back-channels (uh huh, OK, oh oh, oh, I see) to show understanding
P: Very detailed and specific directions, part *n*
NNS: (OK.) Thank you.

Moreover, it can be noted that the pattern for all NS–NNS interactions (both close and easy and far and hard), and for NS–NS, far and hard, is the same: the pedestrian gives very simple directions, segment by segment.

 In summary, the English data analysis clearly revealed three typical patterns: All at once (simple only), and Bit by bit (simple or detailed). When both interlocutors were native speakers, and the destination involved was nearby, the directions most often were given simply and all at once. Occasionally, very detailed directions were given by a NS, bit-by-bit, to another NS. Whenever the destination was far away or the interlocutor was a NNS, the directions were delivered bit by bit, in a simple fashion. These three prototypical dimensions of the English direction-giving discourse are shown in Figure 1, section (a), and will shortly be compared with the counterpart Korean direction-giving data, shown in Figure 1, section (b), to which we turn in the next section. As will be discussed further, the results of the target discourse analysis were applied to the development and sequencing of the nine pedagogic tasks of the *Directions* demonstration module.

Figure 1 Prototypical patterns

a. **English** (Waikiki *Directions*, close and far destinations; NS and NNS direction askers)

All at once		Bit by bit	
Simple **NS–NS** (some) (close and easy)	Detailed 0	Simple **NNS–NS** (close and easy) **NS–NS** (far and hard) **NNS–NS** (far and hard)	Detailed **NS–NS** (some) (close and easy)

b. **Korean** (Youngpoong *Directions*, only one destination; NS and NNS direction askers)

All at once		Bit by bit	
Simple **NS–NS** (a few)	Detailed **NNS–NS** (exclusively some)	Simple 0	Detailed **NS–NS** (most) **NNS–NS** (some)

Sampling of authentic Korean tasks

In order to provide an empirical basis for authentic language use[3] in the two target tasks to be incorporated in the KFL classroom teaching materials (i.e., *Directions*, aimed at the first-year level, and *Shopping*, aimed at the second-year level), (relatively) natural target language samples were collected using participant and non-participant observation, combined with surreptitious audio-recording. One team consisting of a NS (L1 Korean) researcher and a NNS (L1 English) speaker collected recordings of conversations while following street directions and shopping for clothing in Seoul. A team of Korean NSs also went shopping for various items in clothing stores in Honolulu staffed by Korean-speaking shopkeepers, where Korean NSs typically do their shopping. Such elaborate, time-consuming, and labor-intensive data collection would not be required for everyday materials writing, of course. It was conducted in this instance because one of the study's aims was to compare the authenticity of task-related discourse samples gathered by different kinds of speakers, both NS and NNS, and the relative efficacy of each. The target discourse data-collection process, along with some of the findings, will now be discussed, followed by an illustration of their implications for task-based materials writing.

Following street directions in Seoul

Essentially using the same procedures as for the English data collected in Waikiki, two sets of interactions, NS–NS and NNS–NS, were surreptitiously audio-taped in Seoul, Korea during December, 2000. This time, however, directions were only asked to one location (*yengphwung mwunko* or Youngpoong bookstore). All recordings were made in an old palace in downtown Seoul, using a SONY R900 MD recorder. The location was adequate for collecting data, in that it was free from street noise and reasonably distant from the destination chosen for the study. NS–NS data were generated between one of the researchers, who asked the way to a specific building (i.e., the bookstore), and local passers-by, who gave directions to the building. While any participation by the researcher might compromise the naturalness of the data, the threat was arguably lessened, although not completely obviated, in this study in three ways. First, the task was quite authentic, in that the researcher actually did not know the best route to the destination. Second, the researcher's role as a direction-asker was (at least, thought to be) relatively minor, consisting mostly of providing back-channel responses to directions given by the informants. Thirdly, the focus of the study was, in any case, not on the direction-asker but the direction-giver (although the analysis showed otherwise). Thus, while use of sociolinguistically naïve data-gatherers would be desirable in a major materials-writing project, this was not considered essential for a demonstration project, in which the goals were more modest. Ten sample NS–NS conversations were obtained in all.

For the purpose of comparison with the NS–NS baseline data, NNS–NS conversations were recorded under exactly the same conditions with regard to the location where directions were sought and the destination asked about. By holding other elements constant, as had been done in the English data collection, it was possible to isolate the effect of interlocutor type, NS or NNS. A male Canadian in his early twenties asked passers-by in Korean how to get to the Youngpoong bookstore. Any Korean could easily discern that he was not a Korean native speaker, both by his physical appearance and from his Korean language ability, which was limited. As was the case for the NS–NS data, ten sample NS–NNS interactions were collected in this way.

In order to identify prototypical discourse structures for street directions in Korean, and to compare them with the English Waikiki *Directions* data, the sample recorded interactions were analyzed using the same approach as with the English data. Four typical conversations are presented in examples (1) through (4) below, translated by the NS researcher. (↗) indicates pointing.

Example (1): NS–NS

Researcher (NS): Excuse me. May I ask something? If I want to go to Youngpoong bookstore, which direction should I go out?
Pedestrian: Uh, get out of this place and
R: Yes.
P: Go straight to the left and cross an underpass.
R: Yes.
P: Then, you will see Kyobo bookstore (↗).
R: Yes.
P: Passing it, keep going straight, I mean, in that direction.
R: Yes.
P: You only have to go straight in this direction and cross another underpass.
R: You mean by "this direction" the left side when I get out of the gate, right?
P: Yes, go out and go straight to the left.
R: (to herself) Cross an underpass. Then, how should I go from Kyobo?
P: From Kyobo If you get to Kyobo, stop going and to the right, what I mean
R: Keep going in that direction?
P: (Pointing the direction) Kyobo is on this side (↗)
R: Yes, yes.
P: Then to this side, to the right.
R: Then do I only have to go straight? Is it on the same side?
P: Yes, that's right.
R: I see, I see. Thank you.

Example (2): NNS–NS

Researcher (NNS): Hello. Excuse me, but how to get to Youngpoong bookstore?
Pedestrian: Youngpoong bookstore?
R: Yes. Can I get there by subway?
P: Subway?
R: Yes.
P: Yes, you can. Take subway, well, in front of Duksu palace, at Sicheung station.
R: Sicheung station?
P: Si-cheung (loudly and articulately).
R: Sicheung.

P: Yes. Take subway in Sicheung station. And uh, at Chonggak station.
R: Chong-gak station?
P: Yes. Get off and
R: Get off.
P: Uh, cross an underpass and you will see Chonggak there (↗). And
    Chonggak . . .
R: Chonggak?
P: Yes, get off Chonggak and come out in the direction of Chonggak and
R: Yes.
P: If you cross an underpass there.
R: Un-pass?
P: Un-der-pass (loudly and articulately).
R: Underpass.
P: Yes. If you cross it, you will see Youngpoong bookstore.
R: Thank you so much.
P: Yes.

Example (3): NS–NS

Researcher (NS): Excuse me. If I get to Youngpoong bookstore, which way
                should I go?
Pedestrian1:   Youngpoong bookstore, (to her companion) it's in
                Kwanhwamun, isn't it?
P2: Yes.
P1: Go straight to the left and in Chonggak . . . Chonggak is, Youngpoong
    bookstore is right before Chonggak.
R: Right before Chonggak?
R: Yes.
P1: Right before Chonggak, yes.
R: Then do I have to go to this way? To the left?
P1: Yes.
R: Thank you.

Example (4): NNS–NS

Researcher (NNS): Excuse me. I am a stranger here. How can I get to
                 Youngpoong bookstore?
Pedestrian: Youngpoong bookstore?
R: Yes.
P: I know Youngpoong bookstore is near around Chongro bookstore.
    You may find Chongro bookstore first (↗). Go out through the front
    gate. And walk a little bit to the left. Then you will see a statue. If you
    see the statue, go to the other side of the street through an underpass.
    You will see a street sign showing "Chonggak" (↗). If you go down the
    street a little bit more, you will get to Chongro bookstore in Chongro 2.
    I know Youngpoong bookstore is close from there. There you may ask
    passers-by once again.
R: Thank you.

The analysis of transcripts of conversations like these revealed three prototypical discourse patterns, which were similar in some ways, but different in others, from those found in the English Waikiki data. The same basic distinction between directions given all at once or bit by bit was also evident in the Korean data, and as with the English data, directions could be given in simple or in detailed fashion, resulting in three basic patterns: All at once (simple); All at once (detailed); and Bit by bit (detailed). The basic Korean *Directions* discourse pattern distributions are shown in Figure 1b previously.

Korean pattern (1): All at once (simple)

NS: Ask for directions
P: (Identify the destination)
       Give very brief and general directions at once
NS: (Rephrase or confirm P's utterances)
       Thank you.

This general, all-at-once pattern was observed in a few NS–NS interactions, as shown above in Example (3). In this pattern, very brief and overly general directions are given in their entirety. Note that this type of discourse was also found in English NS–NS interactions when they involved close and easy destinations. It may be that Koreans, like other direction-givers, adopt this approach when the direction-giver believes that the destination is easily accessible without detailed information. Although the Korean data included only one, somewhat distant destination, which is rather far from the starting point, it could be that the direction-givers had different perceptions of the distance. This is all the more likely since, despite the distance, the destination is quite famous and easy to recognize. Thus, although not manipulated experimentally in this sampling of *Directions* in Korea, there may have been close-and-easy/far-and-hard variables operating in the data.

Korean pattern (2): All at once (detailed)

NNS: Ask for directions
P: (Identify the destination)
        Give very specific and long directions at once
        a. way to start off
        b. where to turn towards destination
        c. what to do or how far to go
NNS: Thank you

The more detailed all-at-once pattern was found only in the NNS–NS conversations. Example (4) illustrates this pattern, which occurs mostly because the NNS direction-asker is negligent in providing back-channels or seeking confirmations. In turn, this may be attributable partly to the transfer of L1 norms and partly due to the NNS's inadequate language abilities. Canadians tend to back-channel less frequently than Koreans. At times, despite awareness of the norm, the NNS's limited Korean proficiency may have prevented him from providing more frequent back-channels or repetitions to seek confirmation. What makes the situation worse is that the local direction-giver might have felt responsible for providing very detailed and specific information, particularly for a foreigner, who might not know the area at all. These factors conspired to produce very lengthy and far too detailed interaction. It should be pointed out that in the English data, the all-at-once pattern occurs only in the NS–NS interaction, and only when the destination was close and easy (and, hence, involves simple, not detailed directions). In contrast, in the Korean data, this pattern was found only in the NNS–NS interaction, even though the destination was somewhat far (recall that, in the English data, far-away destinations triggered the bit-by-bit approach, regardless of interlocutor). This shows simply that back-channeling is a crucial element in Korean discourse. Furthermore, in Korean, it seems to be the direction-asker rather than the direction-giver who determines how much information should be provided at once. By providing back-channels and seeking confirmation of their understanding, the direction-asker prevents the direction-giver from proceeding too quickly.

The detailed bit-by-bit pattern shown below was characteristic of most NS–NS interactions and some NNS–NS interactions.

Korean pattern (3): Bit by bit (detailed)

R: Ask for directions
P: (Identify the destination)
    (Identify a transportation type)
    Give specific directions, part 1
R: Back-channels or repetition of part of the directions to seek confirmation
P: Confirmation of R's utterances
    Give specific directions, part 2
R: Back-channels or repetition of part of the directions to seek confirmation
P: Confirmation of R's utterances
    Give specific directions, part n
R: Thank you.

Examples (1) and (2) belong to this type. Sometimes, because the direction-givers were anticipating a back-channel, they automatically broke up the directions. However, in most cases, this pattern is attributable to the direction-asker, who back-channels or repeats the direction-giver's utterances to seek confirmation whenever he or she feels that the direction-giver is providing too much information. The direction-asker's frequent interruptions force the direction-giver to stop and go back to his or her previous utterances to confirm or correct the direction-asker's understanding. This was more prevalent among the NS–NS interactions than the NNS–NS interactions. As noted earlier, it might have been due to different L1 conversational norms between Koreans and Westerners, including the tendency of Koreans to provide more frequent back-channels than Canadians. They do so because they consider it polite behavior to show that they are listening to their conversation partner carefully and sincerely.

Asians' strong tendency to provide frequent back-channels is confirmed by the English Waikiki *Directions* data, in which the NNS (male) direction-asker was Japanese. Japanese have the same conversational norm as Koreans regarding back-channels. In his interaction with English-speaking direction-givers, the Japanese NS transferred his L1 norm and supplied frequent back-channels. This tendency was strong enough to override the task complexity variable, i.e., distance to the destination. The Korean NNS direction-asker in this study seemed to be aware of the Korean norm regarding back-channeling. As long as he observed the norm, the resultant discourse structure was similar to the NS–NS interaction. However, he sometimes failed to apply it, resulting in the very odd (and difficult-to-process) discourse pattern involving the giving of very detailed directions all at once.

Shopping for clothes

For the second target task, data were first collected in Honolulu and then in Seoul, as described below. These data will be discussed in brief with regard to another important feature of NA, namely ascertaining features of task complexity for the purposes of pedagogic task design and sequencing.

The Honolulu data

Two females and two males, all native speakers of Korean, participated in the data collection for the *Shopping* target task during the Spring semester of 2000. Carrying tape-recorders concealed in shoulder-bags, the four data collectors entered three different kinds of clothing stores in an area of Honolulu where there is a concentration of Korean businesses. In order to increase the diversity of the sample, they took turns talking to sales clerks, who all happened to be female during this data-collection phase (male customer with female sales clerk, or female customer with female sales clerk). They endeavored to act and talk as naturally as possible in an effort to obtain real-life conversational data in Korean.

After an initial analysis it was determined that the data collected in Hawaii were of limited value, for the following reasons:

(i)   The types of clothing items were insufficiently varied.
(ii) The currency mentioned in the conversations was US dollars, not Korean *won*.
(iii) Some English words (not loanwords) were used in the Korean conversations.
(iv) The quality of recorded data was worse than expected, which would make them difficult to use in pedagogic tasks later as samples of genuine Korean conversations.

Points (ii) and (iii) above, in particular, would not be typical of similar transactions in Korea.

The Seoul data

Accordingly, new sets of shopping-for-clothes conversations were collected in Seoul, in January, 2001. The same Korean researcher and Canadian non-native speaker who had collected the Seoul *Directions* data separately visited a number of shops to buy a few items. All conversations with sales clerks were surreptitiously recorded. Unfortunately, initial recordings were almost all found to be inaudible, mainly due to the loud background music every shop employed for strategic business reasons. Moreover, normal tape-recorders seem more sensitive to music than to human voices. After some alternatives were considered, mini-disc players were employed (SONY R900). Even though mini-disc players cannot eliminate background noise completely, they reduce it to a considerable extent when the sensitivity to sounds within a certain wave cycle range is adjusted. Another advantage of using a mini-disc player is that data are more easily manipulated after recording, e.g., for further minimizing unwanted background noise and for selecting segments for use in materials development. A second round of recording under these conditions yielded eight NS–NS and eight NS–NNS conversations that were much more satisfactory.

The *Shopping* data were submitted to the same type of discourse and task complexity variable analysis as has been described for *Directions*. For reasons of space, rather than discuss the *Shopping* discourse data at length, we will turn our attention primarily to how a task complexity variable analysis was carried out for the purpose of task design and sequencing decisions. In general, the *Shopping* task turned out to be more complex than the *Directions* task, even more so than had originally been envisaged by the research team.

Development of TBLT modules

The purpose of the remaining section of this chapter is to provide an overview of the use of NA data in task-based materials development. The emphasis here is on showing how the information gleaned from the unstructured interviews, questionnaires and target-discourse analysis was used to design and develop the Korean Task Based Language Teaching (KTBLT) modules. Following Long (2000), each module consists of a sequence of pedagogic tasks that gradually increase in complexity and in approximation to the two target tasks, *Directions* and *Shopping*. The Korean *Directions* and *Shopping* modules were based on the English template TBLT module shown in Figure 2 (Waikiki *Directions*), and incorporated the specific results of analysis of the Korean target discourse analysis discussed above.

In *Directions*, the purpose of the module is to raise students' performance to a level at which they can politely request, and understand, street directions to both nearby and distant destinations. In *Shopping*, the aim is to make clothing purchases while considering more and more factors (type, color, size and design, then garment-care instructions, as emerged in the NA data) and, ultimately, also negotiate the price, as the NA data show is the norm in Korean sales transactions. Information from the target discourse analyses is used for many purposes, for instance: to select suitable extracts from the recorded data for use as genuine samples of input; to analyze task complexity factors for use in designing and sequencing the pedagogic tasks; and to prepare scripted materials (based on the genuine samples) for use in the pedagogic tasks.

The first three pedagogic tasks (PTs 1–3) in both *Directions* and *Shopping* are used in a teacher-fronted, whole-class format (although individual students can take the teacher's role after some models). The aim is to provide *intensive exposure* to typical and *elaborated* NS input, using actual recordings and modified interaction. At this stage, the students are not required to produce, but simply to listen. During *Directions* PTs 1–3, they show comprehension by moving their fingers on very simple, two-dimensional street maps. In

Figure 2 Template for TBLT modules (Model target task: Waikiki *Directions*)

PT 1 *The real thing* **Materials:** Tape-recorder and audio-tape.	**Procedure:** Teacher explains that the lesson is on how to obtain and understand street directions to nearby and distant destinations from a passer-by. Teacher then tells students to listen carefully to three sample conversations – real examples of NS giving directions – but not to worry if they do not understand everything. He/she then plays the tape through.
PT 2 *Fragments* **Materials:** OHP (or if unavailable, blackboard) and student worksheets.	**Procedure:** Teacher displays a series of three simple street maps on the OHP, one at a time. Students look at the same map on their worksheets. One at a time, the teacher then reads out five sets of street directions containing fragments from the NA, twice each at first, and students trace that part of the route on their worksheets with their fingers, stopping where they think the direction takes them. The teacher then repeats that direction twice more, moving his/her finger on the OHP, and students thereby receive confirmation or, if that be the case, see where they went wrong. This is not a test. Students are not asked if they were successful. It is assumed they will need numerous hearings before success becomes routine. These early PTs allow for private practice and improvement first. The fragments comprising the sets of directions, which gradually increase in complexity, are genuine excerpts, or only slightly cleaned up versions, or melds, from the target discourse samples obtained as part of the needs analysis. *Sample items:* 1. Go straight down Kalakaua Avenue two blocks, and turn right. 2. Go to the first corner and turn left. 3. Go to the first corner and take a right. 4. Go down Kalakaua Avenue two blocks. Make a right. 5. Go two blocks up Kalakaua. Make a right, and then the first left.

PT 3 *Where are you now?*

Materials: OHP (or blackboard) and three new simple maps on student worksheets. These maps are more detailed, including some additional street names and very simple three-dimensional drawings or symbols of some frequent types of buildings (church, school, bank, museum, etc.) and other typical landmarks (shopping mall, university, railway station, etc.).

Procedure: Same as for PT 2, except that, this time, (i) the directions will tend to be a little more complex because the distances involved will gradually be longer, and (ii) after each one, the teacher will ask the class, gradually shifting to individual students, a question after each one, e.g., What street are you on now? What's the building in front of you? If you are now facing north on Main, is the bank on your left or your right? (Note: Teachers should NOT teach any supposedly unknown vocabulary items first. Students can be expected to learn any such items through doing the task.) Again, allow students to take over the teacher's role if capable of doing so.

Sample items:
1. Go two blocks on Main, and turn left. What street are you on now?
2. Take the first right on Main. Is Trinity Church on your left or your right?
3. Go down Main, past Shipley Road, and take the next right. What street is that?
4. Continue on Redfern Avenue. Make a right, and then an immediate left. What building is in front of you?
5. Go up Main, and make a left on Shipley. Keep going straight on Shipley. How many blocks to the Museum, and is it on the left or right?

PT 4 *Asking the way*

Materials: Tape-recorder and cassette. Worksheets with the same maps as were used in PT 3 and other sheets, each with a mix of three sets of directions and questions used in PT 3, and three new items of the same type (also taken from the original target discourse NA).

Procedure: Teacher replays the original three dialogs, once each, and three additional ones. Then divide the students into groups of four. Students work as two pairs inside each group, each pair with a copy of the map and one of the worksheets. One pair reads out the directions while the other follows them for item 1, then reverses the giver and receiver roles for item 2, and so on. The procedure is demonstrated first if it is a new kind of activity for students. (If more practice is needed, the whole procedure can be repeated with a second pair of worksheets containing another set of items, using the same maps, but with the students this time working in pairs rather than groups of four.)

	Procedure
PT 5 *Follow the route* **Materials:** Real three-dimensional tourist maps of a potential destination town in the L2 environment for the students concerned, (e.g., the map of Waikiki issued to all passengers arriving at Honolulu International Airport; or a map of Seoul, downloaded from the Internet). The map has five different routes marked on it to and from various sites, ideally in different colors. The audio-tape of 10 sets of directions describing the five routes.	**Procedure:** Students hear two versions (A to B, and B to A; C to D, and D to C; etc.) of five sets of taped directions (= 10 in all) while following the routes already marked out by the five colored lines on the map.
PT 6 *Known starting point, unknown destination* **Materials:** The same three-dimensional maps used in PT 5, now one per person, and an audio-tape with five new sets of directions from points marked on the map to destinations not marked on it.	**Procedure:** Students are told they are at point A (B, C, etc.), marked on their maps. They hear taped directions to new unknown destinations, and trace the routes on the map with their fingers. The directions are in segments, with check questions of the sort used in PT 3 (What's the building in front of you? What street are you on now?) as they go. Students complete this task individually, but with answers to the check questions spoken aloud and confirmed or corrected by the teacher or other students. The final question after each set of directions is a variant of "Where are you?" or "What's the building we are now at?"
PT 7 *On your own* **Note:** This PT can also serve as the exit test for this module in lieu of a better simulation or, ideally, the real target task. **Materials:** The same three-dimensional maps as in PTs 5 and 6. Taped versions of five new sets of directions.	**Procedure:** Students do the same as in PT 7, but all at once, i.e., without breaks and check questions along the way, labeling the building/space/etc. on their maps at the end of each route as evidence that they have successfully reached their destinations. To ensure they really have identified the right place, they also answer a check question of the sort used earlier, e.g., "And what's the building next door / across the street?"

Note: The seven PTs are designed to take about two hours to complete, but times are approximate and should be adjusted by the teacher according to student progress. Pedagogic adjustments may also be needed in some cases.

Shopping, they point to items they would or would not buy, given the information understood from the input. PT 4 in both modules continues to employ simple visual support (e.g., two-dimensional maps for *Directions* and clip-art clothing items for *Shopping*), but increases demands on students by requiring some production, albeit sheltered in the privacy of pairwork, and, if necessary, after a demonstration by the teacher. *Directions* PT 4 involves comprehension and production, but the emphasis here and throughout this module is on *following* directions, since this is what visitors need to be able to do and since, as visitors in a strange city, they will rarely be in the role of direction-giver. In contrast, from PT 4 onward, *Shopping*, the more complex of the two target tasks, demands both comprehension and production, because both emerged as important in the target discourse analysis of actual Korean sales transactions. For both *Directions* and *Shopping*, PT 5 and PT 6 increase in task complexity (e.g., of the directions and maps, of clothing features, such as size, color, care, etc., and, for *Shopping*, introducing the requirement to negotiate price). In addition, visual and contextual support are gradually withdrawn. Thus, both PT 5 and PT 6 provide more intensive practice of something now very close to the full target task. The final task in each module, PT 7, is designed to provide practice with as close an approximation to the target task as can easily be completed in most classrooms (unless they have special technical equipment). As such, it can double as a trial run for the exit test.

Clearly, the two modules deal with different target tasks in terms of target language use situation (i.e., following oral directions to a destination with the aid of a map, and making a clothing purchase); in terms of primary skills required for successful task completion (i.e., the focus of *Directions* is on aural comprehension, whereas *Shopping*'s dual focus is on both aural comprehension and oral production); and in terms of features that characterize task complexity (e.g., distance to the destination in *Directions*, and number of purchase decisions in *Shopping*, such as size, color, etc.; and whether or not price is negotiated). Nonetheless, the approach taken to the development of the KTBLT modules for each is similar, particularly with respect to adhering to the template shown in Figure 2, with its series of seven PTs gradually increasing task complexity, and the last serving as an exit test. Accordingly, the Korean *Directions* and *Shopping* recordings described earlier were used for confirmation of the typicality of the discourse structures provisionally identified in the previous prototypical English directions-giving analysis, and to elaborate on the task features involved in following directions and in clothes shopping that would manifest themselves in such conversations. In general, the *Shopping* task turned out to be more complex than the *Directions* task, even more so than had originally been envisaged by the research team.

Task complexity

As the KTBLT *Directions* module largely mirrors the English *Directions* prototype shown in Figure 2, it will not be discussed further here. Rather, we now illustrate how the NA data and the TBLT template were used to design the *Shopping* module from the perspective of task complexity. As had been done in developing the *Directions* module, the transcripts of the target Korean customer–sales clerk discourse (this time only between NS customers and sales clerks) were carefully examined to identify commonly occurring grammatical, lexical, and spoken discourse features. Those features were used to select samples of genuine customer–sales clerk transactions in Korean (for PT 1 and PT 4) and were incorporated into the preparation of the scripts for buying clothes in Korean used in *Shopping* PTs 2, 3, 5, and 6. The scripts were prepared and recorded by two NSs of Korean, taking the roles of customer or sales clerk and referring to the pictures of clothes they were given. Materials and procedures were similar to those in *Directions* (see Figure 2), except that pictures of clothing (along with their size and care 'tags') were used instead of maps, and comprehension was checked by asking questions such as "Which would you buy?" rather than "Where are you now?"

For *Shopping* PT 1, 'The real thing', three genuine samples from the shopping-for-clothing NA data were selected, such that each contained as many instances of the highly frequent features of Korean clothes shopping as possible. As in the *Directions* module, those segments were to be repeated to give students ample exposure to genuine spoken interaction in Korean, and, thus, engender some 'feel' for how people buy clothes in Korean. The instructions to students made it clear, however, that they would not yet be expected to understand the entire clothing purchase transaction.

PT 2, 'Fragments,' employed three simple clip-art pictures each for four different types of clothing (i.e., men's short-sleeved shirts, men's shorts, men's pants, and women's formal wear), which were selected from a clip-art collection. Four conversations between a customer and a sales clerk were recorded, twice each, on the tape. Using an overhead transparency showing all the same pictures, the teacher was to cross out the items one by one that, according to the information given, the customer would not buy, as students listened to the tape to identify the one the customer decided to buy. This was to confirm (without requiring any production) whether students had understood the sales transaction.

In PT 3, 'What are you looking for?', four real pictures each of four different types of clothing (i.e., men's shorts, women's long-sleeved shirts, women's skirts, and women's pants) were downloaded from an Internet shopping catalog. The items could only be distinguished by referring to detailed features, which resulted in slightly lengthened customer–sales clerk interaction and the introduction of more and varied lexical items and expressions. In this respect, the pictures used in PT 3 were more complex than those in PT 2. Once again using overhead transparencies, the teacher was to play the same conversation for a total of four exposures to the somewhat more complex sales transaction. On the third listening, the teacher paused the tape several times and asked students such questions as which item the sales clerk had recommended and which item the customer would not buy, the answers to which were dependent upon an understanding of the customer–sales clerk interaction up to that point.

In PT 4, 'Recommendations,' six samples of genuine conversational data on shopping for clothing in Korean were prepared, as in PT 1. As had been the case for *Directions*, three of them were recycled from PT 1, and the rest were new. The pictures used in PT 3 were also recycled, but the activities students carried out were different. As for *Directions*, *Shopping* PT 4 provided students with two rounds of sheltered pair work. For Group Work 1, referring to pictures of the first two types of clothing (i.e., men's shorts and women's long-sleeved shirts), and working in groups of four, with two sheltered pairs inside each group, one pair role-played the customer and the other, the sales clerk. Then, they reversed roles for another set of pictures. Although referring to the same sets of pictures used in PT 3, the PT 4 scripts of genuine customer–sales clerk interaction provided were different. For Group Work 2, pictures of the remaining two types of clothing (i.e., women's skirts and women's pants) were used. The format was identical to that for Group Work 1, the only difference being that this time students were asked to perform their role-play without any written script support.

The level of task complexity rises in *Shopping* PT 5 and PT 6. Transparencies of five real Internet catalog pictures, are displayed with 'garment tags', i.e., a small box below each illustrated clothing item, listing such information as type, color, size, and design. Two additional pieces of information (i.e., washing method and price negotiation) were used to select the samples of customer–sales clerk interaction, which resulted in much more and different types of information required for successful task completion, compared with previous PTs. Another departure from the previous PTs was that the customer in the selected samples took a more active role in buying clothes. While it had been the case in the previous PTs that the sales clerk recommended clothes, to which the customers only responded by expressing their preferences, starting from PT 5, 'Describe clothes,' customers actively took the initiative to steer the interaction to obtain what they wanted to buy, explicitly mentioning preferences for the type, color, size, design, care instructions, and price of the clothing item to be purchased. Thus, students had to comprehend intricate negotiations rather than follow simple recommendations. They could check their aural comprehension of the interaction by verifying it against the written clothing descriptions and care instructions.

For PT 6, 'Make your purchase,' ten Internet catalog pictures were displayed, five recycled from PT 5 and the rest new, this time with the type, color, size, design, care instructions, and price information not filled in. Students had to ascertain this information themselves, introducing a new, more challenging dimension to the task. Closest to the real-life target task of buying clothes, PT 6 required students to process an increased amount of information *and* to engage in oral production for successful task completion. The teacher took the role of sales clerk, and a volunteer student described an item of clothing already in mind for purchase. At the end, the teacher identified the picture of the clothing item he/she thought the student had wanted to purchase. Accordingly, PT 6 was designed to provide students with a chance to engage in a simulated clothing purchase transaction.

Finally, for PT 7, which can also serve as the exit test for the *Shopping* module, each student was asked to play the role of a customer looking for a particular item. The exit test is a five-item, task-based, criterion-referenced performance test. The test is to be administered individually and audio-recorded. Students are asked to choose among five picture cards, one at a time, and conceal them from the test administrator, who also served as a rater. Students were told to ask about the information in each of the categories in the box, e.g., type, color, size, design, care instructions, and price, i.e., all the information needed to make an appropriate purchase. Students were given 30 seconds to prepare, and one minute to interact.

The Korean TBLT *Directions* and *Shopping* modules were piloted in Fall, 2000, and, subsequently evaluated through classroom observation and by interviewing both students and teachers just after their completion of the entire module (a process reported in detail in

Y. Kim et. al 2001), and by examining the pilot classroom interaction. Revisions to each module were then made in preparation for
their use in subsequent research comparing task-based and traditional classroom discourse, and on the relative merits of TBLT with
and without a focus on form.

Conclusion

The journey from NA to materials design and implementation can be
long and detailed. The effort involved and degree of detail required in
the cases described above were both more extensive than would
normally be necessary, as this was a demonstration project to develop
a prototype NA procedure and teaching materials in a language,
Korean, for which such work was previously unavailable. Also,
experience with English materials writing shows that such work
becomes easier and much quicker with practice. Some may balk at
the prospect of gathering field discourse samples as part of the NA
phase itself, and then balk again at the need to modify them somewhat for use in pedagogic materials. Yet, if this aspect of course
design is to go beyond reliance on notoriously unreliable textbook
writer intuitions, such is the task facing the conscientious materials
writer (and publisher). It is the kind of 'homework' language teachers
and applied linguists routinely expect of purveyors of other social
services, and there is surely no reason for our clients to be satisfied
with lower standards, especially those for whom successful language
learning can seriously affect educational life chances.

Notes

1 The research project reported here was partially supported by a grant
from the US Department of Education under the Language Resource
Centers program (CFDA 84.229, P229A990004). The contents of this
report do not necessarily represent the policy of the Department of
Education, and one should not assume endorsement by the Federal
Government. This chapter is an expanded version of a presentation
given at the National Council of Organizations of Less Commonly
Taught Languages 5th National Conference. Theme: Expanding Our
Capabilities: Focus on Teacher Preparation & Professional Development for Less Commonly Taught Languages. Washington, DC (Chaudron et al 2002).
2 Surreptitious recording causes ethical concerns for some. However,
Varonis & Gass (1982), who also recorded asking for and giving
directions conversations surreptitiously, argued that requests for time
and directions may be freely asked of a stranger without unduly

imposing on her or him. As a basis for their position, they referred to Goffman's (1963) argument that those requests are considered 'free goods' in society (p. 116). In addition, NS interlocutors' identities were never requested.

3 For discussion of varying notions of 'authenticity' in materials design and classroom language use, see Breen (1985); Cathcart (1989); Long (1997); and Widdowson (1996).

References

Breen, M. P. (1985). Authenticity in the language classroom. *Applied Linguistics* 6, 1, 60–70.

Cathcart, R. (1989). Authentic discourse and the survival English curriculum. *TESOL Quarterly* 23, 1, 105–26.

Chaudron, C., Doughty, C., Kim, Y., Kong, D.-K., Lee, J., Lee, Y.-G., Long, M. H., Rivers, R., & Urano, K. (2002). *A task-based needs analysis of a Korean as a foreign language program*. Paper presented at the National Council of Organizations of Less Commonly Taught Languages 5th National Conference, Washington, D.C., April.

Doughty, C. J., & Long, M. H. (2002). Optimal psycholinguistic environments for distance foreign language learning. Plenary address to the conference on 'Distance Learning of the Less Commonly Taught Languages'. February 1–3, 2002. Arlington, VA. *Second Language Studies* 20, 1, 2002, 1–42. Also to appear in a special issue on 'Distance Learning' of *Language Learning and Technology*.

Ferris, D., & Tagg, T. 1996. Academic listening/speaking tasks for ESL students: Problems, suggestions, and implications. *TESOL Quarterly* 30, 2, 297–320.

Goffman, E. (1963). *Behavior in public places: Notes on the social origin of gatherings*. New York: The Free Press of Glencoe.

Kim, Y., Kong, D.-K., Lee, J.-H., & Lee, Y. (2001). *Implementation and evaluation of an approach to task-based Korean language teaching*. National Foreign Language Resource Center, University of Hawai'i at Manoa, appeared in abridged version with the same title in *Korean Language in America* (Proceedings of the 6th Annual American Association of Teachers of Korean) Vol. 6, 2001, 45–51.

Lee, J.-H. (2002). Target discourse analyses in TBLT: NS–NS or NS–NNS discourse? Unpublished paper. Department of Second Language Studies, University of Hawai'i at Manoa.

Long, M. H. (1997). Authenticity and learning potential in L2 classroom discourse. In G. M. Jacobs (ed.), *Language classrooms of tomorrow: Issues and response* (pp. 148–69). Singapore: SEAMEO Regional Language Center.

Long, M. H. (2000). Focus on form in Task-Based Language Teaching. *University of Hawai'i Working Papers in ESL* 16, 2, 35–49. Also in R. L. Lambert & E. Shohamy (eds.), *Language policy and pedagogy* (pp. 179–92). Amsterdam and Philadelphia: John Benjamins.

Long, M. H. (this volume). Methodological issues in learner needs analysis.

Long, M. H., & Norris, J. M. (2000). Task-based teaching and assessment. In M. Byram (ed.), *Encyclopedia of language teaching* (pp. 597–603). London: Routledge.

Varonis, E. M., & Gass, S. (1982). The comprehensibility of non-native speech. *Studies in Second Language Acquisition* 4, 2, 114–136.

Widdowson, H. G. (1996). Authenticity and autonomy. *ELT Journal*, 50, 1, 67–68.

Appendix A: Student needs questionnaire

KOREAN AS A FOREIGN LANGUAGE STUDENT NEEDS
QUESTIONNAIRE
UNIVERSITY OF HAWAI'I AT MANOA SPRING 2000

> This questionnaire is part of a research project into the current and future needs of students taking Korean language classes at the University of Hawai'i at Manoa. The survey is being conducted by faculty and graduate students under the auspices of UH's National Foreign Language Resource Center and with the full cooperation of the Korean Program. We want to identify the reasons you have for studying Korean. What uses do you have for Korean now? What uses do you anticipate having for Korean in the future? The information you provide is very important to the results of the study and for developing materials and courses that best meet the needs of Korean language learners like yourself. The questionnaire will take about 10 minutes to complete. Information you provide on this questionnaire will be used only for the purpose mentioned above. You may answer in English or Korean. If you have any questions or comments regarding this questionnaire or the study, please feel free to contact (Researchers' contact details). Thank you very much for your participation.

Section A: Background Information

1) Course you are currently taking: **KOR** ....

2) Academic status:

  Freshman .... Junior .... Sophomore ....

  Senior .... Grad .... Unclassified Grad ....

3) If an undergraduate student, what is your major (or if undeclared, your anticipated major)?:

  ....

  If a graduate student, what degree and program are you enrolled in (or if an unclassified graduate student, your anticipated degree and program)?:

4) Gender: F .... M ....

5) Native language(s): English .... Korean ....

  Bilingual English and Korean ....

  Other (specify): ....

Section B: Social Uses of, and Needs for, Korean

6) Do you ever use Korean at home, or when you are visiting family members, relatives or friends, or when they are visiting you? If so, who do you use Korean with, and how often? (Circle ALL persons that apply, and the frequency with which you use Korean with them):

Grandmother	always	often	sometimes	never
Grandfather	always	often	sometimes	never
Mother	always	often	sometimes	never
Father	always	often	sometimes	never
Brother	always	often	sometimes	never
Sister	always	often	sometimes	never
Husband/Wife/Partner	always	often	sometimes	never
Roommate	always	often	sometimes	never
Relatives	always	often	sometimes	never
Friends	always	often	sometimes	never
Others (specify):	always	often	sometimes	never

7) Would you like to know Korean (or more Korean) so that you could use it (or use it more) with any of those people at home, or when visiting them, or when they are visiting you? (Circle ALL persons that apply):

Grandmother   Grandfather   Mother   Father   Brother
Sister   Husband/Wife/Partner   Roommate   Relatives
Friends   Others (specify): ....

8) Have you ever visited Korea? Circle ONE: Yes No (If yes, how many times? .... , and, on average, for how long? .... year(s) .... month(s) .... day(s))

9) Do you think you will visit Korea (or visit Korea again)?

Circle ONE: Yes No

10) If your answer to question 8 and 9 was 'No', skip to question 11. If your answer to either question was 'Yes', why did you and/or will you visit? Circle ALL that apply:

Born there   To visit friends or relatives   Church group
Tourism/vacation   Military service
As an escort for other visitors   Sports event (specify: ....)
To study there (if so, circle or specify subject:
Korean language
Other ....)

For business/work (specify: ....)

For academic research (specify: ....)

To attend a conference on .... with papers presented in (circle ALL that apply): Korean English Both

Other reasons (specify):..

Section D: Other Reasons for Studying Korean

11) Which of the following are reasons why you are studying Korean, and how important is each of them for you?

5 = great importance, 3 = average importance, 1 = minor importance, 0 = no importance to you

PLEASE respond to **EVERY** item, **INCLUDING** those that are of no importance to you.

	great importance				no importance
• Communicate better with family members, relatives or friends	5	4	3	2	1	0
• Satisfy a UH language requirement	5	4	3	2	1	0
• Satisfy your interest in some aspect(s) of Korean culture	5	4	3	2	1	0
• Understand your own ethnic heritage	5	4	3	2	1	0
• Use in connection with religious activities of some kind	5	4	3	2	1	0
(Specify: ....)						
• Use in present or future academic work	5	4	3	2	1	0
(Specify: ....)						
• Use in present or future business or employment	5	4	3	2	1	0
(Specify: ....)						
• Use in present or future professional/vocational training	5	4	3	2	1	0
(Specify: ....)						
• Use when visiting Korea for tourism/vacation	5	4	3	2	1	0
• Other (specify: ....)	5	4	3	2	1	0
• Other (specify: ....)	5	4	3	2	1	0

12) Does the following statement apply to you?
"I am studying Korean for no particular reason." Circle ONE: Yes No

Section E: Changes You Would Like to See in Your Korean Language Classes

13) Considering the reasons, if any, you have specified above for studying Korean, and based on the past, current, or anticipated future uses you have for the language, are there any changes you would like to see in your Korean classes at UH? Which parts seem most useful to you? Which parts seem least useful to you? What else would you like to see included that would be relevant to your needs?

Most useful: ....

....

....

....

....

....

....

Least useful: ....

....

....

....

....

....

....

What else you would like to see included: ....

....

....

....

....

....

....

THANK YOU VERY MUCH INDEED FOR YOUR COOPERATION!

Appendix B: Additional Questionnaire Responses

a) Social Uses of Korean

6) Do you ever use Korean at home, or when you are visiting family members, relatives or friends, or when they are visiting you? If so, who do you use Korean with, and how often? (Circle ALL persons that apply, and the frequency with which you use Korean with them):

	always	often	sometimes	never	not circled	total
grandma	24	4	8	31	16	83
grandpa	15	4	2	36	26	83
mother	9	19	24	27	4	83
father	6	8	15	41	13	83
brother	0	0	12	46	25	83
sister	0	1	10	40	32	83
husband ...	2	0	7	38	36	83
roommate	2	0	5	37	39	83
relatives	7	14	17	31	14	83
friends	1	8	35	28	11	83
others	5	2	3	16	57	83

b) Social Needs for Korean

7) Would you like to know Korean (or more Korean) so that you could use it (or use it more) with any of those people at home, or when visiting them, or when they are visiting you? (Circle ALL persons that apply):

	circled	not circled	total
grandma	38	45	83
grandpa	19	64	83
mother	47	36	83
father	28	55	83
brother	12	71	83
sister	8	75	83
husband ...	9	74	83
roommate	4	79	83
relatives	38	45	83
friends	42	41	83
others	9	74	83

Appendix C: Consent form

CONSENT TO PARTICIPATE IN RESEARCH

Task-Based Language Teaching in Foreign Language Education Project

We invite you to participate in an interview that is part of a research project conducted by Professors Michael H. Long, Catherine Doughty and Craig Chaudron, from the National Foreign Language Resource Center at the University of Hawaii at Manoa, Honolulu. You were selected as a possible participant in this project because you are currently enrolled in one of the Korean language courses offered by the Department of East Asian Languages and Cultures at UHM and Korean is one of the target languages of this project.

PURPOSE OF THE PROJECT

This phase of the project involves an analysis of the needs of Korean language learners at university level in the United States.

PROCEDURES

If you decide to volunteer to participate in this study, we will ask you to do the following thing:
You will be asked to participate in a 20-minute informal oral interview only once with one of our project investigators, right before, during, or after your Korean class, or alternatively another time that is most convenient to your schedule. Your interview will be audio-recorded for later reference. Your name will not be associated with the tape – see below.

POTENTIAL BENEFITS TO SUBJECTS AND/OR TO SOCIETY
CONFIDENTIALITY

Any information that is obtained in connection with this interview and that can be identified with you will remain confidential and will be disclosed only with your permission or as required by law.

PARTICIPATION AND WITHDRAWAL

You can choose whether to participate in this interview or not. If you volunteer to participate in this interview, you may withdraw at any time without consequences of any kind. You may also refuse to answer any questions you don't want to answer and still remain in the interview. The investigator may withdraw you from this research if circumstances arise which warrant doing so.

IDENTIFICATION OF INVESTIGATORS

If you have any questions or concerns about the research, please feel free to contact (Researcher's contact details).

RIGHTS OF RESEARCH SUBJECTS

My questions have been answered to my satisfaction, and I agree to participate in this interview. I have been given a copy of this form.

....
Name of Subject

....
Signature of Subject   Date

In my judgment the subject is voluntarily and knowingly giving informed consent and possesses the legal capacity to give informed consent to participate in this interview.

....
Name of Investigator

....
Signature of Investigator   Date

PLEASE INDICATE YOUR PREFERENCE FOR AN INTERVIEW SESSION.

[ ] Right before class.

[ ] During class.

[ ] Right after class.

[ ] Another time. If you prefer this option, then please give us your phone number and e-mail address so that our interviewer can contact you and arrange a meeting.

....
Phone Number   E-Mail Address

PART V:
ANALYZING TARGET DISCOURSE

9 Collecting target discourse: The case of the US naturalization interview

Michelle Winn

Introduction

For years, teachers of English as a Second Language (ESL) / United States (US) Citizenship Preparation courses have wondered how they can best prepare immigrants seeking to become United States citizens for a successful naturalization interview? They have desired more knowledge of the actual interview, while most US Citizenship Preparation texts (e.g., Doran de Valdez, Riedel, & Burgos, 1995) focus almost exclusively on US history and government, with minimal reference to the interview itself,[1] an observation corroborated by Nixon & Keenan (1997). Many teachers of US Citizenship courses were aware that despite having memorized facts about US history and government, students were failing their interviews. Course content was clearly not addressing all that would be demanded of them. But the only resource that provided direct information about naturalization interview discourse was testimony from students who had either passed or failed *their* interviews. Teachers and naturalization applicants alike needed a more accurate description of the specific tasks required.

The history of naturalization

Growing numbers of legal permanent residents[2] were clamoring to naturalize in the last decade of the twentieth century. Between 1990 and 1999, the number of immigrants entering the United States rivaled the previous record of nearly 8.8 million admitted in the first decade of the twentieth century (*INS Yearbook*, 1999). From 1994 to 1997, the number of immigrants applying for naturalization annually rose from a little over half a million to 1.4 million (*INS Yearbook*, 1999).[3]

For those seeking to naturalize, the long-awaited opportunity to apply can be time-consuming, complicated, expensive, and risky. After receiving a green card,[4] immigrants must generally wait five years to apply for naturalization,[5] and then an interview may be scheduled within the next six months to three years, depending on the region. They must gather legal documents, such as birth certificates and marriage licenses. In addition, it costs well over $200 to file an application. Finally, an applicant risks deportation[6] (after a hearing) if criminal or fraud charges or convictions are revealed. Since much may be at stake, the naturalization interview often causes a great deal of anxiety for immigrant applicants, especially native speakers of languages other than English.

US naturalization requirements

An English language production and comprehension requirement for naturalization was introduced in 1906 (*INS Yearbook*, 1999), with the English literacy provision mandated a decade later, in 1917 (Crawford, 1989). With a few exceptions involving a combination of age and extensive residency,[7] the US Citizenship and Immigration Services (USCIS)[8] requires that all applicants demonstrate "an understanding of the English language, including [the] ability to read, write, and speak words in ordinary usage in the English language" (INS Attachment to Form N-335), as well as a basic knowledge of US history and government. Not clearly operationalized, the English speaking and listening requirement is tested incidentally throughout the interview. The test of English writing is given in the form of a sentence dictation, and sentence selection is entirely at the interviewing officer's discretion. Applicants have the right to be dictated up to two sentences, and interviewing officers vary as to whether or not they will accept a minor spelling error. The English reading test entails reading aloud a sentence or short passage from the Application for Naturalization, the list of one hundred US history and government questions, or a basal reader. The test of US history and government is generally administered orally, and applicants must usually answer six questions out of ten correctly to pass. Examples include "What are the colors of our flag?", "Who elects Congress?", and "What are the duties of the Supreme Court?"

The naturalization application process generally involves four steps:

(i)   Filing the Application for Naturalization
(ii) Getting fingerprinted, enabling the Federal Bureau of Investigations (FBI) to conduct a background check
(iii) Being interviewed by an Adjudications officer[9]
(iv) Attending a swearing-in ceremony[10]

The naturalization interview is the only step in the process in which the applicant is required to communicate extensively in English, without assistance;[11] thus, it is almost always the pivotal point in the application process because the outcome determines whether or not the immigrant qualifies to become a US citizen. Therefore, the naturalization interview itself is the key gate-keeping point in the naturalization process.[12]

Theoretical framework: Gate-keeping in the sociolinguistic literature

In the absence of research conducted on the naturalization interview itself, the interactional sociolinguistic research on interviews was consulted in order to provide a conceptual framework for this study. A number of researchers have examined the interplay of differential power relationships and cross-cultural communication. Power relations have been extensively studied in a number of areas: the workplace (Gumperz, 1982; Roberts, Davies, & Jupp 1992; Jupp, Roberts, & Cook-Gumperz, 1986); legal interviews (Eades, in press); medical interviews (Tannen & Wallat, 1982); and interactions between students and academic counselors (Erickson & Shultz, 1982). In gate-keeping interviews, the interviewer often juggles conflicting goals of judging and assisting, with the ultimate aim being acceptance or rejection (Fiksdal, 1990, p. 4).[13] Of course, attending to these competing pressures is problematic, as the gatekeeper ultimately has the authority to make decisions that have a negative or positive impact on an interviewee's life chances.

Not only are power dynamics and cross-cultural issues at play, but linguistic factors can also have a significant impact on an applicant's success. The naturalization interview format – involving information gathering and concurrent assessment of the interviewee – further complicates the interaction by increasing the consequences of misunderstandings and misinterpretations (Jupp, Roberts, & Cook-Gumperz, 1982, p. 255), especially when the participants come from divergent backgrounds, function within divergent "discourses", and hold different implicit expectations of the proper ways to interact in particular environments (Gee, 1996). In addition to overt content, other verbal and nonverbal contextualization cues, such as the immediate physical setting, background knowledge and institutional schema, affect interpretation (Gumperz, 1992; Roberts, 1996).

A lack of overlapping schematic knowledge is especially likely to occur in cross-cultural interactions. A complicating feature of many gate-keeping encounters, and one that is integral to the naturalization interviews examined here, is the challenge of cross-cultural communication. In fact, multiple 'cultures' are at play in the naturalization interview: the interviewee is usually from a different culture or ethnicity from that of the interviewer, with that difference super-imposed upon the potentially unfamiliar culture of US government bureaucracy.

Gumperz (1982) holds that interviewees' success in gate-keeping encounters often depends on how well they have mastered bureau-cratic ways of communicating, rather than exclusively on applicants' grammatical accuracy in English. In their study of interaction between interlocutors of unequal status in multi-lingual British work-places, Roberts, Davies, & Jupp (1992) found that, beyond linguistic accuracy, the way applicants or employees present themselves through discourse influences interviewers' or employers' decisions and evaluations. Likewise, Jupp, Roberts, & Cook-Gumperz (1982) problematize the conventional wisdom that improved fluency in English leads to increased communicative and social power (p. 234). To navigate gate-keeping encounters successfully, not only is language proficiency[14] required, but also language "socialization" (p. 244), which entails knowledge of expected and accepted ways of com-municating in particular domains. Cook-Gumperz & Gumperz (1997) corroborate this finding in their study of job interviews. They observed that candidates whose second language was English tended to be less likely than native speakers of English to recognize the cues provided for them by the interviewer, and thus did not frame their answers (p. 272) in the conventional format, although they may well have provided all of the necessary information.

The methods of interactional sociolinguistics have frequently been used to analyze interactions between those in positions of power who are native speakers of English and those, seeking some kind of benefit, who are native speakers of languages other than English or speakers of 'nonstandard dialects' of English (e.g., Cook-Gumperz & Gumperz, 1997; Eades, in press; Jupp, Roberts, & Cook-Gumperz, 1982; Roberts, Davies, & Jupp, 1992). Each of these studies involved in-depth microanalyses of discourse and cross-cultural conflicts in communication, examining interaction not only in terms of linguistic analysis and task description, but also delving into the "hidden process", including power dynamics (Norton Peirce, 1996) and communicative burden (Lippi-Green, 1997) in cross-cultural com-munication (Jupp, Roberts, & Cook-Gumperz, 1982), with the ultimate goal being to compare successful and unsuccessful inter-actions.

Drawing upon this interactional sociolinguistic research, the study presented here examined causes of misunderstanding within the naturalization interview with the expectation that subtle differences in communication styles or interview expectations were causing difficulties for interviewees. Recorded naturalization interviews were collected as target discourse, the ultimate aim being to contribute to immigrant applicants' efficient and successful preparation for the naturalization interview.

Methodology

Statement of purpose

Because the applied linguistics literature lacked even a basic description of the naturalization interview, much less any kind of discourse analysis, the general question "What actually transpires at the naturalization interview?" guided the research described below. To prepare for the naturalization interview, many immigrants elect to take ESL/US Citizenship Preparation courses sponsored by churches, non-profit organizations, or state governments. The ultimate purpose of this study was to use target discourse analysis to inform the teaching of such courses, as detailed description of the naturalization interview, if made available, would be extremely useful for both ESL/US Citizenship Preparation teachers and the naturalization applicants themselves.

Clearly, a needs analysis (NA) was necessary – a crucial precursor to effective and efficient language teaching, used in the field of applied linguistics to determine, among other things, the precise needs of a definable set of second language learners in a particular employment position or gate-keeping encounter. A critical step in undertaking a NA is the collection and analysis of samples of the discourse surrounding target task completion. In this case, the target task was participation in the US naturalization interview. The target group consisted of immigrants aspiring to become US citizens, a set of individuals especially well suited to a needs analysis because their goal is uniform and obvious: to navigate the naturalization process successfully.

Target discourse collection

The following sections will provide a detailed account of how the researcher gained access to the INS, created rapport with the research participants, and collected data.

Entrée

By chance, the researcher befriended an INS officer[15] late in 1998 and expressed interest in learning more about her job. In June, 1999, the researcher formally requested permission to observe at the INS by writing a letter to the District Director in which the source of her interest in naturalization was explained: a previous position as the ESL/Naturalization Co-ordinator at a non-profit organization. The researcher then explained that she was currently a graduate student in the Department of English as a Second Language [now Second Language Studies] at the University of Hawai'i, and was interested in studying how participants interact and use language in the naturalization interview. The researcher requested permission to observe and video-tape the friend conducting naturalization interviews, assuring the director that the naturalization applicants' permission would be sought in each case. Although the researcher had general research questions about interaction in naturalization interviews, she explained that she would not decide on specific ones until after the initial observations and asked if a particular line of inquiry would be of interest to the INS.

A month later, the District Director responded with a letter stating that, after a review by legal experts, the proposed research was approved, as long as participation was voluntary on the part of applicants; he added that since the friend referred to in the letter would be on leave for the next month, it would be fine to approach other officers about observations. From that point on, the researcher communicated only with the on-site supervisor, the Assistant Director of Examinations.

Preparation for data collection

In the original letter to the District Director, permission to video-tape naturalization interviews was sought. However, after an initial visit to the INS, it was determined that it would be impractical and potentially detrimental to set up a camcorder in the cramped space. The interview cubicles were so small that a video camera could not be unobtrusively placed in a corner, nor could one camera possibly capture both participants simultaneously on film. In addition, it was feared that some applicants' stress might be compounded by the presence of a video camera in such a small area; such a set-up may have impeded some subjects' willingness to participate in the research, or even have hurt their chances of succeeding at the interview.

A decision was made to focus more on verbal interaction than non-verbal communication. Audio-taping, therefore, was selected as the best option because it would provide rich verbal data from both interlocutors without being too obtrusive. The researcher could attend to non-verbal cues, such as facial expression and body movement, while taking field notes.

A form was designed to obtain consent from the applicants for the observation and audio-taping of the naturalization interviews (see Appendix B). The consent form outlined the purpose of the study in 'Plain English'[16] and contained basic information about the researcher's intent: "I want to study how naturalization applicants (like you) and INS (Immigration and Naturalization Service) officers use language in naturalization interviews," as well as the request to observe and audio-tape the interview: "I want to take notes and record (on audio-tape) your naturalization interview." The consent form assured applicants that they would remain anonymous: "I will NOT use your name in my notes. The written version of the interviews will NOT have your name on it. Your name will NOT be used in any paper, article, or presentation. False names will be used. No one will be able to identify you." The consent form also asserted that the decision to participate in the research would not affect interviewees' chances of naturalizing: "I am not an INS employee. I will play NO part in deciding the results of your interview." Applicants were given the option of providing a mailing address to which a brief research report would be sent at the conclusion of the study; only about 25% of the applicants filled in that portion of the document. The consent form concluded by requesting a signature after a summary of the form:

I understand this agreement.
I have had my questions answered concerning this study.
I know that I can ask Michelle to leave the interview at any time.

Before any observations took place, the consent form was shown to the Assistant Director of Examinations and approved.[17]

Recordings

To record the interviews, a small hand-held, battery-operated tape-recorder was placed on the desk between the applicant and interviewer, to the side of the paperwork that was exchanged throughout the interview. The tape-recorder was turned on only after the applicant signed the consent form. The applicant sat across the desk

from the officer, and the researcher generally sat next to the applicant, and occasionally to the side of the desk, taking notes. It was left
up to individual officers to dictate where the researcher should be
positioned, but most officers were flexible and accommodating.
Although being seated next to the applicant made it more difficult for
the researcher to view his or her facial expressions, this position
seemed the least disruptive, and the practical constraints of the
limited space often left no other option.

Field notes

Field notes were made in a bound composition notebook, and each
interview was assigned a number chronologically, as well as an
alphabetical code to designate the interviewer. The corresponding
number was printed on the consent form and, to assure anonymity,
no actual names were used in the field notes. At the beginning of the
interview, the researcher would glance at the application on the desk
to obtain basic personal facts, such as nationality, age, and date of
arrival in the US.

Research participants: Immigrant applicants and interviewing officers

Sixty-seven naturalization applicants, ranging in age from 18 to 79,
participated in the study. They came from 16 different countries,
with the Philippines, China, Korea, Vietnam, and Hong Kong
accounting for the majority (see Table 1).[18] Of the 67 applicants, all
but four consented to being audio-taped, with none objecting to the
researcher's presence. Thus, over the course of the year, 67 naturalization interviews (averaging approximately 15 minutes each) were
observed, 63 of which were audio-taped.

   Those conducting naturalization interviews are district adjudications officers in charge of adjudicating numerous legal issues related
to immigration and naturalization. They conduct inquiries and interviews related to such benefits as immigrant or work visas, green
cards, and certificates of naturalization. The eight officers who
participated in this study – six female and two male – reached their
current position via various routes, such as ascending through the
civil service ranks or making a lateral move from Customs and
Inspections at the airport. Like their clientele, the officers' ethnicities
varied: Japanese-American, Filipino-American, European-American,
and Chinese-American.

Table 1   Naturalization applicants by citizenship

Country or republic of nationality	Number of applicants	Percentage of total applicants
Brazil	1	*
Canada	1	*
China	13	19%
Colombia	1	*
Hong Kong / Great Britain[19]	5	8%
Japan	4	6%
Korea	8	12%
Laos	1	*
New Zealand	1	*
Pakistan	1	*
Panama	1	*
Peru	1	*
The Philippines	20	30%
Taiwan (Republic of China)	2	3%
Venezuela	1	*
Vietnam	6	9%

Bold = The top five countries, which accounted for 78% of the applicants
* = Less than 2%

Research questions and observation protocol

The interviewing officers varied as to whether they introduced the researcher before or after having the applicant raise his or her right hand and swear to tell the truth. Once introduced, the researcher explained "I am studying how people use language in the naturalization interview. Can I sit in on your interview and audio-tape it?" with a gesture towards the tape-recorder. If the applicant agreed to participate, he or she was given a consent form to sign. The research explanation and consent form completion generally took less than thirty seconds.

After a few observations, it was clear that the amount of data being collected was overwhelming. Thus, although numerous questions could have been investigated using such a rich source, this study set out to study the observable factors affecting interview outcomes. More specifically, since it would be impossible to explore all aspects of this communicative event in one study, the focus was on issues that could directly inform curriculum development and classroom practice. In seeking to define learners' needs, the following four questions emerged:

1 How is naturalization interview discourse constructed?
2 What differentiates successful and unsuccessful interviews?
3 Which factors affect applicants' chances of naturalizing?
4 What are the implications for ESL/US Citizenship Preparation courses?

After a few observations, an observation protocol was developed to formalize the researcher's focus of attention in taking field notes, helping to ensure that observations were relevant to the research questions (see Figure 1).

Figure 1   Observation protocol

While observing naturalization interviews, attend to and note:

1 sequence/description of activities.
2 demeanor / eye contact / posture / attentiveness / tone of voice / facial expression of participants.
3 misunderstandings / problem points.
4 extent and type of accommodation and assistance by interviewer.
5 how topic is managed – movement/progression of interview (transitions, explicitness).

Qualitative researchers acknowledge that, by definition, what is observed is "altered". No research can be totally objective. The researcher as participant observer affects the communicative event being observed (Norton Peirce, 1996). In fact, there were a few instances in which either the officer or applicant would address the researcher during the interview.

Ethical concerns and validity of data

One concern in this case was that an outsider's presence – not to mention the presence of a tape-recorder – might increase the stress many applicants already experience. However, the interviewing officers reported that the presence of a third party did not seem to cause extraordinary anxiety on the part of applicants. In fact, some applicants appeared visibly relieved to be introduced to the re-searcher. Perhaps this was due in part to the fact that the 'humanizing ritual' of a personal introduction would have otherwise been absent, as interviewing officers rarely introduced themselves to the applicant by name; indeed, no name plaque even appeared on adjudications officers' desks. For the applicant, having a third person present may also have reduced the tension of the one-on-one power dynamics that typify gate-keeping encounters (see Erickson & Shultz, 1982), although it is impossible to know if all applicants believed they could choose to exclude the researcher without any repercussions on their chances of naturalizing.

A second concern was that the researcher's presence might somehow cause the interview to deviate from its normal course, due to self-consciousness on the part of either party. However, since many applicants were attending their first naturalization interview, they may not have been too surprised by the presence of a third party, or as mentioned above, it may even have put them more at ease. Although a subtle positive shift in the interviewee's comfort level may have benefited interviewees, this did not seem to concern the agency, which professes that it is not attempting to trick applicants but rather discern whether they qualify to naturalize. In addition, since the adjudications officers were accustomed to being observed during interviews by visitors from other states' INS offices, as well as other federal agencies (e.g., the State Department), the adjudications officers would presumably be less inclined to alter their routine for the benefit' of observers; conducting observations regularly over an extended period of time, the researcher built rapport with the adjudications officers, aiming to establish a level of comfort and familiarity that would likewise engender openness. Finally, the adjudications officers themselves reported that the interviews proceeded as usual when the researcher was present, in terms of content, sequence, and tone. Nonetheless, officers asked that the tape-recorder be turned off on two occasions during 'sensitive' questioning related to potential visa fraud. And officers twice asked the researcher not to observe interviews that involved criminal cases, although neither applicant actually appeared for the interview. Applicants with criminal records constitute a small minority of those who apply for naturalization, and such applicants' main hurdle to naturalizing is being able to demonstrate 'good moral character'.[20] Overall, it is believed that the number of recordings led to a representative sample of applicants being observed.

Transcription and analysis

Throughout the eighteen months of audio-taping and observing, the interviews were transcribed using a modified version of Gumperz & Berenz's (1993) transcription key. (See Appendix A for transcription legend.) About half of the 67 interviews were partially or completely transcribed by the researcher, using a transcribing machine with a foot pedal and a variable speed playback feature. Each transcript began with a date, an applicant number corresponding to the consent form, and an alphabetic code showing which officer conducted the interview, as well as a list of basic facts about the applicant (taken from the field notes): the applicant's nationality, age, and length of legal permanent residency in the US. All potentially identifying dates (e.g., birthday) and numbers (e.g., alien registration number[21]) were changed, and all proper names (e.g., places of employment) were likewise altered. The transcripts were then compared to the field notes so that non-verbal gestures and actions (e.g., eye contact, posture, signing forms) as well as other pertinent information (e.g., notes from the applicant's file, preceding occurrences, post-interview comments by the interviewing officer), could be included. Although all interviews were listened to, many repeatedly, some interviews or parts of interviews were not transcribed because they closely resembled other interviews. For example, an officer would often ask identical questions, across interviews, during the initial information verification, such as "Where do you live?" and "When were you born?" Proficient applicants would answer similarly; thus it was not necessary to transcribe these sections repeatedly. Moreover, the research questions led the researcher to focus closely on accommodation (as described in Pica, Holliday, & Morgenthaler, 1989, and Bremer et al, 1996), misunderstandings, and complete communication breakdowns, so these sections of interviews were almost always transcribed both for passing and failing interviews, although passing interviews often provided fewer instances of miscommunication.

Regarding "the openness of qualitative inquiry", Glesne & Peshkin (1992) note that "throughout the research process, [qualitative researchers] assume that social interaction is complex and that they will uncover *some* of that complexity" (emphasis added, p. 7). Initially, factual data were categorized and organized, so as to provide basic descriptive statistics about such matters as interviewees' country of origin and interview outcomes. Later, failure rates by nationality were calculated and the reasons for failure delineated. Various dimensions of the transcripts were examined and coded, including tasks, functions of questions, types of interviewer accommodation, causes of misunderstandings, reasons for communication breakdowns, and instances of negotiation of meaning (as defined in Long, 1996), as illustrated in this exchange:

(I = Interviewer   A = Applicant)
I: . . . When is your birthday?
A: Today is
I: When were you born? (3)

A: China (0.5)
I: What month? (0.5) What day? (2.5)
A: October twenty-ninth nineteen-ninety-nine (1.5)
I: Tell me again your birthday? (4) When were you born? =
A: = Four (2)
I: What month? (4) What month were you born?
A: [Four uh no no no (10) July
I: What day?
A: Thirtieth nineteen-twenty-eight

In the above interaction, the interviewer uses multiple techniques to accommodate the applicant: rephrasing the question, breaking the question down into its component parts, repetition, extended pause time, and elaboration. Much of the discourse analysis in this study focused on such points in the interviews, when negotiation of meaning was evident. Patterns of successful and unsuccessful communication were noted and analyzed with the aim of discovering underlying causes of miscommunication, if any.

Interviewer participation

All of the adjudications officers welcomed the researcher into their offices to observe naturalization interviews. The researcher attributes the adjudications officers' willing participation to five factors:

1 The researcher was genuinely interested in learning more about the naturalization process. Thus, the researcher was not merely conducting research for its own sake, but was gaining information on a topic she was personally invested in as a result of prior experience working with immigrants seeking to naturalize. The adjudications officers welcomed the opportunity to talk about their job, describe applicants, and explain naturalization policy and relevant federal legislation. The adjudications officers were confident in their positions and did not feel that the researcher was judging them but rather that the researcher was learning *from* them. The officers were thus framed as 'experts' from whom the researcher wanted to gain knowledge. (Since this particular office has a co-operative program in which graduate students from local universities majoring in law or criminal justice serve as interns, the officers were familiar with playing a mentoring role.) In fact, the officers generally perceived the research to be focused on the interviewees, not the interviewers.

2 The INS administration views educating and communicating with the community as part of all employees' duties. For example, each

semester, a different adjudications officer does a presentation on the naturalization interview at a training session for volunteers in a Chinese community organization's citizenship tutoring program. Similarly, the Assistant Director spoke at a local conference on naturalization, attended by immigrant service providers; following his presentation, he answered questions frankly.

3 As a result of having gone through official channels, the researcher was provided with administrative support and unequivocal access. The Assistant Director of Examinations, the adjudications officers' direct supervisor, allowed the researcher the freedom to approach officers personally regarding observations.

4 The adjudications officers were accustomed to being observed; as mentioned above, colleagues from other state and federal agencies occasionally sat in on interviews. In addition, the close quarters in the cubicles provided minimal privacy anyway. Frequently, voices from other interviews carried over from an adjacent cubicle, and supervisors or co-workers sometimes leaned into the doorway, interrupting an interview.

5 The researcher had an 'insider connection', since she had been introduced to the other adjudications officers by their colleague. By conducting research for well over a year and by beginning by observing a friend, the researcher gradually built rapport with other adjudications officers before sitting in on their interviews.

In addition to facilitating the observation of naturalization interviews, the rapport between the researcher and interviewing officers enabled informal follow-up interviews to occur after many observed naturalization interviews. The time spent conducting such informal interviews with the officers ranged from approximately thirty seconds to thirty minutes. These informal follow-up interviews were not usually recorded because the researcher sensed that this would have caused officers to hesitate to comment on sensitive matters involving assessment and bias; in fact, officers often asked me to turn off the tape-recorder as the applicant departed.[22] Based on the researcher's perceptions of the sensitivity of the subject matter and the level of comfort and formality, notes were taken either during or after the follow-up interview. The adjudications officers often took on a 'teaching persona' when answering the researcher's questions on policies, although the interviewing officers' personal beliefs and assumptions also emerged. The researcher's occasional presence during lunch breaks also provided opportunities to listen to conversations among officers about specific applicants they had interviewed. In addition to informal follow-up interviews and overheard conversations, more structured interviews were conducted, in which the same personal background questions (e.g., languages spoken, years of government service) were asked of each officer; notes were taken at this time.[23]

Informally interviewing adjudications officers before and after some naturalization interviews created a unique opportunity to discover how they perceived different applicants. While perusing an applicant's file in preparation for the next interview, an adjudications officer would sometimes share his or her predictions about an applicant. This information proved invaluable in follow-up interviews in which the adjudications officer would be able to confirm or refute his or her initial assumptions about an applicant. It also afforded the researcher an opportunity to observe whether different interviewer preconceptions altered the interview proceedings. For example, upon reviewing one applicant's file, an interviewer noted that the applicant was a fish market employee and voiced her prediction that he would not be able to speak and understand English well enough to pass his interview. However, he did pass his interview, and the adjudications officer acknowledged the inaccuracy of her prediction in a follow-up interview.

The researcher was interested in the assumptions that the adjudications officers expressed about applicants and whether these presuppositions in any way affected interview outcome. This information was eventually used to help answer Research Question #3: "Which factors affect applicants' chances of naturalizing?", to define factors leading to interviewers' definitions of success, and to assess whether interviewer bias was affecting applicants' chances of passing. Contrary to the researcher's expectations, interviewers' preconceived notions did not appear to affect interview outcome negatively. Carefully examining potential areas of bias, through interviews with the interviewers themselves and subsequent observations, made it possible to test and confirm or discredit hypotheses about what leads to a successful naturalization interview. Although potentially intimidating tones of voice were used by some officers at times, and although many applicants showed noticeable signs of nervousness, these two factors did not appear to lead to failure in the face of demonstrated English proficiency.

Immigrant input

Despite initial aspirations on the researcher's part, follow-up interviews were not conducted with applicants. Although the researcher was given complete access to naturalization interviews, the subject of conducting follow-up interviews with applicants *after* the actual naturalization interview created some discomfort for the INS administration. Ultimately, the researcher decided not to jeopardize her site access by pushing the issue of post-naturalization-interview discussions with applicants. Not only was the idea politically complicated, but it also would have been difficult to implement logistically – from setting up an interview site off government property to seeking out interpreters. Nonetheless, in this study, the researcher did follow one applicant through the process and conduct a post-interview with her.

Observing several Citizenship Preparation classes and one group tutoring session also provided the researcher with opportunities to question the adult learners and instructors about their impressions of the naturalization interview and definitions of success *before* they attended a naturalization interview. A future study should aim to make the research more complete by also questioning applicants *after* their naturalization interviews, incorporating a naturalization interview playback interspersed with applicant commentary and then follow-up questions from the researcher, thus giving more applicants a voice in naming the causes of their success or failure at the naturalization interview.

Rich description and networking

Out of a desire to inform teachers and students of the naturalization process, the naturalization interview was studied within a larger context; for example, the researcher observed a swearing-in ceremony for new citizens, in order to form a more complete picture of the entire naturalization process. Prior to approaching the INS, the researcher also sought information from, and volunteered at, two non-governmental organizations (NGOs) that assist immigrants in preparing to naturalize: Catholic Charities, and the Chinese Community Action Coalition. Interviewing tutors and a teacher and observation provided valuable first-hand data on the current state of US Citizenship Preparation programs. As a result of the researcher's working relationship with the Naturalization Co-ordinator at Catholic Charities, she was able to attend a local naturalization conference for NGO immigrant service providers, and, in the face of difficulty in finding a US Citizenship Preparation course to observe, used a contact made at the conference to locate one. After the research was completed, pedagogically-oriented reports of the findings were presented to all three organizations, drawing upon the analysis of target discourse and placing it within this detailed broader context.

Findings: Causes of failure

Of 67 interviewees observed, ten did not qualify for naturalization, due to their failing one or more of the tests. Severe difficulties with English speaking, listening, reading, and/or writing were observed in all cases of unsuccessful applicants. Despite the researcher's expectation that interviewer bias might have a negative impact on applicants' chances of naturalizing, the analysis revealed that English proficiency, not cross-cultural differences in communication style, was *the* primary determiner of success or failure (see Tables 2 and 3). As Tables 2 and 3 reveal, contrary to the expectations of many immigrants preparing to naturalize, and the curriculum design of most US Citizenship Preparation courses, no one failed solely the US

Table 2   Observed reasons for failure to qualify for naturalization at the interview

Official reason for failure to naturalize	Number of applicants
Unable to speak/understand English	4*
Unable to speak/understand English + failed *only* the reading test	1†
Unable to speak/understand English + failed *only* the writing test	0
Unable to speak/understand English + failed *only* the US history test	0
Unable to speak/understand English + failed *all three* tests	0
Failed *all three* tests: reading, writing, and US history	3‡
Failed *only* the reading test	0
Failed *only* the writing test	2
Failed *only* the US history test	0

* Usually the interview disintegrated when the applicant was judged to lack basic oral English skills, so the three more formal tests were often not administered.

† The applicant was at a second interview (a re-examination for reading only), failed the reading test, and was not administered any other tests. Since the applicant struggled with understanding English, the interviewer amended the denial letter to read that the applicant was not only unable to read English but also unable to speak or write English (although she was not dictated a sentence). Only the two demonstrated reasons are listed above.

‡ Two of the three were barely able to communicate in English, and could arguably be placed in the category "Unable to speak/understand English + failed all three tests".

Table 3   Number of applicants failing a specific requirement for
naturalization[24]

Requirement	Number* of applicants who failed
Ability to speak and understand English	5†
Ability to write English	5
Ability to read English	4
Knowledge of US history/government	3

* Each applicant may appear up to three times.
† Two more applicants were barely able to communicate in English and
could arguably be placed in this category, as well, although this reason was
not listed on their denial letters.

history and government test; those who did fail to answer enough US
history and government questions correctly always also failed to
demonstrate English proficiency in at least one area. These findings
were corroborated by an INS administrator at an immigrant service
provider conference in 2000; according to him, about 75% of failures
result from a lack of English proficiency, and the other 25% from an
inability to demonstrate 'good moral character'. It is noteworthy that
he did not mention lack of knowledge of US history and government
as a factor contributing to failure. Tables 2 and 3 also show that the
inability to communicate verbally in English was the most common
single reason for failure.

As shown in Table 4, only applicants from the four most highly
represented nationalities (China, Korea, the Philippines, and
Vietnam) failed to naturalize. The Filipino candidates fared exceptionally well as a group, with only one in 20 failing to naturalize,[25]
whereas mainland Chinese applicants had the largest failure rate,
with six out of 13 failing.[26] Referring back to Table 1, Chinese
comprised 19% of the applicants in this study, with an additional 8%
from Hong Kong, Koreans 12%, Filipinos 30%, and Vietnamese
9%. Of course, many factors besides nationality, such as length of
residence, educational background, and exposure to English, most
likely influenced success and failure rates. Overall, ten applicants, or
15%, failed to qualify for naturalization at the observed interviews.
This statistic is in keeping with national averages, as between 1991
and 1997, the number of naturalization petitions denied ranged from
5% to 18% annually, with no statistics reported for 5% of applications (*INS Yearbook*, 1999, p. 142).

Careful analysis of transcripts revealed that, in the naturalization

Table 4 Nationalities of observed applicants who failed to naturalize

Nationality	Number* of applicants who failed	Percentage of applicants within a nationality who failed	Total percentage of applicants (by nationality) who failed
Chinese	6	46%	9%
Vietnamese	2 (+1)*	33% (50%)	3% (4.5%)
Korean	1	12.5%	1.5%
Filipina	1	5%	1.5%
All Nationalities	10 (+1)	15% (16.4%)	15% (16.4%)

* Unable to provide necessary documentation (i.e., adequate medical waiver, court dispositions for misdemeanors, and proof of Selective Service registration) at his first interview, a third Vietnamese applicant was scheduled for a second interview, which he failed to attend; thus, his file was 'closed', and he failed to qualify for naturalization.

interview, fine-tuned skill development in terms of grammar, phonology, and pragmatics was not essential, as long as those components of language development were adequate to ensure successful communication, given some negotiation of meaning. Although many ESL instructors would perhaps define 'language proficiency' using measures of phonological and grammatical competence, and even pragmatic competence, as well, it seems that naturalization interviewers are not concerned so much with applicants' linguistic accuracy as with their ability to convey meaning, albeit with interviewer accommodation at times.

According to the findings of this study, cross-cultural bias or misunderstanding did not determine naturalization interview outcomes. In many ways, naturalization interviews appear to differ from other types of institutional, gate-keeping interactions that have been analyzed, including courtroom, school counseling, and workplace discourse (e.g., Cook-Gumperz & Gumperz, 1997; Eades, in press; Erickson & Shultz, 1982; Roberts, Davies, & Jupp, 1992). This could be attributed to three ways in which the gatekeeper's purpose varies in the different settings:

1 The purposes of the interviews differ. Evaluating English proficiency is a primary goal of the naturalization interview, whereas in other gate-keeping encounters, English proficiency may be taken for granted, with the gatekeeper focusing on more culturally specific aspects of communication, like pragmatics. In job interviews, the interviewer has the responsibility of choosing only one

candidate for each advertised position, whereas there is no ostensible 'cap' on the number of applicants who can qualify to naturalize. Additionally, in many Western contexts, the job applicant bears the burden of promoting him or herself and framing his or her experience, whereas in the naturalization interview, the topic is controlled by the interviewer, with few, if any open-ended questions asked. And whereas courtroom exchanges are deliberately designed to be adversarial and confrontational, this is not an expressed purpose of the naturalization interview. In addition, in interviews other than that for naturalization, more open-ended questions are generally asked (e.g., Gumperz, Jupp, & Roberts, 1979), leaving responsibility for framing and organizing answers in applicants' hands, whereas many questions in the naturalization interview require a simple yes-no answer or another brief response.

2 Interviewers' prior experience with cross-cultural communication varies. Adjudications officers' job description entails interacting with immigrants on a daily basis, whereas the lawyers, judges, academic advisors, and employers in other studies may have had much less experience interacting with those whose language was not 'standard' English.[27]

3 Continuing education and the goals of an organization's leaders may or may not place value on successful cross-cultural communication. Unlike many lawyers, employers, and school counselors, some of the adjudications officers had attended cross-cultural communication courses when working as inspectors at the airport, and the Assistant Director of Examinations, who supervises the interviewing officers, has an interest in cross-cultural communication and keeps a small collection of books on the topic in his office. Presumably, naturalization officers, in contrast to lawyers, employers, and school counselors, are more accustomed to (and perhaps more adept at) interacting with second language speakers of English.

Implications

Although the conclusions of this study focus on the applicants, implications for awareness-raising on the part of the adjudications officers also emerge. After the research was completed, the ways in which different adjudications officers prevented misunderstandings in interviews were highlighted in the thank-you letter and research report provided to each officer who had participated. For example, various interviewing officers were observed reducing the pace of their speech, allowing for extended pause time, using increased volume or articulation to emphasize key words, verbally marking transitions, using gestures to imbue meaning (e.g., holding up a hand horizontally when asking an applicant's height), providing visual aids (e.g., examples of cursive vs. printed signatures), translating legalese into Plain English (e.g., "Have you ever lied and said you're American?" instead of "Have you ever claimed to be an American citizen?"), and explicitly explaining the next step in the interview.[28] Although the research reported here focused more on how to design ESL/US Citizenship Preparation courses to boost applicants' success rates at the naturalization interview, a later study (Seig & Winn, 2003) addressed those in power: the adjudications officers. Transcripts were analyzed to design a course to train new naturalization interviewers in techniques that experienced interviewers use to mark transitions between interview tasks explicitly and to negotiate meaning, thus accommodating second language speakers.

Contrary to many immigrants' impressions, the biggest challenge facing naturalization applicants appears *not* to be recall of basic facts about US history and government but, rather, navigating the other two tests of English reading and writing, as well as interacting in English throughout the interview. In contrast to the conventional content-based ESL course on US history and government usually offered to immigrants seeking to naturalize, this study suggests a task-based approach to teaching a US Citizenship Preparation course.[29] Given the limited time many immigrants have to prepare for their naturalization interview, efficiency is crucial; thus, it is desirable to focus on the specific tasks required at the naturalization interview rather than rely on the typical broad curriculum with a disproportional emphasis on US history and government. A task-based approach will serve to familiarize applicants with the interview process and protocol, while they participate in hands-on activities, like role-plays, practicing the tasks they will need to perform at the actual interview, including use of the necessary vocabulary and linguistic forms.

Adjudications officers seek evidence of comprehensible spoken English and of aural English comprehension during the naturalization interview. In the classroom, this observation should result in an interactionist, communicative approach to language teaching and learning, in which conveying meaning is prioritized. Ideally, rather than presenting prefabricated grammar units, teachers would teach mini-lessons in grammar and pronunciation, addressing issues that emerge from learners' observed communication difficulties.[30] At times, an instructor could choose to use implicit corrective recasts in place of more explicit type of consciousness-raising tasks in address-ing observed learner needs, keeping in mind that grammatical, phonological, and pragmatic *accuracy* do not seem to determine success in the naturalization interview, as long as an applicant's intended meaning can be understood by the interviewer.

Task delineation

Task-based language teaching (TBLT, Long, 1985, and elsewhere) provides an efficient approach to teaching English for specific purposes (ESP), since the real-world tasks learners need to complete form the content of the course. The English language components – from tone and vocabulary to sentence structure and grammar – are integrated into coursework since any problems with these linguistic elements emerge naturally when learners work on the pedagogic tasks and can, if necessary, be highlighted by the teacher through one of TBLT's ten methodological principles, focus on form (see, e.g., Doughty & Long, 2002; Long, 1991, 2000) *in response* to student efforts to use the appropriate target discourse.

In TBLT, a task-based needs analysis, followed by collection and analysis of representative samples of target discourse surrounding target task accomplishment, allows for the identification of appro-priate course content – in this case, the tasks the applicants must accomplish at the naturalization interview. These tasks were ob-served to be fairly consistent across interviews. Although different interviewers varied the order at times, a successful naturalization applicant had to accomplish the following nine, often overlapping, tasks *in English*:

1 swearing to tell the truth during the interview[31]

2 verifying the accuracy of the personal information (e.g., address, marital status, travel outside the US, employment) provided on the Application for Naturalization, and making addendums to the application regarding information that may have changed since it was submitted by the applicant (includes handing over one's alien registration card and pass-port)

I: Are you still living at two zero three three?
A: Yes
I: Maunakea Street?
A: Yes
I: What apartment are you in? (3) What apartment number?
A: Park number?
I: Apartment
A: Apartment oh (3) one eighteen

3 accepting or declining the option to have a legal name change upon
   naturalizing
   I: You said you('re) going to keep your name yeah? (3) You gonna keep
        your name (0.5) you not gonna change yeah?
   A: What ma'am?
   I: Is that right? (0.3) DID YOU SAY you want to keep your name or do
        you want to change your name?
   A: Oh: I uh it will re:main:n uh (1) the same ma'am

4 establishing 'good moral character' (e.g., evidence of Selective Service
   Registration for males ages 18–27, and no evidence of alien smuggling,
   visa fraud, prostitution, or bigamy)
   I: How many wedding ceremonies did you have with your wife? (1.5)
        How many ceremonies did you have? =
   A: = Just one
   I: Just one (1) you didn't (0.3) u::h were you married when you came to
        America? (1.5) Were you already married when you came to America?
   A: No ma'am (2) I went back to marry her[32]

5 professing allegiance to the US Constitution and the American form of
   government (e.g., a willingness to bear arms on behalf of the US and
   perform civilian duties at times of national importance)
   I: Do you believe in the Constitution and form of government of the
        Uni:ted Sta:tes? (0.5)
   A: Yes

6 passing a dictation test of English writing
   I: I want you to write a sentence for me (0.3) a very simple sentence (0.3)
        I have two beautiful children (0.5) OK? (0.5) I have two beautiful
        children (0.3) Just write it down here
   A: (*) =
   I: = Hm: (3) You can print or write (0.5) it doesn't matter (1) for that (3)
        I have (1) two (5) beautiful children (17) good

7 passing a test of English reading
   I: Show me you can read English (0.3) read this sentence to me (0.3) I
        swear ((points to Application for Naturalization)) (4)
   A: I swear that I know (0.3) the contents of this application and (0.3)
        supplemental (0.3) page one to (**)]
   I: [Blank Hmhu
   A: Blank that the correction number one through twelve were made at
        my request (0.3) at this amended application (0.5) is true to the best of
        my knowledge and (0.3) belief

8 passing a test of US history and government
   I: The Bill of Rights guarantees Americans certain rights and freedoms
        can you name some of them? Like freedom of (1)
   A: The right freedom of speech (0.5) press and religion
   I: hmhu:

A: peaceable assembly]
I: [hmh: ((shuffling papers))
A: the government *
I: OK good (0.5) that's good

9 consenting to take the Oath of Allegiance that will be elicited at the Final
Hearing, in which successful applicants are sworn in as US citizens[33]
I: You said earlier that you're willing to take the full oath of allegiance to
America (0.3) this is the full oath here (0.3) it says you will love only
America and no other country (0.3) will you do that? (0.3) Love only
America?
A: Yes
I: Yes OK (0.3) I want you to sign over here[34]

The overarching requirement for these nine tasks is to accomplish
each one *in English*. From verifying one's personal information to
answering questions about US history and government, the entire
interview is composed of information exchanges that the interviewing
officers regard as opportunities to ascertain applicants' English proficiency. Even the reading and writing 'tests' require a degree of aural
English comprehension, as shown in an excerpt from the interview of
an elderly Filipino female:

I: Can you read English? (2.5) Can you read?
A: Can you (0.5) I cannot
I: You cannot read English
A: (*)

This applicant seems not to have initially comprehended the question, as suggested by the substantial pause. The interviewer then
repeats and shortens the question. The applicant then begins to
repeat the question; finally, she pauses briefly and answers the
question by reporting she "cannot" read in English. Nonetheless, the
applicant was still shown a passage from a basal reader; she
attempted to read the sentences. In a follow-up interview the
interviewer revealed, "I was on the verge of passing her on the
reading test," but she missed "a few short simple words" and thus
failed. The applicant also failed the US history and government test
and refused to even attempt to write the dictated sentence.

In TBLT, pedagogic tasks are derived from the identified target
task-types. These pedagogic tasks "are authentic in terms of their
relevance to learners' needs and are defined in terms of *target tasks*,
as established by a task-based needs analysis" (Long, 1997, p. 160).
Pedagogic tasks are simplified approximations – tasks that "teachers
and students ... actually work on in the classroom, at least initially,
until [students] are capable of tackling the full version of the target

task" (Long, 1985, p. 92). In TBLT, pedagogic tasks are sequenced from simplest to most complex, based *not* on intuitive "linguistic criteria grading" but on increased "intellectual challenge", as a function of the amount of cognitive effort required. While still a matter of subjective judgment in many cases, to the extent possible, the grading is based on low-inference criteria, like "the number of steps [required], ... the amount and kind of language required, [and] the number of sources competing for attention" (Long & Crookes, 1992, p. 45; see also Robinson, 2001).

Although several of the tasks outlined above involve answering simple questions, the lexical items in each task vary, and a range of responses may be acceptable. For example, an interviewer seeking the same information could ask "When were you born?" or "What is your birth date?" Thus, actually engaging in listening and speaking pedagogic tasks specifically tailored to each target task could be more useful for learners than merely studying prototypical questions. Sub-tasks are nested within most of the target task-types; thus pedagogic tasks must be designed to address those particular needs, as well.

Pedagogic task (PT) derivation will be illustrated using Target Task 2, above: verifying personal information. The verification of background information in Target Task 2 entails several sub-tasks. Below is a sample sequence of pedagogic tasks for teaching Target Task 2: personal information verification, employing a TBLT approach. Learners begin by listening to genuine recordings of naturalization interviews and then gradually work up to participating in a role play of that segment of the interview. Until their actual interview, learners will only be able to engage in learning tasks that increasingly approximate the authentic communication tasks at the naturalization interview itself (Long, 1997, p. 150).

PT1   Students listen[35] repeatedly to the portion of five naturaliza-tion interviews[36] in which the first few sections of the Application for Naturalization are reviewed. (Due to the lengthiness of this assignment, it could be completed as homework. Students could be given an audio-tape to play at home and could be asked to keep a log of when and for how long they listened to the audio-tape and also answer comprehension questions.) Here is a sample excerpt of a middle-aged Peruvian applicant discussing one portion of Target Task 2: her employ-ment history:

I: Where do you work?
A: Work?
I: M: (huh)

A: My job? (0.5) Um: (0.5) I: I clean a little houses (0.5)
several houses
I: Do what?
A: I clean
I: You **clean** house so this is your own business?
A: No no no (0.5) yeah my own (0.3) for myself an:d uh I work (0.3)
with (0.3) St. Teresa's School
I: You work at St. Teresa's School (0.3) What do you do? =
A: [yeah
A: = the same with the fathers and (0.5) clean * offices
I: So they the school pays you and people pay you
A: No the school pays me
I: So you clean but you clean houses for other people
A: Yeah a few more people
I: Do you work for the school (0.3) or:?
A: No I work for the school (0.5) is a part-time work (0.3)
And then I work (0.3) for myself
I: OK: (1) How long have you been doing this?
A: Um: (0.5) work?
I: M: huh
A: Um (home cleaning)?
I: Uh-huh
A: I've been working about for three years four years

Listening to this extensive interaction would help students to realize
the potential depth and complexity of questioning and explanation
that could follow from the simple question "Where do you work?"

PT2   Students are given the Application for Naturalization and
allowed time to read it over.

PT3   Using an overhead projector, the instructor demonstrates how
to fill out the Application for Naturalization, loosely based on
her/his own situation or on that of someone in the class.

PT4   Students listen again to the personal information verification
portion of one of the recorded naturalization interviews and
fill in information on a partially completed Application for
Naturalization (a cloze activity).[37]

PT5   Students listen to the personal information verification section
of another interview and fill in the information provided on a
blank Application for Naturalization.

PT6   Students fill out the initial sections of the Application for
Naturalization using their own personal information.[38]

PT7   Using the information on the displayed overhead transparency
of a blank Application for Naturalization, the instructor and a
guest instructor role-play the information verification part of
the naturalization interview.

PT8 Students work in pairs to role-play the information verification portion of the naturalization interview, based on their own personal information on the Application for Naturalization.

PT9 The instructor and a guest instructor repeat the role-play based on the information displayed on the overhead transparency, this time including addendums, such as a recent trip outside the US or a change in employment since the application was submitted.

PT10 Ideally, the instructor or another volunteer would then conduct a mock naturalization interview with each student.[39]

The above sequence is an example of how a target task in the naturalization interview can be adapted to the classroom in TBLT. For learners with low English proficiency, the pedagogic tasks could be further divided and repeated. For example, Pedagogic Task 1: listening to naturalization interviews, could be divided into ten separate listening exercises, organized in terms of the required topics:

1 name and address
2 social security number and alien registration number
3 date and country of birth
4 basis for eligibility
5 immigration / green card information
6 absences from the US
7 past addresses
8 past and current employment
9 marital history
10 information about children

Any of these sub-tasks could be further divided for beginning level students. In addition, short, clear interactions could be targeted initially. The complex employment history presented above could be preceded by a much simpler one in which an applicant responded with a single phrase and the interviewer then proceeded to another topic.

Each pedagogic task addressing Target Task 2 works towards Pedagogic Task 7, in which students have an opportunity to role-play both parts: the interviewer and the authentic role of the interviewee, and ultimately, to Pedagogic Task 9, in which students have an opportunity once again to put into practice what they have learned in this module. In the sub-tasks outlined above, pedagogic tasks and more authentic tasks are sometimes combined. For example, although it is not an authentic task for learners to role-play the part of the interviewer, this activity can increase familiarity with the questions asked at the interview, provide opportunities to use relevant vocabulary in a meaningful context, and encourage negotiation of meaning (see Long, 1996).

The pedagogic tasks are sequenced in order of increasing cognitive load and complexity, beginning with an input flood (mere listening), followed by reading, proceeding to a listening and writing task, and finally culminating in role-play. Filling out an application and discussing its contents are collapsed into adjacent pedagogic tasks, although the filing of the Application for Naturalization actually occurs months before the naturalization interview. Nonetheless, for the purposes of role-play, a completed Application for Naturalization needs to be generated. Because an applicant is expected to be familiar with his or her own application, this is an especially important task for learners who had a friend, family member, or lawyer fill out the paperwork for them when applying for naturalization, as well as for those who have not yet applied, for an applicant must answer detailed questions during the interview about the information on his or her application, as well as inform the interviewer of any changes or corrections that need to be made.

Pedagogic Tasks 1, 7, and 9 involve listening to or observing naturalization interviews (or role-plays) that naturally contain instances of negotiation of meaning, including repetition requests, repetitions, clarification requests, elaborations, and restatements. Students are exposed to examples of the negotiation devices generally used in the naturalization interview. These devices can then be highlighted in class discussions and instructor-led role-plays.

The above ideas are merely suggestions for adapting Target Task 2 to a US Citizenship Preparation lesson plan, as the individual instructor's creativity in lesson planning, knowledge about his or her students, and awareness of research findings in the field of second language acquisition should also play a role in determining what kinds of pedagogic tasks are developed to teach each task-type. As Long (2000, p. 188) notes:

> As always in TBLT, the methodological principle is the important thing; the optimal pedagogy for implementing that principle will vary according to local conditions, as assessed by the classroom teacher. He or she is the expert on the local classroom situation, after all.

A future paper, or perhaps a Citizenship Preparation textbook, will describe more fully the other target task-types, provide examples of pedagogic tasks, and discuss further the implementation of such a curriculum in an ESL/US Citizenship Preparation course. Further research should investigate the extent to which increasing familiarity with the interview questions and practicing responses boost applicants' pass rate at the naturalization interview.

Conclusion: Generalizability

Observations of five ESL/US Citizenship Preparation classes and several ESL/Citizenship Preparation tutorial sessions, as well as a review of current Citizenship Preparation textbooks, showed the content in all cases to be US history and government; scant attention was paid to the demands of the interview itself (see, also, Nixon & Keenan, 1997). A lack of descriptive literature on the naturalization interview presumably contributed to this mismatch between typical educational preparation and the target communicative event.

There is an obvious need for an ESL/US Citizenship Preparation course curriculum that addresses some of the glaring disparities between what is currently being taught in the vast majority of such courses and what is actually required during the naturalization interview. The analysis of target discourse and causes for interview failure reported above revealed that a task-based ESL/US Citizenship Preparation course would most likely better meet learners' needs: improved English proficiency for successful completion of target tasks at the naturalization interview.[40] The collection of target discourse made such information available and should serve as a useful resource for naturalization applicants and their teachers,[41] who will no longer have to guess exactly what takes place at the naturalization interview.

Drawing upon the methodology used in this particular study of the naturalization interview, several practical recommendations emerge for target discourse collection in future needs analyses. The following facts and procedures appear to have facilitated collection of target discourse:

- Having an inside connection may have made gaining entrée easier.
- Patiently following official channels in the initial request for permission to observe allowed for broad research access later.
- Gradually getting to know the interviewers over an extended period of time (more than a year) fostered a high level of comfort and camaraderie between the interviewers and the researcher, resulting in an environment of open information sharing during informal interviews.
- Positioning herself as a learner rather than as an expert or

evaluator, the researcher seems to have elicited many comments from interviewers that otherwise might not have been forthcoming.

- Observing a sizeable number of interviews between numerous interviewers and applicants enabled generalizations to be made about routines and variations, thus enhancing the validity of the findings.

- Immediate, informal follow-up interviews, as well as pre-interview conversations, with the interviewers provided unique information that would otherwise have been unlikely to surface. In fact, this information led the researcher to reconsider her initial assumptions regarding the effects of officers' biases.

- Broadening the study to include examination of current curricula, as well as classroom observations, enabled explicit comparisons to be made between what was revealed through analyses of the target discourse and what was being taught in the courses, revealing some of the changes that need to be made.

- Being flexible and creative allowed the researcher to adapt to the challenges that arose in conducting research. For example, the decision to use audio-tape rather than video-tape was made after an initial observation. Also, when seeking permission to conduct follow-up interviews with applicants seemed like it might jeopardize the research site's openness to research, plans were adjusted. Instead, a US Citizenship Preparation course was found to observe and class attended for five evenings. This provided an opportunity to get to know the students and instructor and ask candid questions about their expectations of the naturalization interview. Fortuitously, one student happened to be attending her naturalization interview during the period of the study, making it possible for the researcher to follow that applicant through the process.

- Volunteering and working with two non-profit organizations that provide services to immigrants seeking to naturalize also enabled the researcher to gain access to other sources of information, including interviews with US Citizenship Preparation coordinators and tutors regarding their knowledge of the naturalization interview and their students' self-identified needs. (Those tended to center around the very tangible '100 US History and Government Questions' that have been translated into many languages.)

Overall, being patient, flexible, and personally invested in the research made target discourse collection possible at a seemingly impervious gate-keeping institution. Although analyses of the naturalization interview transcripts revealed great complexity, there is truth in what one officer stated after an interview in which the applicant clearly passed: "They usually do [pass] if they can speak English." This assertion was echoed by several of her colleagues. Reading and writing need to be included in this assertion, however. Despite the fact that many applicants cling almost obsessively to the 100 questions (of US history and government) in preparing for the naturalization interview, the transcripts of the observed and recorded interviews reveal that English language proficiency in oral communication, writing, and/or reading was the deciding factor in success or failure.[42] Now the collected and analyzed target discourse can serve to educate immigrant applicants and US Citizenship Preparation instructors, as well as the interviewing officers. It is hoped that enumerating the steps taken in collecting this corpus of target discourse will benefit others undertaking target discourse collection as part of a NA.

Notes

1 A notable exception is Bliss and Molinsky's (1994) text, *Voices of freedom: English and civics for the US Citizenship exam,* which combines 'authentic' interview dialogues with grammar exercises and US history and government lessons. The video-tape *The US Citizenship interview: Will they pass?* (New Readers Press, 1996) also provides useful role plays of naturalization interviews. In addition, New Readers Press has recently published a separate textbook to accompany the standard US History and Goverment text. *Citizenship: Passing the text* (Weintraub 2002) can now be supplemented with Weintraub's *Citizenship: Ready for the interview* (2002), available with an audio-tape or audio CD; the latter text focuses exclusively on how to answer questions at the interview.

2 Legal permanent residents are immigrants who are legally and permanently residing in the US – without US citizenship.

3 Naturalization was at an all-time high in the 1990s for at least two reasons. First, immigrants who legalized their presence during the Amnesty Program of the 1980s became eligible for naturalization. Second, the benignly titled Personal Responsibility and Work Opportunity Reconciliation Act of 1996 eliminated legal permanent residents' eligibility for certain federal programs, such as Supplemental Security Income (SSI) for the disabled and aged, Social Security for the retired, Medicaid ('health insurance' for low-income individuals), food stamps for the poor, and student loans from the government. Although some of those benefits were subsequently restored, the alarm caused by that legislation resulted in a successful naturalization mobilization effort (Shaw, 1998), including generous grants to non-profit agencies to teach Citizenship Preparation courses, with funding provided by donors such

as George Soros, a financially successful naturalized US citizen from Hungary.

Immigrants are often motivated to naturalize for other reasons, as well; for example legal permanent residents can only petition for immediate relatives: the petitioner's spouse, parents and *unmarried* children to immigrate, whereas US citizens can also petition for siblings and married children, and those family members are given higher priority in receiving immigrant visas. Besides easing immigration of family members, US citizenship also affords the freedom to travel with a US passport, as well as the right to vote in US elections.

4 A 'green card' is the colloquial term for a legal permanent resident card, a photo identification card held by immigrants, who, although not US citizens, are legally and permanently residing in the US.

5 Green card holders married to US citizens need only show three years of continuous, permanent residence to apply for naturalization.

6 Deportation involves requiring a non-US citizen to leave the US because of a violation of the law – usually a breach in immigration status.

7 Applicants can receive English language exemptions based on a combination of length of residence and age. Legal permanent residents aged 50 and over who have been green card holders for at least 20 years, or those aged 55 and over who have had green cards for at least 15 years, can be exempted from the English language requirement and have an interpreter accompany them; however, they still must demonstrate knowledge of US history and government in their native language. In addition, applicants who are at least 65 years old and have been legal permanent residents for 20 years or more can be exempted from the English language requirement and can also be administered a simpler version of the US history and government test (based on a shortened list of 25 questions, instead of the usual 100).

8 The Immigration and Naturalization Service (INS) was renamed on March 1, 2003, following a structural reorganization in response to the events of September 11, 2001. Throughout this paper, the term 'INS' will be used to refer to the agency at the time the research was conducted.

9 There are several potential outcomes of the naturalization interview. An applicant can successfully complete all interview tasks and then be added to the list of applicants waiting to be sworn in as US citizens. Alternatively, an applicant may fail because of an inability to communicate in English, a lack of 'good moral character' or allegiance to the US, or failure of at least one of the three tests.

10 At the entrance to the swearing-in ceremony, applicants are merely asked a few questions to ascertain that personal information (e.g., marital status, police record, and address) has not changed since the naturalization interview. During the ceremony applicants recite the 'Oath of Allegiance' in unison and sign their certificates of naturalization from their auditorium or courthouse seats.

11 A lawyer may be present but can only intervene if the client's legal rights appear to be violated.

12 The swearing-in ceremony is more of a formality, as applicants are sworn in *en masse*.

13 See Erickson & Shultz (1982) for an extensive discussion of gate-keeping encounters.

14 "English proficiency" can be defined as competence in using English for a specific purpose or "the degree of skill with which a person can use [the] language" (Richards, Platt, & Platt, 1992, p. 204).

15 The titles INS officer, interviewer, interviewing officer, and adjudications officer, will be used interchangeably throughout this paper.

16 'Plain English' entails using common, everyday words clearly and concisely, frequently to facilitate understanding of legal matters. See Eagleson (1990) and Tiersma (1999).

17 The consent form that the applicant signed was attached by paper clip to two identical consent forms sandwiched between two pieces of carbon paper. When the interview concluded, the researcher kept the original and then gave one copy to the applicant and one copy to the interviewer for the applicant's file.

18 Nationwide, Mexicans, Filipinos, and Vietnamese compose the largest groups of recently naturalized citizens (Mogelonsky, 1997).

19 At the time this research was conducted, natives of Hong Kong generally held British passports.

20 Possessing 'good moral character' refers to the state of not having violated any US laws, including immigration policies. Although attending an ESL/US Citizenship Preparation course may be helpful for applicants with criminal backgrounds, it would probably not be sufficient to ensure success at the interview, since these applicants most likely need to seek legal advice, as well.

21 An alien registration number is an identification number provided to all non-US citizens who legally reside in the US as immigrants. The alien registration number appears on a photo identification known as the alien registration card, known colloquially as a 'green card'.

22 A few follow-up interviews were recorded because the tape-recorder remained on, with no objection from the interviewing officer.

23 Recording all of the follow-up interviews with adjudications officers could have provided more data to reveal how interviewers define success at the naturalization interview. It is recommended in future studies.

24 Applicants who fail to qualify for naturalization at their first interview are automatically scheduled for a second interview within 60 days; each applicant thus has two chances to qualify for naturalization. Some of the naturalization interviews observed in this study were 're-exams' or second interviews.

25 Presumably, the omnipresence of English in the Philippines played a role in the high success rate among Filipinos.

26 Perhaps the vast linguistic differences between the Chinese and English languages, the ghettoized isolation from English that some may experience living and/or working in China Town, and, possibly, a discomfort with government authorities, could have contributed to the preponderance of difficulties for several Chinese applicants.

27 Also referred to as Mainstream United States English or MUSE (Lippi-Green, 1997).

28 See Bemer & Simonot (1996) for an in-depth discussion of ways to prevent misunderstandings.

29 One could argue that applicants are much more successful navigating the US history and government portion of the interview because this is what is emphasized in US Citizenship Preparation courses. In addition, 'The 100 Questions' are the most tangible and accessible study tool provided by the USCIS.

30 See also Doughty (2000, 2001); Eskey (1997); Grabe & Stoller (1997).

31 The oath was generally not recorded, as applicants' consent was typically sought *after* this step.

32 This questioning of a middle-aged Filipino male applicant focuses on uncovering potential visa fraud; if he had immigrated under single status but actually already been married, his immigrant status would be invalid, and he could be found to be residing illegally in the US.

33 This final step includes signing one's name in a specified manner: in English, in cursive.

34 The young Chinese male applicant passed his interview.

35 A video-tape could be used instead of an audio-tape (e.g., *The US Citizenship interview: Will they pass?* (New Readers Press, 1966), featuring re-enacted naturalization interviews).

36 To protect anonymity, it may be necessary for actual naturalization interviews to be role-played by actors/actresses who have listened to the original audio-tapes for cues as to pace, tone, accent, etc. Transcripts (in which all identifying information was altered) could be used as scripts. Ideally, the part of the immigrant applicant would be played by a non-native speaker of English. However, it would be preferable to secure consent to use actual naturalization interviews.

37 Prior to this step, students could be given a handout to complete, answering questions about the information solicited by the officer in a recorded interview.

38 Students who have not yet applied for naturalization could then be assisted in submitting their applications by mail, if no legal complications exist and the applicant appears proficient enough in English to prepare for the interview within the expected wait time before it is scheduled. A diagnostic interview could also be conducted to ascertain the proficiency level *for this task*.

39 Teachers with large numbers of students would have to adapt, e.g., breaking into different rooms to reduce the noise level during role plays and soliciting help from volunteers, perhaps students in Teachers of

English as a Second Language (TESOL) degree programs and other ESL teachers. In the absence of personnel to conduct mock interviews, students could use audio-tapes at home to record their answers to written interview questions. However, different handouts would have to present the interview questions with slightly different phrasing and ordering to remind students of the variability among interviewers. Applicants' responses cannot be overly scripted.

40 Benesch (1996), an advocate of *critical* NA, points out the limitations of a descriptive NA, in which (she asserts) "the researcher does not look for ways to modify current conditions [and thus make the learning process transformative for the learners] but instead aims to fit students into the status quo by teaching them to make their behavior and language appropriate" (p. 727). (See, too, Fairclough, 1989, for a critique of 'appropriateness' in terms of 'Standard Language Ideology'.) In an ideal world, there should also be an opportunity for the rare learner who actually wants to delve beneath the surface and reach beyond the basic requirements for US citizenship to pursue a course that would encourage a more critical examination of, or an action research approach to, US history, current immigration policy, the naturalization process, and the status of immigrants in American society today.

41 This kind of information is all the more necessary because many teachers of ESL/US Citizenship courses have little or no professional ESL background and have never been present at a naturalization interview.

42 Of course some applicants' English ability may have momentarily decreased under the stress of the interview. At conferences, audience members have suggested that officers in other states may differ significantly in their approach to interviewing, when compared to officers in the state studied, where diversity is ostensibly embraced.

Acknowledgments

I gratefully acknowledge the following University of Hawai'i at Manoa faculty for their assistance with the research reported here: Dr. Graham Crookes, Dr. Kathy Davis, and Dr. Diana Eades, as well as Dr. Cathy Doughty, who provided support on the TBLT portion, and Dr. Mike Long for his guidance and encouragement in completing this chapter. I also extend my thanks to those who provided suggestions for revisions to the paper: Dr. Diana Eades, Ms. Alexandra Johnston, Ms. Linda O'Roke, Ms. Rachel Rivers, and Dr. Mary Theresa Seig. In addition, I am deeply appreciative of those at the Immigration and Naturalization Service who participated in this research, as well as the immigrant applicants who made this study possible. I would also like to thank the adult learners and staff at the

Chinese Community Action Coalition, Adult Education Division, and Catholic Charities for their support.

References

Benesch, S. (1996). Needs analysis and curriculum development in EAP: An example of a critical approach. *TESOL Quarterly* 30 (4), 723–738.

Bliss, B., & Molinksy, S. J. (1994). *Voices of freedom: English and civics for the US citizenship exam.* (Second edition) Englewood Clifs, NJ: Regents Prentice Hall.

Bremer, K., Roberts, C., Vasseur, M.-T., Simonot, M., & Broeder, P. (1996). *Achieving understanding: Discourse in intercultural encounters.* London: Longman.

Bremer, K., & Simonot, M. (1996). Preventing problems of understanding. In K. Bremer et al, *Achieving understanding: Discourse in intercultural encounters.* London: Longman.

Cook-Gumperz, J., & Gumperz, J. (1997). Narrative explanations: Accounting for past experience in interviews. *Journal of Narrative and Life History* 7, 1–4, 291–98.

Crawford, J. (1989). Bilingualism in American: A forgotten legacy. In J. Crawford, *Bilingual education: History, politics, theory and practice.* Trenton, NJ: Crane.

Doran de Valdez, Reidel, C., & Burgos, J. (1995). *Preparation for citizenship.* Austin, TX: Steck Vaughn.

Doughty, C. J. (2000). Negotiating the L2 linguistic environment. *University of Hawai'i Working Papers in ESL* 18, 2, 47–83. Also in C. Munoz (ed.), *Segundas lenguas: Adquisicion en un contexto formal.* Madrid: Ariel Publishers.

Doughty, C. J. (2001). Cognitive underpinnings of focus on form. In P. Robinson (ed.) *Cognition and second language instruction* (206–57). Cambridge: Cambridge University Press.

Doughty, C. J., & Long, M. H. (2002). Optimal psycholinguistic environments for distance foreign language learning. Plenary address to the conference on Distance Learning of the Less Commonly Taught Languages. February 1–3, 2002. Arlington, VA. *Second Language Studies* 20, 1, 2002, 1–42. Also in *Forum of International Development Studies* 23, 2003, 35–73. Also in *Language Learning and Technology.* Volume 7, Number 3 (September) 2003, 50–80. (http://llt.msu.edu)

Eades, D. (in press). The politics of misunderstanding in the legal process: Aboriginal English in Queensland. In J. House, G. Kasper & S. Ross (eds.), *Misunderstanding in spoken discourse* (pp. 196–223). London: Longman.

Eagleson, R. D. (1990). *Writing in plain English.* Canberra, Australia: Australian Government Publishing Service.

Erickson, F., & Shultz, E. (1982). *The counselor as gatekeeper: Social interaction in interviews.* New York: Academic Press.

Eskey, D. E. (1997). Syllabus design in content-based instruction. In M. A. Snow & D. M. Brinton (eds.), *The content-based classroom: Perspectives on integrating language and content* (pp. 132–41). White Plains: Longman.

Fairclough, N. (1989). *Language and power*. London: Longman.

Fiksdal, S. (1990). The right time and pace: A microanalysis of cross-cultural gatekeeping interviews. Norwood, NJ: Ablex.

Gee, J. P. (1996). *Social linguistics and literacies: Ideology in discourse*. London: Taylor & Francis.

Glesne, C., & Peshkin, A. (1992). *Becoming qualitative researchers: An introduction*. White Plains, NY: Longman Publishing Company.

Grabe, W., & Stoller, F. L. (1997). Content-based instruction: Research foundations. In M. A. Snow & D. M. Brinton (eds.), *The content-based classroom: Perspectives on integrating language and content* (pp. 78–94). White Plains: Longman.

Gumperz, J. (1982). *Discourse strategies*. Cambridge: Cambridge University Press.

Gumperz, J. (1992). Contextualization and understanding. In A. Durant & C. Godwin (eds.) *Rethinking context: Language as an interactive phenomenon* (pp. 229–254). Cambridge: Cambridge University Press.

Gumperz, J. & Berenz, N. (1993). Transcribing conversational exchanges. In J. A. Edwards & M. D. Lampert (eds.), *Talking Data: Transcription and coding in discourse research* (pp. 91–121). Hillsdale, NJ: Lawrence Erlbaum Associates.

Gumperz, J., Jupp, T., & Roberts, C. (1979). *Multi-racial Britain: "Cross-talk."* Video-tape. London: National Centre for Industrial Language Training, British Broadcasting Corporation, Films, Inc.

Immigration and Naturalization Service. (1999). *Yearbook*. Washington, D.C.: US Department of Justice.

Jupp, T., Roberts, C., & Cook-Gumperz, J. (1982). Language and disadvantage: The hidden process. In J. Gumperz (ed.), *Language and social identity*. Cambridge: Cambridge University Press.

Lippi-Green, R. (1997). *English with an accent: Language, ideology, and discrimination in the United States*. London: Routledge.

Long, M. H. (1985). A role for instruction in second language acquisition: Task-based language teaching. In K. Hyltenstam & M. Pienneman (eds.), *Modelling and assessing second language acquisition* (pp. 77–99). Clevedon, Avon: Multilingual Matters.

Long, M. H. (1991). Focus on form: A design feature in language teaching - methodology. In K. de Bot, R. B. Ginsberg & C. Kramsch (eds.), *Foreign language research in cross-cultural perspective* (pp. 39–52). Amsterdam: John Benjamins.

Long, M. H. (1996). The role of the linguistic environment in second language acquisition. In W. C. Ritchie & T. K. Bhatia (eds.), *Handbook of second language acquisition* (pp. 413–68). San Diego: Academic Press.

Long, M. H. (1997). Authenticity and learning potential in L2 classroom discourse. In G. M. Jacobs (ed.), *Language classrooms of tomorrow: Issues and responses* (pp. 148–68). Singapore: Regional Language Center.

Long, M. H. (2000). Focus on form in task-based language teaching. In R. D. Lambert & E. Shohamy (eds.), *Language policy and pedagogy* (pp. 179–92). Amsterdam: John Benjamins.

Long, M. H. (this volume). Methodological issues in learner needs analysis.

Long, M. H., & Crookes, G. (1992). Three approaches to task-based syllabus design. *TESOL Quarterly* 26, 27–56.

Mogelonsky, M. (1997). Natural(ized) Americans. *American Demographics,* 19, 45–49.

Nixon, T., & Keenan, F. (1997). *Citizenship preparation for adult ESL learners.* Washington, D.C.: Center for Applied Linguistics, National Clearinghouse for ESL Literacy Education. ERIC EDO-LE-97-04

Norton Peirce, B. (1996). The theory of methodology in qualitative research. *TESOL Quarterly* (The Forum): 569–76.

Pica, T., Holliday, L., & Morgenthaler, L. (1989). Comprehensible input as an outcome of linguistic demands on the learner. *Studies in Second Language Acquisition* 11, 1, 63–90.

Richards, J. C., Platt, J., & Platt, H. (1992). *Dictionary of language teaching and applied linguistics.* Essex: Longman.

Roberts, C. (1996). A social perspective on understanding: Some issues of theory and method. In K. Bremer, et al, *Achieving understanding: Discourse in intercultural encounters* (pp. 9–36). London: Longman.

Roberts, C., Davies, E., & Jupp, T. (1992). *Langauge and discrimination: A study of communication in multi-ethnic workplaces.* London: Longman.

Robinson, P. (2001). Task complexity, cognitive resources, and second language syllabus design. In P. Robinson (ed.), *Cognition and second language instruction* (pp. 287–318). Cambridge: Cambridge University Press.

Seig, M. T., & Winn, M. (2003). Guardians of America's gate: Discourse-based training lessons from INS interviews. American Association of Applied Linguistics Conference. High-stakes Gatekeeping Encounters Panel Presentation.

Shaw, K. (1998). Citizenship services in New York City. *Migration World Magazine* 26, 4, 19–22.

Tannen, D., & Wallat, C. (1986). Medical professionals and parents: A linguistic analysis of communication across contexts. *Language in Society* 15(3): 295–311.

Tiersma, P. M. (1999). *Legal language.* Chicago: University of Chicago Press.

The US citizenship interview: Will they pass? (1996). Video-tape. Los Angeles: New Readers Press.

US Citizenship and Immigration Services. *Naturalization.* Retrieved January 15, 2004, from http://uscis.gov/graphics/services/natz/index.htm

Weintraub, L. (2002). *Citizenship: Ready for the interview.* Syracuse, NY: New Readers Press.

Appendix A:
Naturalization interview transcription legend

Transcription Notation (Adapted from Gumperz & Berenz, 1993)

(1.5)	Pauses by seconds and tenths of seconds*
=	Latching
::	Lengthened phonemes (e.g., fla::g)
-	Truncation (e.g., fla- the flag)
[	Overlap
hh	Audible exhalation (a sigh)
(*)	Unintelligible speech, with * equal to one syllable
i(s)	An informed guess of an unclear segment
(is)	An informed guess of an unclear word
the	Unusual emphasis
THE	Higher volume than the preceding & following utterances
((laughs))	Non-lexical information: prosody or actions

*0.3 seconds is considered a micro-pause. A micro-pause is assumed to have occurred between non-latching, consecutive turns if no pause length is given. All other pauses are estimated at intervals of five-tenths of a second.

All potentially identifying dates and numbers have been changed, and all names are pseudonyms.

A = Applicant for naturalization
I = Interviewing officer

Appendix B: Consent form

Agreement to Participate in an ESL
(English as a Second Language) Study

[Researcher's contact information: university department,
e-mail address, telephone number]

AUDIO-TAPING AND OBSERVATION

- I am a Masters student. I want to study how naturalization applicants (like you) and INS (Immigration and Naturalization Service) officers use language in naturalization interviews.

- I want to take notes and record (on audio-tape) your naturalization interview. I will NOT use your name in my notes. The written version of the interviews will NOT have your name on it. Your name will NOT be used in any paper, article, or presentation. False names will be used. No one will be able to identify you.

- If at any time you want to talk to the immigration officer/interviewer alone, I will leave the room.

- If you would like to receive a short report of my research findings in summer or fall 2000, please print your name and address below.

Name ....

Address ....

....

- I am not an INS employee. I will play NO part in deciding the results of your interview.

- If you agree to be a part of this study, please sign this form.

I understand this agreement.

I have had my questions answered concerning this study.

I know that I can ask Michelle to leave the interview at any time.

....
Your Signature   Date

10 A double shot 2% mocha latte, please, with whip: Service encounters in two coffee shops and at a coffee cart

Nicola J. Downey Bartlett

Introduction

One would think that it is a simple task to order coffee. Intuitively, it is simple. "Can I have a cup of coffee?" seems an appropriate request realization. However, coffee is just not coffee anymore. With the advent of gourmet coffee carts and clever marketing, ordering a coffee is no longer a straightforward process. For the unsophisticated buyer, first-timer, let alone low-proficiency level second language learner, ordering a coffee can be a bewildering experience. There is a myriad of options to choose from: 2% milk, whipped cream, shots of nut or fruit flavored syrups, and double or triple shots of espresso. Your beverage can be iced, either blended, or on the rocks. The sizes are *short* (very small), *tall* (small), and *venti* (extra large). This seems to be a reflection of many service encounters today, where seemingly no order of drinks or food is spared a lengthy list of alternatives.

This study reports on several representative dialogs in two coffee shops and at one coffee cart, which were taken from 168 audio-taped interactions. Their subsequent analysis reveals features found in native speaker to native speaker conversation, common to a variety of specialized and semi-specialized domains of language use. Furthermore, this analysis highlights the inadequacy of model dialogs presented in ESL textbooks, which ill-prepare ESL learners for the realities of everyday interactions. Even though this study focuses on the rather constrained task of 'buying a coffee', dialogs pertaining to the purchase of various drinks and snacks have been included. This type of service encounter was chosen, as coffee shops and carts are a ubiquitous part of everyday American (though not exclusively American) life. These three 'shops' were easily accessible, and the researcher was given *carte blanche* to record, observe, and conduct unstructured interviews with the staff.

Background

Traditional approaches to language teaching have been heavily criticized in the last two decades for providing samples of language that are decontextualized, fail to reflect native speaker conversation and pragmatically appropriate behavior, and may mislead learners rather than help them cope with everyday interactions (e.g., Auerbach & Burgess, 1985; Bardovi-Harlig et al, 1991; Boxer & Pickering, 1995; Cathcart, 1989; Grant & Starks, 2001; Kasper, 1997; Long, to appear, this volume; Myers Scotton & Bernsten, 1988; Williams, 1988; Wolfson, 1981) In addition, Crystal (1995) takes a rather humorous look at the disparities he has observed between "contemporary English in use" and "the somewhat sterile presentation of the language [...] in textbooks and curriculum documents" (p. 120). As textbooks often remain the primary source of L2 knowledge in foreign language settings, the dependence on the information provided therein is even greater.

To master another language a learner needs not only linguistic accuracy, but also communicative competence. Canale & Swain (1980) suggest a model of communicative competence which incorporates grammatical, discourse and sociolinguistic competence, emphasizing that all three are necessary for acquiring the target language. Similarly, Olshtain & Cohen (1991) suggest that a learner needs to acquire a set of sociocultural rules. However, despite this realization, a number of studies have suggested that 'popular' ESL textbooks continue to mislead and deprive learners of the necessary sociolinguistic and pragmalinguistic knowledge, failing to refer to the social strategies that underlie speech behavior. In the early eighties, Wolfson (1981) argued for the inclusion of sociolinguistic information in textbook materials, yet apparently little has been included, as Boxer and Pickering (1995) claim that "[t]here is a critical need for the application of sociolinguistic findings to English language teaching through authentic materials that reflect spontaneous speech behavior" (p. 44). Similarly, Bardovi-Harlig (2001, and elsewhere) argues that learners should have made available to them "pragmatically appropriate input" in their early stages of acquisition. Boxer's (1993) analysis of the speech acts of complaint and commiseration, highlights the importance of demonstrating to ESL learners how the speech acts of complaining and commiserating can be used strategically in making acquaintances. Moreover, she points to the missed opportunity of teaching learners sustained interaction, positing, from an L2 acquisition perspective, "a direct link between the ability to carry on a sustained sequential interaction and increased opportunities for negotiated interaction in which non-native speakers signal their need for and receive input adjusted to their current level of L2 comprehension" (p. 278). (For more detail on negotiated interaction, see, for example, Pica et al, 1989.)

There is a vast literature addressing pragmatic competence, revealing an understanding that native speakers and non-native speakers of a given target language "appear to have different systems of pragmatics" (Bardovi-Harlig, 2001, p. 13). A central issue is whether this warrants pedagogical intervention, and if so, how instruction could influence second language acquisition. (See Kasper, 2001, for a review of research on pragmatic learning in the second or foreign language classroom.) In recent years, there have been a number of proposals to write materials based on empirical studies of native speaker discourse (see Bardovi-Harlig, 2001, for a review).

Ultimately, ESL learners need a course which helps them cope linguistically and pragmatically with everyday events, or tasks, for example, eating out at a restaurant, shopping (both examples of a service encounter), asking for directions, and socializing with speakers of other languages. With these current or future language needs in mind, a task-based approach argues that communicative tasks should be the basic unit of teaching syllabi, where tasks approximate a real world use (e.g., Long, 1985; Long & Crookes, 1992; Long & Robinson, 1998; Robinson, 1999, 2001a, b; Skehan, 1998b). Furthermore, Long (1985) and Robinson (2001a) claim that a needs analysis is essential to identify the tasks that learners will engage in, and the language needed to realize those tasks. Multiple sources and methods should be employed and triangulated for reliability (for discussion, see Lincoln & Guba, 1985; Jasso-Aguilar, 1999; Long, to appear; Svendsen & Krebs, 1984). A second important stage in needs analysis is a target discourse analysis.

A growing number of target discourse analyses comparing textbook dialogs and authentic discourse have shown a mismatch between the two. For example, Williams (1988) recorded and observed informal meetings and compared her findings with the language presented in meetings' textbooks. She found that the textbooks taught language that tended to be too explicit, overly polite, and presented redundant exponents, further adding that "language is complex and our understanding far from complete so that perhaps authentic language is the only safe starting point for teaching" (p. 53). Holmes (1988) found that the textbooks she analyzed were misleading in their treatment of expressing doubt and uncertainty. Bardovi-Harlig et al (1991) studied conversational closings in 20 textbooks finding discrepancies with native speaker data. Likewise,

Grant & Starks (2001), who used Schegloff and Sacks' (1973) description of native speaker conversational closings as a framework for analyzing closings in textbooks, found that scripted material rarely reflects the structures or features of natural spoken discourse. Grant and Starks drew on earlier work by Myers Scotton & Bernsten (1988), who found that direction-giving exchanges were very structured, and not only did native speakers' pre-closing and closings differ from scripted dialogs, but also that there were a large number of confirmation checks, and 'non-fluencies', for example, fillers and hedges, pauses and unfinished sentences, that are underrepresented in textbooks

Service encounters

To be communicatively competent, an ESL learner needs to be aware of language usage in a wide variety of situations, including service encounters. A service encounter is defined as being transactionally or instrumentally motivated, consisting of "limited moments of co-presence" (Coupland, 2000, p. 136) in which the cashier and customer, who are typically strangers, greet and, after a short period of time, take leave of one another. This routine has a beginning, middle and an end, like a conversation (e.g., Schegloff & Sacks, 1973), whereby participants collaborate through talk to carry out a task or a set of tasks. This type of encounter is a conventionalized exchange, in the nature of "ritualized interchanges" (Goffman, 1967).

Service encounter genres may often appear at first sight to involve rather banal exchanges based on the transaction of information, goods and services. However, they provide a rich area for research, and have been analyzed to find general patterns, or shared obligatory elements (e.g., a sale request), non-obligatory elements (e.g., greetings), and when, or if, variation occurs in the realization of those elements.

Foundational work on buying and selling discourses was conducted by Mitchell (1957, cited in McCarthy, 2000), who collected data in markets and shops. He examined the variation in language that took place in market and shop transactions, finding that, while there was variation across different settings, there were recurring sequential stages, typically including such elements as: *salutation – enquiry as to the object of sale – investigation of the object of sale – bargaining – conclusion*. The importance of his proposals endure, in that they enable us to explain why utterance types in different classes of service encounter might vary when other things appear to be equal.

Key studies include Merritt (1976), who examined differences in question-answer and question-question sequences in a small university campus store, and looked at how questions may follow questions to complete a transaction successfully. Focusing on transactional elements found at a greengrocer's, Hasan (1985) identified obligatory elements: *sale request – sale compliance – sale purchase – purchase closure,* and also found that participants added optional elements, or non-obligatory elements, in the sense that they had a relational purpose (e.g., customers giving reasons for their choice). Coupland (1983) looked at travel agency encounters and focused on non-obligatory elements, but also found examples of "encounter evaluation" (p. 472), whereby participants comment on and evaluate how easy or difficult the encounter was to complete. Using Finnish and Australian data collected at a travel agent's and in a post office, Ventola (1983) found that the discourse at each site exhibited a similar schematic structure and that there were cross-cultural differences in schematic expectations. Using Ventola's (1983) scheme, with moves in service encounter talk as the unit of analysis, Marriot & Yamada (1991) analyzed discourse in a duty free shop in Melbourne, and noted that sale opportunities were missed by an Australian speaker of Japanese, owing to a lack of awareness of appropriate discourse structures and pragmatic competence. They concluded that specific training in interactive competence was essential to make a successful sale. In later work, Ventola (1987) analyzed discourse in a travel agency, a post office, and a gift shop; like Hasan (1985), she was concerned with identifying obligatory and non-obligatory elements. Myers Scotton & Bernsten (1988) recorded encounters at a university dormitory desk, in a post office and at two types of fast food restaurants. Their main focus was on the usage of unmarked directive forms (for example, "A twenty-two cent stamp, please."), and found that the unmarked choices differed across the various service encounters. These differences were attributed to the relative status of participants, the setting, and whether the request fell under the definition of the addressee's job. They concluded that textbooks should avoid including in their teaching materials "lists of over-polite, over-explicit, one-sentence-long exponents for functions" (p. 53).

Dialogs recorded at a rural US railway ticket station window were studied by Long (to appear), who found that increased familiarity and shared background knowledge among interlocutors often led to inexplicitness and ellipsis. Long highlights the fact that textbooks tend to offer self-contained language units, which exclude common features of conversation, for example, false starts, interruptions, overlaps, echoic responses and "high degrees of implicitness, open-endedness and inter-textuality" (Long, this volume, p. 58). Likewise, in a British architect's office, Medway & Andrews (1992) were surprised "by the linguistic virtuosity called for in the job" (p. 23). Shared background knowledge, and familiarity with the job and with one another enabled the comprehension of fragmented utterances. In other words, language was used collaboratively to achieve goals. Svendsen & Krebs (1984), who investigated two health care occupations, found that language was much more idiomatic and colloquial than the language models presented in ESL textbooks. Hospital porters needed job-specific terminology and language ability, not only to seek clarification and report on problems, but also to cope with large amounts of social talk. Similarly, Long (this volume) noted greater language ability was needed when, for example, the unexpected occurred, necessitating social talk.

A growing number of studies examine the distribution and functioning of so-called social talk, or relational talk, and the way in which such talk has transactional relevance. Kuiper & Flindall (2000) looked at the talk generated during the brief interactions at supermarket checkouts, where the checkout operators have an "inventory of formulae" that they employ to deal with the opening, payment and closing sequences. But there is also room for a 'free' form of talk, in which the operators and the customers display a limited form of creativity, at least within the confines of 'safe' and non-contentious topics. Similarly, Coupland & Ylänne-McEwen (2000) studied interactions at checkouts in two supermarkets, and found that "even within such a tightly constrained environment [...] there is room for individuality, idiosyncrasy and even for a small measure of creativity" (p. 203), arguing that their findings may be generalized. (For further studies on 'small talk' in service encounters see McCarthy, 2000.)

The importance of naturalistic data

Prior to the study reported below, the researcher conducted informal interviews with several coffee servers (domain experts) and language professionals (teachers and applied linguists) who suggested typical phrases they might encounter in a coffee shop. Their intuitive answers, while not inaccurate, lacked the insights gained from the naturalistic data obtained in the target domain. Many researchers interested in naturalistic data advocate that it is unwise to rely on native speaker intuition about language, as it could be misleading (see, e.g., Auerbach & Burgess, 1985; Boxer & Pickering, 1995;

Long, to appear; Wolfson, 1986). Furthermore, Kasper (1997) points out that native speakers are not fully aware of their pragmatic competence. For example, Wolfson (1986, p. 693) noted that native speaker intuition is not based on speech as it actually occurs in everyday use:

> It has been demonstrated many times that when native speakers are asked to explain or identify forms which they or others in their community use in a given speech situation, their responses do not necessarily coincide with observed speech behavior.

Wolfson, like Cathcart (1989) and Long (to appear), defends the investigation of actual speech in use. Furthermore, Long (1997) asks how, if students are not exposed to real-life communication (such as data recorded between native speakers in service encounters), but are instead offered only simplified versions of such dialogs, learners would be able to "handle the real thing" (p. 148).

Method

Site description

Data were collected from three locations: a coffee cart at the University of Hawai'i at Manoa (HUM), a well-known coffee shop in a military department store (NAVY), and another well-known coffee shop, about one mile from the University of Hawai'i (STAR). At HUM, the cart was frequented not only by students and professors, but also by office workers from the nearby campus center. The NAVY coffee shop was situated immediately by the store exit, and military servicemen and their families, as well as workers from the department store and other shops in the small shopping area (e.g., a hair salon), bought drinks and sundries there. Customers could sit down at a couple of tables, or on stools at a counter. STAR, located near shops and in a somewhat upscale residential area, had comfortable seating; customers often 'drank in'; hence, the frequency of the elliptical question "For here or to go?" During the morning 'rush', customers were typically on their way to work; later in the day, the clientele was diverse, consisting of students, professors and families.

All three operations were fairly small, with two to four employees working at the same time. At HUM, there were three female servers, all local. At NAVY, the four servers were female; three originated from the US mainland and one from Canada. There were four employees at STAR; one was male, and all were local. Each employee was trained to do all aspects of the job (e.g., working at the cash register, making the drinks, preparing food orders, cleaning and stocking). According to Long's (to appear) observations, "the smaller the size of the operation the more the workers function as general-ists" (p. 92). As they were trained to do a variety of activities, the servers moved to different areas behind the serving counter to perform those activities. The physical layout, coupled with their multiple duties, had important consequences for the interactions, as sometimes two or three servers were involved in completing an order. This made several conversations difficult to follow, especially during busy times, when servers moved work stations to give help where needed.

Data collection

The staff of the three shops kindly agreed to being recorded, and the researcher told them that she was a research student interested in what the customers said. As obtaining genuine or unmonitored speech can be difficult, only the servers' permission was gained for recording. It is difficult to know whether the "observer's paradox" (Labov, 1972) operated. There was one server who spoke into the microphone directly. Generally, however, the staff seemed to forget that the recording device was there. Only a few customers were aware of the recording, as evidenced in the data. Once the recording was stopped because of this. In all three locations, the tape-recorder (a small Walkman, with attached microphone which looked like a pen cap) was placed next to the cash register. The recording at the NAVY took place over four consecutive days, between 11am and 1pm, judged by the staff to be the busiest period of the day; at STAR over four consecutive days, between 8.30am and 12pm; and at HUM for six days, between 8.30am and 1.30pm, over a 10-day period. The recording sessions lasted between 30 and 45 minutes. In total, 248 interactions were audio-taped and 168 were transcribed (NAVY: 58; HUM: 39; STAR: 71). Interactions were eliminated from the data set if they could not be fully transcribed, due to background noise (e.g., blender machines, several people ordering simultaneously – especially difficult during the morning rush – or if customers were speaking among themselves while waiting, fiddling with change or ordering while looking through the display cabinet with their voice directed away from the microphone). The researcher sat as close to the register as possible, while trying to remain inconspicuous, taking field notes and sipping numerous lattes.

At least one experienced server from each location was interviewed. Firstly this gave a better understanding of the overall running of the operation, for example, the tasks the workers performed, and the organization of their respective workstations. Secondly, specific terms, not previously understood in the transcripts, could be explained. Thirdly, the servers' intuitions about language use could be verified. The staff members were interested in what the researcher was doing, but only after the data collection did she disclose the exact focus of the study.

Approach

Target discourse analysis can be approached in a number of ways, and by collecting naturally occurring discourse ('real data'), a number of discourse features can be studied. Language can be looked at from a micro-analytic perspective, whereby interactional moves can be studied to investigate types of speech acts, illocutionary force, and features of conversation, such as repetition, feedback and back-channeling. A macro-level view of target discourse analysis can look at how a task is completed, considering, among other things, open-endedness, implicitness, inter-textuality, phatic talk, and structural non-fluencies, such as fillers and incomplete sentences. These features occur in everyday conversations and are generalizable to a wide variety of different situations in everyday life.

Conversation analysis (CA), the most micro-analytical variety of discourse analysis (Wood & Kroger, 2000), has its origins in sociology, in the work of Sacks and his colleagues (e.g., Sacks, Schegloff & Jefferson, 1974), who paid close attention to the structuring and sequencing of turns. CA offers a useful framework for analyzing everyday conversations, such as those recorded in service encounters. As it has a "grounding in the study of ordinary talk between persons in a wide variety of social relations and contexts, CA has been in a particularly strong position to develop analytic tools for the study of talk-in-context" (Drew & Heritage, 1992, p. 16). According to Schegloff, CA "seek[s] to account for the workings of speech exchanges through turn-by-turn examination of their sequential ordering" (Gumperz, 1996, p. 379). The present analysis sought to examine how the transactional task of 'buying and selling a drink item or sundry' was successfully completed. CA offers an approach in which the "interactional accomplishment of particular social activities" (Drew & Heritage, 1992, p. 17) can be considered. The aim is to "seek generalizations about context – and about social conduct and social life – *within* the progression of utterances themselves" (Schiffrin, 1994, p. 10).

For the purpose of the current analysis, no fine-grained transcription was employed. A small number of features were marked in the transcripts, for instance, important pauses, interrupted speech, non-verbal comments and untranscribable speech (see Appendix A for the transcription conventions).

Analysis

In her pioneering work, Ventola (1983) identified general patterns in service encounters, claiming that, if situational variables are held constant, the discourse has a similar schematic structure, regardless of the nature of the interlocutor. In the present data, a generalizable pattern of elements was distinguished across the three coffee sites for the task of 'buying and selling a drink item or sundry'. It typically involved the sub-tasks of either greeting the server, or responding to the service bid ("Can I help you?"), specifying the order, possibly confirming the order and options, sometimes asking additional information about a menu item, responding to the server-initiated "Anything else?" and finally, the predictable sub-task of paying and closing (which was sometimes non-verbal).

The interactions differed in length depending on (i) whether the buyer was a regular – interactions tended to be shorter as the customer knew what he or she wanted, and how to order it clearly and succinctly; (ii) whether the customer needed extra information, or did not understand the drink item on the menu, when more explanation was needed; (iii) whether a problem occurred, for example, when a customer forgot to bring his or her frequent-user card, or when specific names and sizes of drinks were unclear, or an item ran out.

Encounter 1 below is a representative example, demonstrating several features found in the dialogs when ordering a drink.

Encounter 1 (NAVY)

  1 S: Can I help you ma'am?
  2 C: Can I try an iced macadamia latte?
  3 S: Did you want that blended or on the rocks?
  4 C: Blended
  5 S: OK. Did you want whipped cream on that?
  6 C: Yes
  7 S: Anything else for you?
  8 C: ((non-verbal response))
  9 S: OK. That'll be three forty-eight.
10 C: ((customer hands over money))
11 S: Thank you. 50 cents is your change. Would you like your receipt?

12 C: ((non-verbal response))
13 S: OK. It'll be ready for you in just one minute.

In line 1, the server initiates the encounter with a service bid "Can I help you ma'am?" to which the customer responds by specifying their need "Can I try an iced macadamia latte?" A CA analysis is interested in the sequential order of talk (Hutchby & Wooffitt, 1998), and the first two lines illustrate a standard sequence in turn-taking, i.e., an adjacency pair (Sacks, 1973), where the question is responded to by a question, and not an answer, as might be expected. This question–question sequence, also found by Merritt (1976), was used to complete the transaction successfully. The customer confirms two options ("Blended", line 4, and "Yes" for whipped cream, line 6), and gives a non-verbal response, in line 8, to the question "Anything else for you?" The change is given in line 11, and once again the customer responds non-verbally to the question "Would you like your receipt?" The customer produces only three verbal turns (lines 2, 4, and 6), yet the transaction is successfully completed.

Another example of a representative interaction follows in encounter 2.

Encounter 2 (HUM)

1 S: Hi. May I help you?
2 C: Hi. Can I get a double iced chai?
3 S: 2%?
4 C: 2%
5 S: Double iced chai 2%. Do you have a stamp card?
6 C: Yes
7 S: ((stamps card)) There you go.(.) Alright. ((hands over change)) Thank you

The customer greets the server, then responds to the service bid with a question specifying the drink order in line 2. In line 3, the server asks what kind of milk the customer desires by simply stating one type of milk "2%?" The customer confirms that this is her preference by repeating "2%", and in line 5, the server repeats the order to the drink maker, and continues with the transaction by asking the customer whether she has a 'stamp card', i.e., a frequent-user card. The customer responds "Yes". The card is then stamped, and the remainder of the interaction is completed non-verbally by the customer.

There were common patterns found in interactions with regular customers, who tend to be short and 'succinct orderers'. This is illustrated in encounters 3 and 4.

Encounter 3 (STAR)

1 S: Hi. What can I get for you?
2 C: A tall coffee and the Honolulu Advertiser[1]
3 S: 1.91
4 C: ((customer hands over money))
5 S: Out of 2 (.) 9 cents is your change (2) Here's your coffee sir

Encounter 4 (HUM)

1 S: How about for you sir?
2 C: A double latte
3 S: Hot? 2%?
4 C: ((non-verbal))
5 S: ((relays order to drink maker)) Double hot latte 2%. (.) Out of 3
       And your card. ((hands over card and gives change)) We'll see you
       next time after the spring break for your free drink
6 C: Alright
7 S: OK thank you

Both encounters are short and succinct. In encounters 3 and 4, the
regulars take only one turn to specify their order (lines 2), and in
specifying their order a polite request form is omitted (e.g., "Can
I ...?"), a frequent finding in the data for regular customers. In
addition, there is no mention of the word 'coffee', just as the only use
of 'ticket' in Long's data on railway ticket purchases was by a non-
native speaker. Such findings are in sharp contrast to models presented in textbooks. Based on intuition and informal interviews with
native speakers, requesting 'a coffee' would seem appropriate.
However, in all three locations, 'a coffee' is a very specific term,
denoting a brewed or drip coffee of the day. To request this item, the
size is stipulated before the word 'coffee.' Much so-called 'technical'
vocabulary is needed to designate the size of the drink.[2] Sizes are, for
example, *short, tall, grande*, and *venti*. Requesting the size with the
item shortens the interaction (for example, line 2, encounter 3, "A
tall coffee").

Interactions may be lengthened, that is to say, the number of turns
needed to complete a transaction may rise, for a variety of reasons.
Interactions are longer, and confusion is increased when a customer
is not familiar with specific terms, or the 'technical vocabulary', to
specify a drink order, or if the customer is a 'novice' buyer. In
encounter 5, a customer requests a "small frappuccino", but a 'small'
size does not exist in this shop.

Encounter 5 (STAR)

1   C: Hi. Can I have a medium café mocha? And can I put whipped cream
        on it and uhm is there a small frappuccino?
2   S: Tall size?
3   C: Yeah a small
4   S: Another small?
5   C: Yeah I mean tall

The server 'corrects' the customer, wishing to confirm the size, in line
2. The customer appears to refuse to accept that "tall" means 'small'
(line 3). However, in lines 4 and 5, both speakers co-operate, and the
server adopts the term "small" and the customer the term "tall."

In encounter 6, seven turns are needed for the drink order to be
confirmed. This is because the novice customer does not use the
correct lexical item, i.e., "short".

Encounter 6 (STAR)

1   S: Morning. What can I get for you?
2   C: Yeah good morning (.) yeah, can I get a-? Let's see (.) grande coffee of
        the day with whipped cream and your little small coffee
3   S: The tall?
4   C: No the small
5   S: The short?
6   C: Yeah the shortie
7   S: Grande and a short?
8   C: Exactly

After some difficulty revealed in "yeah, can I get a-? Let's see" and
the slight pause following this in line 2, the customer requests a
"grande coffee". In line 3, the server attempts to find out whether the
customer means "tall", and offers "short" in line 5. Finally, in line 8,
after a rather comical exchange, where sizes are referred to as "tall",
"small", "short" and "shortie", the customer confirms that the server
has understood his drink order, managing to avoid using the technical
term 'short'.

In the encounter below, another 'unsophisticated' coffee drinker is
looking at the menu on the wall. He opens the encounter in line 1,
letting the server know that he is not sure what to order, as there are
so many choices on the menu (located in easy sight, on the far wall
behind the counter).

Encounter 7 (NAVY)

1   C: All the different names and (3) Hey
2   S: Oh what are you looking for?

 3 C: XXX the frappuccino?
 4 S: Frio. We have like a chocolate one which says the mocha cappuccino
        (3)
 5 C: Where?
 6 S: Third from the bottom is the iced mocha [that's the] mocha frappu-
        ccino the regular frappuccino is the XXX and cream
 7 C: [Oh right]
        What is the difference between a regular one and a (.) mocha one?
 8 S: That's it one has chocolate in it and the other one doesn't
 9 C: Let me try the: e:r mocha
10 S: Mo[cha? OK]
11 C: [Yeah   ]
12 S: OK (40) three forty eight please
13 C: Three of 'em?
14 S: Forty-eight ((said louder))
15 C: er XXX ((blender noise))
16 S: Yeah (2) There you go (.) thank you very much you have a great day

In fact, the customer is looking for a 'frappuccino'[3], which he cannot
find on the menu (line 3). The server informs the customer that in this
shop it is called a "frio" (line 4). The server explains the different
kinds of "frio" in lines 6 and 8. Finally, the customer specifies his
order in line 9, and the choice is confirmed by the server in line 10.
The paying and closing sequence begins in line 12 when the server
states the price, whereupon the customer jokingly alludes to the high
number of dollars needed for one drink: "Three of 'em?" in line 13,
not taken up by the server.

Interactions are lengthened if the unexpected happens.

Encounter 8 (STAR)

1 S1:   What XXX?
2 C: I guess I want a chai please, a grande chai
3 S1:   Anything else?
4 C: ((non-verbal))
5 S1:   Hot or iced?
6 C: Hot. (.) I was wondering if anyone had found my bag
7 S1:   Oh. You were the one that called yesterday?
8 S2 & 3: XXX
9 C: OK. Good. Thank you.

The customer orders (line 2), and then in line 6 asks if her bag, left in
the shop on a previous day, has been found. Note the politeness, or
the markedness (Myers Scotton & Bernsten, 1988) of the request,
which is due to the relatively high degree of imposition of the inquiry,
as it is not associated with the addressee's primary job. (The bag had
been found, confirmed by two other servers in line 8, but their report

was difficult to transcribe as both speakers were some distance from the microphone.)

Interactions are lengthened due to 'frequent-user card' procedures, which are typical in many shops in America, and are used at HUM and the NAVY. Each time a coffee is purchased, the card is stamped. After a certain number of stamps, the customer receives a free item. At HUM, it is called either a "frequent-user card" or "stamp card," and at the NAVY a "coffee card." In encounter 9, it is referred to as a "stamp card".

Encounter 9 (HUM)

1 S: Do you have a stamp card?
2 C: No. I have it in the office
3 S: Just bring back your receipt and we'll stamp it
4 C: OK thank you
5 S: Thank you

Here, subsequent to ordering the drink (not shown), the customer reveals that the stamp card has been left in the office (line 2), and is informed by the server that if brought back, a stamp can be given as a receipt of the coffee purchase (line 3).

Similarly, in encounter 10, a regular (a hairdresser in the shopping center) has forgotten her card.

Encounter 10 (NAVY)

 1 C: Hi
 2 S: Hi. How are you doing today?
 3 C: Small coffee. I need a new card
 4 S: Small coffee. Are you busy this morning?
 5 C: I don't know I haven't started yet. I keep on forgetting to get my card
 6 S: Do you have a card or do you need a new card?
 7 C: I need a new card. Actually two stamps. With this one it's three stamps
 8 S: You keep forgetting do you?
 9 C: She can vouch for me
10. S: ((hands over coffee)) There you go
11 C: Thank you
12 S: You're welcome
13 C: Thank you
14 S: ((hands over change)) There you go. Have a great day

In line 3, the regular states that she needs a new stamp card. In line 5, she refers to the fact that she keeps forgetting her coffee card. In the next four turns, lines 6, 7, 8 and 9, conversation centers on the forgotten card, and the number of stamps needed.

As seen above, interactions are lengthened when complications arise, e.g., due to wrong usage of vocabulary and card procedures, especially when one is forgotten and small talk, or phatic talk, ensues. This is shown in encounter 10, where the customer jokes about the number of stamps that need to be added to her card, and addresses her comment "She can vouch for me" (line 9) to the second server behind the counter. Earlier in the same interaction, line 4, the server displays routinized, formulaic small talk (Malinowski, 1923) "Are you busy this morning?" and the customer responds in the next turn. This is an example of a safe and non-contentious topic. (Coupland, 2000).

Another example of phatic talk is found in encounter 11. The customer is a non-native speaker, and near the end of the interaction the server initiates small talk.

Encounter 11 (STAR)

 1 S: What can I get for you?
 2 C: I like the white choc#olate mocha[4]
 3 S: Iced?
 4 C: On the rocks (.) And the strawberry croissant (creamed?)
 5 S: Which one?
 6 C: Strawberry cream something
 7 S: Oh the little square one
 8 C: Yeah
 9 S: OK ((server moves over to glass cabinet))
10 C: That one
11 S: Can you make me an iced XXX? ((server repeats order to drink maker)) 5 dollars is your change. That's the right thing right?
12 C: Yeah
13 S: OK. Whipped cream?
14   (60)
15 S: Do you like the iced better or XXX the hot?
16 C: XXX ((blender noise))
17 S: Oh. You do.
18 C: I get XXX
19 S: XXX
20 C: XXX
21 S: OK. There you go. Have a great day.

In line 15, the server asks the customer whether she prefers the drink that she requested iced or hot. This follows a 60-second pause. It is possible that the small talk arises, as the customer is waiting for her drink to be made, and both interlocutors make an attempt to fill the silence. The data revealed many more instances of small talk, but further analysis is beyond the scope this paper.

If an item runs out, more explanation is needed, and alternatives are often suggested.

Encounter 12 (HUM)

```
 1 S:  Hi there
 2 C:  Can I get a double macchiato with caramel?
 3 S:  Hot or iced?
 4 C:  Hot
 5 S:  Right now we're all out of our caramel
 6 C:  Oh
 7 S:  We got the- the vanilla Irish cream-
 8 C:  I'd like vanilla
 9 S:  Vanilla regular or French. French has a little taste of caramel.
10 C:  OK
11 S:  Did you say hot macchiato?
12 C:  Yeah
13 S:  Did you prefer the 2% or the skinny?
14 C:  XXX
```

The server tells the customer that there is no more caramel flavored syrup (line 5). The customer acknowledges receipt of this new information with "Oh", and the server begins to give a list of alternative flavors that are available (line 7). The customer interrupts in line 8, stating that she would like the vanilla, and in line 9, the server explains the different kinds of vanilla flavor, "regular or French", adding that one of the vanilla flavors has a caramel taste, which is the flavor that the customer originally requested, in line 2.

Apart from complications that arise in the encounters, which tend to increase either the number of turns, or the length of individual turns, it takes to complete an order successfully, other features in the encounters were noted. For example, in looking at the sequential order of interactions, servers often initiate the purchase, predicting a regular's drink order. (Long, to appear, found the same phenomenon in the railway ticket purchase data.)

Encounter 13 (STAR)

```
1 S:  Hi. The Americano?
2 C:  Yeah
3 S:  Anything else today?
4 C:  No thanks (hands over money)
5 S:  Three four five ten out of twenty. Thank you.
```

Encounter 14 (HUM)

```
1 S:  Hi there. Your usual?
2 C:  Yes.
```

3 S: OK.
4 C: (Customers pays)
5 S: OK. Thank you.

In line 1 of encounters 13 and 14, the server predicts the drink order and the regular merely has to confirm this prediction in line 2. Such initiation is possible due to shared background knowledge. In interviews with staff, initiating the purchase was seen as good customer service. One worker interviewed said she liked "to make people feel special" by remembering their order.

In addition, to keep a long line moving, the drink-maker, rather than the cashier, typically initiates the purchase with a very different turn of phrase (encounter 15, line 1).

Encounter 15 (STAR)

1 S: Can I get your drink started for you sir?
2 C: A double espresso

Due to the physical layout of STAR, for example, the drink maker shouts across to the person next in line for their order, who remains in line to pay and confirms his or her order at the cash register. (If a regular is next in line, the drink maker may predict the order, then the customer confirms, followed by non-verbal confirmation of the drink by the server. The drink is then made while the customer stays in line to pay.)

Other features concerning how the linguistic realizations of the sub-task, or actions, were performed, were revealed in the analysis. For example, due to shared background knowledge, there is a high degree of implicitness and ellipsis in the server and customer turns.

Encounter 16 (STAR)

1 S: Hi. What can I get for this morning?
2 C: Regular (XXX). Right to the top

In encounter 16, the customer orders a "regular" coffee, and requests that the cup be filled to the top of the cup (line 2), as he does not want to leave room for cream.[5] There is no polite form used, and both parties understand the meaning of "right to the top" in this context. This form of ellipsis is a time-saver when people are in a hurry, or when there is a line. Moreover, to order without a polite request form was not impolite, but pragmatically appropriate in this context. This puts into question the amount of time spent in classrooms teaching polite requests in this type of service encounter. (See the section on textbook evaluation below.) Ellipsis also occurs on the part of the server. Polite question forms are not used; neither are they necessary.

Encounter 17 (NAVY)

1 S: Out of five. 6 cents is your change. Need your receipt?
2 C: Can I take one of your tuna salads?
3 S: Anything else?
4 C: No that'll do it. Thanks
5 S: That's gonna be 4.94

Ellipsis occurs in line 1 "Out of five", "Need your receipt?" and in line 3 "Anything else?"

Another feature found in the sub-task was a large amount of deixis. Similar to findings by Svendsen & Krebs (1984), there is much evidence of pronouns and deictics. Deixis is the language we use to refer to something (e.g., this/that, this one/that one, here/there). Referential talk is little modeled in L2 classrooms, but occurs naturally due to the context-embedded nature of talk. Svendsen & Krebs further noted that nothing is expressed that cannot be seen. Use of deixis was common in all three locations, as each had a large menu, either behind the counter on the back wall (NAVY and STAR), or in front of the counter (HUM), and a display cabinet that customers could point to in order to select the desired food item. For example, in encounter 18, also shown above, there is a great deal of deixis.

Encounter 18 (NAVY)

 1 C: All the different names and (3) Hey
 2 S: Oh what are you looking for?
 3 C: XXX the frappuccino?
 4 S: Frio. We have like a chocolate one which says the mocha cappuccino (3)
 5 C: Where?
 6 S: Third from the bottom is the iced mocha [that's the] mocha frappuccino the regular frappuccino is the XXX and cream
 7 C: [Oh right]
      What is the difference between a regular one and a (.) mocha one?
 8 S: That's it one has chocolate in it and the other one doesn't
 9 C: Let me try the: e:r mocha
10 S: Mo[cha? OK]

Pronouns such as 'those' and 'the big one', explicit or ellipted, replace the full names for items in these conversations. In line 6, above, for example, the server indicates where the "frio" item is written on the menu "third from the bottom", also an example of inter-textuality. The drinks are referred to as "a chocolate one", line 4, and "the regular one and a mocha one" in line 7.

In the following encounter, the customer begins to order, and then sees what she thinks are scones in the display cabinet.

Encounter 19 (NAVY)

1 S: Hi. Can I help you ma'am?
2 C: Yeah. Can I get- are those scones? ((pointing through the glass display cabinet))
3 S: Yuh huh
4 C: The big ones?
5 S: Yeah. We have blueberry or cranberry

In line 2, the customer makes a false start "Can I get-?" as she sees the scones, and points to them through the cabinet, asking "are those scones?" The server confirms, but to make sure, in line 4, the customer once again specifies which items she is referring to with "The big ones?"

Another interesting feature is similar to Long's (to appear) findings, where, in a rural railway station, sundries are held up by customers, but the price is not stated, which affects how the actions are performed. In these data, for example:

Encounter 20 (NAVY)

1 C: I'll have two waters ((the customer is on her cellphone and holds up a piece of banana bread))
2 S: And a banana bread
3 C: I'll be eating those here

In encounter 20, the banana bread is held up (line 1), and accounted for by the server (line 2), who proceeds to put the items in a bag to go. The customer sees this, and in line 3, states that she wishes to eat the sundries in, rather than take them to go.

Concerning the composition of the sub-tasks, or elements, in the service encounters, different uses and functions for several grammatical structures were found. For example, at the NAVY, the servers were trained to ask if a customer required his or her receipt (a shopping center requirement), e.g., "Did you want your receipt?" However, the auxiliary 'did' does not function as a past tense marker, but serves a a mitigation device to lessen the distance between the server and the customer. Other examples are "Did you want whipped cream with that?", "Did you want that blended or on the rocks?" and the examples in encounter 21, lines 1 and 3.

Encounter 21 (STAR)

1   S: 8.91. Out of nine. Thank you sir. Here's your change. Did you want room for cream?
2   C: Pardon me?
3   S: Did you want room for cream?
4   C: Ah no

A final comment pertains to how complex ordering a coffee can be. In informal chats with friends, colleagues (ESL teachers), professors and both native- and non-native-speaking graduate students in the applied linguistics field, it became evident that the majority felt intimidated by the long list of options when ordering coffee. Some even admitted that they tended to "stick to" the same drink, as it was "easier". Furthermore, it was revealed to the researcher, in audio-taped interviews conducted with several servers, that they were sometimes irritated by customers who could not specify their need "correctly", especially regulars they saw frequently, and should have "got it by now". This could be due to the fact that the cashiers have a set sequence in which the options for an order are relayed to the drink makers, which is designed to minimize confusion for the drink makers and speed up service. When a customer's order is not said in the set sequence, the server has, in effect, to reformulate or 'translate' the order for the drink maker, that is, relay the drink requested by the customer in a set sequence. For example:

Encounter 22 (STAR)

1   S: Hi. May I help you?
2   C: Yeah. Can I get a triple latte 2% hot?
3   S: Sure. Triple hot latte 2%. (3.85)
4   C: ((hands over money))
5   S: Thank you. You don't need the receipt yeah?
6   C: No
7   S: Alright
8   C: Thank you

The customer's order in line 2 ("triple latte 2% hot") is reformulated in line 3 by the server ("Triple hot latte 2%"). Similarly:

Encounter 23 (HUM)

1   S: Your usual?
2   C: Uh quad.
3   S: Four shot iced Americano with cream ((relayed to drink maker)) and then e:r XXX (12) Oh let's see where are we? Americano 4 shots
4   C: Yeah
5   S: So that's four shots yeah? With cream and water

The customer is a regular, as evidenced by the server's opening in line 1. In line 2, the drink order is made ("quad"), and this is reformulated for the drink maker in line 3 ("Four shot iced Americano with cream"). In several dialogs in the analysis, for example, in encounters 24 and 25, customers appear to be aware of the existence of a set order and meta-comment about the transaction.

Encounter 24 (STAR)

1 S: Hi. Good morning
2 C: May I have a single iced latte non-fat grande? Did I get it right?
3 S: Uhm yeah (single iced non-fat) grande latte. OK. Anything else?
4 C: XXX
5 S: 3.49

In line 2, the customer asks whether she managed to order correctly, and the server replies in line 3 that she did. However, in repeating the order to the drink maker, we can see that in fact the sequence of the drink order was not correct. Goffmann (1967) views this type of behavior as face-saving, in that the customer does not want to lose face and pre-empts correction; in CA it has been shown that there is a preference for self-repair rather than other repair. The server protects the face of the customer by saying "yeah", but then displays that the order was in fact incorrect. In addition, the analysis reveals findings similar to Coupland's (1983) examples of "encounter evaluations", where participants meta-comment about the success of a transaction. Similarly:

Encounter 25 (STAR)

1 C: Can I get a choc- I dunno how to pronounce it
2 S: (café mocha with) whipped cream?
3 C: Yeah

In line 1, the customer attempts to pronounce the drink name, but prefers to show that she does not know how to say it, in order to save face. The server provides the name in line 2, immediately continuing to ask about the option of whipped cream.

Identifying frequency with concordancing software

With Ventola's (1987) claim in mind that foreign language teaching would benefit from finding out "the most frequent decisions and paths taken and the most frequent [linguistic] realizations of the steps in the schematic structure" (p. 248), a concordancing software program was used, enabling specific target words, phrases or linguistic realizations of sub-tasks to be sought out, which could be easily, and quickly, quantified. In addition, the context in which they appeared could be identified and viewed at the click of a mouse.

Out of the original 168 transcribed interactions, 144 were analyzed by means of a concordancing software program, MonoConc Pro (Barlow, 2000). Interactions were eliminated if the customers were non-native speakers, if the interaction did not result in the sale of a drink or sundry, or, where two conversations proceeded simultaneously, only the 'main' conversation could be completely and accurately transcribed. As a result, it was possible to observe discrepancies between native speaker dialogs and those modeled in several published textbooks.

However, counting the frequency of linguistic realizations of the sub-tasks (e.g., specifying the order, confirming the order and options, asking for additional information) was not straightforward, as several of the service encounters could not be transcribed as 'self-contained units'. The service encounters were transcribed in 'real time', resulting in one (or even two) dialogs, being embedded in one another. For example, customer one (C1) orders, and while waiting for the order to be prepared, customer two (C2) begins his/her order. The closing stages of the service encounter for customer one are thus completed during customer two's encounter. This occurs because there is more than one server behind the counter. Often, one server takes the order and money, and a second makes the drink, sometimes switching roles. It would not be wise to separate each service encounter and present it as a self-contained unit, as this would be a false representation of what took place in real time and it is interesting to look at the embedded dialogs, to see how long it took (in minutes, although not analyzed here, and also turns) to complete a transaction. A closer analysis of the data may reveal a possible explanation for the different linguistic realizations used, for example, why a customer closed non-verbally, elaborately, or even impatiently, or why there was an increased amount of social talk. The following is an example of an embedded dialog, where customer one (C1) is in the closing stages of his transaction with server one (S1), and customer two (C2) is in the opening stages, being attended to by server two (S2).

Sample embedded dialog (NAVY)

1	S2:	What can I get for you?
2	C2:	What kind of sandwich is this?
3	S1:	OK
4	S2:	There's turkey xxx ham XXX cheese or tuna

5 C2:	Yeah. The turkey
6 S1 to C1:	XXX your receipt?
7 S2 to C2:	Do you want the croissant?
8 C2:	[XXX]
9 S1:	[Have a great day]
10 C1:	You too.
11 S1 to C2:	Do you wanna bag for your sandwich?
12 C2:	(No that's fine)
13 S1 to C2:	OK
14 S2 to C2:	Anything else for you?
15 C2:	Mm. That's it.
16 S2:	OK that'll be 5.46.
17 S1 to C2:	There's a napkin in the box for you.
18 Friend to C2:	What did you get?
19 C2:	The turkey er:-
20 Friend:	Panini?
21 C2:	Sandwich thing
22 S2:	OK. 15.05 is your change. Need your receipt?
23 C2:	No
24 S2:	Have a great day
25 C2:	Thanks
26 S1:	Enjoy your lunch

This dialog begins with S2's service bid to C2, and his response. The previous customer (C1) is in the closing stages of his transaction. In line 3, S1 responds to an earlier turn with C1 (not shown), and the closing stages of this encounter follow in lines 6, 9 and 10. S1 is then free to help with C2's order, and asks, in line 11, if he would like a bag for the sandwich, and states that there is a napkin in the box in line 17. While waiting for the order to be ready, C2 and his friend talk (lines 18 to 21).

However, counting linguistic realizations at certain stages of the encounter may not be problematic, for example, in the opening stage, i.e., the service bid or an initial request for an item made by the customer. Using the concordancing software, the most frequent linguistic realizations for requests by a customer, whether initial, or as a second or third request, were identified. The most frequent was "Can I get . . . ?", with 42 matches, followed by "Can I have . . . ?" (32 matches), "I'll have" (7 matches), and "I'd like" (7 matches, but three of which were uttered by one customer in the same dialog, two more by another customer in the same dialog). There was often an absence of so-called 'polite request forms', as the order was simply stated with or without "please". Surprisingly, "Could I . . . ?" was employed as a request strategy only six times. On closer examination, "could" was used three times to specify an initial need (once by a British woman). The remaining three times "could" was used if the request were more imposing. For example, in encounter 26, ten turns (not shown) precede the request in line 2.

Encounter 26 (NAVY)

1   S: There you go XXX is your change.
2   C: Oh. Could I have a coffee card?
3   S: Sure. There you go. There's a stamp already on there. It's kinda faint but-

The customer has already paid, and the server gives the change in line 1. The customer is about to leave, when she remembers (revealed by "Oh") to ask for a coffee card (line 2), and uses the polite form "Could," possibly because the transaction was ending, and the customer had forgotten to mention the card earlier.

Following analysis of the service encounters, the task of ordering a drink or food item does not appear to be so simple. Although there were individual differences, the overall structure is similar across speakers. According to the STAR staff, interactions differed depending on the time of day. To a certain extent these intuitions were verified, as during the early morning 'rush hour' period the customers were mainly regulars, and interactions tended to be shorter with less phatic talk, with more non-verbal confirmation of need and price. However, contrary to intuition, many common features of context-embedded talk were evident at other times of the day. The length of the interactions did differ if (i) the customer was novice and unfamiliar with the item names; (ii) the unexpected happened, for example, an item ran out; and (iii) there was talk concerning a frequent-user card. The sequential order of the interactions was altered depending on whether the server or customer initiated the purchase, and also the positioning of the server, or if there was a long line, for example, in STAR. As for the linguistic realizations of the elements in the encounters, there were differences in the markedness of the requests due to the imposition of the inquiry, which were also reflected in the leave-taking sequences (e.g. when thanking). The latter findings have important consequences for pragmatic appropriacy. Finally, the analysis revealed that authentic discourse contains the following features: ellipsis, implicitness, inter-textuality, deixis, different use of grammatical structure (e.g. did), and structural non-fluencies, (e.g., fillers and incomplete sentences), all too often absent from models presented in textbooks.

This description of the coffee shop, and cart, service encounters is now compared with model interactions presented in textbooks.

Textbook evaluation

When offering a 'survival English' curriculum for ESL learners, many textbook writers state that sample dialogs are modeled on real-life conversations between native speakers of English. However, as mentioned earlier, these models are frequently oversimplified, can contain inauthentic communicative structure and unrealistic situational content, and may mislead learners (see, e.g., Auerbach & Burgess, 1985; Cathcart 1989; Long & Crookes, 1992; Ventola, 1987). Cathcart (1989) concluded that "published materials [should] include language models and activities developed through principled selection and analysis of real interactions" (p. 124).

In the following four sample textbook dialogs (samples A, B, C and D), most of the request strategies focus on "could", "would like," and to a lesser extent "I'll have" and "May ... ?" Most give little or no information concerning the important role context plays in determining the type of request, or response, to be used, or interlocutor information and underlying social strategies of speech behavior. Finally, none of the models presents "Can I get ... ?" the most frequent request strategy found in the present data.

In the 'Social talk – Shopping' unit (Peters, 1991, p. 71), sample conversations take place in what appears to be a canteen (1) and a restaurant (2).

Sample A

1 What would you like? *I'd like some soup.*	2 Good evening, sir. Can I take your order? *Yes, I'd like the chicken curry, please.*

The snippets of conversation in themselves are not inauthentic, but tend to oversimplify the situation by giving mere fragments of speech pertaining to a larger conversation that is not shown. The textbook claims to "prepare non-native ... speakers to understand and use the rapid, idiomatic speech heard outside the classroom." However, these fragments serve only to expose the learners to a simplified question and answer format, and would ill-equip the first-time visitor to deal with, for example, a list of complicated alternatives or a large amount of ellipsis. Furthermore, the dialogs appear to practice the polite request form "would like" by the customer.

A more recent textbook (Kiggell, 1998) "focuses on practical communication through person-to-person network skills" (introduction page). However, in a unit on 'Eating out and making requests', learners adopt the role of either 'wait person' (p. 11) or 'customer' (p. 12), and are asked in pairs, to practice the conversation together. Sample B shows the complete exchange with the two roles.

Sample B

Wait person	Customer
Are you ready to order?	
	Yes. Could I have (*choose an entreé*)?
What kind of potatoes would you like?	
	Let me see. I'd like ...
And would you like peas or asparagus?	
	May I have ...?
Would you like Italian or French dressing with your salad?	
	Could I have ...?
What would you like for dessert?	
	What do you have?
Well, we have ... or ...	
	I'd like ...
And what would you like to drink with your meal?	
	Could I have ...?

The learners are given a model dialog that does little more than practice a variety of linguistic forms for polite requests, with a question–answer, question–question format. Furthermore, there is a lack of generalizable features of context-embedded talk, for example, ellipsis, open-endedness, inter-textuality and inexplicitness. A suggested homework task from the Teacher's guide sample is: "Ask students to learn the conversation and be ready to repeat it in the next lesson" (p. 5). Relying on rote memory learning of formulaic turns of phrase could hardly prepare the students for the unpredictability of language in real life!

Although this textbook fails to fully address pragmatic considerations, the Teacher's guide sample points out that "I'd like the bill, please" is much politer than "I want the bill" (p. 2). In fact, one server interviewed at the NAVY coffee shop considered "I want" to be a 'rude' request. In the native speaker data, "I want" occurred six times, but three times by the same customer, and once by another where the request was modified ("I guess I want") rendering it less direct.

Concerning the request realizations, rather than insisting that learners should use overly polite forms, Myers Scotton & Bernsten (1988) advocate that learners be taught about the usage of the bold imperative form ("five stamps"), which is unmarked and considered polite in certain types of service encounter, whereas the embedded imperative ("Would you give me five stamps?"), a polite request often taught as a 'blanket form' in ESL textbooks, is a marked form and may be perceived as "overly polite at best, or odd at worst." (p. 382). In other words, certain polite forms are only pragmatically appropriate in certain settings or types of service encounters. For example:

Encounter 27 (NAVY)

1 C: Coffee of the day
2 S: Tall?
3 C: Yeah, coffee of the day
4 S: There you go
5 C: Thanks
6 S: You're welcome

In line 1, the customer uses a bold imperative to order the item. The server then asks which size the customer would like by merely asking "Tall?" with rising intonation. In line 3, the customer confirms the size and repeats his order. The transaction is carried out successfully, and is pragmatically appropriate.

In fact, a general criticism made of model dialogs in many EFL/ESL textbooks is that they serve as little more that linguistic drills and exercises in disguise. In a textbook by Denman (2000), for example, it is stated (back page) that "[l]istening and speaking skills in real-life contexts allow students to develop effective communication strategies". On p. 47, there is a picture of two male customers seated at a table, a waiter standing close by with pen and notebook in hand, and a menu listing 11 items, for example, "hamburger", "sandwich", "coffee", and "tea", is on the wall. The model dialog (sample C) appears next to the picture, and learners must fill in the gaps with "*a, an, some, any,* or Ø (for no word)."

Sample C

1 Waiter:	What do you want to drink?
2 Customer A:	I'd like .... coffee, please.
3 Waiter:	Do you want .... milk with that?
4 Customer A:	No, thanks. But I'd like .... sugar.
5 Customer B:	I don't want .... coffee, thanks. I'd like .... tea with .... milk and .... piece of chocolate cake.

Instead of exploiting the menu, e.g., modeling questions regarding the items and deixis (both frequently found in the native speaker data), the dialog presents somewhat stilted language and the rather odd utterance "I don't want coffee, thanks" in line 5. In a later exercise (p. 49), learners are given another model dialog (sample D) and a menu (listing the same items as on p. 47), and asked to talk about their food and drink choices, then to order.

Sample D

1 A:	What can I get for you?
2 B:	I'd like a chicken sandwich and a cup of coffee, please.
3 C:	I want a cheeseburger. Let's have some French fries.
4 B:	Good idea.
5 A:	Would you like any dessert?
6 C:	Let's have some apple pie.
7 B:	Oh, yes!

In line 1, the service bid is very plausible and is frequently found in the present data. In line 2, "a cup of coffee" is also plausible (but "a cup" is improbable in a fast-food encounter). "I want" (line 3) may be a misleading model due to its directness. "Let's have" (lines 3 and 6) shows that persons C and B are discussing their choices, yet they do not appear to confirm their order with the server, and it is not clear who person C is addressing. A feature of service encounter talk, as evidenced in the present data, is frequent checking and confirming of the order by the server, for example, by means of echoic responses. Furthermore, the dialog has been oversimplified, and is unrealistic in that no alternatives or options are offered by the server. The customers ask no additional information about the items, nor is there a closing sequence. It would seem that the model dialog merely exposes the learners to more examples of countable and uncountable nouns (e.g., a chicken sandwich, some French fries, any dessert).

None of the above samples (A, B, C or D) exposes the learners to common features of conversation, e.g., false starts, echoic responses, interruptions or phatic talk. Neither are any of the dialogs wholly complete. That is to say, there is an absence of any kind of closing sequence, which could take the form of, for example, the sub-task of paying, thanking, or a leave-taking exchange.

The following two examples (samples E and F) further exemplify a textbook emphasis to present a variety of polite forms, yet fail to provide a context for their appropriate usage, placing or a beginning, middle or end to the interaction. According to Myers Scotton & Bernsten (1988), service encounters in different settings do not favor the same polite form. Kehe & Kehe's (1994) ESL textbook on conversation strategies (a popular book in a language school where the researcher was employed at the time of writing), offers a unit entitled 'Polite expressions: polite requests, responses, and excuses' in which the following models are given (the bold appears in the textbook):

Sample E

| Informal: | when you are speaking to friends, your family members, waiters, salespeople **Would** you lend me you pen? **Could** I borrow your pen? |
| Formal: | when you are speaking to teachers, police, strangers, your boss, elderly people, important people **Would you mind** lending me your pen? **I wonder if I could** borrow your pen. **Would you mind if I** borrowed you pen? |

Firstly, in the informal section, learners are told to use 'would' and 'could' when speaking to waiters and salespeople, in other words, in service encounters. In the present data, 'could' was only employed if the degree of imposition of the request was greater. Note also the absence of any context (e.g, location, interlocutor status) to situate the models.

The book *Say it naturally* (Wall, 1987) was criticized (Bardovi-Harlig, 1991) for its absence of pre-closings and closing sequences, yet was reprinted in 1998. The present researcher has used both editions of this textbook, which are also in active use in the language school where she was employed at the time of writing. In the unit

'Asking for information', the following models are presented (the bold appears in the textbook):

Sample F

> **Courtesy when asking for information**
>
> In many situations it would be considered almost rude to begin a question without some kind of basic courtesy. We don't just ask a question; we get the person's attention politely in one of these ways first:
>
> Excuse me. When ... ?
> Pardon me, ma'am, but where ... ?
> I hate to bother you but what ... ?
> Sir, could you help me? How many ... ?
> Please, Mr .... Why ... ?
>
> These are just a few ways to start a question. [...] If you begin a question with certain polite phrases like, "Could you tell me ...," "I was wondering ...," "Do you know ..." [...], in the rest of the sentence, the normal verb subject order is reversed.

The polite forms are decontextualized, and no indication is given as to when to use such expressions. For example, in the present data, "I was wondering" (line 6 below) was used once due to the degree of imposition:

Encounter 8 (STAR) (the complete interaction is shown above on p. 318)

5	S1:	Hot or iced?
6	C:	Hot. (.) I was wondering if anyone had found my bag.
7	S1:	Oh. You were the one that called yesterday?
8	S2 & 3:	XXX
9	C:	OK. Good. Thank you.

Another interesting observation in the native speaker data concerned the sub-task 'thanking'. Thanking the server when receiving the ordered item or change, was either expressed non-verbally, or verbally ("thank you" and more rarely "thanks"). "No, thanks" was sometimes used to answer the question "Anything else?" or "Need your receipt?" But compare the following closings. Why would the customer use a more elaborate way of thanking? For example:

Encounter 28 (STAR)

1	S:	Hi
2	C:	Do you have bagels today? Ah there they are ((looks at cabinet)) (.) Yeah I'd like a blueberry bagel. I'd like cream cheese and a plate. I'd like a tall cup (of) coffee in the XXX cup.

3 S: Thank you ((to another customer)) Thank you
4 S2: Have a nice day.
5 C: Thank you ((customer hands over money))
6 S: Thank you
7 C: Oh uhm I forgot to tell you. I need to pick up XXX. Can you just put- pour that into my cup?
8 S: ((Server fills the customer's personal cup))
9 C: Thank you *so* very much.

Encounter 29 (NAVY) (complete interaction not shown)
1 S: The other one is here in the bag. I added some butter
2 C: Oh thank you. That's nice of you.

In fact, the reason lies in the felt need of the customer to show his or her appreciation for the service, for example, the extra imposition on the server to explain items, or render an extra service. In encounter 28, line 9, the customer thanks the server (with emphasis on "so") as the customer requests that her coffee be put in her own cup (line 7). In a previous turn in encounter 29, the order is confused, and it takes several more turns (and some phatic talk) to clarify. In a short amount of time, a rapport is built between the two speakers, and shown in the leave-taking exchanges. A simple routine "thank you" would be insufficient and indeed inappropriate (and is often said earlier in the exchange). Other 'thanking' examples showing greater appreciation were: "You are so kind. Thank you", "Oh, thank you. That's great", "Thanks a lot", "Thanks again". Textbooks rarely explain, or give a context for, the subtle, but pragmatically important, ways of saying 'thank you' uttered by the customer during leave-taking exchanges.

While the above textbook samples were not situated in a coffee shop or coffee cart, the general features of context-embedded talk found in the present data still apply, and should be considered by textbook authors. The findings from the present data suggest that model textbook dialogs should be contextualized and reflect native speaker use. The problem is how to recreate samples of language in real life that are comprehensible to the learner. It may not be possible to expose learners to the 'real thing', but the samples could be either elaborated or simplified to render the meaning explicit, yet all the while ensuring that the dialogs retain their authenticity (see Long, 1997: Yano, Long & Ross, 1993, for discussion).

A prototypical dialog

Subsequent to the analysis of the authentic data, it is possible to identify, and elaborate on, a prototypical dialog, reflecting features common to context-embedded talk in a service encounter.

There is the colloquial language the server uses to state the price ("That'll be 3.41") and idiomatic language when handing over an item ("There you go"). There is a great deal of ellipsis by the server ("Anything else?" "For here?" "Need your receipt?"), and the customer ("Right to the top", "Single Americano", "Small will do"). Much use of deictics and pronouns occur ("the chocolate one", "the one at the front") when referring to items, and when looking at the menu, also an example of inter-textuality, ("third from the bottom is the iced mocha").

Regarding 'technical' lexical items, contrary to native-speaker intuition, "a cup of coffee" did not occur, this generic term being replaced by more specific ones, for example, "two grande café mochas", "coffee of the day", or "the Americano". Idiosyncratic terms are not included in the prototypical dialog, for example, "a skinny," which was only used by employees at HUM.

Grammatical functions sometimes serve a different purpose, for example, "did" does not mark past tense, but serves as a mitigation device in several questions ("Did you want whipped cream with that?", "Did you want room for cream?").

More complex language was needed if an item ran out ("Right now we're all out of our caramel"), if a list of options was offered ("We have fruit flavors or nut flavors. We have raspberry, strawberry, cherry. And then we have hazelnut, amaretto, almond, vanilla"), if there was confusion on the part of the customer ("Blended, I guess. I've never had it that way"), or if the degree of imposition was greater ("I was wondering if anyone had found my bag"). In these cases, interactions tended to be lengthier and more social talk often resulted.

The length of interaction, i.e., the time taken to complete an order, differed. It was considerably shorter, for example, if a regular ordered, especially during the morning rush, compared to when an order made by someone unfamiliar with items and their names.

Below, is a prototypical sample encounter for a customer (not a regular) who orders one drink (a coffee) and a sundry (a scone), which incorporates several features found in the present data, including a false start by the customer (line 12).

Sample prototypical dialog

1 S: Hi. Can I help you?
2 C: Can I get a grande latte with vanilla?
3 S: Did you want that blended or on the rocks?
4 C: Blended, I guess
5 S: 2% or skimmed?
6 C: Uhm 2%
7 S: 2% OK. Any whipped cream?
8 C: Sorry?
9 S: Did you want whipped cream on that?
10 C: Yes
11 S: Anything else?
12 C: No, that's it. Oh no. Can I get- are those scones?
13 S: Yeah, we have cranberry and blueberry
14 C: I think I'll have one of those (pointing)
15 S: A blueberry scone?
16 C: Yeah. The one in the back
17 S: This one
18 C: Yeah that's it
19 S: OK. For here or to go?
20 C: To go
21 S: OK. That'll be three forty-eight
22 C: (hands over money)
23 S: How about a frequent-user card?
24. C: Oh sure
25 S: Thank you. 52 cents is your change (hands over change). And your
      card. OK. It'll be ready for you in just one minute
26 C: Thank you
27 S: There you go (hands over drink). Have a nice day
28 C: You too

Conclusion

This study aims to contribute to the growing number of discourse analyses, highlighting common features found in real-life communicative events. The prototypical interaction is an example of how such features revealed in the data can be incorporated into a model service encounter. As witnessed during the researcher's own language teaching experience and supported by previous target discourse analyses, many current textbook materials ill-equip learners to handle real-life discourse. The present analysis attempts to show that although natural interactions are somewhat complex and reveal variability, there is a predictable overall nature. However, according to findings by Myers Scotton & Bernsten (1988), not all service encounters are equal, and therefore, the present findings cannot be generalized to cover all exchange types. Further research with authentic data is needed, which could greatly benefit by adopting a CA approach, the ultimate aim being to increase our understanding of interactive competence.

Notes

1 A local daily paper.
2 The technical lexicon for different coffee, tea and smoothie drinks is enormous, and the referential terms could be the source of another discourse analysis.
3 A "frappuccino" is the name of a coffee item in another coffee shop, called here a "frio" (line 4). One of the main sources of confusion, confirmed in the interview with the server, is knowledge of the drink names. This is further confounded by the fact that some names are exclusive to certain coffee shops.
4 "I like" was heard on the tape.
5 Cream can be added by customers in an area to the left of the main serving counter.

References

Auerbach, E., & Burgess, D. (1985). The hidden curriculum of survival ESL. *TESOL Quarterly*, 19, 3, 475–95.

Bardovi-Harlig, K. (2001). Evaluating the empirical evidence: Grounds for instruction in pragmatics? In G. Kasper & K. Rose (eds.), *Pragmatics in language teaching* (pp. 13–60). Cambridge: Cambridge University Press.

Bardovi-Harlig, K., Hartford, B., Mahan-Taylor, R., Morgan, M., & Reynolds, D. (1991). Developing pragmatic awareness: closing the conversation. *ELT Journal*, 45, 4–15.

Barlow, M. (2000). MonoConc Pro (Version 2.0) [Computer software]. Houston, TX: Athelstan.

Boxer, D. (1993). Complaints as positive strategies: what the learner needs to know. *TESOL Quarterly*, 27, 2, 277–99,

Boxer, D., & Pickering, L. (1995). Problems in the presentation of speech acts in ELT materials: The case of complaints. *ELT Journal* 49, 1, 44–58.

Canale, M., & Swain, M. (1980). Theoretical bases of communicative approaches to second language teaching and testing. *Applied Linguistics* 1, 1–47.

Cathcart, R. (1989). Authentic discourse and the survival English curriculum. *TESOL Quarterly*, 23, 1, 105–26.

Coupland, J. (2000). Introduction to part II. In J. Coupland (ed.), *Small talk*. Harlow: Longman.

Coupland, N., & Ylanne-McEwen, V. (2000). Talk about the weather: Small talk, leisure talk and the travel industry. In J. Coupland (ed.), *Small talk*. (pp. 163–182) Harlow, UK: Longman.

Crystal, D. (1995). In search of English: A traveller's guide. *ELT Journal 49*, 2, 107–21.

Denman, B. (2000). *In contact 1. Second edition.* White Plains, NY: Addison Wesley Longman, Inc.

Drew, P., & Heritage, J. (eds.), (1992). Talk at work: Interaction in institutional settings. Cambridge: Cambridge University Press.

Goffman, E. (1967). On face-work: An analysis of ritual elements in social interaction. Reproduced in N. Coupland & A. Jaworski (eds.), (1999). *The discourse reader.* (pp. 306–320). London, UK: Routledge.

Grant, L., & Starks, D. (2001). Screening appropriate teaching materials: closings from textbooks and television soap operas. *International Review of Applied Linguistics 39*, 39–50.

Gumperz, J. G. (1996). The linguistic and cultural relativity of conversational inference. In J. G. Gumperz & S. C. Levinson (eds.), *Rethinking linguistic relativity* (pp. 274–406). Cambridge: Cambridge University Press.

Hasan, R. (1985) The structure of a text. In M. A. K. Halliday & R. Hasan, *Language, context and text: Aspects of language in a social-semiotic perspective.* (pp. 52–69). Oxford: Oxford University Press.

Holmes, J. (1988). Doubt and certainty in ESL textbooks. *Applied Linguistics 9*, 1, 21–44.

Hutchby, I., & Wooffitt, R. (1998). *Conversation analysis.* Malden, MA: Blackwell.

Jasso-Aguilar, R. (1999). Sources, methods and triangulation in needs analysis: A critical perspective in a case study of Waikiki hotel maids. *English for Specific Purposes 18*, 1, 27–46.

Kasper, G. (1997). Can pragmatic competence be taught? (NFLRC Network No. 6, HTML document) Honolulu: University of Hawai'i, Second Language Teaching and Curriculum Center. Available at http://nflrc.hawaii.edu/networks/NW6

Kasper, G. (2001). Classroom research on interlanguage pragmatics. In K. Rose & G. Kasper (eds.), *Pragmatics in language teaching* (pp. 33–42). Cambridge: Cambridge University Press.

Kehe, D., & Kehe, P. D. (1994). *Conversation strategies: Pair and group work for developing communicative competence.* Brattleboro, Vermont: Pro Lingua Associates.

Kiggell, T. (1998). *Nexus: Person to person network skills.* Tokyo: Macmillan Languagehouse.

Kuiper, K., & Flindall, M. (2000). Social rituals, formulaic speech and small talk at the supermarket checkout. In J. Coupland (ed.), *Small talk.* (pp. 183–207) Harlow: Longman.

Labov, W. (1972). Some principles of linguistic methodology. *Language and Society*, 1, 97–120.

Lincoln, Y. S., & Guba, E. G. (eds.) (1985). *Naturalistic inquiry.* Newbury Park, Sage.

Long, M. H. (1985). A role for instruction in second language acquisition: Task-based language teaching. In K. Hyltenstam & M. Pienemann (eds.), *Modelling and assessing second language acquisition* (pp. 77–99). Clevedon: Multilingual Matters.

Long, M. H. (1997). Authenticity and learning potential in L2 classroom discourse. In G. M. Jacobs (ed.), *Language classrooms of tomorrow: Issues and responses.* (pp. 148–169) Singapore: SEAMEO Regional Language Center.

Long, M. H. (this volume). Methodological issues in learner needs analysis.

Long, M. H. (to appear). *Task-based language teaching.* Oxford: Blackwell.

Long, M. H., & Crookes, G. (1992). Three approaches to task-based syllabus design. *TESOL Quarterly* 26, 1, 27–55.

Long, M. H., & Robinson, P. (1998). Focus on Form: Theory, research, and practice. In C. J. Doughty & J. Williams (eds.), *Focus on form in classroom second language acquisition.* (pp. 15–41) Cambridge: Cambridge University Press.

Malinowski, B. (1923). On phatic communion. Reproduced in N. & A. Coupland (eds.) (1999). *The Discourse Reader* (pp. 302–05). London, UK: Routledge.

Marriot, H., & Yamada, N. (1991). Language planning and language management for tourism shopping situations. In A. J. Liddicoat (ed.), Language planning and language politics in Australia. Australian Review of Applied Linguistics. Series S, No.8. Melbourne: ALAA.

McCarthy, M. (2000). Mutually captive audiences: Small talk and the genre of close contact service encounters. In J. Coupland (ed.), *Small talk.* (pp.85–109). Harlow: Longman.

Medway, P., & Andrews, R. (1992). Building with words: Discourse in an architect's office. *Carleton Papers in Applied Language Studies* 9, 1–32.

Merritt, M. (1976). On questions following questions. *Language in Society,* 5, 315–357.

Myers Scotton, C., & Bernsten, J. (1988). Natural conversations as a model of textbook dialog. *Applied Linguistics* 9, 4, 372–84.

Olshtain, E., & Cohen, A. D. (1991). Teaching speech act behavior to nonnative speakers. In M. Celce-Murcia (ed.), *Teaching English as a second or foreign language.* (pp. 154–65) Boston, MA: Heinle & Heinle.

Peters, S. (1991). *On a roll: A conversation and listening text.* New Jersey: Prentice Hall Regents

Pica, T., Holliday, L., Lewis, N., & Morgenthaler, L. (1989). Comprehensible output as an outcome of linguistic demands on the learner. *Studies in Second Language Acquisition* 11, 1, 63–90.

Robinson, P. (1999). Task complexity, task difficulty and task production: Exploring interaction in a componential framework. *Applied Linguistics, 22*, 1, 27–57.

Robinson, P. (2001a). Task complexity, cognitive resources, and syllabus design: A triadic framework for examining task influences on SLA. In P. Robinson (ed.), *Cognition and second language instruction.* (pp. 287–318). New York: Cambridge University Press.

Robinson, P. (2001b). Task complexity, task difficulty, and task production:

Exploring interaction in a componential framework. *Applied Linguistics* 22, 1, 27–57.

Sacks, H., Schegloff, E. A., & Jefferson, G. (1974). A simplest systematics for the organization of turn-taking for conversation. *Language, 50,* 696–735.

Schegloff, E. A., & Sacks, H. (1973). Opening up closings. Semiotica 7. Reproduced in N. & A. Coupland (eds.) (1999). *The discourse reader.* (pp. 263–274) London, UK: Routledge.

Schiffrin, D. (1994). *Approaches to discourse.* Cambridge: Cambridge University Press.

Skehan, P. (1996). A framework for the implementation of task based instruction. *Applied Linguistics* 17, 1, 38–62.

Skehan, P. (1998a). *A cognitive approach to language learning.* Oxford: Oxford University Press.

Skehan, P. (1998b). Task-based instruction. *Annual Review of Applied Linguistics* 18, 268–86.

Svendsen, C., & Krebs, K. (1984). Identifying English for the job: Examples from healthcare occupations. *The ESP Journal* 3, 153–64.

Ventola, E. (1983). Contrasting schematic structures in service encounters. *Applied Linguistics* 4, 3, 242–58.

Ventola, E. (1987). *The structure of social interaction: A systemic approach to the semiotics of service encounters.* London: Frances Pinter.

Wall, A.P. (1987). *Say it naturally! Verbal strategies for authentic communication.* New York: CBS College Publishing.

Williams, M. (1988). Language taught for meetings and language used in meetings: Is there anything in common? *Applied Linguistics* 9, 1, 45–58.

Wood, L,. & Kroger, R. O. (2000). *Doing discourse analysis: Methods for studying action in talk and text.* Thousand Oaks, California: Sage.

Wolfson, N. (1981). Compliments in cross-cultural perspective. *TESOL Quarterly,* 15, 2, 117–124.

Wolfson, N. (1986). Research methodology and the question of validity. *TESOL Quarterly,* 20, 689–699.

Yano, Y., Long, M. H., & Ross, S. (1993). The effects of simplified and elaborated texts on foreign language reading comprehension. *Language learning,* 44, 189–219.

Appendix A: Transcription conventions

The transcription symbols here are from Hutchby & Wooffitt (1998), based on the original work of Gail Jefferson.

(6)	The number in brackets indicates the length of pause.
(.)	A dot enclosed in a bracket indicates a brief pause.
[ ]	Square brackets indicate the onset and end of a spate of over-lapping talk.
(( ))	A description enclosed in a double bracket indicates a non-verbal activity.
-	A dash indicates the sharp cut-off of the prior word or sound. For example:
	C: Can I get- are those scones?
:	Colons indicate that the speaker has stretched the preceding sound or letter.
XXX	indicates the presence of an unclear fragment on the tape.
(whipped)	The words within a single bracket indicate the transcriber's best guess at an unclear utterance.
.	A full stop may indicate the end of a sentence or phrase.
?	A question mark indicates a question with rising intonation.

11 *When small talk is a big deal: Sociolinguistic challenges in the workplace*

Janet Holmes

Introduction

Any sociolinguistic analysis of the needs of language learners will place socio-pragmatic skills high on the list. From a sociolinguistic perspective, learners need to be able to manage on-going, dynamic social interaction in a wide range of settings, and this entails the ability to accurately analyze the relative weight of different dimensions such as power, solidarity, formality and function (Holmes 2001). Long (this volume) argues for *task* as the fundamental unit of needs analysis, rather than linguistic units, notions or functions, on the basis that this provides a basis for coherent syllabus design. This paper makes a case for also paying attention to the social demands on workers, especially those in blue collar workplaces or small businesses. Any thorough needs analysis of the language demands on workers in their work contexts will identify the pervasiveness of small talk or social talk, and the crucial importance of managing this well for acceptance in the workplace.

Interpersonal interaction provides a range of challenges for anyone joining a new place of work and workplace small talk certainly represents one such challenge. Skilful management of small talk is extremely important in accounting for successful integration into the workplace, but it is an area that is often overlooked. This paper examines the challenges presented by social talk at work for two particular groups: newly immigrant workers for whom English is a second language, and workers with an intellectual disability. While the social situations of these two groups are in most respects very different, the kinds of difficulties they face in managing some aspects of social talk at work are surprisingly similar. Thus, applied sociolinguists have a useful role to play in examining the sociolinguistic demands made of such workers as they attempt to fit into a new workplace. The paper describes the results of an analysis of the social demands made on employees in a range of workplaces, including workplaces employing recent immigrants and workers with intellectual disabilities. The analysis focuses on aspects of the management

344

of social talk which present a challenge to both groups. Some common topics of small talk, typical distributional patterns, and some of the functions of small talk at work are identified, as well as the problems each of these areas may raise for new employees. Finally, some suggestions are provided for ways in which teachers and trainers may assist workers acquire some of the sociolinguistic skills required to manage small talk effectively in their workplaces.[1]

Example 1[2]

Context: Factory workers are standing around waiting for their early morning meeting.

1 Henry: that was a shit of an afternoon wasn't it +
2 Stuart: could've been worse
3 Henry: do you think?
4 Stuart: yeah they could've messed up the bins too
5   [laughter]

This brief interaction illustrates a number of the features of workplace small talk – it fills a gap while people wait for work to begin; the topic is a work-related event (a minor disaster on the production line caused by a different department which resulted in extra work for these men); it assumes shared experience and background information (e.g., both participants know that the relevant "afternoon" occurred the previous day); and its function is primarily social and interactive, as reflected, for instance, in the two questions (lines 1, 3), and the humorous comment which is intended to amuse (line 4). A newcomer or an outsider would find it difficult to join in. Interpersonal workplace interaction provides many challenges for anyone joining a new place of work. Successful integration typically involves learning local ways of being sociable and local norms for managing small talk, humor, and friendly chat more generally. Indeed, in some cases, success at work depends as much on a competent social performance in these areas, as on more obvious aspects of task fulfillment. Many workers from non-English-speaking backgrounds (NESB) are very skilled at their jobs, but they do not always know how to manage the social and interpersonal aspects of workplace interaction. Similarly, those with an intellectual disability may be perfectly capable of completing the tasks assigned to them, but the social demands made by their fellow workers are much more problematic. Actual ability to perform work tasks is just the tip of the iceberg in terms of success at work, with social and interpersonal skills underpinning the structure as much more significant predictors of workplace success (Black & Langone, 1997; Butterworth &

Strauch, 1994; Hagnar, 1993; Huang & Cuvo, 1997). In both cases, because the problems are typically subtle, as well as social, workers may not realize precisely how they are failing to meet expectations of workplace performance.

Employers, by contrast, are generally very aware that it is lack of social proficiency that often lets their workers down, rather than weaknesses in their task performance, or even their formal linguistic skills (Clyne, 1994). Interviews undertaken by members of our research team with factory managers employing NESB workers (Brown, 2000), and with the proprietors of small businesses employing workers with an intellectual disability (Fillary, 1998), clearly identified interpersonal social skills as a common area of concern. These employers commented that workers often have all the skills necessary to do the job, but that they seem unfriendly or uncomfortable at work; they do not seem to fit in smoothly. It is sociolinguistic and pragmatic skills which often determine whether people are perceived as good workmates, and even as good workers. Most people acquire these skills in their native language(s) from years of immersion in the culture, mixing and working with others, but they can present real challenges for second language learners (e.g., Thomas, 1983). And for those with intellectual handicaps and inadequate interactional skills, exposure alone, no matter for how long, does not seem to help them acquire the ability to relate to others easily. In both cases, then, though for different reasons, assistance is needed in acquiring the socio-pragmatic skills that are needed for establishing good social relationships in the workplace.

Workers from non-English-speaking backgrounds

There is considerable evidence that speakers from non-English-speaking backgrounds often face difficulties with social interaction in a new culture, and particularly in a new workplace (e.g., Clyne, 1991, 1994; Gumperz, Jupp & Roberts, 1979; Roberts, Davies & Jupp, 1992). And, as Clyne points out, typically:

> inter-cultural communication breakdown occurs at the discourse and pragmatic levels, rather than being caused by phonological, lexical and morphosyntactic questions.
>
> (1994, p. 211).

Problems arise, for example, with culturally specific assumptions about appropriate ways of apologising, complaining, refusing, complimenting, giving instructions, and with making small talk. Misunderstandings occur because workers mistake moans or whinges for genuine complaints, or interpret friendly social talk as intrusive cross-questioning about personal matters (Clyne, 1994, p. 180). Clyne describes the puzzlement of a Chinese factory hand in Melbourne at the explicit and extensive apology that a colleague provided for holding up his work by being a little late. In Chinese languages, apologies are often conveyed through body language rather than verbally; consequently, Clyne notes, the Chinese are often surprised by the amount of explicit apologizing that takes place between Australians of British and European descent (Clyne, 1994, p. 179). And, similarly, he relates the relative absence of apologies among Asian workers in his Australian workplace corpus to "their collectivist values", where relationships, rather than "sin and guilt" are the basis for social control.

Relatively little research explores these socio-pragmatic problems using ethnographic data from authentic workplaces which employ workers for whom English is a second language. And, surprisingly little attention is paid to such socio-pragmatic skills in textbooks designed for NESB workers. A small survey which I undertook of 50 textbooks aimed at teaching English for the workplace revealed that most devoted less than 15% of their content to social and inter-personal aspects of workplace interaction such as small talk. More advanced textbooks often ignored this area completely; apparently small talk is considered too basic to deserve serious attention in such books.

Workers with an intellectual disability

Greenspan & Shoultz (1981) cite extensive research, including their own, which supports the claim that "it is an inability to interact effectively with other people, rather than an inability to operate machines or perform job tasks that often causes many mentally retarded adults to get fired from competitive jobs" (p. 23). There is evidence that workers with intellectual disabilities typically interact less with co-workers at break-times (Parent et al, 1992), engage with a smaller range of co-workers (Storey et al, 1991), engage in more inappropriate interactions (Parent et al, 1992), and are less involved in workplace joking and teasing (e.g., Hagnar, 1996). Reviewing this literature, Hatton (1998) concludes that while people with intellec-tual disabilities are generally accepted by co-workers, they typically do not achieve "a high degree of social integration" (p. 91). More recently, research on factors affecting the success of workers with intellectual disabilities stresses the crucial role played by social skills or social behaviors in the *perceptions* of others as competent; in other

words, socially competent workers are often more positively perceived, whatever their level of task-related ability (Butterworth &
Strauch, 1994; Hatton, 1998).

Again, while the literature on the relationship between social
competence and success at work is extensive, there is relatively little
research which involves direct observation of workers in their actual
places of work. Earlier research has been based on reports of worker
behavior collected through interviews or questionnaires. With a few
exceptions (e.g., Clyne, 1994; Roberts, Davies & Jupp, 1992), more
recent workplace research has tended to focus on professional and
institutional contexts, such as interactions between clients and
doctors, social workers, lawyers, and counselors (e.g., Boden, 1994;
Drew & Heritage, 1992a).

There is ample scope, then, for research that examines everyday
interactions among workers in their normal places of work. The
research reported in this paper was designed with this in mind. The
analysis is based on extensive tape-recorded data of workplace
interactions collected in a wide range of New Zealand workplaces,
including organizations employing NESB workers, and businesses
employing workers with intellectual disabilities. As described below,
this data was collected using a very rich range of methods (see Long,
this volume), including a period of preparatory participant observation followed by a period of recorded data collection, with follow-up
interviews and de-briefings to help illuminate the analysis. In what
follows, I first present our analytical framework, and then outline the
methodology developed to collect authentic workplace interactions.
In the central section of the paper, some distinctive features of small
talk in New Zealand workplaces are outlined. Finally the implications of the research are examined in terms of potential input to
programs for prospective workers, including specific suggestions for
how teachers may assist workers to acquire some of the relevant
sociolinguistic skills in the area of small talk that they need to
operate effectively.

Analytical framework

Language plays an important part in creating a particular kind of
work environment. Using language appropriately for each particular
workplace is a crucial aspect of becoming an accepted participant
(Roberts, Davies & Jupp, 1992). Wenger (1998) suggests that a
workplace is a typical "community of practice", with its own
repertoire of resources, including linguistic and discourse resources.
When we join a new workplace we need to learn not only the

technical terminology and the in-group jargon, we also need to acquire the norms for interaction – the appropriate ways of addressing and referring to people, the acceptable levels of formality for use in meetings of different sizes, and involving people of different status. Joining a new workplace entails learning how to use language to negotiate new meanings with new colleagues. Interaction is a dynamic process and language is a crucial resource in managing social relations at work (Drew & Heritage, 1992b). All this suggests that learning how to communicate effectively in a new workplace will take time and sensitive observation, even for a competent native speaker. And facilitating this process will ideally involve teachers spending time observing in the kinds of workplaces in which their learners will be working.

Sociolinguistic theory also emphasizes the fact that the particular context in which an encounter takes place significantly affects how we interpret what is said. Participants bring a great deal of background knowledge to any interaction, which enables them to understand what is going on, and assists them in making effective and appropriate contributions. As Gumperz (1992, p. 303) points out:

> interpretation of what a speaker intends to convey at any one point rests on socially constructed knowledge of what the encounter is about and what is to be achieved.

Background knowledge about the role relationships involved, as well as the kind of talk appropriate in each setting, are always relevant to how participants interpret utterances in their sequential context. Moreover, what people want to convey is generally skilfully tailored to the specific social context and negotiated between participants (Gumperz, 1982, 1992). So participants take account of relationships of power and solidarity, paying attention to the 'face' needs of others in interaction (Brown & Levinson, 1987; Holmes, Stubbe, & Vine, 1999).

The analytical framework adopted in this paper thus draws predominantly on an interactional sociolinguistic model, within a broader social constructionist model of communication. This approach emphasizes that an understanding of the wider context is crucial for interpreting the discourse at a local level. As Wenger (1998) indicates, workplace interactions tend to be strongly embedded in the business and social context of a particular work group, as well as in a wider social or institutional order. The approach also assumes that discursive interaction is a dynamic process where meanings and intentions are jointly and progressively negotiated between the individuals involved in a given interaction. The focus in the analysis which follows is thus on discourse at the micro-level of individual workplace interactions. The data has been 'triangulated' (see Long, this volume) to the extent that it constitutes authentic recorded data which has been the focus of reflection and comment from those involved in teaching the workers who are the focus of the study.

Finally, it is important to put the analyses which are the particular focus of this paper in a broader perspective. The sociolinguistic competence which underlies the ability to use talk in interaction successfully is typically acquired gradually over years of experience and exposure to language in different contexts. Those who move to a country where an unfamiliar language is used at work have not had this experience and exposure. And, as indicated above, people with intellectual disabilities have often not fully developed this aspect of social competence. The analysis below provides some empirical evidence of the kinds of problems which arise in workplaces employing NESB workers and workers with intellectual disabilities. However, it should also be borne in mind that, although the focus here is areas of potential difficulty, many of the interactions we recorded indicated that such workers manage interactions quite successfully. Conversely, the sociolinguistic and pragmatic problems we identify can also be observed in the behaviors of native speakers and those without intellectual disability. Nevertheless, the fact that employers perceive such problems as presenting particular difficulties for the groups I am focussing on, provides a strong rationale for the analysis, as well as for the practical applications discussed in the final section. Finally, it should be noted that the analysis is qualitative and indicative rather than quantitative and definitive (cf. Hagnar & Helm, 1994).

Methodology

Database

Over the last seven years, researchers involved in the Victoria University of Wellington Language in the Workplace Project (LWP) have collected data from a range of different New Zealand workplaces, including government agencies, large private organizations, small businesses and factories (Holmes & Stubbe, 2003). We have recorded over 2000 different interactions and more than 500 hours of talk at work. Nearly 400 women and men have contributed, from a range of ages and levels within each organization, and from a variety of ethnic backgrounds, including Samoan, Chinese, Maori and Pakeha (New Zealanders with European origins). The database also includes 84 interactions collected in workplaces where young workers with intellectual disabilities had been placed.[3]

The bulk of the data consists of small, relatively informal interactions ranging in time between twenty seconds and two hours. It includes not only task-oriented or business talk, but also the kind of social talk that occurs at the start of the day, at tea breaks and at lunchtime. This is the material that provides the basis for the qualitative analysis below.

Data collection

At all the sites where we have collected data, the methodology has been designed to give participants the maximum control possible over the data-collection process (see Holmes, Fillary, McLeod & Stubbe, 2000; Holmes & Stubbe, 2003, Stubbe, 1998). Moreover, all those involved, and all those whose voices have been recorded, have provided information on their ethnic background, home language, age and so on, as well as detailed contextual information, and permission for the data to be used for linguistic analysis.

When we began designing the data collection for the LWP project, our goal was to collect as wide a spectrum of workplace interaction as possible, but, ideally, we did not want the data collection process to influence or alter the way people normally spoke to each other at work. Inevitably, however, observers with tape-recorders *do* alter the way people interact. We resolved this "observer's paradox" (Labov, 1972) by devising a way of minimising the unavoidable effects: we asked a group of volunteers from a number of workplaces to do the tape-recording for us. They were asked to record a range of their everyday work interactions over a period of about two weeks. This included social and task-oriented talk, telephone interactions and formal meetings, with the aim of providing between four hours and ten hours of recorded talk. In order to collect this data some kept a tape-recorder and microphone on their desks, while others carried the equipment round with them. In addition, we video-taped complete sets of meetings of some project teams. Two video cameras with long-playing tapes were set up in the meeting rooms in advance, and in this way we recorded valuable pre-meeting and post-meeting talk, as well as the meeting itself. After several days, the cameras were ignored and regarded as part of the furniture.

Throughout the data-collection process, participants were free to

edit and delete material as they wished. Even after they had completed recording and handed over the tapes, they could ask us to edit
out material that they felt, in retrospect, they did not wish us to
analyze. Over a period of time, however, people increasingly ignored
the recording equipment, and there are often comments at the end of
interactions indicating people had forgotten about the tape-recorder.
Also over time, the amount of material they deleted, or which they
asked us to edit out, decreased dramatically. By handing over control
of the recording process in this way, an excellent research relationship developed with our workplace participants. In return for
guarantees of anonymity and confidentiality, the volunteers provided
a wide range of fascinating material.

Of particular relevance for any research involving manual workers
is the methodology devised for collecting data in the environment of
a busy factory, where machine noise threatened to drown out most
talk, and where verbal interaction was often brief, intense and
typically sporadic. In one factory, we confined data collection to
offices and avoided the factory floor. In the other, however, we
worked with a factory production team, and this unavoidably
involved dealing with the problems of high levels of noise and activity
(Stubbe & Ingle, 1999).

Given the nature of their factory work, it was not possible for
people to record themselves. We therefore used a young friendly
fieldworker (Ingle) to collect the data. Initially, she simply accompanied the team manager on her factory rounds, noting features of the
lay-out and procedures, logistical and technical problems, potential
recording opportunities, and so on. Later, as she became increasingly
familiar to the team members, she began to record interactions as
opportunities arose. Another variation of the methodology was the
use of radio microphones carried by more peripatetic team members,
which further reduced the intrusiveness of the recording process.
Portable digital mini-disc recorders (Sony MZ-N707 Net MD
Walkmans) improved the quality of the spoken material. Initially,
recording was undertaken for a rolling three to four hours a day over
successive shifts, in order to obtain samples from each part of a
typical day, and each day of the four-day shift (Stubbe & Ingle,
1999). Subsequent recording extended to a wider range of interactions, including one-to-one discussions, briefing meetings, and
communication via the factory intercom, and in the control room for
one entire four-day shift.

These methods provided a unique and richly diverse set of workplace interactions, ranging from the formal strategic planning

sessions of a group of regional managers, to the early morning briefing meetings of a soap factory production team, and including talk during a break as well as interactions involving some very highly paid Chief Executive Officers. In the next section, some of the small talk recorded in the various workplaces is discussed.

Small talk at work

Small talk serves a range of functions in the workplace. It is often used for primarily social functions, expressing friendliness, establishing rapport, and maintaining solidarity among people in the workplace, as illustrated in example 2.

Example 2

Context: Diana, a manager, enters the office of her administrative assistant, Sally, at the beginning of the day to collect mail.

1 Diana: good morning Sally lovely day
2 Sally: yes don't know what we're doing here we should be out in the sun
3 Diana: mm pity about the work really
4 Sally: how are your kids?
5 Diana: much better thank goodness + any mail?

On the basis of our extensive sample of workplace interactions collected in a wide range of different kinds of workplaces, we can confidently state that this is a typical example of small talk at work. It covers standard small talk topics – the weather, complaints about work, mention of family, health; it occurs as two people meet for the first time that day, and its main function is to oil the social wheels, to maintain good relations between Diana and Sally. I will briefly discuss each of these aspects of workplace small talk – the topics or content of small talk, the distribution of small talk, and the functions of small talk at work, illustrating with data from a range of workplaces, including those employing NESB workers and young people with intellectual disabilities. (See Holmes, 2000, for more detailed discussion.)

Topics of small talk at work

Small talk in New Zealand workplaces typically focuses on non-controversial topics: the weather (e.g., 'cold eh', 'lovely day'), ritualized inquiries about health (e.g., 'how are you?'), out-of-work social activities (e.g., 'wonderful concert last night'), sport (e.g., 'great match on Saturday, eh'), generalized complaints about the economy (e.g., 'stock market's crashed again I see'), positive comments on appearance (e.g., 'wow you're looking great'), work (e.g., 'how's it going?'), and so on. There is some skill involved in selecting appropriate topics for a particular workplace. In some workplaces, for example, sport was a perennial and safe topic of small talk. In others it was not so successful. (Compare examples 3 and 4.)

Example 3

Context: Ann is delivering mail to the office of young administrative assistant, Bea.

1 Ann: great match on Saturday eh
2 Bea: yeah awesome

Example 4

Context: Carl, a factory supervisor and Ben, a newly arrived immigrant are taking a tea break.

1 Carl: great match on Saturday eh
2 Ben: what match?

In example 4, the speaker has wrongly assumed shared background knowledge. Common ground in the form of shared background knowledge, experience and/or attitudes, is an important basis for successful small talk. Although we found examples of this kind involving NESB workers and workers with intellectual disabilities, in fact, any worker in a new workplace may make such a false assumption. Developing an awareness of the interests of your co-workers is important for all workers.

Social factors, such as how well you know someone, also influence the choice of possible topics of small talk. In the New Zealand workplaces in which we observed, comments on very personal topics typically occurred only between those who knew each other very well and who had long-established good work relationships. This sometimes proved a problem for those with different cultural norms, as well as for workers with intellectual disabilities. One such example involved a young man asking detailed questions about the marriage plans of a co-worker, followed by a request to be invited to the wedding. It was clear from the reactions of other workers that he had over-stepped the bounds of what was considered acceptable small talk. Example 5 illustrates a comment from an NESB worker that was intended as a compliment.

Example 5

Context: Showing family photographs at tea break.

1 Recent Chinese immigrant:	Such a big family!
2 Pakeha New Zealander:[4]	Yes, but it has advantages too

The rather defensive response of the Pakeha New Zealander indicates the comment was interpreted as a criticism. Large families are regarded more positively in Asian and Polynesian cultures than in Pakeha culture, hence the miscommunication. In general, then, very personal comments tended to be restricted to exchanges between people who knew each other very well. Comments on such topics as false teeth or false hair (e.g., 'I like your toupee') were rare, except between workmates who had established a close relationship, often expressed through mutual jocular abuse.

Gender and status are also relevant social factors. Comments on appearance between women are common small talk tokens (e.g., 'what a lovely blouse!'), while between males they are very rare indeed in New Zealand (Holmes, 1988), and they are infrequent in our workplace data. However, we did find examples of young males being teased by co-workers on aspects of their appearance, and this included NESB workers and young men with intellectual disabilities. There are more and less acceptable ways of responding to compliments. Many Asian cultures prescribe overt modesty, including denials and disagreements as appropriate responses to compliments, whereas western cultures tend to prescribes a gracious acceptance of some kind (Chen, 1993; Herbert, 1989; Holmes, 1986; Manes, 1983; Pomerantz, 1978; Ylanne-McEwen, 1993). Clearly, it would be useful if new workers were given advice on how to handle compliments, as well as teasing.

Relative status is also important. Wolfson (1983) noted that compliments from a woman on a man's appearance occurred only when the man was much younger than the female. In our New Zealand workplace data, when people are of different status, small talk tends to be restricted to bland, impersonal, uncontroversial topics. If personal topics, such as family health or relationships, occur, it is usually the subordinate's family, not the superior's, which is the focus of discussion (as illustrated on p. 358 below). This was another aspect of small talk that proved especially problematic for workers with intellectual disabilities. We identified examples where such workers asked questions about members of their supervisor's family which were clearly experienced not as harmless small talk tokens, but as intrusive. Learning the appropriate limits is a challenging aspect of managing small talk at work.

What is considered a bland and 'safe' topic is, of course, also culturally variable. One particularly frequent and 'safe' small talk topic in the workplaces where we recorded was work itself. As example 6 illustrates, routine small talk questions frequently elicited equally ritualistic responses about work.

Example 6

Context: Joan and Elizabeth pass in the passageway.

1 Eliz: hi Joan
2 Joan: hi how are you?
3 Eliz: oh busy busy busy
4 Joan: mm terrible isn't it

Example 7, by contrast, illustrates a response that clearly surprised the supervisor in the small business where it was recorded.

Example 7

Context: Supervisor, George, to worker with disability.

1 Geo: you been busy Ron?
2 Ron: not much

Reference to how busy one is serves in the workplace as an ideal small talk token – a perfect topic for small talk at work. The appropriate response to a question such as George's is generally a positive one, since this indicates an orientation to the 'proper' goals of the workplace. However, Ron's reply would be acceptable in the context of social talk during a work-break.

What is also noticeable in such examples is the considerable skill involved in selecting the appropriate level of detail for the discussion of small talk topics. In most cases, especially when they take place in passing, such interactions are very short. This is an area where newcomers to the New Zealand workplace sometimes err. In response to a formulaic small talk token, such as "How are you?", some of our participants launched into a detailed account of their current medical worries. Getting the level of detail of the response right requires some judgment. The same is true for other small talk formulae, such as "how's things", "been busy", "what have you been up to?", and so on. A detailed analysis of why one considers that one's workload is unreasonably high is not appropriate when the speaker's intentions are clearly social, to establish rapport and get the day started in a friendly way. More extensive social talk occurs in some contexts, of course: in fact, it is obligatory at morning teatime and lunchtime.

Distribution of small talk

Small talk is typically, but not exclusively, found at the boundaries of interaction, as well as at the boundaries of the working day (Hagnar, 1993; Holmes, 2000). It is almost mandatory to exchange small talk when people who work together first arrive at work, or meet for the first time in the working day, as example 2 demonstrates. An emergency or urgent task can displace it, but, generally in the workplace, the first encounter of the day between work colleagues can be considered an obligatory site for small talk. The omission of small talk at such points appears marked, and is likely to be interpreted as evidence of bad manners or bad humor. This seems to be a culturally very widespread phenomenon, but it is clearly not a sociolinguistic universal. One New Zealand employer noted, for example, that a very shy young Asian woman was regarded as rude because she did not look directly at people or respond verbally to greetings. Generally, however, the NESB workers we recorded did use some kind of greeting on first encounter with a co-worker (although the length and choice of greeting form was not always standard). However, failure to produce or respond to small talk at this important point in the day was a problem identified in some of the interactions involving workers with intellectual disabilities. In example 8, Jim fails to respond appropriately at a couple of points.

Example 8

Context: Supervisor, Helen, greets Jim, who has an intellectual disability, at the start of the day.

```
1  Hel:   morning Jim
2  Jim:   what's that?
3  Hel:   er it's a big tank it's a pressurized tank full of water
          /that's gonna\
4  Jim:   /er er\
5  Hel:   help clean our trays +
6         how are you ++
7         how are you ++
8         cut your hair?
9  Jim:   yeah
```

Analysis of this brief excerpt identifies a number of signals that Jim is not behaving as expected of a participant in early morning workplace small talk. He fails to respond to Helen's greeting "morning". Instead, he asks a direct question oriented away from the social relationship and focussed on some workplace equipment. At line 4, he interrupts with a hesitation noise, indicating he wants to say something, but when Helen finishes her utterance at line 5, he fails to pick up the conversation. She then tries again with small talk "how are you?" but again Jim fails to respond. There is a two-second pause after each of her repeated attempts to engage Jim at lines 6 and 7. Finally, she manages to elicit a brief response by focussing on something more personal, "cut your hair?" Jim consistently ignores the formulaic small talk tokens that are so important at the start of the day's interactions. It was clearly considered unfriendly by co-workers if overtures such as "good morning", "chilly eh?", or "nice day" were met by silence. Small talk is important at such points in the day: it warms people up socially, oils the interpersonal wheels, and gets work started on a positive note.

In some work contexts, small talk develops beyond a couple of ritualistic utterances into more extended social talk, as illustrated by example 9.

Example 9

Context: Manager (i.e., the head of department) Hana, with her administrative assistant, Beth, who has just returned after a holiday.

1 Hana: well it's nice to have you back welcome back
2 Beth: yes had a very good holiday
3 Hana: and feel well rested? so where did you go
4 Beth: no [laughs]
5 Hana: oh well
6 Beth: it's just just been busy with my mum and then she had me
7   take her here and take her there and [laughs]
8 Hana: oh
9 Beth: so no it was good I didn't have to worry about meals I didn't
10   have to worry about bills or kids or um work or anything just
11 Hana: (just) a holiday for you
12 Beth: yeah + it was UNREAL [laughs]
13 Hana: now listen are you going to be wanting to take time off during
14   the school holidays

Despite what is suggested by the occurrence of "welcome back", this interaction occurred at the end of the meeting between Hana and Beth. Urgent business had displaced it from the beginning of the encounter. Small talk develops or expands in this way for a number of possible reasons: the participants may know each other well, or the period since they last had contact may be considerable, or they may be aware that there is nothing urgent awaiting the immediate attention of either, or the meeting they have just had (or are anticipating) may have been very long or problematic. In all these cases, a brief ritualistic small talk exchange at the boundaries of the speech event is likely to be experienced as inadequate. In example 9, Beth and Hana had not seen each other for a while and they are doing some obligatory 'catching up'.

Example 10 (from Clyne 1994, pp. 148–9)[5]

Context: Vietnamese woman Giao shows her Austrian shop steward Liesl some broken parts.

1 Giao: [shows broken parts to Anna]
2 Liesl: hallo Giao
3 Giao: /hallo Liesl\
4 Liesl: /I haven't seen you\ for ages ++ what's wrong? ++
5 Giao: (...................................) so like this
6 Liesl: ooh they're breaking?
7 Giao: yeah see ++ I beg your pardon what you want?
8 Liesl: I haven't seen you for a long time

Clyne notes that workers from India, Croatia and the Philippines handled the mixing of social and work routines more easily.

Workers with intellectual disabilities sometimes did not realize that it was important to sustain the small talk for a longer period when they or their co-worker had been away from work ill, for instance, or when they had been away on a trip. Nor did they always pull their weight when a co-worker engaged them in such talk. They sometimes failed to respond adequately, answering in monosyllables or non-verbally, thus allowing the topic to drop inappropriately quickly. In other words, they did not keep up their end of the social conversation. Example 11 illustrates this pattern.

Example 11

Context: Mary is working alongside Heath, a worker with an intellectual disability. They are taking a break between tasks.

1 Mary: how's your mum
2 Heath: good
3 Mary: is she ++ has her knee fixed up yet ++
4 Heath: no
5 Mary: has her knee got better now
6 Heath: yes
7 Mary: that's good

Mary is doing all the conversational 'work' here, carrying the conversation. Heath is answering minimally, rather than supplying extra information to keep the conversation alive. This was a common pattern: the worker with a disability does not take any conversational initiatives. On some occasions when a worker with a disability did initiate small talk, they did so at an inappropriate moment – in the middle of a complicated task, for example, rather than at the boundaries of work episodes. Getting the timing right is clearly an aspect of managing small talk that requires attention and practice.

It is worth noting that the more senior person generally brings workplace small talk to a close. The superior in an interaction has the deciding voice in licensing small talk (Clyne, 1994, p. 87; Tannen, 1994, pp. 223–4). In example 2, for instance, the superior is the person who shifts the talk back to task-oriented business talk. This is an important aspect of workplace interaction for workers to be aware of. The worker who persists in trying to maintain social interaction when their supervisor clearly wishes them to get on with their work is not likely to be positively perceived. While this clearly applies to all workers, we found that workers with intellectual disabilities occasionally missed the cues that their boss was ready to proceed to work. Utterances such as "what are you going to do today?" or "what are you doing next?" may seem obvious clues, but they did not always elicit a prompt appropriate response. It is very common for superiors to indicate how much small talk is acceptable by taking the initiative in shifting to business. Subordinates and fellow workers need to recognize such signals and respond appropriately. Prolonging small talk at such points may cause irritation.

Functions of small talk

It is clear from the discussion and examples provided above that the major functions of small talk are social. The most obvious function, and the reason why it is so important that new workers learn to manage small talk, is its social function in establishing and maintaining interpersonal relationships between those who work together. Small talk is an indispensable component of being a good workmate.

Example 12

Context: Jon and May pass on the stairs.

1 Jon: hello hello /haven't seen you for a while\
2 Mary: /hi\
3   well I've been a bit busy
4 Jon: must have lunch sometime
5 Mary: yeah good idea give me a ring

Jon and May indicate mutual good intentions as they make brief social contact through small talk. Jon's use of "sometime" in his invitation is an indication of the largely symbolic status of the interchange, and this is ratified by May's equally non-specific suggestion that he ring her; no precise time or date is mentioned. These are crucial clues that may be missed by workers from different sociocultural backgrounds or lacking in social experience. Pressing for a precise date and time would generally be an inappropriate response. There were examples in our data where workers failed to 'read' the signals that no specific social commitment was being made, despite a co-worker's friendly offer. Responses such as "when?" are too specific in such contexts.

In general, both NESB workers and the workers with intellectual disabilities in our data typically managed very basic small talk, such as simple greetings, and responses to unthreatening questions, e.g., "had a good weekend?". They sometimes had more problems with the extended social talk that developed at break-time and lunchtime. Yet these are precisely the social contexts that have been identified as problematic in terms of successful integration into the workplace (e.g., Greenspan & Shoultz, 1981; Hagnar, Rogan, & Murphy, 1992; Hatton, 1998). In such contexts, small talk is an appropriate bridge to more extended social talk, as in the following example from a plant nursery, where Hal is a worker with an intellectual disability.

Example 13

Context: Tea break in a garden center. Caroline, Sharon, Hal and Des are present.

```
 1 Car:    cold eh
 2 Sha:    chilly
 3 Car:    I know it's like that all over the area
 4 Sha:    need my morning cuppa to warm me up
 5 Car:    would you like a biscuit Hal?
 6 Hal:    no
 7 Des:    they eat nice cake don't they
 8         you on a diet Hal?
 9 Hal:    yeah
10 Des:    are you? gotta lose weight do you
11         you're getting a bit of a pot there
```

Our analysis shows that the kind of banter illustrated in lines 8 and 10 is common at sanctioned social breaks in many workplaces, but it is one of the most difficult aspects of work for those joining an established working team. The fact that Hal is an integral participant in the workplace banter is a sign of his acceptance as a co-worker (cf. Hagnar, Rogan & Murphy, 1992). But he has not acquired skills which enable him to respond appropriately, and is generally silent in response to such comments. It is important to be able to participate in order to signal that you 'belong' to the work team. Yet getting the tone right and keeping contributions appropriately short are real challenges for would-be participants.

The analysis of our observational and recorded data from workplaces where NESB workers operated, and from where those with intellectual disabilities were placed, suggests, then, that these employees may have trouble with each of the features of small talk discussed. Some very shy young workers regularly failed to greet fellow workers at all, looking at the floor and avoiding eye contact. This is clearly not a good way to start the day. Others were sporadic in their level of response. They sometimes selected inappropriately personal topics for small talk or provided inappropriate responses: e.g., some workers did not recognize the formulaic status of "how are you?" and responded with a detailed discussion of symptoms of illness. The analysis suggests that new employees may not be confident or accurate in their judgments about the relative status of small talk in different work contexts – is it crucial or peripheral, indispensable or optional? Some workers treated small talk as if it was the main business, even when they were engaged in a task, whereas managing small talk effectively generally involves using it in ways which indicate its secondary status much of the time, e.g., dropping it when the task becomes complex, or the meeting begins, or the boss indicates there has been enough of it.

Dimensions of analysis	Examples of relevant consideration
Content	• What topics are appropriate? • What level of detail is appropriate?
Distribution	• Where does it occur in an interaction? • How much is appropriate at any point? • Who has the right to start/end small talk?
Functions	• What can be achieved through small talk? e.g. strengthening collegial relationships, easing workplace tensions

Figure 1 Small talk in the workplace

Implications and applications

To what extent can the ability to interpret the subtleties and complexities of everyday talk in context be taught? Is it possible for NESB workers to acquire socio-pragmatic skills in a formal teaching context? How can workers with intellectual disabilities be helped to acquire the sociolinguistic skills needed for successful interaction at work?

Experienced native speakers of a language learn to analyze the interactions they observe and deduce the sociolinguistic rules from extensive exposure. But natural exposure to an adequate range of workplace interactions is most unlikely for either NESB workers or for those with intellectual disabilities. The amount of exposure and the level of generalization required is likely to prove too demanding. What is possible, however, is a combination of preparatory training, together with on-the-job practice of what has been learned.

The challenge for ESOL teachers, as for those involved in work skills training preparation for workers with intellectual disabilities, is therefore to devise efficient ways of assisting workers acquire basic socio-pragmatic skills as preparation for genuine workplace interaction. Teachers and trainers need to demonstrate some ingenuity in providing opportunities for learners to observe, practice, and acquire the sociolinguistic skills involved in successfully managing small talk in the workplace. I focus here on the preparatory aspect of this equation, and suggest two complementary methods of approaching the challenge. The suggestions are at a relatively high level of generality, and therefore have the potential for being adapted to a wide range of preparatory courses and contexts.

Using the soaps

One method that has been successfully used for teaching English to New Zealand NESB immigrants makes use of local television "soap operas" (Grant & Devlin, 1996). These also offer possibilities for teaching ways of managing small talk to workers with intellectual disabilities. While scripted material has obvious limitations as a model for developing production skills, it is ideal for developing skills in identifying different kinds of talk and different speech functions, and for practising skills in accurately interpreting sociolinguistic meaning. For this purpose, realistic soap operas set in workplaces, such as hospitals, police stations, and offices, provide very valuable material focussing on interactions at work. Moreover, the formulaic nature of much small talk means that the scripted aspect of the talk is less problematic than it might be for developing socio-pragmatic skills in relation to other speech functions. Using such materials as resources, teachers can usefully explore the following issues with those preparing for the workplace. Where appropriate, comparison with native-speaking norms or previous experience can be very useful.

Topics

• What are considered appropriate topics for use as small talk?

Learners can observe small talk interactions between different people in the program and note the range of topics that occur, e.g., weather, sport, family, work. Comparison with patterns in their native language can be particularly valuable for NESB workers.

• How much detail should be provided?

Learners can observe how long each topic is discussed, and note the level of generality and degree of detail with which topics such as health, weather, sport, weekend activities are discussed.

Distribution

• Where is small talk placed in the speech event?

Learners can observe where in an interaction the small talk occurs, e.g., at the beginning of the first encounter, at the end before people part, or between other topics.

• When is small talk required/optional/prohibited?

Teachers can draw learners' attention to situations where small talk is dispensed with, e.g., in an emergency situation, compared to where it is normally regarded as obligatory, e.g., on first meeting for the day.

• How frequently does small talk occur in the course of the working day?

Teachers can use TV programs to stimulate reflection on the frequency with which small talk occurs in different work contexts: e.g., when and how often does it occur after the first meeting of the day?

• How long does it last in different contexts?

Teachers can draw learners' attention to the fact that small talk is brief in some contexts and longer in others, e.g., longer at morning tea break, shorter in passing someone when engaged in a work task.

Functions

• How can small talk be used to express positive feelings to another?

Learners can observe in soap operas that small talk lasts longer among those who know each other well, who are friends, etc. They can note when it is brief, and discuss why.

- How can small talk be used to oil the wheels in a tricky encounter?

Teachers can identify examples of people using small talk to smooth the way in a tricky encounter, or to make their peace after relations have been difficult, or to lead into a request for a favor. Discussion of such examples can assist learners to recognize the usefulness of small talk in maintaining good relations.

Role-playing small talk at work

A second very important method of developing socio-pragmatic skills for the workplace is role-play. Role-play provides the opportunity to simulate a much wider range of workplace interactions than a worker will typically encounter in their normal everyday experience. Exercises which encourage young workers to develop automaticity with small talk should be the goal (cf. Holmes & Brown, 1987).

We have found that the following three exercises are particularly useful in developing workers' skills in managing small talk in a variety of workplaces: (i) practicing automatic and brief responses; (ii) practicing extended small talk; and (iii) spotting the errors.

Practicing automatic and brief responses

In this exercise the learners are greeted and farewelled by others playing the role of manager, cashier, co-worker, tea-lady, and so on. They learn to provide brief, appropriate responses without delay and without elaboration, no matter what the 'feeder' line. So, for example, young workers learn to respond with "fine" or "great" to "how" feeders as varied as "how are you today?", "how's things?", "how are you doing?", "how are you going?", "how was your weekend?", "how was your holiday?", and "how was your meal?". And with not much to "what" feeders such as "what have you been up to?", "what's new?", and "what's the latest gossip then?"

Practicing extending small talk

This exercise is aimed at developing the worker's ability to maintain small talk beyond a single exchange. At morning tea, during breaks or at lunch, it is appropriate for co-workers to engage in more extensive small talk. This is where NESB workers in workplaces where there are no co-workers from similar backgrounds can often get left out, and where workers with intellectual disabilities are frequently marginalized and isolated. The role-play exercise involves learners practicing making a simple response and then adding a question to that response. They are taught to add questions, such as "how about you?", "what about you?", or "what have you been doing?", in order to extend the interaction.

Example 14

Manager role:	hi Tom how are you?
Learning worker role:	fine, how about you?
Cashier role:	hi Sally how was your weekend
Learning worker role:	great what have you been doing?
Co-worker role:	gidday Ron what have you been up to?
Learning worker role:	not much, what about you?

These simple devices provide the learning workers with socio-linguistically acceptable ways of extending the small talk in appropriate contexts. This takes the pressure off the other person to 'carry' the conversation by asking questions, and makes the interchange far more of a shared enterprise.

Spotting the errors

A third exercise which can work well with more linguistically advanced or more able workers is to role-play interchanges between people involving sociolinguistic errors, or gaffes. The learner's task is to 'spot the error' and correct it in a subsequent role-play. The questions listed above in relation to using soap operas in skills training can provide ideas for possible errors. So errors may involve such behaviors as

- use of an inappropriate topic in small talk
- inappropriately long responses, or no response where one is clearly required
- inappropriately detailed responses
- insertion of a small talk formula at an inappropriate point within an exchange

In discussing errors, learners become aware of the importance of such factors as status differences, as well as length of acquaintance, and degree of friendship in determining what can be said, and how, and what is inappropriate in different contexts.

There are obviously many more ways in which an innovative teacher can use the information on the features of small talk provided in this paper to develop the socio-pragmatic skills of workers new to particular workplaces. We have stressed here the importance of keeping things simple and developing automaticity in useful sociolinguistic routines for all workers, while offering more able workers the possibility of further understanding the factors involved in the good management of small talk at work.

ESOL teachers have long been aware of the value of preparation, reflection and practice in developing socio-pragmatic competence (e.g., Bardovi-Harlig, 1999; Boxer, 1993; Byrnes & Candlin, 1991; Cohen & Olshtain, 1993; Holmes & Brown, 1976; Schmidt & Richards, 1980). There is an extensive literature providing suggestions for use in work-skill preparation for NESB workers. There is now also considerable evidence that focussed social skills training both before and during work placement contributes to improvements in the management of interpersonal interaction by workers with intellectual disabilities (Hatton 1998, Hughes, Killian & Fischer, 1996; La Greca, Stone & Bell, 1983; Schloss & Wood, 1990). In particular, the combination of carefully designed preparation along with the provision of 'natural supports' (i.e., sympathetic and helpful co-workers) in the workplace appears to be a very effective way of addressing the acquisition of the kinds of social skills outlined in this paper (Hagnar, 1993, 1996; Hagnar, Rogan & Murphy, 1992; Huang & Cuvo, 1997).

Conclusion

Employment is a central aspect of participation in the community, fulfilling societal expectations that community members be productive, as well as the individual's need for financial independence. It is clearly crucial for workplace success that all workers acquire the sociolinguistic skills which will enable them to establish good relations with co-workers. An attractive and outgoing social manner can have a major impact in pre-disposing co-workers positively, and can even over-ride irritation when tasks are not done with maximum efficiency. The value of effective socio-pragmatic skills in the workplace cannot be over-estimated.

The data from the Wellington Language in the Workplace project provides invaluable information on the way workers actually interact in a number of genuine New Zealand workplaces. This paper has illustrated some of the specific socio-pragmatic and sociolinguistic skills needed to function effectively. The skills described provide a basis for developing materials that will better prepare workers for the kinds of interaction they encounter daily in their workplaces. Exercises can assist workers in understanding the importance of these skills and their impact on fellow workers, as well as help them establish the kinds of automatic social routines that will provide for a good start at work. Making a good beginning is important; it establishes a sound basis for developing, with the assistance of supportive and understanding co-workers, more sophisticated aspects of social competence that are most effectively acquired in the workplace context itself.

Notes

1 This paper draws on material from the following published papers: Holmes (2000), Holmes & Fillary (2000), and Holmes, Fillary, McLeod, & Stubbe (2000). I am very grateful to Meredith Marra for useful comments on a final draft.
2 Transcription conventions are provided. (See Appendix A.) Some examples have been slightly edited for ease of reading where the detail is irrelevant for the discussion.
3 The research described in this paper has been funded by the New Zealand Foundation for Research, Science and Technology, with support from the Eastern Institute of Technology for the research on workers with intellectual disabilities. I here express appreciation to the Language in the Workplace project team, and especially Rose Fillary, Maria Stubbe, and Bernadette Vine, for their contributions to the research on which this paper is based.
4 Pakeha is a Maori word which is widely used to refer to New Zealanders of European, and especially British, origin.
5 I have edited Clyne's example for ease of reading.

References

Bardovi-Harlig, K. (1999). Exploring the interlanguage of interlanguage pragmatics: A research agenda for acquisitional pragmatics. *Language Learning* 49, 4, 677–713.

Black, R. S., & Langone, J. (1997). Social awareness and transition to employment for adolescents with mental retardation. *Remedial and Special Education* 18, 214–22.

Boden, D. (1994). *The Business of talk: Organizations in action*. Cambridge: Cambridge Polity Press.

Boxer, D. (1993). Complaints as positive strategies: What the learner needs to know. *TESOL Quarterly* 27, 2 277–99.

Brown, P. (2000). *Directives in a New Zealand factory*. M.A. thesis. Wellington: Victoria University of Wellington.

Brown, P., & Levinson. S. C. (1987). *Politeness: Some universals in language usage*. Cambridge: Cambridge University Press.

Butterworth, J., & Strauch, J. D. (1994). The relationship between social competence and success in the competitive workplace for persons with mental retardation. *Education and Training in Mental Retardation and Developmental Disabilities* 29, 118–33.

Byrnes, F. & Candlin, C. (1991). *English at work*. Sydney: National Centre for English Language Teaching and Research.

Chen, R. (1993). Responding to compliments: A contrastive study of politeness strategies between American English and Chinese speakers. *Journal of Pragmatics* 20, 49–75.

Clyne, M. (1991). Patterns of inter-cultural communication in Melbourne factories. *Language and Language Education* 1, 1, 5–30.

Clyne, M. (1994). *Inter-cultural communication at work*. Cambridge: Cambridge University Press.

Cohen, A. D. & E. Olshtain (1993). The production of speech acts by ESL learners. *TESOL Quarterly* 27, 1, 33–56.

Drew, P., & Heritage, J. (eds.) (1992a). *Talk at work. Interaction in institutional settings*. Cambridge: Cambridge University Press.

Drew, P., & Heritage, J. (1992b). Analyzing talk at work. In P. Drew & J. Heritage (eds.), *Talk at work. Interaction in institutional settings*. (pp. 1–65). Cambridge: Cambridge University Press.

Fillary, R. (1998). Language in the workplace for students with intellectual disability: Research methodology issues. *Te Reo 41: Special Issue* (191–95). Proceedings of the Sixth Language and Society Conference 28–30 June 1998.

Grant, L. E. & Devlin, G. A. (1996). *Kiwi conversation: the "Shortland Street" way: A video/workbook for teachers and students*. Auckland: Auckland Institute of Technology: School of Languages.

Greenspan, S., & Shoultz, B. (1981). Why mentally retarded adults lose their jobs: Social competence as a factor in work adjustment. *Applied Research in Mental Retardation* 2, 23–38.

Gumperz, J. J. (1982). *Discourse strategies*. Cambridge: Cambridge University Press.

Gumperz, J. J. (1992). Interviewing in intercultural situations. In P. Drew & J. Heritage (eds.), *Talk at work*. (pp. 302–27). Cambridge: Cambridge University Press.

Gumperz, J. J., Jupp, T., & Roberts, C. (1979). *Crosstalk: A study of cross-cultural communication*. Southall, Middlesex: National Centre for Industrial Language Training.

Hagnar, D. (1993). *Working together: Workplace culture, supported employment and people with disabilities*. Cambridge: Brookline Books.

Hagnar, D. (1996). Social skills at work. Paper presented at the Association of Supported Employment NZ Conference, Wellington, New Zealand. September, 1996.

Hagnar, D. C., & Helm, D. T. (1994). Qualitative methods in rehabilitation research. *Rehabilitation Counselling Bulletin* 37, 290–303.

Hagnar, D., Rogan, P., & Murphy, S. (1992). Facilitating natural supports in the workplace: strategies for support consultants. *Journal of Rehabilitation* 58, 29–34.

Hatton, C. (1998). Pragmatic language skills in people with intellectual disabilities: A review. *Journal of Intellectual and Development Disability* 23, 79–100.

Herbert, R. K. (1989). The ethnography of English compliments and compliment responses: a contrastive sketch. In O. Wieslaw (ed.), *Contrastive Pragmatics* (pp. 3–35). Amsterdam: John Benjamins.

Holmes, J. (1986). Compliments and compliment responses in New Zealand English. *Anthropological Linguistics* 28, 4, 485–508.

Holmes, J. (1988). Paying compliments: A sex-preferential positive politeness strategy. *Journal of Pragmatics* 12, 3, 445–65.

Holmes, J. (2000). Doing collegiality and keeping control at work: Small talk in government departments. In J. Coupland (ed.) *Small talk* (pp. 32–61). London: Longman.

Holmes, J. (2001) *Introduction to sociolinguistics*. second edition. London: Longman.

Holmes, J., & Brown, D. (1976). Developing sociolinguistic competence in a second language. *TESOL Quarterly* 10, 4, 423–31.

Holmes, J. & Brown, D. (1987).Teachers and students learning about compliments. *TESOL Quarterly* 21, 3, 523–46.

Holmes, J. & Fillary, R. (2000). Handling small talk at work: challenges for workers with intellectual disabilities. *International Journal of Disability, Development and Education* 47, 3, 273–91.

Holmes, J. & Stubbe, M. (2003). *Power and politeness in the workplace.* London: Pearson.

Holmes, J., Fillary, R., McLeod, M., & Stubbe, M. (2000). Developing skills for successful social interaction in the workplace. *New Zealand Journal of Disability Studies* 7, 70–86.

Holmes, J., Stubbe, M., & Vine, B. (1999). Constructing professional identity: "doing power" in policy units. In S. Srikant & C. Roberts (eds.), *Talk, work and institutional order. Discourse in medical, mediation and management settings* (pp. 1–35). Berlin, NewYork: Mouton de Gruyter.

Huang, W., & Cuvo, A. (1997). Social skills training for adults with mental retardation in job-related settings. *Behavior Modification* 21, 3–44.

Hughes, C., Killian, D. J., & Fischer, G. M. (1996). Validation and assessment of a conversational interaction intervention. *American Journal on Mental Retardation* 100, 493–509.

Labov, W. (1972). Some principles of linguistic methodology. *Language in Society* 1, 1, 97–120.

La Greca, A. M., Stone, W. L., & Bell, C. R. (1983). Facilitating the vocational-interpersonal skills of mentally retarded individuals. *American Journal of Mental Deficiency* 88, 270–78.

Manes, J. (1983). Compliments: A mirror of cultural values. In N. Wolfson & E. Judd (eds.), *Sociolinguistics and language acquisition* (pp. 96–102). Rowley, MA: Newbury House.

Parent, W. S., Kregel, J., Metzler, H. M. D., & Twardzik, G. (1992). Social integration in the workplace. *Education and Training in Mental Retardation* 27, 28–38.

Pomerantz, A. (1978). Compliment responses: notes on the co-operation of multiple constraints. In J. Schenkein (ed.), *Studies in the organization of conversational interaction* (pp. 79–112). New York: Academic Press.

Roberts, C., Davies, E. & Jupp, T. (1992). *Language and discrimination: A study of communication in multi-ethnic workplaces.* London: Longman.

Schloss, P. J., & Wood, C. E. (1990). Effect of self-monitoring on maintenance and generalization of conversational skills of persons with mental retardation. *Mental Retardation* 28, 105–13.

Schmidt, R. & Richards, J. (1980). Speech acts and second language learning. *Applied Linguistics* 1, 2, 129–57.

Storey, K., Rhodes, L., Sandow, D., Loewinger, H. & Petheridge, R. (1991). Direct observation of social interactions in a supported employment setting. *Education and Training in Mental Retardation* 26, 53–63.

Stubbe, M. (1998). Researching language in the workplace: A participatory model. *ALS 98 Proceedings of the Australian Linguistics Society Conference.* Brisbane University of Queensland, July, 1998. http://www.cltr.uq.edu.au/als98.

Stubbe, M. & Ingle, M. (1999). Collecting natural interaction data in a factory: Some methodological challenges. Paper presented at Murdoch Symposium on Talk-in-Interaction, Murdoch University, Perth, September, 1999.

Tannen, D. (1994). *Talking from 9 to 5.* London: Virago Press.

Thomas, J. (1983). Cross-cultural pragmatic failure. *Applied Linguistics* 4, 2, 91–112.

Wenger, E. (1998). *Communities of practice.* Cambridge: Cambridge University Press.

Wolfson, N. (1983). Rules of speaking. In J. C. Richards & R. W. Schmidt (eds.) *Language and communication* (pp. 61–87). London: Longman.

Ylanne-McEwen, V. (1993). Complimenting behavior: A cross-cultural investigation. *Journal of Multilingual and Multicultural Development* 14, 6, 1–20.

Appendix A

Transcript conventions

All names are pseudonyms.

YES	Capitals indicate emphatic stress
[laughs]	Paralinguistic features in square brackets
[drawls]	
+	Pause of up to one second
++	One to two second pause
..../......\...	Simultaneous speech
..../........\...	
(......)	untranscribable or missing words
(hello)	Transcriber's best guess at an unclear utterance
?	Rising or question intonation
publicat-	Incomplete or cut-off utterance
—	Some words omitted

Index

ACTFL (American Council of Teachers of Foreign Languages) 106, 122 fn. 6
ACTFL/ETS proficiency scale 106
analytic syllabuses 4, 21–2

business language needs 159–81

community of practice 348–50
concordancing 326–9
consent and consent forms 260–1, 271, 297 fn. 17, 304, 351–2
conversation analysis 313
cost-benefit analysis 80, 160
Council of Europe 21

Delphi method 167–8
Dictionary of Occupational Titles 22, 26, 49–50, 63, 68
discourse community 185
DLI (Defense Language Institute) 6–7, 85, 105, 122 fn. 1
domain experts 23, 27–8, 35, 62–3, 110, 115, 120–1, 123 fn. 12, 131, 188, 191, 197

ETS (Education Testing Service) 106

flight attendants 48–65
focus on forms 3, 12 fn. 2, 24
frequency of linguistic forms 326–9
FSI (Foreign Service Institute) 106

goal analysis 129, 229, 231–2

history of NA 2, 5

ILR language proficiency scale 106, 122 fn. 6, 123 fn. 12
interlanguage development 3
intellectually disabled workers 347–8

job advertisements 167
job analysis 129

language for specific purposes 19

market forces in NA 82–100
Maryland, State of 90–100
methodology of NA 5, 19–76, 117–22
methods for NA 30–2
    ethnographic methods 43–4, 133, 150
    interviews 33, 35–7, 51–2, 96, 166, 186–9, 191, 228–30; (unstructured) 51, 59–60, 63, 115, 135, 138, 143, 186, 197
    introspection 51–2, 58–9, 135, 197
    journals and logs 44–5
    language audit 33, 40–2
    language tests 167, 266
    multiple 32–4, 64, 149, 193–7
    non-participant observation 33, 42, 195–6
    participant observation 33, 42–3, 135–6, 139, 166
    proficiency tests 34, 45–8
    questionnaires 33, 38–40, 63–4, 91–2, 135, 147–9, 153–4, 161–2, 166, 168–70, 171–4, 180–1, 188–9, 203–8, 216–22, 230–2, 255–9 (anonymous) 167–8; (response rate) 40, 65 fn. 2, 91–2, 189–90, 203, 230–2; (telephone) 216–7
    reliability 117–9, 120–22
    retrospection 120–1
    sequencing of methods 33–4, 64, 188, 193–4, 226
    shadowing 132
    triangulated methods 25, 29–30, 128
    validity 119–22

373